Scottish Highlands and the Atlantic World

Histories of the Scottish Atlantic
Series Editors: S. Karly Kehoe and Chris Dalglish

This series showcases new research into the history of Scotland's relationship with the Atlantic World and promotes understanding of the present-day legacies of this past. It analyses how interactions between diverse Atlantic communities influenced the development of particular landscapes and regions, both in Scotland and on the other side of the ocean. It interrogates the ways in which these past interactions and developments continue to resonate with people today, as an aspect of their identity and a factor influencing their lives and life chances.

'Histories of the Scottish Atlantic' reveal and explore the legacies of a complex past and advance understanding of how this at-once positive and negative heritage might be harnessed for the future development of communities on both sides of the Atlantic.

Available titles

Reappraisals of British Colonisation in Atlantic Canada, 1700–1930
Edited by S. Karly Kehoe and Michael Vance

Scottish Highlands and the Atlantic World: Social Networks and Identities
Edited by S. Karly Kehoe, Chris Dalglish and Annie Tindley

edinburghuniversitypress.com/series/hsa

Scottish Highlands and the Atlantic World

Social Networks and Identities

Edited by
S. KARLY KEHOE, CHRIS DALGLISH
AND ANNIE TINDLEY

EDINBURGH
University Press

Edinburgh University Press is one of the leading university presses in the UK. We publish academic books and journals in our selected subject areas across the humanities and social sciences, combining cutting-edge scholarship with high editorial and production values to produce academic works of lasting importance. For more information visit our website: edinburghuniversitypress.com

© editorial matter and organisation S. Karly Kehoe, Chris Dalglish and Annie Tindley, 2023, 2025
© the chapters their several authors, 2023, 2025

Edinburgh University Press Ltd
13 Infirmary Street
Edinburgh EH1 1LT

First published in hardback by Edinburgh University Press 2023

Typeset in 10/13 Giovanni by
Cheshire Typesetting Ltd, Cuddington, Cheshire

A CIP record for this book is available from the British Library

ISBN 978 1 4744 9430 4 (hardback)
ISBN 978 1 4744 9431 1 (paperback)
ISBN 978 1 4744 9432 8 (webready PDF)
ISBN 978 1 4744 9433 5 (epub)

The right of S. Karly Kehoe, Chris Dalglish and Annie Tindley to be identified as editors of this work has been asserted in accordance with the Copyright, Designs and Patents Act 1988 and the Copyright and Related Rights Regulations 2003 (SI No. 2498).

Contents

List of Illustrations vii
Acknowledgements viii
Notes on the Contributors ix
Foreword by James Hunter xi

Introduction: Scottish Highlands and the Atlantic World: Social
Networks and Identities 1
S. Karly Kehoe, Annie Tindley and Chris Dalglish

PART ONE Land

1 'I prefer to establish myself in my own colony': The Translation of
   Aristocratic Thinking on Land and Governance between Highland
   Scotland and Atlantic Canada, c. 1803–1910 15
   Annie Tindley

2 Tripped up by Tartan: Settler Colonialism and the Highland Scots
   on Cape Breton Island 31
   S. Karly Kehoe

PART TWO Language and Culture

3 Gaelic Heritage, Language Revitalisation and Identity in Present-day
   Nova Scotia 47
   Stuart Dunmore

4 'Drochaid eadar mis' agus mo dhùthaich' ['A bridge between
   me and my country']: Transatlantic Networks and the
   Nineteenth-century Gaelic Periodical Press 71
   Sheila M. Kidd

5   The Scottish Highlands and Warfare in the British Atlantic World,
    c. 1740–1815   91
    Matthew Dziennik

PART THREE Networks of Empowerment and Oppression

6   Christian Robertson (1780–1842) and a Highland Network in the
    Caribbean: A Study of Complicity   115
    David Alston

7   The Gaelic Club of Glasgow: Gateway from the Scottish Highlands
    to the British Atlantic World, 1780–1838   148
    Stephen Mullen

8   Family, Society and Highland Identity in an Industrial World   170
    Don Nerbas

Epilogue: Contested Boundaries – Documenting the Socio-cultural
Dimensions of Empire   195
Dara Price

Index   200

Illustrations

Figure 2.1	Detail, map of the island of Cape Breton by John L. Johnson, 1831	36
Figure 8.1	Detail, map of the island of Cape Breton compiled from Recent Surveys (1868)	174
Figure 8.2	William McDonald, MP, April 1873	177
Figure 8.3	Senator's Corner, Glace Bay, 1906	184
Table 3.1	Key to transcription conventions	70
Table 7.1	Residence of Atlantic world-based 'Strangers' at Gaelic Club, 1780–1838	164

Acknowledgements

This volume has been a collaborative and transatlantic effort and the co-editors have a number of acknowledgements and thanks to make. Firstly, we would like to thank all of our wonderful contributors, whose intellectual efforts have made this volume what it is, but also who delivered their work in circumstances of great difficulty due to the COVID-19 pandemic. We would also like to thank the anonymous reviewers of the proposal and the text, who have helped us to improve it and we would like to give a very warm thank you to the team at Edinburgh University Press, who have been ever supportive of this project. Lastly, we would like to acknowledge the financial support of the School of History, Classics & Archaeology at Newcastle University towards the final production.

Notes on the Contributors

David Alston is an independent scholar who pioneered research on the role of Highland Scots in the exploitation of enslaved people on the plantations of the British Caribbean and South America. His book *Slaves and Highlanders: Silenced Histories of Scotland and the Caribbean* was published by Edinburgh University Press in 2021.

Chris Dalglish is a Director of Inherit, the Institute for Heritage & Sustainable Human Development. Inherit supports community development through cultural heritage. Working around the world, the Institute provides practical help to communities, carries out purposeful research and advocates evidence-based policy change. It is part of a UK-based charity, the York Archaeological Trust.

Stuart Dunmore teaches in language and culture at the University of Edinburgh and held a Fulbright scholarship at Harvard University. His research focuses on the sociolinguistics of contemporary Gaelic communities and speaker networks in Scotland, Nova Scotia and New England.

Matthew Dziennik is an Associate Professor of British and British Imperial History at the United States Naval Academy in Annapolis, Maryland. His research focuses on military recruitment in the British Empire in the age of revolutions.

James Hunter is Emeritus Professor of History at the University of the Highlands and Islands and has written extensively about the Scottish north and the region's worldwide diaspora.

S. Karly Kehoe is Professor of History and Canada Research Chair in Atlantic Canada Communities at Saint Mary's University in Nova Scotia. Her work concentrates on Scottish and Irish Catholic settlement and colonisation in the north Atlantic.

Sheila M. Kidd is Senior Lecturer in Celtic and Gaelic at the University of Glasgow. Much of her research to date has dealt with Gaelic literature from the eighteenth century to the twentieth century with a particular focus on Gaelic periodicals and newspaper columns.

Stephen Mullen is a historian based at the University of Glasgow. His research focuses on slavery and its legacies in the British Atlantic world with an emphasis on Scotland and the Caribbean. His monograph *The Glasgow Sugar Aristocracy: Scotland and Caribbean Slavery, 1775–1838* was published in 2022.

Don Nerbas is Associate Professor and the St Andrew's Society/McEuen Scholarship Foundation Chair in Canadian-Scottish Studies in the Department of History and Classical Studies at McGill University.

Dara Price is the Director of History and Heritage for Canada's Department of National Defence. She was previously Director General of Archives at Library and Archives Canada. Her research interests focus on the role of heritage institutions in social change initiatives.

Annie Tindley is Professor of British and Irish Rural History at Newcastle University and Head of the School of History, Classics and Archaeology. Her work interrogates land issues in the modern period, including ownership, management and reform.

Foreword
The Scottish Highlands and the Atlantic World
James Hunter

Much the most striking feature of this collection, to someone of my vintage, is its scope and diversity. When, in 1971, I began researching the doctoral thesis published, five years later, as *The Making of the Crofting Community*, academic enquiry into the post-Culloden Highlands and Islands was notable mainly by its absence. There was little on the clearances, next to nothing on the famine era, a couple of sketchy articles on the Land League period and still less on early twentieth-century land settlement – despite such settlement then being within living memory. Nor was migration from the region, whether to the rest of the UK or to overseas destinations, much better served. In 1971, it followed available academic analysis of the topics I was looking to explore could be got through in days. This, from my perspective, was a good thing. It meant that I was able, with the brash confidence of youth, to set about constructing, more or less from scratch, my own crofter-centred take on the history of the West Highlands and Islands in the period between the 1790s and the 1920s. Today that would be difficult. As can be seen from this book's contents, academic explorations of Highlands and Islands history – a history seen increasingly to have been influenced by Highlands and Islands involvements with the wider world – has uncovered nuance and complexity of a kind that, half a century ago, was utterly unknown to me.

In 1974, my thesis completed, I quit the world of academic history and wouldn't re-enter it until, from 2005, I spent five years helping to provide the University of the Highlands and Islands with its Dornoch-based Centre for History. But during the later 1970s and throughout the 1980s, when working as a journalist and when employed for a period by the Scottish Crofters Union, I continued to be intrigued by the north of Scotland's past and by the way an understanding of this past, or so I've long thought, can aid efforts to provide the region and its population with a worthwhile future. And so, on a freelance basis now, I began again, in the 1990s and subsequently, to write history – with a view, in part, to looking into the experiences of the many people who left the Highlands and Islands to make new lives for themselves in North America. In this connection I managed to visit localities where substantial Highlands and Islands settlement had occurred – North Carolina, the Mohawk Valley, Ontario's Glengarry County, Prince Edward Island, Cape Breton Island, mainland Nova Scotia. Further travels would take me to the prairies and points west; not least to the Flathead Indian Reservation in Montana where I'd spend time with a family of part-Highland and part-Nimiipuu or Nez Perce extraction; a family, McDonald by name, whose story, freely shared with me, took a whole book to tell.

Much of what I had to say in the 1990s about the Highlands and Islands diaspora in the United States and Canada would have profited from exposure, had that been possible, to what's to be read here. While I was aware – how could I not be after meeting and talking with folk on the Flathead Reservation? – of the extent to which white settlement in North America was preceded by the removal, and worse, of the continent's Indigenous inhabitants, it's clear to me, on reading Karly Kehoe's contribution to these pages, that I'd not now write about the Highlands and Islands presence in places like Cape Breton in quite the way I did in *A Dance Called America*, a book put together in 1993.

Yes, many Highlands and Islands emigrants to North America had suffered greatly, as I stressed, when clearing lairds deprived them of both homes and land. But what of the Mi'kmaq whose presence in Cape Breton, Kehoe notes, had endured for millennia? By getting themselves across the Atlantic, as Kehoe underlines, people who had been victims of one set of dispossessions, became – in their new guise of landholding settlers – the beneficiaries of those other, far more extensive, dispossessions that, whether in Cape Breton Island or elsewhere in Canada and the US, have left those countries' original occupiers with vanishingly small proportions of their former territories. This needs more recognition than, some thirty years ago, it got from me.

Cape Breton, I confess, has fascinated me since I first spent time there in 1980 and 1981. Once it was my intention to embark on a comparative study of Cape Breton and the Scottish north; a study of how neither Highlands and Islands crofts nor Cape Breton farms were reliable sources of income; of how resulting out-migration was characteristic of both regions; of how Boston was to late nineteenth-century Cape Bretoners what Glasgow was to their Highlands and Islands counterparts; of how the tourist trade, as Kehoe notes from a Cape Breton standpoint, saddled both localities with tartanised distortions of their Gaelic heritages; of how resources such as Cape Breton coal or Highlands and Islands land have been exploited largely for the benefit of external interests; of how late twentieth-century state agencies, the Highlands and Islands Development Board on one side of the ocean, the Cape Breton Development Corporation on the other, set about the task of combating disadvantage, marginalisation, lack of opportunity. That there might be gains to be got from comparative studies of this kind is suggested here by the results of Stuart Dunmore's meticulous account of divergent approaches to, and outcomes of, Gaelic-medium teaching in Nova Scotia and Scotland. More comparative exercises of this sort would be most welcome.

My long-abandoned excursion into Cape Breton history would have touched on the extent to which miners of Highlands and Islands descent, many of them Gaelic-speaking, helped provide Cape Breton with one of North America's most militant labour movements. But for all that a Cape Breton mining town like Glace Bay was very much a working-class community, it was also a place, as Don Nerbas demonstrates, where a man like William McDonald, whose origins were much the same as those of many Glace Bay miners of Highlands and Islands background, could establish a commercial dynasty of a sort seldom featured in accounts of industrial Cape Breton – a dynasty whose emergence was greatly assisted by McDonald being able to look for support to a kinship network of a type entirely characteristic of the Highlands and Islands diaspora.

Nerbas references Hugh MacLennan, who grew up in early twentieth-century Glace Bay and on whose novels and essays I've drawn extensively. This pleases me. And having myself tried to find ways of deriving wider historical insights from the experiences of a single family, a very different set of McDonalds in my case, I'm equally pleased to see this approach deployed here by David Alston as well as by Nerbas – Alston adding to his already extensive explorations of the Highlands and Islands presence in the Caribbean by focusing on a group of closely related individuals whose family origins were in the Highlands and Islands and who were beneficiaries of wealth generated from the exploitation of enslaved people in an area that was, in the decades around 1800, a key component of the British Empire.

A similar, if more varied and extensive, transatlantic network came to be centred, as Stephen Mullen shows, on the Gaelic Club of Glasgow. In this instance, as in the transatlantic linkages described by Alston, network members were primarily engaged in trade and commerce. But similar sets of ocean-spanning connections were eventually to be made, as Sheila M. Kidd demonstrates, by those journalists and others who, from the mid-nineteenth century onwards, made huge efforts to foster contact between Gaelic speakers still in Scotland and those other Gaelic speakers who, by that point, were rooted firmly in North America.

Among the earliest Gaelic speakers to reach what are now the United States and Canada, as Matthew Dziennik demonstrates, were soldiers recruited in the Highlands and Islands for service in one or other of the several wars fought by Britain in the North American theatre during the later eighteenth and early nineteenth centuries. Gaelic songs made by such soldiers – perhaps unsurprisingly in that few military men fall in love with places where they're likely to die – are often a lot less positive about North America, as Dziennik underlines, than songs created by Gaelic-speaking settlers. In contrast to settlers, of course, soldiers were transients – something also true of the landed aristocrats who, as Annie Tindley shows, were to find in Canada a means of sustaining, for a period at least, self-images rooted in the notion that men like them were uniquely fitted to rule.

From Tindley, Dziennik and their colleagues there's so much in this book that's new and valuable that it's maybe churlish to raise, in conclusion, the need for further work. But any comprehensive account of how the Highlands and Islands came to be so enmeshed in the Atlantic World ought ideally to recognise that the overwhelming bulk of the ties that came to bind the Scottish north so closely to Canada and the US were put in place by the untold thousands of people who made one-way voyages westwards in the holds of sailing ships or on the lower decks of steam-powered liners. Individually, these folk might seem of little account. Collectively, their impact was immense. They, their children, grandchildren and great-grandchildren would supply North America with homesteading farmers, cowboys, lumberjacks, river pilots, trappers, railroad builders, locomotive engineers, schoolteachers, stevedores, cops, clerks, cooks, steelworkers and a whole lot more besides. These people's lives, hopes and ambitions require rescuing from what a great historian, Edward P. Thomson, so memorably called 'the enormous condescension of posterity'. There's a job in that for somebody.

Introduction
Scottish Highlands and the Atlantic World: Social Networks and Identities

S. Karly Kehoe, Annie Tindley and Chris Dalglish

Just as I belong to the last Canadian generation raised with a Highland nostalgia, so also do I belong to that last which regards a trans-Atlantic flight as a miracle …

Now eating a filet mignon and sipping champagne in the supreme luxury of this Pan-American aircraft, I looked down on the waste of seas which, together with the mountains of British Columbia, had divided the clansmen from their homes over a century ago …

I looked out there, in a semi-circle of sunshine, the only sunshine apparently in the whole northern hemisphere at that particular moment, lay Cape Breton Island, the plane sloped down to eighty thousand feet and I saw beside Bras d'Or Lake the tiny speck which was the house where my mother and sister at that very moment lay asleep …

Am I wrong, or is it true that it is only now, after so many years of not knowing who we were or wanted to be, that we Canadians of Scotch descent are truly at home in the northern half of Canada?[1]

These excerpts come from the last couple pages of *Scotchman's Return*, a short story by Hugh MacLennan, a Nova Scotia-born author of Highland descent. MacLennan uses this story to explore the legacy of his father's Highlandism and to share the essence of a personal journey that many others in the Scottish Highland Diaspora must have experienced when they realised that 'home' was not the Highlands. It reveals something of that moment of consciousness when the significance of place is recognised as defining identity; that moment when it comes to be understood that how and who one is depends upon an ability and willingness to interrogate assumptions about one's ancestors and the spaces they occupied.

---

[1] H. MacLennan, *Scotchman's Return and Other Essays* (New York: Charles Scribner's Sons, 1960), pp. 10–12.

It can be a transition of agonising complexity. MacLennan was born in 1907 in Glace Bay, a Cape Breton mining town, and many of his stories, including this one, are autobiographical in how they confront the inherent tensions of understanding oneself in the broader context of the Scottish Highland Diaspora. The fact that Highlanders ended up in a place like Cape Breton Island, for example, was a consequence of empire. The story of Highland emigration to Cape Breton represented, on the one hand, Highlanders' own rejection of profound and irreversible socioeconomic and cultural change, and, on the other hand, their opportunism and desire to exploit colonial opportunities for their own benefit.

It is this complex and multi-layered legacy of empire and colonisation that the chapters in this volume come together to explore. Each of the chapters in the three sections of the book presents new historical research on how Highland Scots engaged with the British Empire and how this shaped their lives, the lives of their descendants and the lives of the peoples they encountered and displaced.[2] The idea for this volume emerged out of a curiosity with the social dimensions of Highlanders' entanglements with empire and how a variety of relationships that were forged and sustained over time and space affected people's lives and life chances. It also emerged from an awareness of the growing body of research in this field, and from seeing how that research is informing and provoking public discussion and helping to promote action to address the ongoing impacts of this past on people's lives today.

Highland migrants, who crossed the Atlantic willingly and unwillingly and set themselves up either permanently or temporarily, immediately encountered Indigenous peoples in the colonies of north-eastern British North America or enslaved African and African-descended peoples in the Caribbean. The relationships that many of the chapters consider were central to the opportunities and benefits that empire offered to Highlanders and other Britons and the colonial privilege they enjoyed. They were also central to the ways in which others were displaced and disenfranchised, exploited and oppressed.

Highland settlement was one part of a larger Scottish process and researchers are confronting the legacies of this; in fact, how people today are or are not engaging with this past is at the forefront of academic debate.[3] More widely, Scottish institutions are beginning to acknowledge and reckon with the country's colonial past, especially with its slavery and enslaver past. The University

---

[2] The Irish migration story is much better served: see, for example, C. Wilson, *A New Lease on Life: Landlords, Tenants and Immigrants in Ireland and Canada* (Montreal and Kingston: McGill-Queen's University Press, 1994), pp. 3–7, 38; D. Wilson (ed.), *Irish Nationalism in Canada* (Montreal and Kingston: McGill-Queen's University Press, 2009), pp. 3–21.

[3] Z. Laidlaw, *Colonial Connections, 1815–45: Patronage, the Information Revolution and Colonial Government* (Manchester: Manchester University Press, 2005), pp. 13–35; S. K. Kehoe, *Empire and Emancipation: Scottish and Irish Catholics at the Atlantic Fringe, 1780–1850* (Toronto: University of Toronto Press, 2022); A. Mackillop, *Human Capital and Empire: Scotland, Ireland, Wales and British Imperialism in Asia, c.1690–c.1820* (Manchester: Manchester University Press, 2021).

of Glasgow, for example, has acknowledged that it benefited financially from slavery and it has brought forward its Historical Slavery Initiative as a form of reparative justice.[4] National, city and local museums – including in the Highlands – have begun to explore the colonial and slavery links of their collections in more depth and to raise public awareness and understanding through exhibitions.[5] National and regional archives and libraries have published guides to researching and learning about enslavement and the trade in enslaved people through their collections and have mounted public exhibitions and held events such as public lectures and panels as well.[6] The landowning heritage charity, the National Trust for Scotland, has audited the enslavement connections of its properties, and Community Land Scotland – a community landownership and land reform charity – has published research into the historical relationship between plantation enslavement and privately owned landed estates in the Highlands and Islands.[7]

These developments have only taken us a few steps down the road to recognising the full truth of the Scottish, and Highland, colonial past and to addressing its legacies of inequality and injustice, which persist to this day. Each in their own way, the authors in this book are adding to the ongoing collective and cumulative effort to recognise, understand and address this past. They are engaging in an overdue exploration and, while their work will continue long after this volume is published, what they present here is intended to open new conversations by bringing into clearer view some of the nuances of transatlantic and transplanted Highlandism. Collectively, they consider how the preservation of the Gaelic language, the tradition of military service, the inherent tensions over the ownership and exploitation of land and the networks of

---

[4] Available at <www.gla.ac.uk/explore/historicalslaveryinitiative> (last accessed 30 April 2022).
[5] See for example 'Legacies of Slavery in Glasgow Museums and Collections', Glasgow Museums, available at <https://glasgowmuseumsslavery.co.uk> (last accessed 30 April 2022); 'The Matter of Slavery in Scotland', National Museums Scotland, available at <www.nms.ac.uk/collections-research/our-research/highlights-of-previous-projects/the-matter-of-slavery/> (last accessed 5 May 2022); 'Slaves and Highlanders', Cromarty Courthouse Museum, available at <www.antislavery.ac.uk/items/show/519> (last accessed 5 May 2022).
[6] See, for example, National Library of Scotland, available at <www.nls.uk/collections/topics/slavery> (last accessed 5 May 2022); 'Slavery and the Slave Trade', National Records of Scotland, available at <www.nrscotland.gov.uk/research/guides/slavery-and-the-slave-trade> (last accessed 5 May 2022); 'Landscapes and Lifescapes Project', High Life Highland, available at <www.highlifehighland.com/landscapes-and-lifescapes-symposium> (last accessed 5 May 2022).
[7] 'Facing our Past', National Trust for Scotland, available at <www.nts.org.uk/stories/facing-our-past> (last accessed 25 April 2022); 'New Research Reveals Extent of Historical Links between Plantation Slavery and Landownership in the West Highlands and Islands', Community Land Scotland, available at <www.communitylandscotland.org.uk/2020/11/new-research-reveals-extent-of-historical-links-between-plantation-slavery-and-landownership-in-the-west-highlands-and-islands> (last accessed 5 May 2022).

people, places and cultures supported and extended the tangible and intangible colonial structures that were constantly in flux.[8]

Our hope is that this volume will encourage a discussion of the peculiarly Highland dimension of Scottish and British colonisation in ways that will prompt new questions and more research and support contemporary efforts to acknowledge this past, understand it more deeply and address its ongoing consequences. As it stands, the detailed case studies and episodes presented in the book connect to some of the larger debates about colonial encounters and postcolonial legacies in ways that highlight the lived experiences of specific people and places and enable interrogations of motives, drivers, experiences and legacies. We have made room in this volume for perspectives that will help underpin future research which is both historically grounded and assists contemporary societies and peoples to consider their current and future directions.

Out-migration had long been a feature of Highland society, but there was a marked acceleration from the 1770s as large groups of people began actively to reject the widespread socioeconomic changes that were sweeping through their region and to identify new opportunities beyond Scotland. The decision to leave, it needs to be remembered, was an extremely complex and deeply personal one to make. It was not taken lightly and often caused distress when ties to community and landscape had to be severed permanently. Highlanders went to a range of places, but the Maritime colonies in what would later become Canada, and various locations in the Caribbean were favoured locations; because of this, they have been highlighted. In choosing to pay special attention to these regions, we enable a more focused interrogation of two places where Highlanders had a particularly significant impact. The northern Atlantic colonies, for example, witnessed heavy levels of migration and settlement between the early 1770s and the 1850s and again in the early twentieth century as new employment opportunities opened in industries such as mining.[9] Yet, across all phases of migration, the civic, religious, economic, educational and other structures that Highlanders established remained an important constant that extended, utilised and relied upon the tight social and familial networks they already possessed. Although meant as a criticism at the time, General George Wade's 1724 observation about the 'extensive adherence to one another as Highlanders' is instructive when trying to understand how Highlanders acted in colonial settings.[10] Adherence to one another could be

---

[8] As the shift to transnational historical perspectives has shown: C. A. Bayly, S. Beckhert, M. Connolly, I. Hoffmeyr, W. Kozol and P. Seed, 'AHR conversation: On transnational history', *American Historical Review*, 111:5 (2006), pp. 1440–64.

[9] See for global context: J. C. Weaver, *The Great Land Rush and the Making of the Modern World, 1650–1900* (Montreal and Kingston: McGill-Queen's University Press, 2003).

[10] General Wade, 'Report & c. Relating to the State of the Highlands, 1724', in J. Allardyce (ed.), *Historical Papers Relating to the Jacobite Period, 1699–1715*, Vol. 1 (Aberdeen: New Spalding Club, 1895), pp. 132–3.

and was both a defence mechanism and an extension of authority in the process of colonisation. As will be seen, the construction of settlements and the survival of communities relied heavily upon pre-existing networks and it was these networks, and the relationships that underpinned them, that normalised empire, cemented British authority and extended the reach of the imperial state.[11] Despite numerous exceptions, and the emergence of clear Catholic and Presbyterian clusters, Highlanders settled among other Highlanders.[12] As Gaelic speakers, they shared a vital cultural possession that not only provided them with a buffer against Anglicisation but also with a linguistic space to tell their own stories. Class also affected prospects, with some having more opportunities than others, but like their Lowland counterparts, the Highland migrant stream included people from every social category, and it was this diversity, as the chapters that follow demonstrate, which enabled such an extensive programme of settler colonialism.

Themes and coverage

The essays in this collection explore how Highland migration and the networks Highlanders possessed connected with the broader process of British imperialism.[13] The authors were brought together because their work offers interventions which, in various ways, progress understanding of the present-day legacies of Highland engagements with colonialism and the long-term and ongoing process of forging real and imagined identities. Despite numerous natural overlaps and connections among and between many of the chapters, we felt compelled to arrange them loosely around three key themes: land; language and culture; and networks of empowerment and oppression. Each theme is far-reaching and has multiple meanings according to place, time and lived experience.

Land and landed assets are one of the fundamental building blocks of modern colonial expansion and imperialism, as recognised and prioritised by European migrants and governments, both home and colonial, from the

---

[11] C. A. Bayly, *The Birth of the Modern World, 1780–1914: Global Connections and Comparisons* (Oxford: Blackwell, 2004), pp. 290–9.

[12] K. Kehoe, 'Catholic identity in the diaspora: Nineteenth century Ontario', in T. Bueltmann, A. Hinson and G. Morton, *Ties of Bluid, Kin and Countrie: Scottish Associational Culture in the Diaspora* (Guelph: Centre for Diaspora Studies, 2009), pp. 83–9; T. Murphy and G. Stortz (eds), *Creed and Culture: The Place of English-speaking Catholics in Canadian Society, 1750–1930* (Montreal and Kingston, McGill-Queen's University Press, 1993), pp. 171–80; L. H. Campey, *'A Very Fine Class of Immigrants': Prince Edward Island's Scottish Pioneers, 1770–1850* (Toronto: Natural Heritage Books, 2001); S. J. Hornsby, *Nineteenth-Century Cape Breton: A Historical Geography* (Montreal and Kingston: McGill-Queen's University Press, 1992).

[13] A. Behm, 'Settler historicism and anticolonial rebuttal in the British World, 1880–1920', *Journal of World History*, 26:4 (2015), pp. 787–813.

late sixteenth to the early twenty-first centuries.[14] Land is a finite resource and, as such, it was and is critical to the power of elites to leverage economic, political and cultural capital.[15] It was a fundamental reality that in order to improve one's circumstances in life, access to or ownership of land was vital and this reality was – via the networks of empowerment and oppression that we explore below – exported to the colonial setting in a variety of ways.[16] In those colonial spaces, European interests and practices clashed with Indigenous systems of governance, belief, knowledge and practice relating to the land and its use and stewardship. The consequences were profound, and they are still shaping how we all live now.[17] This was in part because land, in the European context, was a driver and enabler that spoke to all social levels. It was a unifying factor across European – including Scottish and Highland – societies and cultures.[18] The acquisition of land in colonial territories was done by violence, by dubious legal means and even by lottery, and it happened at both the British and colonial governmental levels.[19] It also happened over time, with the early stages of acquisition marked by opportunism, violence, limited regulation or oversight, and certainly without permission from Indigenous peoples such as the Mi'kmaq. Consequently, and as part of wider movements in the nineteenth century across Britain, Ireland and Europe, land reform became a dominant political force in colonial territories and land rights remain one of the most critical issues for people in colonised territories today.

How people perceived their position in the world was not only linked to land and place but also to their communities of language and culture, our second main theme. This becomes particularly complicated and nuanced when

---

[14] D. B. Swinfen, *Imperial Control of Colonial Legislation 1813–1865* (Oxford: Clarendon Press, 1970), pp. 95, 103–5; J. W. Cell, *British Colonial Administration in the Mid-Nineteenth Century: The Policy-Making Process* (New Haven: Yale University Press, 1970), pp. vii–xi.

[15] Z. Laidlaw and A. Lester (eds), *Indigenous Communities and Settler Colonialism: Land Holding, Loss and Survival in an Interconnected World* (Basingstoke: Palgrave Macmillan, 2015), pp. 3–15.

[16] R. Bittermann and M. McCallum, *Lady Landlords of Prince Edward Island: Imperial Dreams and the Defence of Property* (Montreal and Kingston: McGill-Queen's University Press, 2008), pp. 4–6.

[17] P. Dwyer and L. Ryan, 'Reflections on genocide and settler-colonial violence', *History Australia*, 13:3 (2016), pp. 335–42; J. McLaren, A. R. Buck and N. E. Wright, *Despotic Dominion: Property Rights in British Settler Societies* (Vancouver: University of British Columbia Press, 2004); A. Nettlebeck, 'Colonial protection and the intimacies of Indigenous governance', *History Australia*, 14:1 (2017), pp. 32–46; A. Perry, *Colonial Relations: The Douglas-Connolly Family and the Nineteenth-Century Imperial World* (Cambridge: Cambridge University Press, 2015); K. Kehoe and M. E. Vance (eds), *Reappraisals of British Colonization in Atlantic Canada, 1700–1900* (Edinburgh: Edinburgh University Press, 2020).

[18] R. Gibson and M. Blinkhorn (eds), *Landownership and Power in Modern Europe* (London: HarperCollins Academic, 1991).

[19] I. R. Robertson, *The Tenant League of Prince Edward Island, 1864–1867* (Toronto: University of Toronto Press, 1996), pp. 271–84; B. Messamore, *Canada's Governors General, 1847–1878: Biography and Constitutional Evolution* (Toronto: University of Toronto Press, 2006); for a comparative study, see C. Harris (ed.), *The Resettlement of British Columbia: Essays on Colonialism and Geographical Change* (Vancouver: University of British Columbia Press, 1997).

examining Highland colonial settlement, where – as Hugh MacLennan's work explored – new contexts and societies change the parameters of tightly held views about what culture and language are and mean. Understanding Scottish Gaelic in this context is critical and debates – sometimes acrimonious – have raged between scholars. What we hope to achieve in this volume is to present perspectives and historically grounded case studies that help to develop further that debate.

According to the Scottish Government, the decline in Gaelic speakers has begun to slow since the 2001 census.[20] But this comes after a long period of attrition driven by active government and church policies in the eighteenth and nineteenth centuries as well as more insidious changes in social and cultural expectations generated around the Scottish Enlightenment and notions of 'Improvement' – economic and moral – and an association of Gaelic-speaking with 'backwardness'. Ironically, of course, many of these ideas would be exported throughout the empire and applied to the peoples and societies encountered there. Many migrants from the Gaelic-speaking areas were encouraged to learn and speak English, as the 'true' language of empire and to smooth their passage away from the Highlands and out into the colonies. There was no regard for the languages already present, let alone Gaelic. These were long-standing and powerful drivers in the decline in the number of Gaelic speakers. Still, the Scottish Government's figure that, in 2020, there were an estimated 87,000 people who could understand, speak and/or read Gaelic represents a noticeable deceleration and it is testament to the efforts of campaigners and educators and structural and investment funding from the European Union.[21]

We can trace both a parallel and an echo in the Canadian Gaelic experience. Estimates from the 1901 Canadian Census suggest a Gaelic-speaking population of around 50,000 in Nova Scotia, though this declined rapidly over the course of the twentieth century. Today, there are no more than 2,000, with a number of those being new learners.[22] Widespread discrimination forced Gaelic to become a language of the home and, adding to that, many descendants of

---

[20] Scottish Government Gaelic Language Plan 2016–2021, available at <https://www.gov.scot/publications/scottish-government-gaelic-language-plan-2016-2021/pages/4/> (last accessed 15 February 2022).

[21] R. Herault and C. Willis, 'European Union Structural and Investment Funds and Celtic Language: An analysis of the 2007–2020 funding period in relation to Breton, Irish, Scottish Gaelic and Welsh', 2021, available at <https://mpra.ub.uni-muenchen.de/107324/> (last accessed 5 May 2022).

[22] The 2016 census, recording 910 individuals in Nova Scotia with 'knowledge of Gaelic in private households' and 145 reporting Gaelic as mother tongue. Equivalent totals for Canada are 1,090 and 3,980 respectively. See Census Profile, 2016 Census, Nova Scotia, Canada, available at <https://www12.statcan.gc.ca/census-recensement/2016/dp-pd/prof/details/Page.cfm?Lang=E&Geo1=PR&Code1=12&Geo2=&Code2=&SearchText=Nova%20Scotia&SearchType=Begins&SearchPR=01&B1=All&GeoLevel=PR&GeoCode=12&type=0> (last accessed 22 March 2022).

the original settlers felt that English would offer them more opportunities for social and economic advancement.[23] Schools did not teach Gaelic and the language was not used in public administration nor civil society: English and French became the official Canadian languages of business and government, though French and its speakers experienced significant discrimination and were consistently overshadowed by the dominance of English; and Gaelic was almost completely marginalised.[24] Just as Scotland has experienced a resurgence in Gaelic, there has been a revival of Gaelic education and language instruction in parts of Canada due to demand both from people in traditionally Gaelic-speaking areas such as western and central Cape Breton Island and from new learners. This is one of the reasons why several chapters in this book explore the linguistic and cultural dynamics of social networks and identities and how they were challenged and changed over time.

Vital to our understanding of how social identities were constructed and translated are the structures we loosely term networks of empowerment and oppression.[25] These were the sinews through which people, goods and ideas moved – or were obstructed – between the Scottish Highlands and the rest of the Atlantic world. Highlanders were embedded in networks which were hugely diverse in structure and operation, with some being constructed along family and kinship lines, some along racial or linguistic or cultural lines and yet others built around economic or political interests.[26] Each network was constructed and adjusted according to the immediate context of place and space and, as our contributors demonstrate, what was required at that precise point in time. Still, generalisations are possible, and we can point to some common features of Scottish Highland networks including language, cultural touchstones

---

[23] E. Mertz, 1982, '"No Burden to Carry": Cape Breton Pragmatics and Metapragmatics' (PhD thesis, Duke University, 1982), p. 36; E. Mertz, 1989, 'Sociolinguistic creativity: Cape Breton Gaelic's linguistic "tip",' in N. Dorian (ed.), *Investigating Obsolescence: Studies in Language Contraction and Death* (Cambridge: Cambridge University Press), pp. 103–16.

[24] 'French Canadians', in P. R. Magosci (ed.), *Encyclopaedia of Canada's Peoples* (Toronto: University of Toronto Press, 1999), pp. 538–86; N. Landry and N. Lang, *Histoire de l'Acadie*, 2nd end (Québec: Éditions du Septentrion, 2014); J.-H. Blanchard, 'L'Enseignement du français dans les écoles publiques de l'Île-du-Prince-Édouard', *Deuxième Congrès de la langue française au Canada* (1937), pp. 221–30; R. Cooney, *A Compendium History of the Northern Part of the Province of New Brunswick* (Place, 1832); B. LeBlanc, 'Tête à tête et charivari à Moncton: Rencontre inter-culturelle entre les Acadiens et les anglophones de Moncton', *Les Cahiers de la Société historique acadienne*, 27:1 (1996), pp. 4–18; P. M. Charbonneau and L. Barrette, *Contre vents et marées. L'histoire des francophones de Terre-Neuve et du Labrador* (Moncton: les Éditions d'Acadie, 1992).

[25] C. Hall, *Cultures of Empire: A Reader: Colonizers in Britain and the Empire in the Nineteenth and Twentieth Centuries* (Manchester: Manchester University Press, 2000).

[26] J. A. Mangan, *Making Imperial Mentalities: Socialisation and British Imperialism* (Manchester: Manchester University Press, 1990), pp. 1–3; M. Francis, *Governors and Settlers: Images of authority in the British Colonies, 1820–60* (Basingstoke: Palgrave MacMillan, 1992), pp. 1–17; A. Porter, 'Empires in the mind', in P. J. Marshall (ed.), *The Cambridge Illustrated History of the British Empire* (Cambridge: Cambridge University Press, 1996), pp. 185, 218–19.

(Burns, Scott), military service and the importance of land in cultural as well as economic terms.[27] The interplay of oppression and empowerment was experienced differently and at multiple levels by Highland Scots, other migrant groups, Indigenous peoples and enslaved peoples. This is the other major theme explored in this volume.

These three major themes of the book – land; language and culture; and networks of empowerment and oppression – are picked up in the epilogue, which explores the present-day legacies of these subjects. It offers big-picture and challenging thinking about the significance of these histories and their relevance to people's lives today.

Structure and chapters

The book has eight research chapters organised under the foregoing three themes. Two chapters address the first theme of Land, looking at the colonial histories and relationships associated with this vital but finite resource from different perspectives. Annie Tindley examines those aristocratic networks and drivers that led some of those from the upper social echelons in the Highlands, and Britain more widely, to investigate and lead in the purchase or lease of land in Atlantic Canada and, often, to follow up with elaborate migration schemes to populate that land, with both intended and unintended consequences. As among the humble Highland clansmen, one of the key drivers for this activity was class or social identity-building among the gentry and aristocracy.[28] In a period when their traditional activities and privileges were under increasing attack, the Scottish and British elite classes were searching for new roles and meanings, and one of the most important was the translation of their status and activities to the colonial context.[29] Karly Kehoe tackles the question of land and identity from a very different perspective – land appropriation and

---

[27] A. Tindley, '"All the arts of a Radical agitation": Transnational perspectives on British and Irish landowners and estates, 1800–1921', *Historical Research*, 91:254 (2018), pp. 705–22; A. Tindley, *The Sutherland Estate, 1850–1920: Aristocratic Decline, Estate Management and Land Reform* (Edinburgh: Edinburgh University Press, 2010); A. Mackillop, *More Fruitful than the Soil: Army, Empire and the Scottish Highlands, 1715–1815* (East Linton: Tuckwell Press, 2000); J. Hunter, '"You must fire on them": Protest and repression in Pultneytown, Caithness, in 1847', *Studies in Scottish Literature*, 46:1 (2020), pp. 40–5; J. Hunter, 'History: Its key place in the future of the Highlands and Islands', *Northern Scotland*, 27 (2007), pp. 1–14.

[28] See for comparison, R. Ansell, 'Educational travel in Protestant families from post-Restoration Ireland', *Historical Journal*, 58:4 (2015), pp. 932–40.

[29] G. Bolton, 'The idea of a colonial gentry', *Historical Studies*, 13 (1968), p. 307; P. Dunae, *Gentlemen Emigrants: From the British Public Schools to the Canadian Frontier* (Toronto: University of Toronto Press, 1981), pp. 1–10; A. Taylor, *Lords of Misrule: Hostility to Aristocracy in Late Nineteenth and Early Twentieth Century Britain* (Basingstoke: Palgrave Macmillan, 2004), pp. 1–15; and see, for example, A. Kirk-Greene, 'The Governors-General of Canada, 1867–1952: a collective profile', *Journal of Canadian Studies*, 12 (1977), pp. 35–44.

Indigenous displacement. The Scottish Highland settlement of Cape Breton Island resulted in widespread Mi'kmaq displacement and dispossession. Kehoe offers a deeper interrogation of the island's development to unpack some of the colonial dimensions of Highland settlement and to explore how landownership among Highland settlers advanced the power structures in the nineteenth century and how, later, this enabled the Highland image to be sympathetically reimagined in romantic terms to enhance their standing as respectable citizens and to bolster an emerging tourism industry in the twentieth century.

The second theme, Language and Culture, is explored by three contributors, covering a wide range of perspectives and sources, from the linguistic, press, military service and song. Stuart Dunmore marries contemporary heritage issues with historical legacies in his chapter on Gaelic heritage and revitalisation in Nova Scotia today. His work assesses the language learning and life experiences that inform Scottish and Nova Scotian new speakers' decision to acquire and use Gaelic, and, relatedly, their cultural identifications with the language to present a comparative analysis of new speaker motivations, identities and linguistic ideologies in both places. Sheila Kidd's chapter moves the analysis back to the nineteenth century and to one of the major technological and cultural shifts of the period – the growth of a mass, cheap and global periodical press. Initially inextricably entwined with the agendas of landlords in promoting emigration, it expanded to create embryonic transatlantic literary networks which developed a shared common cause of cultural rehabilitation and reinvigoration. Lastly, Matthew Dziennik links military service, the traditional outlet of Highland migrants, to cultural song traditions. As he shows, while lauding the contributions of Gaels to British imperialism, many songs also acknowledged the brutality of war and the limitations of North America as a land of opportunity, and he concludes by suggesting that these Gaelic songs must be viewed critically as part of the framework of military recruitment and the exploitative use of Gaelic labour by the British state in order to oppress other peoples.

The final theme, Networks of Empowerment and Oppression, begins with David Alston's chapter on a case study of a Highland network in the Caribbean during the late eighteenth and early nineteenth centuries. The central figure of this network was a woman who never left Britain and yet whose entire life, and that of her family, was shaped by Caribbean involvement and complicity in the enslavement of Black Africans. This focus on a woman in Scotland as part of a Caribbean network reveals something of the extent to which middle-class families were invested in and involved with the vast international system of enslavement and how it was accepted as part of everyday life in the north of Scotland. Stephen Mullen also considers the opportunities and restrictions offered by networks, with a case study of the Gaelic Club of Glasgow, one of a range of such associations, networks and clubs that acted as conduits, charitable enterprises, identity builders and commercial operations. His chapter shines an important light on an elite Highland–Caribbean nexus in Glasgow with high-level connections stretching across the British Atlantic world. Lastly, Don Nerbas takes us back to the start of this volume and the reflections of Cape Breton's Hugh MacLennan, but from the perspective of a growing middle and professional class. His chapter reconstructs the making of a prominent family from the composite Highland community that developed in industrial Cape Breton's coalmining district to help us understand how industrialism, class formation and colonial nationalism recast Highland identities in the Atlantic world during the long nineteenth century.

The opening and closing reflections were invited to engage with the issues raised throughout the book. James Hunter and Dara Price have responded to all three themes covered in the volume and help us to frame the historical analysis and case studies explored in the chapters into a contemporary context. From this we hope that scholars will ask new questions, assess new evidence and explore new perspectives on transatlantic networks and identities. And we hope that their thoughts will help readers more generally to identify and reflect upon the connections that exist between histories of the Highland Atlantic and the lives of people today, both in Scotland and in Canada, the USA and the Caribbean. These histories are not dead and gone, they are active in the present through the structures, institutions, relationships, identities and inequalities they set in train. In that sense, they remain unresolved. In bringing to light new evidence and looking in depth at the stories of real people and their relationships, we hope that the contributions in this book help to advance understanding of the truth – and something of the true complexity – of Highland entanglements in the Atlantic world.

Part One

Land

ONE

'I prefer to establish myself in my own colony': The Translation of Aristocratic Thinking on Land and Governance between Highland Scotland and Atlantic Canada, c. 1803–1910[1]

Annie Tindley

Introduction

In the early nineteenth century, emigration from the Scottish Highlands to Atlantic Canada was at the heart of a heated, acrimonious debate among some of the wealthiest and most powerful Scottish landowners.[2] Lord Selkirk, an influential supporter of emigration as the solution to the economic and demographic problems of the Highland region, found himself in direct opposition to the house of Sutherland, whose tenants he was proposing to assist to emigrate to Nova Scotia and Prince Edward Island (hereafter PEI) in the first decade of the nineteenth century.[3] As he later wrote, 'the prejudices entertained against the situation I proposed, were industriously fomented by some persons, who had conceived a jealousy against my undertaking; and, in consequence of this obstruction I found it necessary to extend my offers of encouragement as far as I could.'[4] The obstructions and jealousies referred to consisted of a well-organised and well-supported campaign by Highland landowners to prevent emigration from their estates, a campaign which culminated in the 1803 Passenger Vessels Act. This legislation increased the cost of emigration by imposing minimum standards of food and other supplies on emigrant passages, thereby reducing the numbers who could afford to leave. Highland landowners had been keen to prevent emigration to retain the growing population on their estates for work

---

[1] *Highland News*, 2 September 1911.
[2] M. Harper, *Adventurers and Exiles: the Great Scottish Exodus* (London: Profile, 2003), pp. 78–88; J. M. Bumstead, *The People's Clearance: Highland Emigration to British North America, 1770–1815* (Edinburgh: Edinburgh University Press, 1982), pp. 196–203.
[3] Bumstead, *People's Clearance*, pp. 193–4.
[4] Lord Selkirk, *Observations on the Present State of the Highlands, With a View on the Causes and Probable Consequences of Emigration* (London, 1805), p. 168.

in the burgeoning kelp and fishing industries, and so were entirely opposed to Lord Selkirk's plans to settle Cape Breton and PEI.[5]

Just over a hundred years later, in 1910, a prospective emigrant to Canada from the Highlands of Scotland explained his reasoning to a newspaper reporter. He was leaving Scotland because, he said, 'I prefer to establish myself in my own colony.'[6] It was a classic statement of emigrant aspiration from the common person: to start a new life of freedom, with access to land free from the shadow of landlords. Ironically, this statement was made by Cromartie Granville Leveson-Gower, the 4th Duke of Sutherland and great-grandson of the anti-emigration 1st Duke, one of the richest and largest patrician landowners in Britain, about his recent decision to sell land in the Scottish Highlands and use the capital freed up to purchase land in Alberta, Canada. The Duke gave away his patrician background with his use of the possessive, 'my own colony'; this turn of phrase was perhaps the result of generations of being western Europe's largest landholding family, unable to understand the appeal of places like Canada to ordinary working men and women, who saw it as a place of refuge away from feudalistic landlords. Indeed, in many cases, they had very little choice but to emigrate to Atlantic Canada, as the tidal wave of the Sutherland Clearances had pushed those who could afford, or were assisted, to emigrate.[7]

This chapter is framed by class and the transnational movement of people and ideas in the later nineteenth and early twentieth centuries. It examines the interconnections between ideas and people outwith national frameworks and boundaries, but maintains a focus on the roles played by political and landed elites, as opposed to the more widely researched mass movement of lower- and middling-class emigrants.[8] This gives the historian an opportunity to examine

---

[5] J. Hunter, *Set Adrift upon the World: The Sutherland Clearances* (Edinburgh: Birlinn, 2015), pp. 104–7.

[6] Reported in the *Highland News*, 2 September 1911; 5th Duke of Sutherland, *Looking Back* (London, 1953), pp. 86, 98, 164; A. Tindley, *The Sutherland Estate 1850–1920: Aristocratic Decline, Estate Management and Land Reform* (Edinburgh: Edinburgh University Press, 2010), pp. 131–6; D. Spring, 'The role of the aristocracy in the nineteenth century', *Victorian Studies*, 4 (1960), p. 63; D. Wilson, *United Irishmen, United States: Immigrant Radicals in the Early Republic* (Ithaca: Cornell University Press, 1998), pp. 1–2, 8.

[7] Hunter, *Set Adrift*, pp. 319–22; E. Richards, *The Highland Clearances* (Edinburgh: Birlinn, 2008), pp. 16, 25–6.

[8] See D. Cannadine, *The Decline and Fall of the British Aristocracy* (London: Penguin, 1990), pp. 8–25; F. Campbell, *The Irish Establishment, 1879–1914* (Oxford: Oxford University Press, 2009), pp. 2, 19–20. See the European comparative analysis that demonstrates this approach: E. Frie and J. Neuheiser, 'Introduction: Noble ways and democratic means', *Journal of Modern European History*, 11:4 (2013), pp. 433–48; N. Whelehan, 'Playing with scales: Transnational history and modern Ireland', in N. Whelehan (ed.), *Transnational Perspectives on Modern Irish History* (London: Routledge, 2015), pp. 7–8; C. A. Bayly, *The Birth of the Modern World, 1780–1914: Global Connections and Comparisons* (Oxford: Oxford University Press, 2004), pp. 2, 27–9, 395–431; S. Rose and C. Hall (eds), *At Home with the Empire: Metropolitan Culture and the Imperial*

colonial elite formation and the transnational opportunities and restrictions imposed by class structures, and what the challenges to those in the Canadian context were.[9] There are two areas of analysis: firstly, the impact *of* Atlantic Canada and the wider empire on how British and Irish elites operated and saw themselves in times of change and challenge to old certainties. Secondly, the impact *on* Atlantic Canada of these elites: how did they attempt to mould the dominion into their own image and align it to their expectations? The chapter will consider these elements through two frameworks: first, emigration and settlement, and second, land agitation and legislative reform. Both themes are central to the history of British North America and to Britain and Ireland in the nineteenth and early twentieth centuries. Although Scotland was one of the fastest industrialising and urbanising nations on earth in the nineteenth century, the Highland region saw a continued attachment to land, so much so that the 1880s witnessed a violent Land War, with the aim of securing legislative reform and increased security from the great landowners.[10] Atlantic Canada was of course a destination regarded as land-rich; a place to settle to become a master of one's own destiny, free of landowners. Land – both the physical reality and its management and ownership – is one of the most important binding aspects between Atlantic Canada and Highland Scotland, not least as seen in the movement of people, including landowning elites.[11]

David Cannadine has examined the impact of the landed and aristocratic classes on the wider British Empire in the nineteenth and twentieth centuries and has argued that their role in it became increasingly ornamental.[12] He suggests that the empire initially presented aristocrats with an opportunity to protect and exercise their accustomed influence, which was rapidly declining domestically from the 1880s, especially in the Irish context.[13] As the empire was constructed on fundamentally unequal and autocratic power structures and required 'rule by the best' as one of its much-vaunted 'benefits', aristocrats saw themselves as perfectly placed to undertake this role.[14] This was because they regarded themselves as a *service* aristocracy; that is, their wealth, status and position was based on an implicit social contract of duty and reward.

World (Cambridge: Cambridge University Press, 2006); C. A. Bayly, S. Beckhert, M. Connelly, I. Hoffmeyr, W. Kozol and P. Seed, 'AHR conversation: On transnational history', *The American Historical Review*, 111:5 (2006), p. 1444.

[9] A. Kirk-Greene, *Britain's Imperial Administrators, 1858–1966* (Basingstoke: Palgrave, 2000), pp. 7–11, 202–9.

[10] For the classic account, see J. Hunter, *The Making of the Crofting Community* (Edinburgh: John Donald Ltd, 1976), especially pp. 146–64.

[11] Hunter, *Set Adrift*, p. 319.

[12] D. Cannadine, *Ornamentalism: How the British Saw their Empire* (London: Penguin, 2001), p. 95.

[13] For an overview of this interpretation, see Cannadine, *Decline and Fall*, pp. 25–31.

[14] B. Knox, 'The Earl of Carnarvon, empire and imperialism, 1855–90', *Journal of Imperial and Commonwealth History*, 26:2 (1998), pp. 48–9.

They were also used to performing the more ornamental duties of the figurehead; the pomp and ceremony required as part of imperial postings was second nature to them, having been educated and brought up in the ceremonial world.[15] They firmly believed they were the natural political leaders and statesmen of society, representative of what was best about British political culture and morals. This view had a long history, stemming from aristocratic military service to the crown which persisted from the Norman invasion well into the early modern period. As the armed forces professionalised in the eighteenth and nineteenth centuries, the focus shifted to politics, governance and diplomacy, but the service ethos remained definitive to the aristocracy's self-identity.[16]

Not everyone agreed, however. The landed classes were also under sustained attack by the later nineteenth century, as pressures from the lower and middle classes for political and social reform slowly squeezed out old aristocratic certainties. Their territorial and financial dominance was also under pressure, as agricultural depression set in from the 1870s and new industrial wealth began to catch up.[17] One area where their influence endured a little longer was the empire, at least in part due to its fundamentally undemocratic structures, which suited the aristocratic outlook, and required the sheen and veneer of the ornamental that aristocrats could provide.[18] Cannadine and F. M. L. Thompson have also noted more prosaic reasons for imperial place-hunting among aristocrats: the opportunity it afforded for cheap overseas living and comfortable salaries, a kind of outdoor relief for the landed aristocracy, who often found themselves short of cash and resources.[19]

The nineteenth century saw great tension and even conflict around the roles played by elites in the management of their land and the people who lived on it, both in Scotland and Canada (as elsewhere).[20] These tensions were translated between Scotland and Canada via people – emigrants, settlers, campaigners – moving from the old world to the new, and sometimes back again. It was something of a cliché, but a durable one, that many people left the Scottish

---

[15] Cannadine, *Ornamentalism*, pp. 1–7, 92–6.

[16] F. M. L. Thompson, 'English landed society in the twentieth century: II: New Poor and New Rich', *Transactions of the Royal Historical Society*, 6:1 (1991), p. 11.

[17] Cannadine, *Decline and Fall*, pp. 1–25; Z. Laidlaw, *Colonial Connections, 1815–45: Patronage, the Information Revolution and Colonial Government* (Manchester: Manchester University Press, 2005), pp. 17–21.

[18] Cannadine, *Ornamentalism*, pp. 1–13.

[19] F. M. L. Thompson, 'English landed society in the twentieth century: III: Self-Help and Outdoor Relief', *Transactions of the Royal Historical Society*, 6:2 (1992), pp. 1–24; F. M. L. Thompson, 'English landed society in the twentieth century: IV: Prestige without Power', *Transactions of the Royal Historical Society*, 6:3 (1993), pp. 1–26.

[20] See Hunter, *Crofting Community*; T. Dooley, *The Decline of the Big House in Ireland: A Study of the Irish Landed Families, 1860–1960* (Dublin: Wolfhound Press, 2001), pp. 3–10; O. Purdue, *The Big House in the North of Ireland: Land, Power and Social Elites, 1878–1960* (Dublin: UCD Press, 2009), pp. 1–12.

Highlands and Islands and came to Canada because it offered an opportunity to own and work the land outright. It was a chance to escape to a better world, where no rent was due, a farm could be established and improved, the benefits of which went direct to the farmer rather than being translated into higher rent to pay. As well as this more positive rationale, there was a less rosy one where people were refugees, fleeing the tyranny of their landowners, or if not fleeing, forced to leave via clearance and eviction policies, or emigration schemes which in some cases were backed by the British state.[21]

This chapter will examine these themes through the prism of elite, landed experience. Firstly, it will examine aristocratic and landed influences on emigration and settlement in Atlantic Canada, principally Cape Breton Island and PEI. It will trace the interplay between rural revolution in Highland Scotland and settlement in Atlantic Canada, and the shifting attitudes of Scottish landowners towards this mass movement. Secondly, it will examine the relationship between land reform agitation in Scotland and Atlantic Canada from the 1860s to the 1880s and the ways in which the landed and governing classes linked the two to create a perceived transnational threat to their dominance.[22]

Section I: Aristocratic influences on emigration and settlement in Atlantic Canada

The range of aristocratic influence and experience on the emigration to and settlement of Atlantic Canada was extensive, but this section will focus on two elements. First, the type of estate management policies introduced in the Scottish Highlands that led to the emigration of people over the Atlantic, and second, the influence and impact the aristocratic and landed had on thinking about those emigrant groups once in Atlantic Canada and their expectations and norms.

One of the most controversial and most discussed aspects of landed and aristocratic influence on emigration to and settlement in Atlantic Canada from the Scottish Highlands comes from the Highland Clearances. One of the most bitterly contested and politically charged episodes in modern Scottish history, the Highland Clearances were no doubt at the root of much emigration across the Atlantic, whether voluntary and opportunistic or forced and traumatic.[23] Although the later eighteenth century had seen those Highlanders with some

---

[21] Hunter, *Set Adrift*, p. 319.
[22] See P. J. Cain and A. G. Hopkins, *British Imperialism: I: Innovation and Expansion* (London: Routledge, 1993), pp. 3–52.
[23] Richards, *Highland Clearances*, pp. 16, 25–6; R. Bitterman, 'On remembering and forgetting: Highland memories within the Maritime diaspora', in M. Harper and M. Vance (eds), *Myth, Migration and the Making of Memory: Scotia and Nova Scotia, c.1700–1990* (Halifax and Edinburgh, 2000), pp. 254–6, 257, 261; E. Richards, *Debating the Highland Clearances* (Edinburgh: Edinburgh University Press, 2007), pp. 3–25.

capital take advantage of the opening up of the North American colonies – and indeed, these were the people that Highland landowners were keen to prevent from migrating via the 1803 Passengers Act – by the early nineteenth century and particularly after the end of the Napoleonic Wars, the drive reversed and growing populations of so-called 'redundant' people were seen as best removed.[24] By the time the Highland Famine was afflicting large parts of the region in the mid-1840s, it was a matter of orthodoxy among landowners and their agents that the population of the region had grown too large and the best solution was to assist (or encourage the government to help assist) them to establish new lives overseas.[25]

One of the most infamous episodes of clearance took place from around 1806 to 1821 on the enormous Sutherland estates of the Earls (later Dukes) of Sutherland, during which they completely transformed the existing tenurial arrangements on their 1.2 million acre northern estates. Thousands of people were directly affected, and a large proportion of these either left under their own steam or were assisted to emigrate. This was a pattern that would repeat itself all over the Highlands and Islands well into the 1850s.[26] Some – indeed many – of those from Sutherland chose Nova Scotia as their ultimate destination, with Pictou as their initial gateway. In 1814 seventeen of them petitioned the governor of Nova Scotia, Sir John Sherbrooke, explaining how the introduction of commercial sheep farming in their home country meant they decided 'to look for asylum in Nova Scotia', and were now requesting land grants in the Pictou area.[27] They were a small number of many more Sutherland people who came to the same part of Nova Scotia, setting up what were effectively transplanted Sutherland communities. In a sense then, the aristocratic and landed classes of Britain and Ireland had a direct impact on the settlement of Atlantic Canada through their clearance policies, precipitated by a shift to a more commercial outlook on their landed estates. Sutherland was probably the most significant example of this: an estate which saw its owners pick up the reins of capitalistic and imperial economic opportunity and make the fundamental – and highly controversial – adjustments required to transform their Highland estates.[28]

---

[24] F. Albritton Jonsson, *Enlightenment's Frontier: The Scottish Highlands and the Origins of Environmentalism* (New Haven: Yale University Press, 2013); Bumstead, *People's Clearance*, pp. 198–203.

[25] See, for example, Argyll, 8th Duke of, *Crofts and Farms in the Hebrides: Being an Account of the Management of an Island Estate for 130 Years* (Edinburgh, 1883); T. M. Devine, *The Great Highland Famine: Hunger, Emigration and the Scottish Highlands in the Nineteenth Century* (Edinburgh: John Donald Ltd, 1988). For an Irish comparison, see T. Dooley, 'Landlords and the Land Question, 1879–1909', in C. King (ed.), *Famine, Land and Culture in Ireland* (Dublin: UCD Press, 2001), pp. 116–18.

[26] Bitterman, 'On remembering and forgetting', pp. 254–5.

[27] Hunter, *Set Adrift*, pp. 320–1.

[28] Tindley, *Sutherland Estate*, pp. 1–13; E. Richards, 'An anatomy of the Sutherland fortune: Income, consumption, investments and returns, 1780–1880', *Business History*, 21:1 (1979), pp. 45–78.

The collective memories of loss and bitterness created in the early to mid-nineteenth century around the Highland Clearances and the blame attached to landowners for those hated evictions spilled into popular discourse in Canada and made a long-standing impact on perceptions of Highland Scottish landed elites in the country. One of the most famous attacks on the governance of landed estates in Scotland was a series of letters published in book form in Toronto in 1857 by Donald MacLeod, an emigrant from Sutherland who saw as a boy the clearances carried out at first hand. His *Gloomy Memories of the Highlands of Scotland* was a bestseller both in Canada and in Britain and has remained influential.[29] In his view, rather than representing 'rule by the best', the landed classes were dangerous, self-interested and foolish. These criticisms were translated more directly to those imperial aristocrats in posts: as the individuals holding official office, they became conduits for colonial dissatisfaction and pressure for greater constitutional freedoms from Britain.

Some landowners were ahead of this curve and were passionate supporters of emigration when it was far from fashionable to be so. Lord Selkirk was one of them. He encouraged through active measures a future for those cleared Highlanders in North America, but was sufficiently critical of the clearance policies he witnessed in the Highlands to write and publish extensively on the matter. Selkirk recognised the deeply held view among the people that although they might not legally own their plots of land in the Highlands, they had some moral rights to it and the right of long occupancy. It was this feeling which – Selkirk argued – when overturned by a new generation of capitalistic landowners such as the Sutherlands, had created the social conflict dividing the Highlands and driving its population overseas.[30] For Selkirk this was an opportunity, and one he hastened to support, putting him in direct opposition to most Highland landowners in this period.[31] One of his first efforts towards supporting emigration took place in PEI in 1803, when he bought land to settle no fewer than eight hundred Highland settlers, mainly from the Hebrides and west Highlands.[32] In his publications on the subject, Selkirk never glossed over the challenges faced by emigrants, even in the relatively populated parts of Atlantic Canada, which included administrative delays to land grants, the enormous environmental challenges, and the adjustments required from a people used to a treeless land to the heavily forested Canadian landscape.[33] As he put it himself: 'though his mental energy should remain unimpaired, the

---

[29] C. W. J. Withers, '"Give us Land and Plenty of it": The ideological basis to land and landscape in the Scottish Highlands', *Landscape History*, 12 (1990); D. MacLeod, *Gloomy Memories in the Highlands of Scotland* (Toronto, 1841).

[30] Hunter, *Set Adrift*, p. 104.

[31] Bumstead, *People's Clearance*, pp. 195–202.

[32] Hunter, *Set Adrift*, pp. 104–6; Selkirk, *Observations*, p. 173.

[33] Selkirk, *Observations*, pp. 168–70.

practical difficulties that await him are sufficient to discourage the most hardy. In every work he has to perform, he is unpractised, and has all the awkwardness of a novice.'[34] However, the risks and efforts were worth the candle, according to Selkirk and the settlers.

Interestingly, Selkirk was able to buy into PEI land due to an unusual foundational land system established on the island in 1767. This had taken the form of a land lottery, held in London, by which large lots of land were secured by principally absentee landowners.[35] As Selkirk said, these landowners 'paid no attention to their improvement, and in consequence many extensive tracts are totally uninhabited'.[36] Selkirk saw an opportunity for settlement, although this wider issue would come back to haunt PEI and the federal government by the 1850s, as described below. The immediate challenges facing the settlers were more pressing, but Selkirk attributed their ultimate success to 'the hardy habits of these Highlanders', and – critically – to the incentive each settler had, 'from the nature of their tenures'. This was, of course, the ultimate prospect of 'independence' from any landowner; what Selkirk called the 'pride of landed property'. This was the ultimate draw for many a Highland settler in Atlantic Canada, particularly those who, as Selkirk said, 'though of little service as manufacturers, they may be made excellent colonists'.[37]

Selkirk was in the vanguard of a new attitude to the opportunity presented by emigration to Canada, and in effect translated his traditional leadership role away from the nucleus of his estate to the new world, with mixed results. Another example of this can be seen in John Ramsay of Kildalton, an Islay landowner, who also assisted some of his tenants to emigrate to Canada. He framed this as a policy for their own benefit, having purchased land on Islay in 1855 from the bankrupted Sir Walter Campbell, a personal friend and landowner whose financial position had been pushed past the point of no return due to his generosity in supporting his tenantry through the famine years of the 1840s.[38] Ramsay was more business-minded, having made a fortune as a Glasgow entrepreneur.[39] He assisted many of the tenantry to emigrate to Canada, but faced a good deal of criticism and controversy in the press and parliament for doing so.[40] In 1870 he decided to travel to Canada to investigate the fates of those he had assisted years before to emigrate, and his diary was circulated privately on his return. In it (perhaps unsurprisingly) he noted his pleasure at the improved living standards he saw, especially housing, despite

[34] Ibid. p. 168.
[35] I. R. Robertson, *The Prince Edward Island Land Commission of 1860* (Acadiensis, 1986).
[36] Selkirk, *Observations*, p. 173; Bumstead, *People's Clearance*, pp. 192–5.
[37] Selkirk, *Observations*, pp. 178–80, 185.
[38] F. Ramsay (ed.), *John Ramsay of Kildalton: Being an Account of his Life in Islay and Including a Diary of his Trip to Canada in 1870* (Toronto, 1969), pp. 18–20.
[39] Ibid. pp. 13–17.
[40] Ibid. pp. 39–41.

the bitter winters. Levels of education, food and health were all improved, and the emigrants were more 'independent-spirited' than those who remained on Islay in his view, echoing Lord Selkirk seventy years before.[41]

Aristocratic agendas were important in driving emigration, but they also informed perceptions of Canadian governance and the constitutional structures of government.[42] Aristocracy was inherently linked to monarchy by principle, constitution and often by blood relation.[43] As such, aristocrats were great promoters of hereditary principles and royal governance, something we can see in the governor-general Lord Dufferin's attempts to convince Canadians and his Colonial Office masters in the 1870s that the governor-generalship should be promoted to a viceroyalty, a move met with caution in Britain and rejected in Canada.[44] In making this suggestion, Dufferin both exposed his aristocratic mindset and misjudged public opinion on both sides of the Atlantic. Although there was broad support for the British connection in Canada, as a confederated, self-governing dominion, the spectre of a viceroyalty – by which non-self-governing territories like Ireland and India were ruled over – was distasteful, and for those Canadians further along the road to independence, it was downright insulting. Dufferin was also exercised by the possibility of the creation of a 'native' hereditary Canadian aristocracy, to cement 'English' values and systems. In part this was proposed to counteract the perceived dangers of American democracy and was informed also by the structures of British India, where 'native' princely states had been co-opted to support British interests in the subcontinent. However, it was also informed by Irish arrangements, themselves informed by the Anglo-Irish Ascendancy, a powerful, hereditary group planted to exercise British control in Ireland. Although increasingly challenged in this period, most Irish aristocratic and landed families understood their role to be supportive of the British establishment, and by definition, to be supported by it in turn. As Dufferin said:

> It would be undoubtedly beneficial if we could introduce into our own social organisation an element which should fulfil some of the functions discharged by the best

---

[41] Ibid. pp. 61–140, esp. pp. 96–101.
[42] A. Kirk-Greene, 'The Governor-Generals of Canada, 1867–1952: A collective profile', *Journal of Canadian Studies*, 12 (1977), p. 48; B. Messamore, *Canada's Governors General, 1847–1878: Biography and Constitutional Evolution* (Toronto: University of Toronto Press, 2006), pp. 148–9.
[43] B. Messamore, '"The line over which he must not pass": Defining the office of Governor General, 1878', *Canadian Historical Review*, 86:3 (2005), p. 461; M. Francis, *Governor and Settlers: Images of Authority in the British Colonies, 1820–60* (Basingstoke: Palgrave, 1992), p. 3.
[44] For Dufferin's entry in the *Oxford Dictionary of National Biography*, see R. Davenport-Hines, 'Blackwood, Frederick Temple Hamilton-Temple-, first marquess of Dufferin and Ava (1826–1902)', *Oxford Dictionary of National Biography*, Oxford University Press, 2004; online edn, January 2008, available at <http://www.oxforddnb.com/view/article/31914> (last accessed 18 October 2018).

aristocracies of an old country, and which should serve to remind the people that there are other titles open to respect and consideration than mere wealth.[45]

We can unpick this aristocratic mindset in other ways too, for instance in the conceptualisation and framing of the colonial environment, which was compared unfavourably to 'home', or at least, a romantic ideal of that home. For instance, take Lord Dufferin's description of PEI after his visit there in 1873: 'It is a pretty little place, about 130 miles long by 16 broad and would make a snug estate.'[46] This conception of PEI was of course the opposite of that held by its emigrant settlers and, on the face of it, to that of Lord Selkirk. But, in fact, there is less of a difference between the visions of Selkirk and Dufferin than it first appears. Framing the world through notions of property was part of the mental furniture of aristocratic men, and they often spoke of their colonial responsibilities as though they were estates of which they were the absentee owners, as Dufferin elucidates for us: 'I have put rather a constraint upon myself, for it is a great and obvious temptation to endeavour to rule the destinies of five millions of people without having to leave one's comfortable armchair at home.'[47] This was, of course, exactly the kind of governance that thousands of emigrant Highlanders were seeking to leave behind. As one Highland newspaper editorial put it:

> this is indeed adding insult to injury – this progeny of a noble family whose ancestors burned the poor Highlanders' cottages etc. about their ears, evicted them without remorse, and now has the impudence to offer a 'settlement' in some far off country for the remnant of those whose forefathers escaped the Sutherland Clearances.[48]

Conceptions of governance from within Canada and those translated from the aristocratic mindset created points of disagreement and challenge, but also arguably of creative tension, which helped Canadians define what they did and did not want from their governing classes. Those sacrosanct principles of the British and Irish aristocracy – property, service, the primacy of the hereditary principle – were not always a comfortable fit when translated to Canada. Men like Dufferin could confidently assert that at least Canada was not like the United States of America, with (in their view) its corrupt democracy and anti-aristocratic demagoguery, but in truth, aristocratic principles were by no means welcome in Canada either. Popular and communal memory in Highland communities in Atlantic Canada focused around the horrors of the Highland

---

[45] That is, the rights that hereditary power brought: Dufferin to Carnarvon, 27 July 1876, D1071, H/H/1/5, Dufferin papers, Public Record Office of Northern Ireland [hereafter PRONI], Belfast.
[46] Dufferin to Lord Kimberley, 23 July 1873, D1071, H/H/2/1b, ff. 52, Dufferin papers, PRONI.
[47] Dufferin to Kimberley, 23 July 1873, D1071, H/H/2/1b, ff. 52, Dufferin papers, PRONI.
[48] Letter to the editor from 'A Highland Land Leaguer', *Highland News*, 15 October 1910.

Clearances, the blame for which was laid firmly at the door of landed elites, particularly those in the vanguard of industrial capitalism. Atlantic Canada, and other settlement colonies, were seen by many as refuges from the machinations of aristocratic control, something to which the aristocratic promoters of settlement or governors of Canada – men like Dufferin and Ramsay – were often blind, and which would generate serious consequences.

Section II: Land reform and agitation – the landed perspective

> If of any property it ever was true that it was robbery, it is literally true of the property of the British aristocracy.[49]

As noted above, the appetite for land among all classes was a powerful draw for migrants to Canada: not least elite migrants. Linking the constitutional to the political through an examination of the contested issue of land on PEI is a useful way of exposing the underlying assumptions of elite men such as Lord Dufferin, an Ulster landowner and Canada's governor-general between 1872 and 1878, and how they were challenged.[50] Part of the mystique of Canada to the emigrant was its offer of cheap or even free land, with no landlords. However, not everywhere was it so simple, as the wrangling over land rights in PEI from the 1830s to the 1870s demonstrates.[51] There were really a number of different issues at stake during this period in the island province. First was the legacy of the land lottery held in eighteenth-century London that left large portions of the island's 1.4 million acres of excellent arable land in the ownership of around a hundred mainly absentee, private individuals and families.[52] The history of their ownership was not a happy one, being characterised by one historian as 'frustration on one side and unaccountability on the other'.[53]

---

[49] K. Marx, 'The Duchess of Sutherland and slavery', 8–9 February 1853, in J. Ledbetter (ed.), *Dispatches for the New York Tribune: Selected Journalism of Karl Marx* (London: Penguin, 2007), p. 113.

[50] See also R. Bitterman, *Sailor's Hope: The Life and Times of William Cooper, Agrarian Radical in an Age of Revolution* (Montreal: McGill-Queen's University Press, 2010).

[51] I. R. Robertson, 'Political realignment in pre-confederation Prince Edward Island, 1863–1870', *Acadiensis*, 15:1 (1988), pp. 25–58; Bitterman, 'On remembering and forgetting', pp. 262–3.

[52] Absenteeism was a critical issue in Irish politics in this period also. Robertson estimates that only 40 per cent of occupiers in PEI in 1861 were freeholders; see Robertson, 'Political realignment', p. 36; Robertson, *The Prince Edward Island Land Commission of 1860*, pp. ix–xxiii; R. Bitterman (with Dr M. McCallum), 'Upholding the land legislation of a "Communistic and Socialist Assembly": The benefits of confederation for Prince Edward Island', *Canadian Historical Review*, 87:1 (2006), p. 3; J. McLaren, A. R. Buck and N. E. Wright, 'Property rights in the colonial imagination and experience', in J. McLaren, A. R. Buck and N. E. Wright (eds), *Despotic Dominion: Property Rights in British Settler Societies* (Vancouver: UBC Press, 2004), p. 3; R. Bitterman and M. McCallum, *Lady Landlords of Prince Edward Island: Imperial Dreams and the Defense of Property* (Montreal: McGill-Queen's University Press, 2008), p. 4.

[53] Robertson, *The Prince Edward Island Land Commission of 1860*, p. x; see also p. xi.

Spurred on by an active land agitation, a royal commission was appointed in 1860 to investigate the issues and make recommendations, which condemned the original settlement and recommended the application of a Land Purchase Act to all the original holdings.[54] The commissioners suggested that the British government guarantee a loan of £100,000 to fund this policy, but this recommendation was rejected by the Colonial Office.[55] A further period of tenant agitation ensued, including rent strikes, as no action was taken at all.[56] Having been failed by Canadian politicians on both ends of the political spectrum and by the imperial government, PEI tenants took matters into their own hands and founded a Tenant League in May 1864, with a programme of rent strikes, resisting sheriff officers and enticing soldiers to desert.[57]

They were facing an uphill battle, however, as their compatriots in the Scottish Highlands and Ireland would a decade later. Against them was the full weight of the landed and constitutional establishment, but by the 1860s, cracks in the armour were appearing, not just in Atlantic Canada, but in Scotland and Ireland. Examining landed responses transnationally demonstrates some striking similarities. PEI's landowners behaved in almost exactly the same fashion as Irish landlords such as Dufferin. Tenant agitation had long been part of Irish rural life, and in the 1840s and 1850s Dufferin had experienced stiff turbulence during the Irish Tenant Right agitation, which was especially strong in Ulster where his Clandeboye estate was located.[58] The issues at stake were similar too: land hunger, lack of security of tenure, landowner absenteeism, compensation for improvements made by tenants, and desire for fair rents.[59] Land agitation was a global issue: in British India, for instance, extensive reforms had been made by this period, and acrimonious and controversial settlements were being conducted in South Africa, New Zealand and Australia.[60] A critical linkage

[54] Ibid. pp. xviii–xxii.
[55] Ibid. p. xxii.
[56] Robertson, 'Political realignment', pp. 36–8; A. Lyall, *The Life of the Marquess of Dufferin and Ava* (London, 1905), p. 244; C. E. Drummond Black, *The Marquess of Dufferin and Ava* (London, 1903), p. 100; Bitterman, 'Upholding the land legislation', pp. 3–4, 7–8. There are direct comparisons to be made in terms of tactics with the Highland Land War of the 1880s: see Hunter, *Crofting Community*, pp. 147–9, 153, 158, 160.
[57] Robertson, *The Prince Edward Island Land Commission of 1860*, p. xxv.
[58] M. W. Dowling, *Tenant Right and Agrarian Society in Ulster, 1600–1870* (Dublin: Irish Academic Press, 1999), pp. 290–7; P. Bull, 'Irish land and British politics', in M. Cragoe and P. Readman (eds), *The Land Question in Britain, 1750–1950* (Palgrave: Basingstoke, 2010), p. 128; A. Casement, 'The management of landed estates in Ulster in the mid-nineteenth century', unpublished PhD thesis (Queens University Belfast, 2002).
[59] Bitterman and McCallum, *Lady Landlords*, pp. 10–11.
[60] E. D. Steele, 'Ireland and the Empire: Imperial precedents for Gladstone's First Irish Land Act', *Historical Journal*, 11:1 (1968), pp. 64–83; W. P. Morrell, *British Colonial Policy in the mid-Victorian Age* (Oxford: Clarendon Press, 1969); E. Delaney, 'Directions in historiography: Our island story? Towards a transnational history of late modern Ireland', *Irish Historical Studies*, 37:148 (2011), pp. 599–621; T. Brooking, *Lands for the People?: The Highland Clearances and the*

in this global picture were the aristocratic landowners who acted as imperial governors, such as Lords Dufferin, Lorne, Lansdowne, Mayo and Elgin, whose transnational mobility gave them an overview of land questions globally. Their views on land were conflicted: on the one hand, their landowning instincts placed them firmly in the camp of property rights and privileges, and their defence in any location was made on both principled and practical grounds.[61] After all, if concessions were made in PEI or Bengal, why not in Ireland, Scotland or England?[62] But on the other hand, as British imperial administrators, they were keenly aware of their responsibility to ensure good governance, including liberal and progressive reform, in order to justify British dominion.[63] In the case of PEI, tenant agitation had a long history before the 1860s and 1870s, and resistance to landlordism had long been part of the formal politics of the island, including by re-emigrating to Cape Breton Island and eastern Nova Scotia.[64]

Land was one of the truly transnational issues of this period. In every nation, region, dominion or colony, land was at one time or another a critical and often divisive political, economic, social and cultural question.[65] This is unsurprising, given that it is a resource both finite and fundamental, especially in settlement colonies such as Canada, or agricultural economies like those in Highland Scotland, Ireland and India.[66] Of interest here are the perceived duties,

---

Colonisation of New Zealand: A Biography of John Mackenzie (Otago: University of Otago Press, 1996).

[61] P. J. Cain, 'Capitalism, aristocracy and empire: Some "classical" theories of imperialism revisited', *Journal of Imperial and Commonwealth History*, 35:1 (2007), pp. 25–6.

[62] C. A. Bayly, 'Ireland, India and the Empire, 1780-1914', *Transactions of the Royal Historical Society*, 6:10 (2000), pp. 390–1; see also E. Rothschild, *The Inner Life of Empires: An Eighteenth Century History* (New Jersey: Princeton University Press, 2011), pp. 1–11 for an example of the transnational activities of a minor Scottish gentry family.

[63] M. Bentley, *Lord Salisbury's World: Conservative Environments in Late Victorian Britain* (Cambridge: Cambridge University Press, 2001), p. 72. Dufferin oversaw a major land reform bill for Bengal while Indian viceroy, for example; see B. Martin, *New India, 1885: British Official Policy and the Emergence of the Indian National Congress* (Berkeley, 1969). Gladstone also idealised the concept of an 'aristocracy redeemed by service', itself a historicist proposition: C. Dewey, 'Celtic agrarian legislation and the Celtic revival: historicist implications of Gladstone's Irish and Scottish Land Acts, 1870–1886', *Past and Present*, 64:1 (1974), p. 60.

[64] R. Bitterman, *Rural Protest on Prince Edward Island: From British Colonisation to the Escheat Movement* (Toronto: University of Toronto Press, 2006), pp. 1–3; R. Bitterman and M. McCallum, 'When private rights become public wrongs', pp. 144–68.

[65] See Bitterman and McCallum, 'When private rights become public wrongs'; A. Ali, *The Punjab Under Imperialism, 1885–1947* (New Jersey: Princeton University Press, 1988); L. P. Curtis, 'Landlord responses to the Irish Land War, 1879–87', *Eire-Ireland*, 38:3 (2003), pp. 137–46; S. Gopal, *British Policy in India 1858–1905* (Cambridge: Cambridge University Press, 1965).

[66] See, for example, Argyll to Dufferin, 12 November 1873, D1071/H/B/C/95/67, Dufferin papers, PRONI: 'I must go to write about land tenures on India, a subject which engrosses me much'; B. Crosbie, *Irish Imperial Networks: Migration, Social Communication and Exchange in Nineteenth Century India* (Cambridge: Cambridge University Press, 2012), pp. 3–14; S. Cook, 'The Irish Raj: Social origins and careers of Irishmen in the Indian Civil Service, 1855–1914', *Journal of Social*

rights and privileges conferred by ownership (if not necessarily occupation) of land and its inheritance.⁶⁷ We can trace a locus of tension between the British and Canadian interpretations: the Canadian ideal of owner-occupier, as opposed to the aristocratic hereditary tradition of the old world, where tenants worked the land and the landowner enjoyed the fruits of their labour through rent payment. As Donald MacLeod put it in relation to Highland Scotland in his *Gloomy Memories*, 'these aristocratic locusts, who were, and will continue to be, the desolating curse of every land and nation they are allowed to breed in'.⁶⁸ Tension had been evident long before MacLeod published his influential work in the 1840s. These challenges accelerated from the 1870s in rural Britain and Ireland and contextualise why aristocratic governors and administrators in the imperial territories were often opposed to land reform in the empire, as Dufferin was in PEI.

Before turning to PEI, we must turn back to the anti-emigration policies of the great Highland landowners at the turn of the nineteenth century. Due to a host of factors, Highland (and British and Irish) landowners had changed their minds about emigration by the 1840s and were assiduously promoting it, as well as encouraging the government and charities to do the same. This was primarily for reasons of political economy and fears of 'over' population, particularly in the famine years of the late 1840s. However, there was also significant encouragement from Canadian authorities seeking to populate the provinces, supported by aristocratic and landed governors, including Dufferin.⁶⁹ But those emigrating had certain expectations and hopes of a new relationship to land, fuelled by the growing emigration promotion industry, which stressed repeatedly the benefits of an independent life in Canada.⁷⁰ 'Just fancy yourselves possessed of real property, on such terms – no yearly tenancy,' extolled the *Edinburgh Journal* in 1832.⁷¹ It was this promise and the expectation of a modest prosperity which fuelled discontent on PEI, which was dominated by large, absentee and unimproving landowners demanding the hated rents.

Midway through his tenure as governor-general, Dufferin was horrified to see tenant agitation deepening in PEI, leading to proposed land reform legislation

---

History, 20:3 (1987), 507–10; S. B. Cook, *Imperial Affinities: Nineteenth Century Analogies and Exchanges between India and Ireland* (New Delhi: Sage Publications, 1993), pp. 9–15; E. Delaney and C. O'Niall, 'Introduction: Beyond the nation: Transnational Ireland', *Eire-Ireland*, 51:1–2 (2016), p. 10; Whelehan, *Transnational Perspectives on Modern Irish History*, especially pp. 7–29; D. Wilson (ed.), *Irish Nationalism in Canada* (Toronto: McGill-Queen's University Press, 2009), pp. 178–89.

67 Tindley, *Sutherland Estate*, pp. 1–13; E. Richards, *The Leviathan of Wealth: the Sutherland Fortune in the Industrial Revolution* (London: Routledge, 1973), pp. ix–xviii.
68 MacLeod, *Gloomy Memories in the Highlands of Scotland*, p. 164.
69 See, for example, his praise of a pro-emigration speech made by his successor Lord Lorne in 1873: Dufferin to Argyll, 15 March 1873, D1071/H/B/C/95/65, Dufferin papers, PRONI.
70 Harper, *Adventurers and Exiles*, p. 79; see also pp. 86–8.
71 Cited in Harper, *Adventurers and Exiles*, p. 80.

to remove the influence of absentee proprietors under legal compulsion. Dufferin reported to the Colonial Office in appalled tones:

> There has also come up from the Local Legislature of Prince Edward Island a Bill expropriating land owners in the Island under very unfair conditions. I have told my Government that I could not consent to it becoming law, and I have no doubt I shall obtain their concurrence in this view.

Laid bare here are the underpinning assumptions of the governing landed elite, who saw all land-related questions, in any geographical or historical context, as interconnected. We can note too an implicit trust in the government; as governments were usually comprised of their peers, they could be trusted to do the right thing. However, as Dufferin swiftly realised in the PEI context, this was not in fact the case: 'I find my Ministers are very unwilling to take upon themselves the responsibility of advising me to disallow the Prince Edward Island Land Bill.' This opposition came as a shock to Dufferin, who had, on his initial arrival in Canada, been confident of 'a generally peaceful and contented population; even my Brother Paddies are without a grievance.'[72] To Dufferin's dismay, things were going against the landowning classes in Canada. In his view, any backsliding on fundamental questions of property had to be combated in whatever context they were found. It was not enough to wave through reform in Canada because the context was 'different' there. As he well knew, radical reform was translated across geographies with ease, and precedents were set globally.[73] Canada presented a double-edged sword for landed elites like Dufferin. On the one hand their relevance and powers as governors remained more robust than in Britain and Ireland, where their role as a service aristocracy was in steep decline. On the other, they found much in the attitudes and expectations of Canadians towards key economic and political issues, such as land, to be disappointingly radical. They looked on as the contagion of agitation and state-led land reform reduced their powers, both at home and in the empire.

Conclusions

By the early to mid-nineteenth century, Atlantic Canada was one of the most important destinations for migrants of all classes from the Scottish Highlands and Islands. The roles played by landed elites in this process were critical, if often contradictory. For those like Lord Selkirk, emigration was an opportunity not to reject the traditional, paternalistic duties of the landowner, but a new field in which to play this role out. By providing the leadership – social as well

---

[72] Dufferin to Argyll, 27 November 1872, D1071/H/B/C/95/62, Dufferin papers, PRONI.
[73] See, in comparison, Wilson, *United Irishmen, United States*, pp. 1–2, 8.

as financial – required to help establish small tenant farmers in the new world, Selkirk and Ramsay saw themselves as protecting and enhancing the position of their class in a changing world. Others took a very different view, however: they wished to retain the traditional sphere of their influence in Highland Scotland and saw the exodus of their tenantry as a defeat. This sense of failure was further enhanced when those who left began to agitate for land reform and generated an impression of a global threat to landed rights and the heritable principles it had been based on in Scotland, Britain and Ireland. Perhaps these two conflicting views tell us one important fact: that the desire to own land – whether for security, for status or for income – was the most powerful transnational impulse of them all.

TWO

Tripped up by Tartan: Settler Colonialism and the Highland Scots on Cape Breton Island

S. Karly Kehoe

Growing up in Cape Breton, an island that is part of the province of Nova Scotia on Canada's Atlantic coast, it felt like history was always around me. I come from a little village in Inverness County called Margaree Forks. It is distinctively rural, was originally inhabited by the Mi'kmaq and had a mix of settling groups: Acadian, Loyalist, Scottish (predominantly Highland) and Irish. Many residents today can still trace their families back to the original settlers; they have their own stories and traditions, and many have a genuine interest in who 'their people' were. On this western or sunset side of the island, a strong Scottish Highland identity tends to dominate and often gets projected over the other groups. That Cape Breton is home to many ethnicities is thanks also to the rise of heavy industry in the early twentieth century, when a variety of people arrived to work in coal and steel and set up as merchants.[1] I remember, as an undergraduate student in the 1990s, reading Anne Marie MacDonald's award-winning novel, *Fall on Your Knees*, and being shocked to discover that Cape Breton had a Lebanese community. It was not something that anyone locally ever mentioned nor anything we were taught about in school. It was a similar situation with the island's African Caribbean community, though I do recall one confusing incident in junior high when a class project on family tartans was announced.[2] Those of us with no Scottish ancestry protested, including a young woman who highlighted her African Caribbean heritage as an example, but an annoyed teacher ignored our arguments and told us to find

---

[1] L. MacKinnon, *Closing Sysco: Industrial Decline in Atlantic Canada's Steel City* (Toronto: University of Toronto Press, 2020); E. Rosenblum, 'Jewish Life and Belonging on Cape Breton Island', *Diversitycapebreton.ca Blog*, 4 June 2015, available at <http://diversitycapebreton.ca/content/jewish-life-and-belonging-cape-breton-island> (last accessed 15 September 2021).

[2] Claudine Bonner's work is illuminating; see C. Bonner, '"Likely to become a Public Charge": Examining Black Migration to Eastern Canada, 1900–1930', in F. Aladejebi and M. Johnson (eds), *Unsettling the Great White North: African Canadian History* (Toronto: University of Toronto Press, in press); C. Bonner, 'A Caribbean Community in the North Atlantic: Caribbean Migration to Whitney Pier, Nova Scotia, 1900–1930', *Social History* (forthcoming).

one we liked and use that. This is a small example, but it reveals how a Scottish Highland identity could dominate.

To the Mi'kmaq, the region's Indigenous people, Cape Breton Island is known as Unama'kik, which loosely means 'Land of Fog', and if you arrive on the island by road via the Canso Causeway, two signs will greet you: the English 'Welcome to Cape Breton' followed by the Mi'kmaw 'Pjila'si Unama'kik'.[3] The Mi'kmaw welcome was only added in the summer of 2021 as a step towards reconciliation and an acknowledgement of their historic presence. According to the Mi'kmaw elder and scholar, Daniel Paul, the Mi'kmaq occupied much of what we now know as the Canadian Maritimes for somewhere between 5,000 and 10,000 years. There were seven districts, each with its own government comprised of a chief and council which included female and male elders, the most revered and respected people in Mi'kmaw society.[4] Each district had 'conditional authority to make war or peace' and resembled what we understand a country to be today. There was a grand council which connected all the districts, but its function was primarily diplomatic – it was not an overarching authority. According to Paul, political corruption was 'unknown' because 'any leader who engaged in such dishonourable practices would have soon found himself deposed and disgraced'.[5]

Some time ago, Steve Murdoch observed that our ability to understand how the settling Scottish Highlanders influenced the development of Cape Breton Island has been limited by the exclusion of the Mi'kmaw perspective.[6] I cannot provide this perspective, but I can use this chapter to highlight some important dimensions that should prompt new questions. Using Scottish Highland settlement to interrogate the island's development more broadly requires a major recalibration and a willingness to dispense with the romance that tends to cloud our judgement. Adopting more critical perspectives will enable us to probe and unpack the deeply complex colonial dimensions of Highland

---

[3] 'Land of Fog' is Cape Breton University's Unama'ki College's translation; see <https://www.cbu.ca/indigenous-affairs/unamaki-college/> (last accessed 21 July 2021); L'Nu Affairs, Government of Nova Scotia, 'New Sign at Canso Causeway Welcomes Motorists to Unama'kik', 9 July 2021, available at <https://novascotia.ca/news/release/?id=20210709002> (last accessed 3 August 2021).

[4] D. N. Paul, *We Were Not the Savages: A Mi'kmaq Perspective on the Collision between European and Native American Civilizations* (Halifax: Fernwood Publishing, 2000), pp. 15–16; F. Metallic, 'Treaty and Mi'gmewey', in M. Battiste (ed.), *Living Treaties: Narrating Mi'kmaw Treaty Relations* (Sydney: Cape Breton University Press, 2016), pp. 42–9.

[5] Paul, *We Were Not the Savages*, p. 18.

[6] S. Murdoch, 'Cape Breton, Canada's "Highland" island?', *Northern Scotland*, 18:1 (1998), p. 40. A very good blog from Angela Tozer outlines the legacy that settlement and the continual 'erosion of Mi'kmaw sovereignty' has had on the fishery; see A. Tozer (2020), 'Settler Colonial violence and the Maritime fisheries', available at <https://earlycanadianhistory.ca/2020/11/23/settler-colonial-violence-and-the-maritime-fisheries/> (last accessed 23 November 2020).

settlement and community formation.⁷ This is not to question the suffering caused by the clearances, the protracted process of change to land use and occupation in the Highlands that included, at times, the forcible removal of people. That they were so destructive to so many aspects of Highland society is undeniable and, particularly after 1810, many cleared Highlanders migrated to and settled in Cape Breton Island and the Maritimes more widely because they had very little, if any, choice. What we cannot do, however, is allow that historic suffering to eclipse the pivotal role that Highland settlers played in the British colonisation of the Maritimes. In the case of Cape Breton Island, access to land was foundational to the process of settler colonialism and unpacking the legacy of the Scottish Highland presence requires us to start there. This chapter uses settlement and Mi'kmaq dispossession to explore how land use and landownership among Highland settlers advanced the power structures of the settler colonists in the early to mid-nineteenth century, and how, later, this enabled the Highland image of the twentieth century to be sympathetically reimagined in romantic terms to enhance their standing as respectable citizens and to bolster an emerging tourism industry.

In the late eighteenth and early to mid-nineteenth centuries, the maritime colonies of north-eastern British North America were a popular destination for thousands of Scottish migrants. A significant proportion of them were from the Highlands and Islands and many ended up settling on Cape Breton Island, either directly from Scotland or indirectly via Prince Edward Island and/or Nova Scotia. Cape Breton was a separate colony between 1784 and 1820; Highland migration to the island began as a trickle in the mid-1770s but sped up dramatically after 1800, peaking in the late 1820s.⁸ Cape Breton offered many a 'home away from home', and the critical mass of Highlanders that had emerged on the island after 1800 made the prospect of emigration far less daunting. New arrivals joined or formed communities with fellow Gaelic speakers, co-religionists, friends and relatives.⁹ While some of the migrants lamented the land they had left behind, others relished where they ended up and the freedom they gained as a result.¹⁰ Yet, even with the networked

---

⁷ Some work has started; see A. Parnaby, 'The cultural economy of survival: The Mi'kmaq of Cape Breton in the mid-19th century', *Labour/Le Travail*, 61 (2008), pp. 69–98; S. K. Kehoe, 'Catholic Highland Scots and the colonisation of Prince Edward Island and Cape Breton Island, 1772–1830', in S. K. Kehoe and M. E. Vance (eds), *Reappraisals of British Colonisation in Atlantic Canada, 1700–1930* (Edinburgh: Edinburgh University Press, 2020), pp. 77–92; W. C. Wicken, *The Colonization of Mi'kmaw Memory and History, 1794–1928: The King v. Gabriel Silliboy* (Toronto: University of Toronto Press, 2012), particularly Chapter 1.
⁸ L. H. Campey, *After the Hector: The Scottish Pioneers of Nova Scotia and Cape Breton 1773–1852* (Toronto: Natural Heritage Books, 2004), p. 110.
⁹ Campey, *After the Hector*, pp. 145, 153, 163.
¹⁰ K. Fenyo, *Contempt, Sympathy and Romance: Lowland Perceptions of the Highlands and the Clearances during the Famine Years, 1845–1855* (East Linton: Tuckwell Press, 2000); J. Hunter, *Scottish Exodus: Travelling among a Worldwide Clan* (Edinburgh: Mainstream, 2007), p. 157.

support systems, settlement was difficult. People struggled with the intimidating and heavily forested landscape, with the wild animals and with a climate of extremes. Accounts of the Highlanders being a 'hardy and stout-hearted' people with an 'instinct for survival' who were 'capable of enduring much bodily fatigue' were common.[11] True enough, perhaps, but it is also likely that most dreaded the agonising winters of freezing temperatures, food shortages and isolation. Despite these very real hardships, and whether they recognised it or not, the communities they built became the pillars of the colonial enterprise. They paved the way for the civil and administrative structures that cemented their own authority and that of the state.[12]

The hope of landownership was a major inducement to prospective settlers. Writing to Henry Bathurst, secretary of state for war and the colonies, Cape Breton's Scottish-born lieutenant governor from 1816 to 1820, George Robert Ainsley, used the arrival of one group of Highlanders from Barra in the summer of 1817 to argue that land needed to be offered as an enticement to stay:

> The redundant populations are ready enough to emigrate – on landing, finding themselves much deceived, they become discontented, in that state of mind they will write home and the next batch of Emigrants go to the United States depriving thus the Empire of the services of the hardiest race of fishermen in His Majesty's Dominions and of unshaken loyalty.[13]

The migrants, desperate for land, put colonial officials like Ainsley under tremendous pressure to give it to them. In fact, Ainsley had encountered the 'unanimous and daily expressed wishes of the settlers', who wanted government to recognise the 'expediency of giving them a permanent interest in the land they settle on by a Crown Grant instead of the present mode of lease'.[14] The settlers were reacting against a system that excluded the majority of them by limiting actual grants of land to Loyalists and discharged military personnel; everyone else, including the Mi'kmaq, was forced to accept temporary licenses

---

[11] L. Stanley, *The Well-Watered Garden: The Presbyterian Church in Cape Breton, 1798–1860* (Sydney: University College of Cape Breton Press, 1983), p. 22.

[12] S. Y. MacDonald, 'Dh'fheumadh iad àit' a dheanamh' (They Would Have to Make a Place): Land and Belonging in Gaelic Nova Scotia (PhD thesis, Memorial University of Newfoundland, 2017), pp. 102, 115. Jim Phillips and Philip Girard note the treacherous tracks and how it put off judges in 'Courts, communities and communication: The Nova Scotia Supreme Court on Circuit, 1816–50', in H. Foster, B. L. Berger and A. R. Buck (eds), *The Grand Experiment: Law & Legal Culture in British Settler Societies* (Vancouver: University of British Columbia Press, 2008), pp. 130–1.

[13] Letter from George Robert Ainsley, Sydney, Cape Breton Island, to Earl Bathurst, London, England, 24 July 1817, CO 217/135/201, Cape Breton, The National Archives (hereafter TNA).

[14] Letter from George Robert Ainsley, Sydney, Cape Breton Island, to Earl Bathurst, London, England, 9 July 1817, CO 217/135/90, Cape Breton, TNA.

of occupation.¹⁵ A turning point came in 1817 and lasted for about a decade, when people could get a grant of land for a cost of between £3 and £5, which made it accessible to most newcomers. From the early 1830s, land was still accessible but it needed to be purchased at reserved and higher prices set by the government.¹⁶ The loosened restrictions in 1817 meant that people could obtain land grants of 100 or 200 acres, provided the grantee(s) met the conditions of building a house, of 'clear[ing] and cultivat[ing] 3 of every 50 acres' and of having at least three cows. An update in 1820 made it possible for land to be granted jointly to multiple people to enable poorer migrants to pool resources.¹⁷ Historic Crown Land maps held by the Nova Scotia Department of Lands and Forestry show that for the Margaree area alone, numerous grants were issued jointly. Most went to two, three or four people, but some plots show as many as six names, including one to David Ross, Jacob Ross, David Ross, William Ross, Elizabeth Ross and her children, and John Ross.¹⁸ The majority of grants were issued to white settler men, but some went to women, including one shared by Dorothy Ross and Susan MacPherson, and another shared by Margaret Fraser and Malcolm Fraser, presumably siblings since wives were not usually named as co-grantees.¹⁹ Despite these examples coming from one part of Inverness County, where there were also sizeable Acadian, Irish and Loyalist populations, it is indicative of the broader pattern of familial settlement that characterised most Scottish Highland communities in Cape Breton, and is borne out by the maps for other districts and communities.²⁰

These maps show us where the Scots were and the kind of land they sought or could afford, but they also reveal significant clustering – although the Scots, the Irish, the Loyalists and the Acadians were neighbours, each group tended to stick to their own though the settlement pattern in south-eastern Cape Breton Island reveals that mixing could and did occur. The fact that so many Highland Scots could settle together and create communities that replicated, in many ways, the ones they had left behind in Scotland, was one of the main reasons why the island was so popular with Highlanders, particularly those

---

[15] Cape Breton County Registry of Deeds records, Nova Scotia Registry of Deeds fonds, Nova Scotia Archives [hereafter NSA], available at C:\Users\s9569529\Downloads\Cape <https://memoryns.ca/cape-breton-county-registry-of-deeds-records> (last accessed 22 July 2021); 'Mi'kmaw Timeline', Cape Breton University, available at <https://www.cbu.ca/indigenous-affairs/mikmaq-resource-centre/mikmaq-resource-guide/mikmaw-timeline/> (last accessed 22 July 2021).

[16] L. Campey, *After the Hector*, pp. 109, 321; R. Bittermann, 'The hierarchy of the soil: Land and labour in a 19th century Cape Breton community', *Acadiensis*, 18:1 (1988), p. 39.

[17] S. J. Hornsby, 'An Historical Geography of Cape Breton Island in the Nineteenth Century' (PhD thesis, University of St Andrews, 1986), pp. 83–4.

[18] Index Sheet 121, Crown Land Index Maps 1750–1850, available at <https://novascotia.ca/natr/land/indexmaps/121.pdf> (last accessed 22 July 2021).

[19] Ibid.

[20] Available at <https://novascotia.ca/natr/land/grantmap.asp> (last accessed 3 August 2021); for the relevant map sections, see blocks 108–40, excepting 118.

Figure 2.1 Detail, map of the island of Cape Breton by John L. Johnson, 1831

from the Western Isles, throughout the 1830s and 1840s.[21] Unsurprisingly, such extensive and rapid settlement took its toll on the physical landscape and it was not long before the pressure on land and resources became a problem. In fact, population growth was so rapid that by the early 1840s there were an estimated 50,000 people on the island, which was one-fifth of the Nova Scotia total. Most were Gaelic-speaking Highlanders drawn from across the social spectrum; they were 'people from the upper echelons of Highland society, tacksmen and tenants of substance and people much closer to the bottom of the heap'.[22] While many of those who arrived after the mid-1820s were comparatively poor, the tight and protective Highland networks gave them an important sense of security by enabling them to recreate the communities they had lost. The ability to connect with co-religionists was an important part of this and so most settlements were organised along religious lines, as another historic map shows.[23]

While the 1831 Johnson map, named after the cartographer John L. Johnson, reveals where the 'English, Scotch Presbyterians, Scotch Catholics, Irish and Acadians' were mostly located, it also shows 'Indian tracts' and how by the early 1830s the island's original inhabitants had been restricted to just five areas around the Bras d'Or Lakes.[24] Enabling Highlanders to settle together in the safety and comfort of reconstituted communities was at the expense of the Mi'kmaq.

The rapid influx of Highland migrants upset the delicate balance of carefully managed resources and cut off, incrementally, the Mi'kmaq people's access to food, water and to the lands of their ancestors. More specifically, it disrupted their ability to undertake the ceremonies required of them to show their appreciation to the earth for its gifts.[25] The Highlanders were aggressive, land hungry and in a position to lobby for land effectively, and if they did not receive what they wanted, many simply took it. A case study of Middle River, a

---

[21] Campey, *After the Hector*, pp. 145–7, 153–7.
[22] R. Bitterman, 'On remembering and forgetting: Highland memories within the maritime diaspora', in M. Harper and M. E. Vance (eds), *Myth, Migration and the Making of Memory: Scotia and Nova Scotia, c. 1700–1900* (Edinburgh: John MacDonald, 2000), p. 261; R. C. Macdonald, *Sketches of Highlanders: With an Account of their Early Arrival in North America, their Advancement in Agriculture, and some of their Distinguished Military Services in the War of 1812, &c. & c* (Saint John, New Brunswick, 1843), p. 47; I. McKay, 'Tartanism triumphant: The construction of Scottishness in Nova Scotia, 1933–1954', *Acadiensis*, 21:2 (1992), p. 7.
[23] F/201 – Cape Breton 1831, Nova Scotia Archives Map Collection, NSA, available at <https://archives.novascotia.ca/maps/archives/?ID=16> (last accessed 18 May 2021).
[24] Ibid.
[25] S. J. Augustine, 'Negotiating for life and survival', in M. Battiste (ed.), *Living Treaties: Narrating Mi'kmaw Treaty Relations* (Sydney: Cape Breton University Press, 2016), pp. 16–23; J. G. Reid, 'Scots, settler colonization, and Indigenous displacement: Mi'kma'ki, 1770–1820 in comparative context', *Journal of Scottish Historical Studies*, 38:1 (2018), pp. 178–96; L. F. S. Upton, 'Indian policy in colonial Nova Scotia, 1783–1871', *Acadiensis*, 5:1 (1975), pp. 14–15, 28.

predominantly Scottish Highland settlement to the north-east of the Margaree River valley, exposes that even where the land rights of the Mi'kmaq were supposed to be ensured, squatters overran them.[26] Notwithstanding the fact that many Highlanders were there because they themselves had been displaced, they had few qualms about settling on land in use by the Mi'kmaq.[27] Writing to a fellow priest back in Scotland, Augustin McDonald – younger brother of John MacDonald, the tacksman who established the first mass Scottish Catholic settlement at Glenaladale in Prince Edward Island in the early 1770s – showed little concern for the Mi'kmaq. His observation that 'it was hard to say when they will be induced to give it up or imitate surrounding examples into civilisation … here are not Countrys [sic] but Kingdoms challenging to be possessed' was not unique.[28]

As James Hunter observes, 'there are many parts of North America where emigrants from the Highlands and Islands, despite the hardships faced initially, managed to better themselves in a remarkably short time. Cape Breton Island was not like that.'[29] A culture of survival and perseverance was clear, and there is something to be said for the observation that the 'mythology that all Highlanders were driven from their homelands … appears to be more prominent in narratives written in English than in memories preserved in Gaelic'.[30] Cape Breton Island was a new landscape where they could live landlord free and that was enormously appealing, yet while many Highland Scots petitioned for and were granted large tracts of land, there were many more whose wounds were raw from the clearances and who found themselves, and probably preferred to be, on the geographic and social fringes in their new home. Consequently, squatter settlements were ubiquitous, and many were in parts of the island that were difficult to access.

The settlers cultivated a sense of self-sufficiency that would get them through the harsh winters, which might see them cut off from other communities for as many as five or six months. Those living along the mountainous coasts, at settlements such as Pollet's Cove (the front cover of this volume) or Lowland Cove on the north-western tip of the island, relied heavily upon water for transport and communication; it was much faster and far more convenient. Rough tracks existed sometimes, but overland travel along precarious stony trails up and down mountainsides was arduous and could be extremely dangerous at

---

[26] Bittermann, 'The hierarchy of the soil', pp. 33–55.
[27] Kehoe, 'Catholic Highland Scots', pp. 77–92.
[28] Quoted in I. Allan, M.-A. Macinnes, D. Harper and L. G. Fryer (eds), *Scotland and the Americas, c.1650–c.1939: A Documentary Source Book* (Edinburgh: Scottish History Society, 2002), p. 185.
[29] Hunter, *Scottish Exodus*, p.10.
[30] C. Calloway, *White people, Indians and Highlanders: Tribal Peoples and Colonial Encounters in Scotland and America* (New York: Oxford University Press, 2008), p. 265.

certain times of the year.³¹ Around 1887, for example, the residents of Pollet's Cove petitioned the Nova Scotia government for road improvements and the construction of two bridges to make crossing the rivers during the big spring floods easier.³² Subsistence agriculture combined with hunting, fishing and good root cellars sustained families and kept people from starving, though the potato blight that ravaged the Scottish Highlands and Ireland in the late 1840s wreaked havoc in Cape Breton too.³³ There were accounts of people 'reduced to indigency and scavenging for carrion along the shoreline ... of families subsisting on one meal per day of curds and milk to stave off starvation'.³⁴ It is estimated that about 50 per cent of Cape Breton's entire population at mid-century were squatters and their 'fierce reputation' meant that they faced little government interference.³⁵ The Committee on Crown Property reported in 1860 that 'a half a million of acres of the crown lands, representing a capital of over £50,000, are in the hands of squatters' and that such a state of affairs was 'pregnant with most serious mischief'.³⁶ The image of the Cape Breton Highlander, like their Scottish counterpart, went through a process of romanticisation and softening that was largely complete by the 1880s, but initial impressions of many as intimidating and lawless enabled the culture of land squatting to go unchecked.³⁷ That these settlers initially had no legal title to the lands they occupied did not deter them, nor did the presence of the Mi'kmaq.

When it comes to understanding how the Scottish Highlands connect with Cape Breton, we need to accept that there are two irreconcilable Highland pasts at play – colonised and coloniser – and they could be and were both conscious and unconscious. Squatting, while a common feature of colonial life, was an acute problem on Cape Breton.³⁸ From the 1860s, there were deter-

---

[31] Jim Phillips and Philip Girard note the treacherous tracks and how it put off judges in 'Courts, communities and communication: The Nova Scotia Supreme Court on Circuit, 1816–50', in H. Foster, B. L. Berger and A. R. Buck (eds), *The Grand Experiment: Law & Legal Culture in British Settler Societies* (Vancouver: University of British Columbia Press, 2008), p. 131.

[32] Nigel Maney included this petition in his 'History of Pollett's Cove'. The original petition, which was submitted around 1887 and signed by John M. Fraser, has not yet been located.

[33] S. J. Hornsby, *Nineteenth-Century Cape Breton: A Historical Geography* (Montreal and Kingston: McGill-Queen's University Press, 1992), pp. 48–84; Robert Campbell, 'The truck system in the Cape Breton fishery: Philip Robin and Company in Cheticamp, 1843–1852', *Labour/Le Travail*, 75 (2015), p. 181.

[34] L. Stanley, *The Well-Watered Garden: The Presbyterian Church in Cape Breton, 1798–1860* (Sydney: University College of Cape Breton Press, 1983), p. 24.

[35] 'Emigration to Nova Scotia, New Brunswick, Prince Edward Island, and the Canadas', in *Chambers's Information for the People* (Edinburgh, 1842), p. 28.

[36] 'Report of Committee on Crown Property', in *Journals of the House of Assembly of Nova Scotia* (1860), p. 220.

[37] J. I. Little, '"A fine, hardy, good-looking race of people": Travel writers, tourism promoters, and the Highland Scots identity on Cape Breton Island, 1829–1920', *Acadiensis*, 44:1 (2015), p. 27.

[38] D. Samson, *The Spirit of Industry and Improvement: Liberal Government and Rural-Industrial Society, Nova Scotia, 1790–1867* (Montreal: McGill-Queen's University Press, 2008), p. 189; D. C. Harvey, 'Scottish immigration to Cape Breton', *Dalhousie Review*, 21:3 (1941), p. 323.

mined efforts by government to normalise all land occupation, but it was a struggle, since opposition to state intervention was strong.[39] The heavy squatter presence in nineteenth-century Cape Breton has been noted by researchers, but there has been no consideration of the broader ramifications or long-term effects. For example, patterns of social exclusion and economic deprivation are rooted deeply in the process of settler colonialism and continue to plague many Cape Breton communities, but how this process evolved across multiple levels and numerous constituencies requires interrogation. The work of James Hunter is helpful for identifying certain markers. In his *On the Other Side of Sorrow: Nature and People in the Scottish Highlands*, he notes the consequences of the 'inferiorisation' of the Highlands and its people. They witnessed a 'belittling' of everything about them, 'not just their language, but their entire culture, their music, their traditions – all those things, in short, which render them distinctive, are scorned, derided, denigrated'.[40] This was not restricted to the Highlands. The Highland migrants and their descendants across the British Empire faced significant prejudice as they tried to re-establish themselves in various colonies; sectarianism and racism were strong undercurrents. During a visit to the province in the 1850s, the American travel writer, Frederick Cozzens, denigrated the Scots of northern Cape Breton as 'a canting, covenanting oat-eating money-gripping tribe of Scotch Presbyterians: a transplanted degenerate, barren patch of high cheek-bones and red hair with nothing cleaving to them of the original stock, except covetousness and that peculiar cutaneous eruption for which the mother country is celebrated.'[41] Another writer, Thomas Chandler Haliburton, hailed by some as 'the Province's most celebrated 19th Century writer', observed scornfully that 'the great number ... are indigent and ignorant Scotch islanders, every year receiving an increase of a thousand or two fresh emigrants, equally poor and illiterate, and almost all of the Roman Catholic persuasion'.[42]

Negative descriptions and stereotypes were damaging, but they spurred efforts by those of Highland descent to reclass the Highland Scots as respectable and productive citizens – St Francis Xavier University, for example, which was ostensibly the first Scottish Highland university in the world, is one example. The legacy of this, however, is the omission, deliberate or not, of their active participation in the process of colonisation. Some of the work on Highland settlement, land, identity and belonging in the Maritimes that has drawn attention

[39] D. Nerbas, 'Scots, capitalism, and the colonial countryside: Impressions from nineteenth-century Cape Breton', *History Compass*, 18:11 (2020), p. 4; Hornsby, *Nineteenth-century Cape Breton*, pp. 126–8.
[40] J. Hunter, *On the Other Side of Sorrow: Nature and People in the Scottish Highlands* (Edinburgh: Birlinn, 2014), p. 35.
[41] F. S. Cozzens, *Acadian or, A Month with the Blue Noses* (New York: Derby & Jackson, 1859), p. 151.
[42] Quoted in Little, '"A fine, hardy, good-looking race of people"', p. 22.

to the significance of the oral tradition in creating memory around the issue of Mi'kmaq displacement should encourage deeper interrogations of the collaborative role played by the Highlanders in extending the process of British colonisation in the region.[43] That the Mi'kmaq often pushed back and sought recognition for their right to land has been overshadowed by the more palatable settler narrative which tends to stress collaboration and mutual support.[44] Of course, there were numerous instances of mutual support, but reciprocity was not the norm for the Highland settlers and we should not assume that it was. Instead, the reality this created for the Mi'kmaq across the Maritimes was widespread displacement and dislocation, as the petition that Chief Oliver Thomas LeBone sent to Queen Victoria in 1838 highlights. The loss of 'hunting grounds without receiving any remuneration' on Prince Edward Island, he pointed out, 'reduced the much numerous Tribes in this Island to a skeleton of Five Hundred Individuals who collectively are not inferior to any other denomination of Your Majesty's subjects'.[45] In 1859, Chief Francis Tomah's petition to Nova Scotia's lieutenant governor stressed the problem of settler spread, explaining that the lands his people had been allotted were 'in an unsatisfactory state, much encroached upon by squatters and trespassers, and yielding no benefit whatever to the tribe'. To rectify the situation, he requested that a survey be taken of 'all the lands reserved' for Mi'kmaq use so that the government could see 'the encroachments made on each reserve, with the names of the parties trespassing. The nature and value of their improvements, if any, and the damage they have done.'[46] Aware of the toll unregulated settlement had taken on their communities, these Mi'kmaq leaders were asserting their rights. The problem they faced was the settlers' blatant disregard for all attempts to control where they lived and what they lived upon. As I have shown elsewhere, there are numerous examples of settler petitions requesting land they knew to be occupied or in use by the Mi'kmaq.[47]

---

[43] S. Y. MacDonald *'Dh'fheumadh iad àit' a dheanamh'* (*They would have to make a Place*): *Land and Belonging in Gaelic Nova Scotia* (PhD thesis, Memorial University of Newfoundland, 2017).

[44] See various chapters in M. Battiste (ed.), *Living Treaties: Narrating Mi'kmaw Treaty Relations* (Sydney: Cape Breton University Press, 2016); see also the interview between the author and the composer and musician, Ian McKinnon, February 2021, available at <https://www.youtube.com/watch?v=v5N0as8jY1o&list=PLWz2XwDtse7G4c4J9Dj3iPxMJs8F1n2r1&index=7> (last accessed 2 June 2021). For a general discussion, see T. Bueltmann, A. Hinson and G. Morton, *The Scottish Diaspora* (Edinburgh: Edinburgh University Press, 2013), pp. 95–113.

[45] R. Bitterman, 'Mi'kmaq land claims and the Escheat Movement in Prince Edward Island', *University of New Brunswick Law Journal*, 22 (2006), pp. 173, 176.

[46] 'Petition of the Micmac Indians of the island of Cape Breton, in council assembled, on the Festival of St Anne, at Chapel Island, 1859', *Journal and Proceedings of the House of Assembly of the Province of Nova Scotia* (1860), pp. 327–8.

[47] Kehoe, 'Catholic Highland Scots', pp. 77–92. Specifically, see 1812 Charles McNab, Cape Breton No. 854, mf. 15791, and 1822 Archibald McPhagan, Cape Breton No. 2874, mf. 15798, Cape Breton Island Petitions, 1787–1843, NSA.

Michael Newton's point that 'the shame of dispossession is transformed onto a narrative of self-determination and triumph' bears particular consideration here since the process of memory construction was and remains a tool of colonisation.[48] Prioritising the recollections of descendants, which extrapolate visions of 'good relations', is inconsistent with the reality of colonialism.[49] Mary Mullen's work on Ireland makes a similar point, and her argument that such an approach 'perpetuates colonialism by too easily smoothing over differences and confusing affective connections with material realities' is relevant here, since it reflects the reality that many had to overcome the exclusion they had faced first in Scotland and then in north-eastern British North America.[50] A figure who played a major role in this in Nova Scotia was Angus L. MacDonald, an early twentieth-century politician and premier whose people came from Moidart in the western Highlands, but who himself had been born at Dunvegan, Inverness County, Cape Breton. His 'rather hazily conceived Scottish tradition', and the fact that the province was somehow reimagined as the Scotland of North America, speaks to the deeply entrenched colonial power structures that enabled the invention of an identity that made little room for the other resident ethnicities.[51] Myth-making and memory (re)construction played a central role. The tendency of immigrants, regardless of their nation of origin, to undertake the construction of historical memory is a natural part of the process of adjusting and resettlement. When looking at the Highlanders who went to the Canadian Maritimes, we must be mindful of how understandings of the past have evolved over time and why. Nineteenth-century needs, for example, differed markedly from twentieth-century ones. In the Scottish Highland case, the ability to prosper and be active participants in a growing economy required migrants and their descendants to 'forget' or dissociate themselves from the humanitarian distress that had been caused by the rise of a more aggressive commercial economy in the Highlands.[52] Fair enough, but this raises a few questions: how did this manifest in the subsequent generations who did not experience the clearances themselves; how was trauma carried by the migrants and their descendants; and to what extent did this mask the colonialism they knowingly and unknowingly extended?

So, how do we, as modern-day historians, deal with this complex legacy? The best way to start is by approaching it from the dichotomous and irreconcilable

---

[48] M. Newton, *Seanchaidh na Coille / The Memory-Keeper of the Forest* (Sydney: Cape Breton University Press, 2015), p. 145.

[49] MacDonald, 'Dh'fheumadh iad àit', p. 119.

[50] M. L. Mullen, 'How the Irish became settlers: Metaphors of indigeneity and the erasure of Indigenous peoples', *New Hibernia Review*, 20:3 (2016), p. 83.

[51] McKay, 'Tartanism triumphant', pp. 16–18; P. Basu, *Highland Homecomings: Genealogy and Heritage Tourism in the Scottish Diaspora* (Abingdon: Routledge, 2007), p. 42; Cozzens, *Acadia*, p. 151.

[52] Bitterman, 'On remembering and forgetting', p. 257.

perspective that both colonised and colonising Scottish Highlanders were the reality. This will enable us to acknowledge the trauma of the clearances, to position Scottish Highland settlement as an act of colonisation upon the Mi'kmaq, and to see the invented and mythologised elements of Highland Diasporic culture more clearly. Beyond these developments and linking back to a point made at the start of the chapter about the projection of a Scottish Highland identity over other groups, this kind of approach will illuminate the authentic traditions that exist at local, familial and community levels. It will stop us from misidentifying the Scottish essence or thinking that there is such a thing. It would render our searches 'for the signs which today mark the Scots and by extension the Nova Scotian' redundant.[53] We would see that rather than using tartan, as my junior high teacher did, as a marker of Scottishness, it is to the familial and community-based networks that we must turn because before 'Scottishness' was marketable, it was the people's private world.

Before his death in 1997, the well-known Margaree storyteller, teacher and fiddler, Archie Neil Chisholm, explained the private world of ethnicity. Disabled as a child from polio, he wrote of how traditions sustained him: 'momma beguiled my hours at home with Gaelic songs, and she truly relished telling a good story. Fiddle music and kitchen rackets were part of life ... when I was young.'[54] Other traditions such as marriages, naming practices, lullabies and funerals were similarly influential. This intangible heritage was an intricate part of community formation because it built people's lives.[55] The 'Scottishness' of Cape Breton Island has a distinctively Highlands and Islands character, but it has very little to do with tartan and everything to do with colonisation. Identifying and untangling the threads of Britain's imperial programme, in which Highlanders were deeply invested, is a responsibility that we all bear, and those of us with intimate connections to the rural world do not have the luxury of time. Only by confronting the inherently complex legacies of clearance, colonialism and rural exclusion collectively as a research community, and as individuals who need to understand our own positionality, can we build sustainable communities.

---

[53] McKay, 'Tartanism triumphant', p. 14.
[54] M. A. Ducharme, *Archie Neil: A Triumph of Life!* (Wreck Cove: Breton Books, 1992).
[55] The work of Richard Mackinnon is invaluable here. See, for example, R. Mackinnon, *Discovering Cape Breton Folklore* (Sydney: Cape Breton University Press, 2009); R. Mackinnon, 'The UNESCO Convention for the Safeguarding of Intangible Cultural Heritage and its Implications for Sustaining Culture in Nova Scotia', in M. Stefano, P. Davis and G. Corsane (eds), *Safeguarding Intangible Cultural Heritage* (Woodbridge: Boydell & Brewer, 2021), pp. 153–62.

Part Two

Language and Culture

THREE

Gaelic Heritage, Language Revitalisation and Identity in Present-day Nova Scotia

Stuart Dunmore

The creation of 'new speakers' via education and language policy interventions has become an increasingly crucial objective in many contexts of minority language revitalisation. The phrase was initially coined in respect of L2 users of the Galician and Catalan languages, and has since been employed frequently in the sociolinguistics of other minoritised language groups.[1] The concept of 'new' speakers refers to individuals who have acquired high levels of oracy in an additional language to that of their principal childhood socialisation, and make frequent use of it in the course of their daily lives. At the respective levels of national and provincial government, policymakers in Scotland and Nova Scotia make frequent reference to the role that such individuals may play in the future of the Gaelic language. In addition to Scotland's 57,600 Gaelic speakers, the 2011 Canadian census recorded 1,275 Gaelic speakers in Nova Scotia, or just over 0.1 per cent of the total population of the province.[2] Of that number, only 300 individuals reported Gaelic as their mother tongue.[3] The Nova Scotia

---

[1] On Galician and Catalan see, for example, B. O'Rourke and F. Ramallo, 'Competing ideologies of linguistic authority amongst new speakers in contemporary Galicia', *Language in Society*, 42 (2013), pp. 287–305; B. O'Rourke, J. Pujolar and F. Ramallo, 'New speakers of minority languages: the challenging opportunity – Foreword', *International Journal of the Sociology of Language*, 231 (2015), pp. 1–20; J. Pujolar and I. Gonzàlez, 'Linguistic "mudes" and the de-ethnicization of language choice in Catalonia', *International Journal of Bilingual Education and Bilingualism*, 16 (2013), pp. 138–52. On new speakers of other minority languages, see also C. Smith-Christmas, N. Ó Murchadha, M. Moriarty and M. Hornsby (eds), *New Speakers of Minority Languages: Linguistic Ideologies and Practices* (Basingstoke: Palgrave, 2018).

[2] See National Records of Scotland, *Statistical Bulletin: 2011 Census – Key Results on Population, Ethnicity, Identity, Language, Religion, Health, Housing and Accommodation in Scotland – Release 2A*, 2013, available at <www.scotlandscensus.gov.uk/documents/censusresults/release2a/Stats Bulletin2A.pdf> (last accessed 26 September 2019); Statistics Canada, *National Household Survey Profile: Nova Scotia 2011*, 2015, available at <https://www12.statcan.gc.ca/nhs-enm/2011/dp-pd/prof/> (last accessed 13 December 2019); Statistics Canada, *2011 Census: Detailed Mother-tongue – Nova Scotia*, 2017, available at <https://www12.statcan.gc.ca/census-recensement/2011/> (last accessed 14 December 2019).

[3] Ibid.

Gaelic community is thus substantially smaller than that of Scotland relative to the total population, having declined from an estimated population of over 80,000 in the early twentieth century.[4] In both polities, policymakers have emphasised the importance of Gaelic language teaching as a mechanism for revitalising Gaelic. New speakers have thus emerged in both contexts as a significant element in the Gaelic language community.

Notably, Gaelic educational opportunities in Nova Scotia are limited by comparison with Scotland, where over 6,000 children are currently enrolled in Gaelic-medium immersion education. Immersion programmes have been available to Indigenous Mi'kmaw children and to Acadian children for some years, and in September 2021 North America's first Gaelic immersion school opened its doors to nine primary school pupils in Mabou, Cape Breton. For the most part, however, Gaelic language teaching in the province remains largely limited to a small number of schools teaching the language as a subject, evening classes, residential immersion courses and university classes.

Given this disparity, a major objective of the present research has been to assess the language learning and life experiences that inform Scottish and Nova Scotian new speakers' decision to acquire and use Gaelic, and, relatedly, their cultural identifications with the language. In spite of the small overall numbers of reported Gaelic speakers in Nova Scotia, the provincial Office of Gaelic Affairs has estimated that at least 230,000 Nova Scotian inhabitants claim descent from families who spoke Gaelic historically.[5] As a response to policymakers' present priorities in both contexts, and building on research that has previously examined language ideologies in respect of Gaelic and Scottish identity, this chapter presents a comparative analysis of new speaker motivations, identities and linguistic ideologies in both countries.[6]

---

[4] M. Kennedy, 'Gaelic Nova Scotia: An Economic, Cultural, and Social Impact Study', Report for Nova Scotia Government, 2002, Halifax, NS, Nova Scotia Museum.

[5] See Office of Gaelic Affairs, 'Our community', 2018, available at <https://gaelic.novascotia.ca/community> (last accessed 15 October 2021).

[6] For the author's previous research concerning language ideologies and Gaelic identity in Scotland and Nova Scotia, see also S. Dunmore, 'Immersion education outcomes and the Gaelic community: Identities and language ideologies among Gaelic-medium educated adults in Scotland', *Journal of Multilingual and Multicultural Development*, 38 (2017), pp. 726–41; S. Dunmore, 'New Gaelic Speakers, New Gaels? Language ideologies and ethnolinguistic continuity among Gaelic-medium educated adults', in C. Smith-Christmas, N. Ó Murchadha, M. Moriarty and M. Hornsby (eds), *New Speakers of Minority Languages: Linguistic Ideologies and Practices* (Basingstoke: Palgrave, 2018), pp. 23–44; S. Dunmore, 'Bilingual life after school? Opportunity, choice and ideology among former Gaelic-medium students', *Transactions of the Gaelic Society of Inverness*, 63 (2018), pp. 287–316; S. Dunmore, *Language Revitalisation in Gaelic Scotland: Linguistic Practice and Ideology* (Edinburgh: Edinburgh University Press, 2019).

Language acquisition, identities and Fishmanian views of language revitalisation

Language shift, loss and revitalisation have become matters of increasingly urgent concern internationally.[7] Efforts to stem the decline of minoritised languages have turned increasingly to second language acquisition – and especially bilingual, 'revitalisation immersion education' – as a strategy for increasing numbers of speakers.[8] In part this development, observed in diverse contexts across Oceania, North and Latin America and Western Europe, is reflective of policymakers' understanding that once interrupted, the organic, intergenerational transmission of languages in the home domain is very difficult to influence or to reinstate.

In Scotland, Gaelic-medium immersion education (henceforward 'GME') is regarded by policymakers as one of the principal mechanisms for the generation of new Gaelic speakers.[9] Nevertheless, it has been widely theorised on the basis of research from the international context that the potential impact of (bilingual) education on language revitalisation may be undermined by a complex interplay of social, linguistic and psychological factors. Evidence from this wide-ranging literature – and especially that drawing on French immersion education in Canada – provides a mixed picture of target language use by past students after their completion of bilingual schooling.[10]

Prefiguring much of this linguistic research, Fishman consistently theorised that school-based language policy interventions would ultimately prove

---

[7] For a sample of the growing literature on global language loss, see D. Nettle and S. Romaine, *Vanishing Voices: The Extinction of the World's Languages* (Oxford: Oxford University Press, 2000); S. Romaine, 'Linguistic diversity, sustainability, and the future of the past', in K. King, N. Schilling-Estes, L. Fogle, J. Lou and B. Soukup (eds), *Sustaining Linguistic Diversity Endangered and Minority Languages and Varieties* (Washington, DC: Georgetown University Press, 2008), pp. 7–21; S. Romaine, 'The bilingual and multilingual community', in T. K. Bhatia and W. C. Ritchie (eds), *The Handbook of Bilingualism and Multilingualism*, 2nd edn (Oxford: Blackwell, 2013), pp. 445–65; J. A. Fishman and O. García (eds), *Handbook of Language and Ethnic Identity: Disciplinary and Regional Perspectives*, Vol. 1, 2nd edn (Oxford: Oxford University Press, 2010); J. A. Fishman and O. García (eds), *Handbook of Language and Ethnic Identity: The Success–Failure Continuum in Language and Ethnic Identity Efforts*, Vol. 2, 2nd edn (Oxford: Oxford University Press, 2011); J. Costa, *Revitalising Language in Provence: A Critical Approach* (Oxford: Blackwell and Philological Society, 2017).

[8] The phrase 'revitalisation immersion' education is attributed to O. García, *Bilingual Education in the 21st Century: A Global Perspective* (Oxford: Blackwell, 2009).

[9] Relevant policy statements are contained in the following key documents: Bòrd na Gàidhlig, *The National Gaelic Language Plan, 2018–2023*, 2018, Inverness; Scottish Government, *Consultation Paper on a Gaelic Medium Education Bill*, 2014, Edinburgh.

[10] See, for example, B. Harley, 'After immersion: Maintaining the momentum', *Journal of Multilingual and Multicultural Development*, 15 (1994), pp. 229–44; R. Johnstone, *Immersion in a Second or Additional Language at School: Evidence from International Research*, Stirling: Scottish Centre for Teaching and Research, 2001; A. MacFarlane and M. Wesche, 'Immersion outcomes: Beyond language proficiency', *The Canadian Modern Language Review*, 51 (1995), pp. 250–74.

unsuccessful without adequate support outside the classroom.[11] Fishman stressed of minoritised languages at which RLS ('reversing language shift') efforts are directed, that habitual usage is required 'before school begins, outside of school, during the years of schooling and afterwards, when formal schooling is over and done with'.[12] His recommendations on behalf of endangered languages were particularly persistent in emphasising the importance of minority language use in the home. In Nova Scotia, 'core Gaelic' second language teaching in schools, extra-curricular immersion programmes and adult language acquisition initiatives have tended to form the basis of revitalisation efforts in recent decades.[13] It is particularly noteworthy, however, that both the province-funded *Gàidhlig aig Baile* ('Gaelic in the home') immersion programme and *Bun is Bàrr* ('root and branch') master-apprentice scheme place heavy emphasis on encouraging meaningful and ongoing interaction between fluent or L1 Gaelic speakers and (L2) learners for creating new speakers of the language.

Such initiatives clearly resonate with Fishman's recommendations vis-à-vis the reattainment of diglossia and intergenerational interaction at the fundamental, lower-level stages of his model for assessing and reversing language shift.[14] In that sense, the bottom-up and community-centred focus of current Gaelic revitalisation efforts in Nova Scotia may be seen, from a Fishmanian perspective, as theoretically more sustainable in the long term than school-focused initiatives which tend to dominate in Scotland. As I demonstrate below, an emphasis on ethnolinguistic identity and discourses of cultural distinctiveness currently dominating in Nova Scotia's Gaelic community also closely parallel recommendations advocated by Fishman.

Yet Fishman's RLS model and his recommendations on behalf of threatened minority languages rest largely on a conception of language and ethnic identity which contemporary sociolinguists increasingly regard as problematic.

---

[11] Fishman's consistent approach advocating his models and theories of RLS are laid out in full in the following works: J. Fishman, *Reversing Language Shift: Theoretical and Empirical Foundations of Assistance to Threatened Languages* (Clevedon: Multilingual Matters, 1991); J. Fishman (ed.), *Can Threatened Languages Be Saved? Reversing Language Shift Revisited: A 21st Century Perspective* (Clevedon: Multilingual Matters, 2001); J. Fishman, 'From theory to practice (and vice versa): Review, reconsideration, and reiteration', in J. Fishman (ed.), *Can Threatened Languages Be Saved? Reversing Language Shift Revisited: A 21st Century Perspective* (Clevedon: Multilingual Matters, 2001), pp. 451–83.

[12] Fishman, 'From theory to practice (and vice versa)', p. 471.

[13] F. MacEachen, 'Am Blas Againn fhìn: Community Gaelic Immersion Classes in Nova Scotia – An evaluation of activities in 2006–2007', report for Office of Gaelic Affairs, 2008, Halifax, NS, Office of Gaelic Affairs; R. Dunbar, 'Minority language renewal: Gaelic in Nova Scotia, and lessons from abroad', report for NS Govt Office of Gaelic Affairs, 2008, Halifax, NS, Office of Gaelic Affairs; S. Watson and M. Ivey, 'Nàisean cultarach nan Gàidheal: Ath-chruthachadh tìr-dhùthchasaich ann an Albainn Nuaidh', in W. McLeod, A. Gunderloch and R. Dunbar (eds), *Rannsachadh na Gàidhlig 8* (Edinburgh: Dunedin Academic Press, 2016), pp. 183–94.

[14] Fishman, *Reversing Language Shift*, p. 395.

The feasibility of positing a straightforward relationship between the minority language ('Xish') and its traditionally defined, ethnolinguistic speaker community ('Xmen/Xians') has been questioned at length by various authors.[15] Jaffe, for instance, critiqued essentialist interpretations of the language–identity nexus, in which 'both "language" and "identity" and their iconic relationships are seen as fixed, ascribed/natural and unproblematic'.[16] Contemporary scholars tend to distance themselves from such essentialist positions, which often presume that members of a given identity category are 'both fundamentally similar to one another and fundamentally different to members of other groups'.[17]

While his theoretical stance regarding the importance of the home context to intergenerational transmission remains influential in the contemporary literature, many of Fishman's ideas draw on such an unproblematic, iconic conception of language and identity. Fishman's RLS model rests to a large degree on the 'premises that Xmen are not Ymen and that Xish culture [...] is not Yish culture'.[18] He states that 'prior ideological clarification' of these fundamental premises 'must not be skipped over' if revitalisation initiatives are to succeed.[19] The notion of 'prior ideological clarification' leads us inevitably to a discussion of language ideologies and their role in the development of ethnolinguistic identities. Silverstein defined linguistic ideologies as 'sets of beliefs about language articulated by users as a rationalisation or justification of perceived language structure or use'.[20] Linguistic ideologies circulate systematically as cultural products, and are reproduced through sociocultural interaction, coming to be viewed as 'natural or as common sense', through processes that obscure the reality of their subjectivity and socially negotiated dissemination.[21]

---

[15] See the following: J. Edwards (ed.), *Linguistic Minorities, Policies and Pluralism* (London: Academic Press, 1984); J. Edwards, *Minority Languages and Group Identity: Cases and Categories* (Amsterdam: John Benjamins, 2010); M. Heller, *Linguistic Minorities and Modernity: A Sociolinguistic Ethnography*, 2nd edn (London: Continuum, 2006); M. Heller, *Paths to Postnationalism: A Critical Ethnography of Language and Identity* (Oxford: Oxford University Press, 2010); A. Jaffe, *Ideologies in Action: Language Politics on Corsica* (Berlin: Mouton de Gruyter, 1999); A. Jaffe, 'Discourses of endangerment: Contexts and consequences of essentializing discourses', in A. Duchêne and M. Heller (eds), *Discourses of Endangerment: Ideology and Interest in the Defence of Languages* (London: Continuum, 2007), pp. 57–75; S. Romaine, 'Planning for the survival of linguistic diversity', *Language Policy*, 5 (2006), pp. 441–73.

[16] Jaffe, 'Discourses of endangerment', p. 8.

[17] M. Bucholtz, M. Hall and K. Hall, 'Language and identity', in A. Duranti (ed.), *A Companion to Linguistic Anthropology* (Oxford: Blackwell, 2004), pp. 369–94, see esp. p. 374.

[18] Fishman, *Reversing Language Shift*, p. 394.

[19] Ibid.

[20] M. Silverstein, 'Language structure and linguistic ideology', in R. Cline, W. Hanks and C. Hofbauer (eds), *The Elements: A Parasession on Linguistic Units and Levels* (Chicago: Chicago Linguistic Society, 1979), pp. 193–247, see esp. p. 193.

[21] A. Boudreau and L. Dubois, 'Français, Acadien, Acadjonne: Competing discourses on language preservation along the shores of the Baie Sainte-Marie', in A. Duchêne and M. Heller (eds), *Discourses of Endangerment: Ideology and Interest in the Defence of Languages* (London: Continuum, 2007), pp. 99–120, see esp. p. 104.

In recent years, scholars have frequently observed that ideologies of this kind can be advanced in speakers' discourse as attempted rationalisations for language practices, which may in turn reinforce those practices.[22] In particular, research on language ideologies has often addressed the relationship of speakers' linguistic practices and perceptions to their sociocultural identities.[23] On this basis, linguists and anthropologists have theorised that language ideologies can have an important influence on the ways in which bilingual speakers in minority language settings identify and engage with the multiple varieties that make up their linguistic repertoires. Such considerations regarding the role of language ideologies in speakers' linguistic practices are central to the analysis I present below.

New speakers, identities and paths to new speakerhood in Scotland and Nova Scotia

Research on new speakers of Gaelic in Scotland has previously examined the nature of such speakers' language learning trajectories, motivations and linguistic practices. McLeod et al. employed semi-structured interviews and focus groups to analyse speakers' discourses surrounding the phenomenon from an emic perspective, while third-wave variationist studies by Nance and colleagues also assessed phonetic productions by new Gaelic speakers.[24] These studies emphasised Scottish new Gaelic speakers' association with the term 'Gaelic community'/*Coimhearsnachd na Gàidhlig* in preference to the more circumscribed, ethnonymic term 'Gaels/*Gàidheil*'. Furthermore, while most new speakers, by definition, make frequent use of Gaelic in their day-to-day lives, different linguistic behaviours were reported (and analysed) in interviews. While on the one hand, L1 native speakers were widely viewed as the best model for new speakers in terms of pronunciation and *blas* ('accent/taste'), L1

---

[22] See, for example, Bucholtz and Hall, 'Language and identity'; P. Kroskrity (ed.), *Regimes of Language: Ideologies, Polities, and Identities* (Santa Fe, NM: School of American Research Press, 2000); P. Kroskrity, 'Language ideologies', in A. Duranti (ed.), *A Companion to Linguistic Anthropology* (Oxford: Blackwell, 2004), pp. 496–517; M. Makihara, 'Anthropology', in J. A. Fishman and O. García (eds), *Handbook of Language and Ethnic Identity: Disciplinary and Regional Perspectives* (Vol. I), 2nd edn (Oxford: Oxford University Press, 2010), pp. 32–48; J. Cavanaugh, 'Language ideologies and language attitudes', in P. Auer, J. Caro Reina and G. Kaufmann (eds), *Language Variation: European Perspectives IV* (Amsterdam: John Benjamins, 2013), pp. 45–55.

[23] See G. Valdés, S. Gonzàlez, D. García and P. Márquez, 'Heritage languages and ideologies of language', in D. M. Brinton, O. Kagan and S. Bauckus (eds), *Heritage Language Education: A New Field Emerging* (New York: Routledge, 2008), pp. 107–30; García, *Bilingual Education in the 21st Century*.

[24] W. McLeod, B. O'Rourke and S. Dunmore, *New Speakers of Gaelic in Edinburgh and Glasgow: Soillse Research Report*, 2014, Sleat, Isle of Skye: Soillse, p. 39; C. Nance, W. McLeod, B. O'Rourke and S. Dunmore, 'Identity, accent aim, and motivation in second language users: new Scottish Gaelic speakers' use of phonetic variation', *Journal of Sociolinguistics*, 20 (2016), pp. 164–91, see esp. p. 181.

speakers' greater use of English loan words and frequent code-switching tended to be something new speakers tried to avoid.[25]

A number of principles pertinent to second language acquisition are of particular relevance here, most notably Gardner and Lambert's 'integrativeness' model.[26] Based on long-standing research on French–English bilingualism in Canada, Gardner and Lambert defined integrative motivation as L2 learners' 'sincere desire' to culturally integrate with the community. This desire was frequently observed to exert an influence on learners' successful acquisition of the L2. Yet there exist a number of questions as to the model's applicability to the context of heritage language learners of Gaelic in Scotland and Canada, however distant such heritage connections may be. In Nova Scotia, the provincial government-supported *Gàidhlig aig Baile* and *Bun is Bàrr* programmes emphasise the importance of regular interaction between L1 and fluent L2 Gaelic speakers and L2 learners, both for socialising new speakers in the language, and developing their identities as Gaels, an objective rarely observed in contemporary Scotland.

A particularly relevant consideration in this connection concerns the various ways in which contemporary notions of fluid and nested linguistic identities may influence this model's applicability in contemporary society. One possible solution to these questions was developed by Dörnyei and Ushioda.[27] Their concept of the 'motivational self-system' proposes that second language learners' acquisition of an additional language is guided largely by their imagined identities in the language in question, conceived of in terms of the 'ideal' and 'ought to' L2 self. The distinction between these two notional 'selves' is characterised by, on the one hand, second language speakers' internal conceptions of their desired identity in the target language, and, on the other, identity they feel they 'ought to' enact externally while interacting with other speakers (whether teachers, other learners or L1 speakers). Also crucially for the purposes of this chapter, MacIntyre et al. investigated language learning motivations among a sample of L2 Gaelic learners in Nova Scotia. They conceptualise Nova Scotian L2 Gaelic speakers' motivations in terms of the 'rooted' L2 self, distinguishing their orientations toward the language – which drew heavily on understandings of heritage, kinship and ancestry – from L2 learners for whom such identity

---

[25] Ibid.
[26] R. Gardner and W. Lambert, 'Motivational variables in second language acquisition', *Canadian Journal of Psychology*, 13 (1959), pp. 266–72; R. Gardner and W. Lambert, *Attitudes and Motivation in Second Language Learning* (Rowley, MA: Newbury House, 1972).
[27] See the following: Z. Dörnyei, *The Psychology of the Language Learner: Individual Differences in Second Language Acquisition* (Mahwah, NJ: Lawrence Erlbaum, 2005); Z. Dörnyei and E. Ushioda (eds), *Motivation, Language Identity and the L2 Self* (Bristol: Multilingual Matters, 2009); E. Ushioda, 'Language learning motivation, self and identity: Current theoretical perspectives', *Computer Assisted Language Learning*, 24 (2011), pp. 199–210.

associations may be more abstract, or less keenly felt.[28] The notion of the 'rooted' self in acquisition of Gaelic in Nova Scotia, in particular, is extremely apt, resonating closely with the analysis I outline below.

Research context 1: Gaelic in Nova Scotia

The name Nova Scotia ('New Scotland') was first applied to the traditional territories of the Mi'kmaw First Nation, lying between what had become 'New England' and 'Newfoundland' in 1621, when a royal charter for their colonisation was issued to William Alexander, Earl of Stirling.[29] The first Gaelic-speaking Scots to emigrate to Nova Scotia arrived as early as 1629, and while Alexander's attempts to establish a sizeable Scottish colony in the region proved unsuccessful in the short term, Highlanders continued to migrate in small numbers during the seventeenth and early eighteenth centuries.[30] Kennedy even cites evidence that Scots constituted the largest minority group in the Acadian colony of 'New France' after the territory was ceded by British colonists to the French in 1632.[31] Migration from the Scottish Highlands to eastern Nova Scotia accelerated in earnest from the 1770s, as the middle-class Gaelic 'tacksmen' sought new livelihoods in North America in response to declining living standards at home. Migration continued over the next fifty years, but by the 1840s Highland migrants increasingly comprised the displaced and largely homeless tenant classes left destitute as a result of the clearances.

Peak emigration to Nova Scotia occurred between about 1770 and 1850, when over 50,000 Highland Scots are estimated to have arrived into eastern Antigonish, Victoria, Inverness and Cape Breton counties. MacKinnon notes that Gaelic speakers first settled en masse in Pictou County from 1773, having been preceded by Gaelic emigration to Prince Edward Island from 1769, and being followed by mass migrations to south-eastern Cape Breton between 1791 and 1795, Antigonish County and western Cape Breton between 1803 and 1815, and to north-western Cape Breton between 1802 and 1843.[32] Other important foci of Gaelic settlement in eastern Canada included Glengarry

---

[28] P. MacIntyre, S. Baker and H. Sparling, 'Heritage passions, heritage convictions and the rooted L2 self: Music and Gaelic language learning in Cape Breton, Nova Scotia', *Modern Language Journal*, 101 (2017), pp. 501–16.

[29] D. Campbell and R. MacLean, *Beyond the Atlantic Roar: A Study of the Nova Scotia Scots* (Toronto: McClelland and Stewart, 1974), p. 35; E. Mertz, '"No Burden to Carry": Cape Breton Pragmatics and Metapragmatics' (PhD thesis, Duke University, 1982), p. 36.

[30] T. Ó hIfearnáin, 'Doimhne an dúchais: éagsúlacht san aistriú teanga i gCeap Breatainn na hAlban Nua', *Taighde agus teagasc*, 2 (2002), pp. 62–91, see esp. p. 64.

[31] Kennedy, 'Gaelic Nova Scotia', pp. 25–7; see also Campbell and MacLean, *Beyond the Atlantic Roar*, p. 35.

[32] K. MacKinnon, 'Gaelic in Canada: Haki and Hekja's inheritance in "The Land of Promise"', in P. Sture Ureland (ed.), *Global Eurolinguistics: European languages in North America – Migration, Maintenance and Death* (Tübingen: Niemeyer, 2001), pp. 19–47, see esp. p. 20.

County, Ontario, parts of eastern Quebec, and settlements in south-western Newfoundland resulting from secondary migration from Cape Breton.

The settlement patterns that these successive waves of migration produced were diffuse and overwhelmingly rural in nature, in contrast to the urban settlement of mostly Anglophone settlers who moved into the burgeoning towns and industrial centres of Nova Scotia.[33] In sociolinguistic terms, Gaelic-speaking communities thrived as sites for language socialisation in these relatively isolated conditions, although their socioeconomic circumstances were often fragile.[34] The cultural homogeneity of Gaelic-speaking communities in Nova Scotia was amplified by the chain migration patterns that characterised Gaelic speakers' settlement in the nineteenth century; communities that were relatively uniform in terms of their (Gaelic-dominant) linguistic practices and religious observances – whether Catholic or Protestant – were frequently transplanted into similarly homogeneous communities in eastern Nova Scotia.[35]

Kennedy remarks that 'the nature of the migrations from Scotland ensured that large, nearly homogeneous communities were established [in Nova Scotia], dominating nearly a third of the province's area'. Lowland Scots' settlement patterns in Nova Scotia were similarly consistent, with Scottish English speakers forming homogeneous blocks distinct from Gaels in town and country. As a result, the Gaelic speakers of Nova Scotia fared somewhat better than their contemporaries in the old country; Kennedy argues that within this 'richly Gaelic environment', a unique, 'truly Canadian and North American Gaelic community' developed and flourished in the nineteenth century.[36]

Patterns of chain migration to Nova Scotia accelerated through the mid-nineteenth century, as a consequence of the processes of mass displacement that became known as the Highland Clearances. Shaw has estimated that by 1880 over 80,000 Gaelic speakers were present in Nova Scotia, and by the time of the 1871 census, Scots were the largest ethnic group in Nova Scotia, having temporarily overtaken ethnic English settlers.[37] Furthermore, the majority of Scots to have immigrated into the province were Gaelic speakers, who formed the linguistic majority over large parts of eastern Nova Scotia.[38] Even at this stage, however, Edwards has reviewed evidence for the weakening of intergenerational transmission of Gaelic and subsequent language shift to English

---

[33] Kennedy, 'Gaelic Nova Scotia', pp. 22–3.
[34] E. Mertz, '"No Burden to Carry"'; MacKinnon, 'Gaelic in Canada'; Kennedy, 'Gaelic Nova Scotia'.
[35] Edwards, *Minority Languages and Group Identity*; Kennedy, 'Gaelic Nova Scotia'; MacKinnon, 'Gaelic in Canada'; Ó hIfearnáin, 'Doimhne an dúchais'.
[36] Kennedy, 'Gaelic Nova Scotia', p. 277; Campbell and MacLean, *Beyond the Atlantic Roar*, p. 46.
[37] J. Shaw, 'Bithidh iad a' moladh na Gàidhlig, ach 'sann anns a' Bheurla', 23 September 1977, *West Highland Free Press*.
[38] Kennedy, 'Gaelic Nova Scotia', p. 25.

in Gaelic communities.[39] The seeds of language shift may already have been sown at this early juncture, therefore. Demand for the provision of education through Gaelic was minimal, and when state schools were established in 1864 no provision was made for any form of Gaelic education.[40] As such, Kennedy argues, children of Gaelic speakers in the nineteenth century subsequently learned next to nothing (and certainly nothing positive) of their language in schools, and internalised negative attitudes regarding the relevance and importance of Gaelic in (Anglophone) Canadian society.[41]

Edwards states that only in 1921 was Gaelic permitted in the education system for study as an optional subject 'if the majority of students demanded it', by which time the language was unarguably undergoing language shift.[42] Again, demand for uptake of Gaelic was limited, partly due to the internalisation of hostile official attitudes in the nineteenth century described above, and partly due to an already declining Gaelic population.[43] MacKinnon observes that from a population of over 70,000 in the mid-nineteenth century, Cape Breton's Gaelic population had declined to just 24,000 by the 1931 census.[44] Numbers of recorded Gaelic speakers in Nova Scotia continued to decline by around 50 per cent in each subsequent census throughout the twentieth century, until just under 1,500 were recorded in 1971.[45]

Mertz investigated the pragmatics of Gaelic language shift in Nova Scotia in great detail, identifying a 'metapragmatic filter' through which Gaels came to attribute relative values to their languages, and which in turn impacted on their willingness to speak and transmit the Gaelic language in the crucial domains of daily life. The 1920s and '30s transformed the prevailing socioeconomic circumstances in Nova Scotia, hastening and enhancing the ideological association of Gaelic with rurality, economic immobility and low social cachet.[46] Mertz argues that the particular metapragmatic filter – that is, the sets of language attitudes, ideologies and 'folk theories' concerning Gaelic – that had the greatest consequence for the future trajectory of the language in Nova Scotia was that prevailing at the time of the Great Depression.[47]

---

[39] J. Edwards, 'Gaelic in Nova Scotia', in C. Williams (ed.), *Linguistic Minorities, Society and Territory* (Clevedon: Multilingual Matters, 1991), pp. 269–97, see esp. p. 273.

[40] Edwards, *Minority Languages and Group Identity*, pp. 156–7; MacKinnon, 'Gaelic in Canada', p. 19.

[41] Kennedy, 'Gaelic Nova Scotia', p. 51.

[42] Edwards, *Minority Languages and Group Identity*, pp. 156–7.

[43] Kennedy, 'Gaelic Nova Scotia'.

[44] MacKinnon, 'Gaelic in Canada', p. 19; Edwards, 'Gaelic in Nova Scotia', p. 278.

[45] R. MacLean, 'The Scots: Hector's cargo', in D. Campbell (ed.), *Banked Fires: The Ethnics of Nova Scotia* (Port Credit, ON: Scribblers' Press, 1978) pp. 51–72.

[46] Mertz, '"No Burden to Carry"'; E. Mertz, 'Sociolinguistic creativity. Cape Breton Gaelic's linguistic "tip"', in N. Dorian (ed.), *Investigating Obsolescence: Studies in Language Contraction and Death* (Cambridge: Cambridge University Press, 1989), pp. 103–16.

[47] Mertz, '"No Burden to Carry"', pp. 311–12.

The harsh economic climate of the 1920s and '30s essentially prompted Nova Scotia Gaels to re-evaluate their relationship with Gaelic, a language they increasingly viewed via the 'metapragmatic filter' of linguistic ideology as an irrelevance to their children's future success and wellbeing, and at worst a hindrance. The linguistic 'tip' was reached, and language shift to English subsequently accelerated. The situation was compounded as Gaelic-speaking Nova Scotians continued to migrate in large numbers to the urban centres of Sydney, Antigonish, Pictou and Inverness, or further afield, to Halifax, New England; or still further, to Ontario or the prairies.[48] Kennedy states the urban environments that were increasingly the destination for Gaels 'proved particularly hostile to the socialisation of children in Gaelic', while rural populations continued rapidly to decline.[49]

Contemporary policy to revitalise Gaelic can be traced to bottom-up, grassroots efforts to stem the decline of Gaelic that started in the 1970s.[50] Such grassroots initiatives were joined at the start of this century by 'top-down', institutional supports for the language community. Crucially in 2006, Rodney MacDonald, then Premier of Nova Scotia, established *Oifis Iomairtean na Gàidhlig* (The Office of Gaelic Affairs) as a civil service unit within the provincial government, along with a ministerial portfolio for Gaelic Affairs. *Iomairtean na Gàidhlig* exists, in its own words, for the purpose of helping 'Nova Scotians [to] reclaim their Gaelic language and identity as a basis for cultural, spiritual, community and economic renewal ... by creating awareness, working with partners and providing tools and opportunities to learn, share and experience Gaelic language and culture'.[51] These objectives are in turn to be achieved by:

- Creating awareness of Gaelic language, culture and history and its contribution to Nova Scotia's diversity, community life and economy.
- Providing language training, support materials, innovative programming, strategic advice, research, translations and communications services to enable appreciation, acquisition and use of Gaelic language and culture.
- Building partnerships within government to ensure investment in and stewardship of these language and cultural resources that are uniquely Nova Scotian.[52]

The aims of Nova Scotian policymakers with responsibility for Gaelic can therefore be interpreted to go far beyond generating new speakers, and the principle of promoting the language as an aspect of the province's distinctive

---

[48] Kennedy, 'Gaelic Nova Scotia', p. 73; Edwards, *Minority Languages and Group Identity*, p. 154.
[49] Kennedy, 'Gaelic Nova Scotia', p. 75.
[50] Dunbar, 'Minority language renewal'.
[51] Office of Gaelic Affairs, 'Our community'.
[52] Ibid.

identity is clearly discernible in the above extracts. Stimulating awareness and ownership of the language and its associated identity even among the estimated 230,000 Nova Scotians of Gaelic heritage is no small task, let alone among the rest of Nova Scotia's almost one million inhabitants. Yet the emphasis on language training, programming and materials highlights the importance of new speakers to the future of the language in the province. Very little is currently known about either the size or linguistic practices of the new speaker population. Watson and Ivey summarised this deficiency in a seminal conference paper, asking 'who are these speakers? Why are they learning Gaelic? How fluent are they? And how often do they use it?' (my translation).[53]

Research context 2: Gaelic in twenty-first-century Scotland

The 2011 UK census showed a 2 per cent decline in the number of people claiming an ability to speak Gaelic in Scotland compared to the 2001 census. This constituted a sharp diminution in the rate of decline from ten years previously, when the equivalent loss was 11 per cent from the 1991 figure. In total 57,602 people over the age of three reported being able to speak Gaelic in 2011, approximating to 1.1 per cent of the total population of Scotland.[54] In spite of this, the census also showed growth, for the first time, in the proportion of Gaelic speakers under the age of twenty. Although the rate of this growth was just 0.1 per cent compared to the percentage of speakers recorded for this age-group in 2001, a great deal was made of its importance in demonstrating the growth of GME in Scotland. The then chief executive of *Bòrd na Gàidhlig* – the statutory agency charged with the promotion of Gaelic – stated of the figures that:

> the number of Gaelic speakers in Scotland has almost stabilised since the census of 2001. This is mainly due to the rise in Gaelic-medium education ... [and] shows that within the next ten years the long term decline of the language could be reversed.[55]

The significance attached to the development of GME as a key priority for strategic policy objectives is similarly emphasised in the Scottish Government's consultation paper on a Gaelic education bill.[56] The most recent iteration of *Bòrd na Gàidhlig*'s National Gaelic Language Plan states in similarly unambiguous terms:

---

[53] Watson and Ivey, 'Nàisean cultarach nan Gàidheal', p. 184.
[54] National Records of Scotland, *Statistical Bulletin: 2011 Census*.
[55] Bòrd na Gàidhlig, 'Gaelic Education Helps Reverse Decline of the Gaelic Language', 2014, available at <http://www.gaidhlig.org.uk/bord/en/news/article.php?ID=474> (last accessed 9 July 2020).
[56] Scottish Government, *Consultation Paper*.

> Gaelic education is central to the ambition of Gaelic growth and for this reason education and learning will remain central to this Plan, as they were to the previous Plan ... Our clear view is that Gaelic education makes an important contribution to the aim of increasing the numbers of those speaking, using and learning the language.[57]

Contemporary policy statements of this kind therefore indicate the degree to which policymakers view GME as a mechanism by which not only to increase rates of Gaelic language acquisition in school, but also to generate new speakers who will later carry forward their bilingualism into the domains of home and work. In essence, the intention is that GME will substantially increase the numbers of new speakers of Gaelic in Scotland, equipping students to use the language to a considerable degree throughout their adolescent and adult lives. Yet little empirical evidence has previously assessed whether GME does impact lastingly on past students' linguistic practices in this way. Indeed, while various scholars have observed that the impact of immersion education in other contexts of language revitalisation appears to be limited, research on the long-term outcomes of bilingual programmes is notable by its scarcity.

On the basis of various meta-analyses of the effectiveness of French immersion education in Canada,[58] Edwards notes that in spite of their greater command in the target language, immersion pupils generally appear not to seek out opportunities to use their second language to a greater extent than, for instance, students studying it as a subject.[59] As Baker phrases it, there is always a chance that '[p]otential does not necessarily lead to production; skill does not ensure street speech'.[60] Although it is the hope and intention of many that bilingual education systems will equip children to lead a bilingual life after school, this had not hitherto been clearly demonstrated.

In the remainder of this paper I would like to draw attention to some of the language ideologies that Scottish and Nova Scotian speakers from these two studies convey when describing their current identifications with Gaelic. I argue that while the language clearly plays an important role in the professional lives of Scottish new speakers, the ideologies that they express tend to militate against their association with the traditionally defined, ethnolinguistic Gaelic community. By contrast, Nova Scotian new speakers seem generally more eager to embrace their heritage identities as Gaels. A clear distinction will be demonstrated between Scottish new speakers' negative perceptions and lack

---

[57] Bòrd na Gàidhlig, *The National Gaelic Language Plan*, p. 32.
[58] See B. Harley, 'After immersion'; MacFarlane and Wesche, 'Immersion outcomes'; R. Johnstone, *Immersion in a Second or Additional Language at School*.
[59] Edwards, *Minority Languages and Group Identity*, p. 261.
[60] C. Baker, *Foundations of Bilingual Education and Bilingualism*, 5th edn (Bristol: Multilingual Matters, 2011), p. 265; see also Fishman, *Reversing Language Shift*; Fishman, *Can Threatened Languages Be Saved?*

of association with the term 'Gael(s)', and their Canadian counterparts' relative ease in employing that term as an element of their cultural heritage.

Method

The interview corpora upon which I draw for the following analysis were collated over seven years of research throughout Scotland and three months of fieldwork in Novia Scotia.[61] The study that informs the present analysis is an ethnographic investigation of new speaker practices and identities in Scotland and Nova Scotia, drawing on 60 semi-structured interviews (30 in each country), 4 focus groups (2 in each), 80 questionnaire responses (51 from Scotland, 29 from Nova Scotia) and participant observation within Gaelic communities and social networks in the two contexts. In Scotland, seven of the thirty new speakers interviewed were educated through Gaelic-medium classes in the late 1980s and early 1990s. Of this seven, the first two new speakers I discuss below are identified by the pseudonyms Alasdair and Euan, both raised in settings with very little Gaelic spoken by either parent at home. In a sense, these seven individuals are 'outliers' compared to the broad picture of limited day-to-day Gaelic language use among the majority of Gaelic-educated adults in my earlier study, especially those not substantially socialised in Gaelic by their parents in childhood. Similarly, their identifications with the Gaelic language as an aspect of their cultural identities varied widely, but were never described in terms analogous to the 'Xians-with-Xish' ideal emphasised in Fishman's theoretical work.

New speakers of Gaelic and ethnic identity: Gàidheil? Gaels?

As with previous research on new Gaelic speakers in Scotland, a sense of disaffection (and occasionally open hostility) was generally conveyed by Gaelic-educated, Scottish interviewees when discussing the term 'Gael'. In the cases of both new speakers discussed below, in fact, a sense of identification with this term is rejected outright. While elsewhere, 'Euan' described his sense of gratitude for the opportunity to work through the medium of Gaelic in his professional life, his explanation in the following extract of his own identity – and his reaction to my prompt regarding the term Gael – provide a clear account of his lack of association with that label:

---

[61] For a fuller discussion of new speaker issues and immersion education outcomes in the Scottish context, see Dunmore, 'Immersion education outcomes'; Dunmore, 'New Gaelic Speakers, New Gaels?'; Dunmore, 'Bilingual life after school?'; Dunmore, *Language Revitalisation in Gaelic Scotland*.

Extract 1

Euan: [T]ha mis' gam fhaicinn fhìn mar Albannach gun teagamh (.) dìreach- tha an teaghlach agam ann an sheo- sin far a bheil an (.) an dachaigh againn
I certainly see myself as Scottish (.) just- my family is here- that's where our (.) our home is [...]

SD: Dìreach (.) an e Gàidheal a th' annad cuideachd mar sin?
Exactly (.) are you a Gael as well then?

Euan: ((laughs)) Chan e uill ((laughing)) cha chanainns' gur e Gàidheal a th' annam idir **no** (.) 's e Gall a th' annam [...] a tha air tionndadh mar gum biodh ((laughs)) em **yeah** bidh mise an-còmhnaidh ag ràdh gur ann à Dùn Èideann a tha mi
*((laughs)) No well ((laughing)) I wouldn't say I am a Gael at all **no** (.) I'm a Lowlander [...] who has 'turned' as it were ((laughs)) em **yeah** I always say I'm from Edinburgh*

Euan's description of his civic Scottish identity in unproblematic terms – as the place where his family lives and where their home is – reflects a widespread sentiment throughout the 2015 dataset. Overwhelmingly, interview and questionnaire informants self-identified as Scottish, reflecting an association with a civic national identity that they perceive as banal but inclusive. When I ask Euan if he is a Gael as well as a Scot, his response is one of surprise and amusement. He laughs at the suggestion, and even uses the oppositional (and, in Fishmanian terms, 'Yian') Gaelic designation '*Gall*' ('foreigner; Lowlander') to explain his lack of affinity with the traditional ('Xian') identity category 'Gael'. The limited currency and attractiveness of this traditionally defined identity is reflected right across the sample of Gaelic-medium educated adults I surveyed. Taken as a whole, the majority of Scottish new speakers interviewed described their cultural identities in terms, principally, of their self-identification as Scots. Possible reasons for this explicit rejection of the term 'Gael' are suggested by Alasdair in the following extract:

Extract 2

Alasdair: Anns an obair seo /tha/ mise (.) ann an dòigh (2.0) you know an ginealach ùr
In this job I'm (.) in a way (2.0) you know the next generation [of Gaelic]

SD: hmm

Alasdair: Ged nach eil mise a' smaoineachadh orm mar Ghàidheal airson tha seòrsa stigma attached a tha mise faicinn
Although I don't think of myself as a Gael because there's a kind of stigma attached that I see

SD: Tha
Yeah

Alasdair: **Identity** 's chan eil mi airson a bhith a' dol a-staigh dhan a' chòmhradh a tha sin idir [...] cha do smaoinich mi riamh gum bi mi nam oifigear na Gàidhlig agus ma bhruidhinneas tu ris na tidsearan a bh' agam cha-nadh iad an aon rud [...] **so** a thaobh fèin aithneach/adh/ tha mise smaoineachadh- chan e Gàidheal a th' annam idir idir

*An **identity** and I don't want to get into that discussion at all [...] I **never** thought I'd be a Gaelic officer and if you speak to the teachers I had they'd say the same thing [...] so in terms of identity I think- I'm not a Gael at all*

While reflecting that in his current job (as Gaelic officer at a local authority) he is part of a new generation (*'ginealach ùr'*) of Gaelic speakers, Alasdair states in no uncertain terms his lack of identity as a Gael, because, in his own words, of the 'stigma attached' to that label. He neglects to elaborate here, stating that he does not 'want to get into that discussion at all'; I suggest that this reluctance may indicate negative affect surrounding his and other new speakers' percep-tions of this 'stigma', and their subsequent rejection of the identity. Alasdair reflects that as a school pupil he would never have imagined being a Gaelic officer in the future – and that his teachers in GME would have been similarly surprised! In terms of his identity, he claims that he is not a Gael 'at all'. Such discourses neatly encapsulate the experience of most new speakers of Gaelic in Scotland.[62]

While such a clear rejection of a social identity as Gaels is by no means uniformly expressed by all members of this group, the ethnolinguistic category is overwhelmingly avoided or problematised by most Scottish new speakers in my research. By contrast, Nova Scotian new speakers' Gaelic identities are fre-quently expressed in enthusiastic terms, and it is clear that most new speakers in Nova Scotia embrace the Gael(ic) label when describing their identification with the language and motivations for having learned it. In the following extended extract, the informant 'Seonaid' explains the varying ways in which contrasting Scottish and Gaelic identities are regarded in the province, both by herself and by other Nova Scotians of Highland extraction:

---

[62] See also McLeod et al., *New Speakers of Gaelic in Edinburgh and Glasgow*; Dunmore, 'Immersion education outcomes'; Dunmore, *Language Revitalisation in Gaelic Scotland*.

Extract 3

Seonaid: Bruidhinn orm fhìn cha robh- chanainnsa gu làidir a-nis gur e Gàidheal a th' annam- gur e bana-Ghàidheal a th' annam ach cha robh fios agam gu dè a bha ann an Gàidheal mun a thòisich mi air Gàidhlig ionnsachadh agus a-nis nuair a bhios mi coimhead air mo theaghlach tha fhios- ged nach eil Gàidhlig acasan tha mi faicinn cho Gàidhealach 's a tha iad sna dòighean aca. Agus mar sin chanainn gu bheil <u>mòran</u> ann an Alba Nuadh (.) a tha gu math Gàidhealach, ged nach eil Gàidhlig aca tuilleadh, bha Gàidhlig a's na <u>teaghlaichean</u> aca o chionn – fhios agad – ginealach no dhà… ach cha bhiodh iadsan ag aithneachadh (.) uh: (.) ag aithneachadh (.) uh (.) an ainm 'Gàidheal' (.) **you know** chanadh iad dh'fhaoidte **'oh we're Scottish- we're Scotch'**

> *Speaking about myself- I'd say strongly now that I'm a Gael- that I'm a Gaelic woman but I didn't know what a Gael was before I started learning Gaelic and now when I look at my family I know – although they don't speak Gaelic – I can see just how Gaelic they are in their ways. And therefore I'd say <u>lots</u> of people in Nova Scotia are quite Gaelic, even though they can't speak Gaelic anymore, their <u>families</u> spoke Gaelic – you know a generation or two ago… But they wouldn't recognise uh the name 'Gael' you know, they'd maybe say* **'oh we're Scottish- we're Scotch'**

This extract highlights the speaker's changing awareness and appreciation of her Gaelic identity as her exposure to the language increased. On the other hand, she identifies in the (extralinguistic) cultural practices of the people she was surrounded by while growing up as being quintessentially 'Gaelic'. She notes that this sense of cultural distinctiveness, however, was understood by such individuals as reflective of their 'Scottish' (or 'Scotch') heritage, rather than of any distinctively Gaelic ethnolinguistic identity. This quality of Gaelic distinctiveness among certain Nova Scotians forms a frequently occurring trope across the thirty interviews conducted in the province. Whereas the previous interviewee traces a fluctuating trajectory in her identification with the term 'Gael', the following speaker, 'Mairead', twenty years her junior, expresses absolute certainty in her own association with the word, reflecting the increased prevalence of the term since the turn of the century:

Extract 4

SD: An e Gàidheal a th' annadsa?=
    Are you a Gael?=

Mairead: ='S e
    =Yes

SD: 'S e=
    Yes=

Mairead: ='S e
          =Yes
SD: An ann air sgàth a' chànain fhèin a tha sin air no air sàilleabh chultair agus òrain 's a h-uile càil mar sin?
          Is that because of the language itself or because of the culture, the songs and so on?
Mairead: (1.1) Ah uill (2.4) 's e um (.) cànan (1.9) mo shinn- mo shinnsearan a bh' ann
          (1.1) Ah well (2.4) it was um (.) the language (1.9) of my ancest- my ancestors
SD: Dìreach
          Exactly
Mairead: Agus (2.7) siud as coireach! ((laughs)) [...] Bidh mi a' cleachdadh Beurla air sàilleabh 's gu bheil (2.2) feum agam air a bhith (.) a' bruidhinn còmhla ri (1.9) daoine ach is fheàrr leam Gàidhlig
          And (2.7) that's why! ((laughs)) [...] I use English because (2.2) I have to (.) speak it with (1.9) people but I prefer Gaelic
SD: Carson a tha sin nad bheachd?
          Why do you think that is?
Mairead: ^Chan eil mi cinnteach um
          ^I'm not sure um
SD: Hmm
Mairead: 'S e um (.) cànan (1.1) mo shinnsearan a th' ann an Gàidhlig (.) um (.) 's e cànan (5.1) chan e cànan mo shinnsearan ((laughs)) a th' ann am Beurla!
          Gaelic is the language (1.1) of my ancestors (.) um it's the language (5.1) English is not the language of my ancestors!

When questioned as to her own identity as a Gael, Mairead replies without a moment's hesitation that she is (the '=' symbol denoting latched speech, with no identifiable pause between question and answer). A greater degree of hesitation is notable when in the following speech acts she explains the reasons for this, regularly producing pauses of over two seconds' duration when considering the basis of her Gaelic identity (pauses are recorded in parentheses in tenths of a second). The importance of heritage and ancestry for this speaker – and her perceived lack of any ancestral connection to the English language (in spite of having grown up with only English at home) is key to understanding her motivations for having learned Gaelic to fluency as a second language. This stands in stark contrast, as previously noted, to the majority of new speakers in Scotland. The realisation of this aspect of the second language learner's own identity in Gaelic is likened by 'Joy' in the following extract to a kind of epiphany; a moment of astounding self-discovery on the road to fluency in the language:

Extract 5

Joy: Dar a thòisich mi air a' Ghàidhlig bha iad a' bruidhinn air um (.) sloinnidhean agus dìreach bha '<u>bing</u>!': 'O! Siud as coireach gu robh iad ag eigheadh Sarah Archie Angus ris an t-seann tè a bha sin dar a bha mi òg!' Agus rudan eile mar sin agus aig ceann na seachdain thuirt mi '^**Oh my god I think I'm Gaelic**!' ((laughs)) Mura biodh ceangal ann le Gàidhlig air bith (x) cha- cha b' <u>urrainn</u> dhomh cumail orm ann an Alba Nuaidh […] feumaidh (.) Gàidhlig a bhith nad chridh', air neo (0.8) feumaidh tu ceangal a- a dhèanadh (.) um:: do fèin aithne aig duine an dòigh air choreigin (.) uh ach chan eil mi bruidhinn air **DNA**

> *When I started [learning] Gaelic they were talking about um (.) patronymics [/ancestry] and it was just like <u>bing</u>: 'Oh! That's why they called the old lady Sarah Archie Angus when I was young!' And other things like that and at the end of the week I said '^***Oh my god I think I'm Gaelic***!' ((laughs)) If I hadn't had any connection to Gaelic I wouldn't- I <u>couldn't</u> have continued [learning] in Nova Scotia […] Gaelic has to be in your heart, or (0.8) you have to- to make some sort of connection (.) um:: with a person's identity (.) uh but I'm not speaking about **DNA***

This interviewee's understanding of her Gaelic identity is therefore described as having occurred to her as suddenly as the ring of a bell ('<u>bing!</u>'). Without this sudden discovery of her own connection to the language, through the familiarity of distinctive naming practices and other characteristics of her community in childhood, she states that she wouldn't have been able to carry on learning Gaelic in the province. Motivation of this kind – connection to the language in one's 'heart' (if not formally in one's 'DNA') is thus seen as key to understanding the decision to learn Gaelic to fluency. Yet for the following speaker, 'Mòrag', a sense of identity as a Gael is problematised, and the necessity of such an ethnolinguistic or community connection is rejected. In this way Mòrag avoids excessively relying, in her own words, on 'purism' in discussing her relationship with the Gaelic language:

Extract 6

SD:	Bheil thu coimhead ort fhèin mar bhana-Ghàidheal?
	Do you regard yourself as a Gael?
Mòrag:	Uh huh (.) ^uill [[ann an ^<u>dòigh</u>]
	^well [[in a ^<u>way</u>]
SD:	[[An canadh tu sin?]
	[[Would you say so?]
Mòrag:	Ann an <u>dòigh</u> […] ach tha cuimhne agam nuair a bha mi aig an t-Sabhal Mhòr bhiomaid <u>daonnan</u> a-mach air a' chuspair seo

> *In a <u>way</u> [...] but I remember when I was at Sabhal Mòr [Ostaig; Gaelic College on the Isle of Skye] we were <u>always</u> discussing that issue*

SD: Yeah

Mòrag: Agus <u>uaireannan</u> bhithinn ag ràdh (.) 'carson?' [...] tha mise smaointinn (.) orm- tha mi coimhead orm fhìn mar bana-Ghàidheal math dh'fhaoidte air sàilleabh 's gu bheil mi ag obair airson cor na Gàidhlig [...] bidh mi ag ràdh gur e (.) bana-Ghàidheal a th' annam [...] tha e gu ^math cudromach an-seo- tha sinn a' feuchainn a bhith cleachdadh an fhacail siud- Gàidheal

> *And sometimes I would ask (.) 'why?' [...] I do think of (.) myself- I see myself as a Gael perhaps because I work on behalf of Gaelic [...] I do say I am a Gael [...] it's ^quite important here- we try to use that word- Gael*

SD: Hmm

Mòrag: Uh (.) o tha e air atharrachadh tro na linntean

> *Oh but it's changed over the years*

SD: Sheadh

> *Yeah*

Mòrag: Bho- you know- 'Highlander' [[no 'Scots']

> *From- you know- 'Highlander' [[or 'Scots']*

SD: [[Highlander yeah]

Mòrag: 'Scottish', 'Celtic' – diofar- diofar rudan [...] tha mi faireachdainn gu bheil um (1.4) tha:: hh: tha (.) tha sinn a' siubhail tro ^**purism** an-seo ^uaireannan

> *'Scottish', 'Celtic' – different- different things [...] I feel that um (1.4) there's:: th:: that (.) we rely too much on ^**purism** here ^sometimes*

In the above extract, Mòrag therefore qualifies her assertion of ethnocultural identity as a Gael with the phrase 'in a <u>way</u>' (*ann an dòigh*), producing rising intonation and heavy emphasis of the last word to convey this stance clearly. These paralinguistic cues in her speech reveal that her possession of this identity is viewed as potentially problematic. She recounts a sense of disillusionment at how prevalent discussion of the term seemed to her while studying at Sabhal Mòr Ostaig, Scotland's Gaelic college on the Isle of Skye. Nevertheless, she goes on to explain that she habitually does in fact describe herself as a Gael ('*bidh mi ag ràdh gur e bana-Ghàidheal a th' annam*') and, indeed, notes that language advocates in Nova Scotia consciously attempt to encourage the use of that term, where in the past Gaels in the province themselves might have identified to a greater degree as Highlanders, Scots or, perhaps rather less precisely, as 'Celtic'.

Discussion: Gaels and Gaelic in twenty-first-century Scotland and Nova Scotia

The foregoing analysis has sought to demonstrate that while the linkage envisaged between language and ethnolinguistic identity in Fishman's RLS model fails to mobilise in the case of new Gaelic speakers who graduated from GME programmes in Scotland, the term has substantially greater currency among new speakers in Nova Scotia. The traditional 'Xian' ethnolinguistic community indexed by the term 'Gael(s)' seems not to be one with which Scottish new speakers readily associate as part of their 'ideal' L2 selves.[63] The apparent degree of 'stigma' attached to the term in Scotland, as 'Alasdair' discusses in extract 2, above, is rarely explicitly clarified. Nevertheless, it appears from extracts discussed above that conceptions and definitions of the term that privilege a direct ancestral connection to the language in the negotiation of 'Gael' identity are viewed very differently in Scotland and Nova Scotia. In Scotland, the ideological association of the 'Gael' identity with rurality, tradition and the past contributes to its perception as a stigmatised social category with which new speakers do not readily identify.

Yet the relative enthusiasm with which Nova Scotian new speakers of Gaelic appear to construct and negotiate their ethnolinguistic identities as Gaels stands in stark distinction to the Scottish speakers' apparent disillusionment with the term. The definition of the 'Gael' identity that Nova Scotian participants convey in discourses discussed above does appear to pertain to ancestry and ethnolinguistic socialisation within authentically Gaelic communities. In that sense, the definition of what it means to be a 'Gael', and which Nova Scotian speakers embrace so readily, is not far removed from that which Scottish new speakers overwhelmingly shun.[64] While the evidence from Scotland I have discussed here thus tends to corroborate the view that essentialist conceptions of language and ethnolinguistic identity fail to capture new speakers' identifications with minority languages, the Nova Scotian evidence clearly challenges this thesis.

Thus, while the feasibility of positing a straightforward relationship between a minority language and its traditional speakers as a strategy for revitalising minority verities has been problematised by authors such as Jaffe, Edwards, and Duchêne and Heller, most Nova Scotian speakers' clear desire to embrace their ethnolinguistic identity as Gaels, and to privilege their ethnic heritage in negotiating this identity, does lend support to Fishmanian conceptions of the

---

[63] cf. Dörnyei, *The Psychology of the Language Learner*; Dörnyei and Ushioda, *Motivation, Language Identity and the L2 Self*; MacIntyre et al., 'Heritage passions, heritage convictions and the rooted L2 self'.

[64] c.f. Dunmore, 'Immersion education outcomes'; Dunmore, *Language Revitalisation in Gaelic Scotland*.

language–identity nexus.⁶⁵ Yet Fishman's models of language and ethnicity sit uneasily with contemporary conceptions which problematise essentialism.⁶⁶ Jaffe advocated approaches to language and identity 'that acknowledge the political and social character of all identity claims and that leave room for the multiple forms of language practice', without positing any direct relationship between the two.⁶⁷ This stance was informed by many years of ethnographic research within a context in which 'an essential relationship between language, culture and identity is posited as a given'.⁶⁸ In such cases, Bucholtz and Hall argue, essentialist perspectives should not be altogether dismissed, since they continue to possess salience and meaning for the speakers whom linguists study.⁶⁹ Bourdieu commented that contested definitions of ethnic identity and the nature of its 'reality' can be understood 'only if one includes in reality the representation of reality'.⁷⁰ On this basis, Joseph argues that while ethnic identity categories may essentialise arbitrary differences between groups, they become socially 'real' when speakers deploy them as 'mental representations' of reality.⁷¹ Jaffe thus advises against interpreting essentialist outlooks as entirely separable from meaningful representation; where essentialist positions are reflected in informants' language ideologies, they frequently are in fact socially meaningful constructions.⁷² Appreciating the social reality of essentialist perspective does not mean assuming such a perspective in one's own theoretical approach. Indeed, Dorian cautions on the basis of her feted East Sutherland Gaelic research that the situated realities linking language and identity are in fact rarely as straightforward as essentialist conceptions would envisage.⁷³

From such a perspective, neither Nova Scotian speakers' somewhat essentialist outlook on Gaelic, nor Scottish new Gaelic speakers' apparent lack of a clear identity as Gaels need be viewed as problematic in or of themselves. For Nova Scotian new Gaelic speakers, ethnic identities are constructed within a wider North American context in which perceived heritage often forms the basis

---

[65] Jaffe, *Ideologies in Action*; Jaffe, 'Discourses of endangerment'; A. Jaffe, 'Minority language movements', in M. Heller (ed.), *Bilingualism: A Social Approach* (London: Palgrave Macmillan, 2007) pp. 50–95; Edwards, *Minority Languages and Group Identity*; A. Duchêne and M. Heller (eds), *Language in Late Capitalism: Pride and Profit* (London: Routledge, 2012).
[66] Bucholtz and Hall, 'Language and identity'; Jaffe, 'Discourses of endangerment'.
[67] Jaffe, 'Discourses of endangerment', p. 70.
[68] Ibid.
[69] Bucholtz and Hall, 'Language and identity', p. 376.
[70] P. Bourdieu, *Language and Symbolic Power*, trans. G. Raymond and M. Adamson (Cambridge: Polity Press, 1991), p. 221.
[71] J. Joseph, 'Identity', in C. Llamas and D. Watt (eds), *Language and Identities* (Edinburgh: Edinburgh University Press, 2010), pp. 9–17, see esp. p. 12.
[72] Jaffe, 'Discourses of endangerment', p. 57.
[73] N. Dorian, 'Linguistic and ethnographic fieldwork', in J. Fishman and O. García (eds), *Handbook of Language and Ethnic Identity* (Oxford: Oxford University Press, 2010), pp. 89–106, see esp. p. 89.

of cultural identity claims in general. In Scotland, on the other hand, if new speakers' principal identification with and use of the Gaelic language derives from their professional lives, it is clear no such heritage-oriented ethnic identity should be expected to develop.

Yet without a strong social identity in the language outside of the professional sphere, it would similarly seem unlikely that such new speakers could take the language forward as a vital aspect of their domestic and family lives, and to transmit it to children in the home-community context in future. On the other hand, while Nova Scotian new speakers may well possess the requisite ethnolinguistic commitment to Gaelic to desire that their own children acquire a sense of heritage and identity as Gaels, the relative paucity of support mechanisms for intergenerational transmission in the province, combined with the fast-dwindling network of native speakers, provide clear challenges for the socialisation of young people in the language itself.

If it is hoped that new Gaelic speakers in each country will attain fluency, and then progress to using the language in the home-community sphere, while simultaneously developing a strong identity in the language, additional attention and resources should be focused on that specific objective in Scotland, as seems to be the case in Nova Scotia. While Nova Scotians often look enviously at current provision for Gaelic-medium immersion education in Scotland, it is clear in that respect that policymakers in Edinburgh and Inverness would benefit from ongoing dialogue with language teachers and advocates in Halifax and Cape Breton. As a response, Scottish children currently in GME schools and classes should clearly be encouraged to socialise in the language outside of class as much as possible, to interact with fluent speakers wherever possible, and to better understand the relevance of Gaelic to their (keenly felt) civic identities as Scots in a modern, multicultural Scotland.

Conclusions

In terms of speakers' bilingual development, issues of linguistic practice, ideology and identity are central to much research that has already been produced on the phenomenon of new speakers of minority languages. The findings presented in this chapter are perhaps suggestive of Scottish and Nova Scotian new speakers' cultural identifications with Gaelic, although they are by no means exhaustive. In Scotland, most new speakers' rejection of the label 'Gael' is significant inasmuch as it does not distinguish them from the majority of former GME students, who tend to make only limited use of Gaelic in the present day.[74] As noted above, these new Gaelic speakers' lack of identification as Gaels is not problematic for language policy objectives as such. As my analysis has

---

[74] Dunmore, *Language Revitalisation in Gaelic Scotland*.

Table 3.1 Key to transcription conventions

[[words]	overlapping speech
(.)	perceivable pause <1s duration
(2.0)	perceivable pause >1s duration
(word)	uncertain transcription
(x)	unintelligible
xxx	(place)name omitted
/word/	non-concordant morphosyntactic usage
((word))	analyst's comments
[...]	material omitted
wo::	elongation
word	emphatic speech
word=	latched speech, no pause
words	codeswitch

demonstrated, however, functional fluency in Gaelic and constant use of the language appear not to be accompanied by strong social identity in Gaelic. If, as contemporary policy statements suggest, new speakers with strong ideological commitment to the language, and to passing it onto children, are among the intended outcomes of GME, additional resources should be directed specifically at encouraging students' development of the concomitant practices and identities in school and at home.

In Nova Scotia, by contrast, developing the ethnolinguistic identity component of new speakers' Gaelic language acquisition appears to be foregrounded in efforts both to instruct students' linguistic practices and secure a future for the language in the province. Yet even notwithstanding such explicit objectives in language policy, heritage and ancestry appear from interviewees' own accounts to form the principal motivations of Nova Scotian new speakers' attempts to acquire and use the language. As a consequence, their expressions of identity as 'Gaels' are notably stronger than the majority of their Scottish counterparts, who tend to problematise or reject the term as a facet of their own identities. The clear contrast between the two settings reflects the divergent histories and social geographies of Scotland and Nova Scotia. It makes for a source of intriguing diversity in the twenty-first-century transatlantic Gaelic community, of which ever greater numbers of new speakers in both countries are a part. Crucially, it is clear that language advocates and policymakers on both sides of this community have much to learn from one another.

FOUR

'Drochaid eadar mis' agus mo dhùthaich' ['A bridge between me and my country']: Transatlantic Networks and the Nineteenth-century Gaelic Periodical Press

Sheila M. Kidd

The dispersal of Gaelic speakers throughout the colonies of the British Empire in the course of the nineteenth century coincided with, and to an extent contributed to, a rise in Gaelic secular publishing, and in particular the emergence of a Gaelic periodical press. The contribution of emigrant Gaels to nineteenth-century Gaelic literature took a variety of forms including, for example, subscribing to Gaelic dictionaries, with a substantial proportion of the subscribers to two Gaelic dictionaries published in the 1820s based in the West Indies.[1] These were for the most part temporary migrants and this financial support for Gaelic scholarship and publishing provided them with an opportunity to retain a cultural connection with a homeland to which they hoped to return. Periodicals, on the other hand, offered an opportunity for an ongoing connection and commitment and, as Jude Piesse has noted in the wider context of the English language press, 'played a crucial and overlooked role in performing and dramatizing the central dynamics that characterized settler emigration'.[2]

There is a growing body of scholarship on Gaelic literature in North America and indeed on the maintenance of diasporic Gaelic identity more generally.[3]

---

[1] Sheila M. Kidd, 'Gaelic books as cultural icons: The maintenance of cultural links between the Highlands and the West Indies', in Carla Sassi and Theo van Heijnsbergen (eds), *Within and Without Empire: Scotland across the (Post)colonial Borderline* (Newcastle: Cambridge Scholars Publishing, 2013), pp. 46–60.

[2] Jude Piesse, *British Settler Emigration in Print, 1832–1877* (Oxford: Oxford University Press, 2016), p. 2.

[3] See, for example, Michel Newton (ed.), *Seanchaidh na Coille: The Memory-keeper of the Forest. Anthology of Scottish Gaelic Literature of Canada* (Sydney, NS: Cape Breton University Press, 2015); Robert Dunbar, 'The poetry of the emigrant generation', *Transactions of the Gaelic Society of Inverness*, 64 (2008), pp. 22–125. For an interesting new direction in this scholarship, see Laurie Stanley-Blackwell and Michael Linkletter, 'Inscribing ethnicity: A preliminary analysis of Gaelic headstone inscriptions in Eastern Nova Scotia and Cape Breton', *Genealogy*, 2.3 (2018).

This includes work which deals specifically with diasporic literary networks such as Robert Dunbar's on the first weekly Gaelic newspaper, Cape Breton's *Mac-Talla* (*Echo*) (1892–1904), and Michael Linkletter's on the networks of the Canadian Gaelic scholar and writer, Rev. Alexander Maclean Sinclair.[4] This chapter takes a broader perspective in considering the pre-*Mac-Talla* period, concentrating on two periodicals, *Cuairtear nan Gleann* (*The Traveller of the Glens*) (1840–3) and *An Gaidheal* (*The Gael*) (1871–7), and considers the emergence, and nature, of Gaelic literary networks in the course of the century.

The focus of the chapter is initially on the periodicals of the first half of the century, periodicals with aims which were frequently inextricably entwined with the agendas of landlords in promoting emigration. It moves on to consider the ways in which the embryonic literary networks nurtured by these journals expanded in the middle decades of the century through the work of Glasgow publishers with discussion of Islay–Glasgow–Ontario links in particular. The final section considers the ways that periodicals and newspapers in the 1870s nurtured and expanded transatlantic literary networks in a shared common cause of cultural rehabilitation and reinvigoration, considering some of the individuals at the centre of these networks and their role in sustaining these transnational literary networks.

Gaelic publishing had expanded rapidly in the course of the nineteenth century, with Glasgow publications gradually coming to outnumber those emerging from Edinburgh as the city's Gaelic-speaking population increased.[5] Glasgow was not just a physical gateway to the Atlantic world for Gaels but became a literary one. While the emergence of a Gaelic periodical press in the city in the late 1820s was a faltering one, Glasgow was well situated to take advantage of the increasing opportunities for distribution up the western seaboard of the Highlands and across the Atlantic.

Piesse has described the periodical press as 'an intrinsically migratory form' and has noted the way that the 'new technologies of motion' which facilitated its development were frequently addressed within the publications themselves.[6] In Gaelic journals this sense of motion, the movement in tandem of both

---

[4] Robert Dunbar, 'Gaelic periodicals and the maintenance and creation of networks: Evidence from the Eastern Canadian Gàidhealtachd', in Michel Byrne and Sheila M. Kidd (eds), *Lìontan Lìonmhor: Local, National and Global Gaelic Networks from the 18th to the 20th Century* (Glasgow: Roinn na Ceiltis is na Gàidhlig, University of Glasgow, 2019), pp. 108–52; Michael D. Linkletter, '*Bu dual dha Sin*' (That was his birthright): Gaelic scholar Alexander Maclean Sinclair (1840–1924)' (Unpublished doctoral thesis, Harvard University, 2006). For an overview of the nineteenth-century Gaelic press, see Sheila M. Kidd, 'The Scottish Gaelic Press', in David Finkelstein (ed.), *The Edinburgh History of the British and Irish Press, Vol. 2* (Edinburgh: Edinburgh University Press, 2020), pp. 337–56.

[5] Donald E. Meek, 'Gaelic printing and publishing', in Bill Bell (ed.), *The Edinburgh History of the Book in Scotland Volume 3: Ambition and Industry 1800–1880* (Edinburgh: Edinburgh University Press, 2007), pp. 107–22 (108).

[6] Piesse, *British Settler Emigration in Print*, pp. 2, 23.

publication and people, found expression in a number of ways. The periodicals were anthropomorphised, not just in names such as 'Teachdaire' ('*Messenger*'), 'Cuairtear' ('*Traveller*') and 'An Gaidheal' ('*The Gael*'), but in their depiction as itinerants. *Cuairtear nan Gleann* is described by Rev. Alexander MacGregor as a welcome 'aoigh' ('*guest*') '[nach] àill am baile fhàgail ach uair sa mhìos' ('*who only likes to leave the city once a month*') and by John Maclean (Bàrd Thighearna Chola / *The Laird of Coll's Poet*) in his eulogy to the journal as a warrior, 'àrmann dealbhach' ('*a comely hero*');[7] *An Gaidheal* is a pedlar, 'a' giulan dà mhàileid lom làn de gach gnè bhathair a chordadh ri clann nan Gaidheal' ('*carrying two packs stuffed full with every sort of ware which would appeal to the Gaels*').[8] Ship metaphors also appear frequently. When the first sustained attempt at a periodical, *An Teachdaire Gae'lach* (*The Gaelic Messenger*) (1829–31) ceased publication, its editor, Rev. Norman MacLeod, in his final words to readers, described the periodical as an old galley: 'tha 'n t-sean bhìrlinn air a tarraing gu tìr car tamuill, sann chum calcaidh, tha dòchas agam [...] Cha bhi i fada dol 'na h-uidheam – cha mhò bhios dì làmhan chum a cur gu sàile an latha thuigear gu'm bi feum oirre' ('*the old galley has docked for a while, for caulking, I hope [...] she won't be long until she is ready to set sail – nor will there be a lack of hands to launch her on the day it's seen she's needed*').[9] MacLeod's next venture into periodical publishing almost a decade later, *Cuairtear nan Gleann*, picked up where the *Teachdaire* had left off with the periodical introduced to readers with the same metaphor: 'tha mi 'n diugh air stiùir na bìrlinn ùir so tha dol air sàile' ('*today I am at the helm of this new galley that's setting sail*').[10] The metaphor retained its relevance in the later decades of the century when *An Gaidheal* drew on Mac Mhaighstir Alasdair's epic eighteenth-century seafaring poem, 'Birlinn Chlann Raghnaill' ('*The Galley of Clanranald*'), which depicted the heroism of the crew on their journey between South Uist and Antrim, linking sea-divided Gaels, just as the periodicals would: 'Bidh aige [*An Gaidheal*], uime sin, sgioba air nach tugadh barr eadhon leòsan a thug gu "cala réidh" Birlinn ainmeil Chlann-Raonuill; agus bidh e iongantach mur eirich gu math do 'n luing a bhios fo'n curam' ('*It* [An Gaidheal] *will, therefore, have a crew that could not be surpassed even by those who brought Clanranald's famous galley to a "safe harbour"; and it will be a wonder if the ship under their care does not fare well*').[11]

---

[7] *Cuairtear nan Gleann* 29 (July 1841), p. 118; Donald E. Meek (ed.), *The Wiles of the World. Caran an t-Saoghail. An Anthology of 19th Century Scottish Gaelic Verse* (Edinburgh: Birlinn, 2003), p. 202. For a discussion of Maclean's eulogy, 'Oran don "Chuairtear"', see Dunbar, 'Gaelic periodicals', pp. 126–8.
[8] *An Gaidheal*, 3.36 (1874), p. 378.
[9] *An Teachdaire Gae'lach*, 24 (April 1831), p. 281.
[10] *Cuairtear nan Gleann*, 1 (March 1840), p. 2.
[11] *An Gaidheal*, 3.36 (1874), p. 378. For a discussion of 'Birlinn Chlann Raghnaill', an excerpt from the poem and accompanying translation, see Ronald Black, *An Lasair. Anthology of 18th Century Scottish Gaelic Verse* (Edinburgh: Birlinn, 2001), pp. 202–17, 469–75.

The ship has been a multi-faceted symbol in the Gaelic literary imagination over the centuries as Meg Bateman has discussed, including as 'a symbol of communication, potential, absent and achieved'.[12] While its use in the emigrant context remains to be explored, one of the foremost examples in Gaelic prose is in MacLeod's 'Long Mhòr nan Eilthireach' ('*The Emigrant Ship*'). First published in his 1828 school reader and, since then, firmly embedded in the Gaelic emigration narrative, it describes a poignant, shipboard scene in Tobermory Bay with a minister preaching to those departing, a scene most likely based on the experience of his father, Rev. Norman MacLeod of Morvern.[13] It was a scene which the younger MacLeod would replicate in later decades as emigrant ships left the Clyde, preaching, for example, on board the *Blenheim*, headed for New Zealand in 1840 and, particularly relevant in the context of this chapter, presenting the emigrants with 'fifteen volumes of the most valuable books in the Gaelic language, with a view to found a Celtic Library in New Zealand'.[14] Gaelic books also featured in the departure of two hundred emigrants for Canada in 1847, with MacLeod presenting them with 'bibles and other books in the Gaelic language', both as suitable reading material for their voyage and as a tangible cultural connection with their homeland.[15]

While Gaelic books were being carried to Canada on emigrant ships, Gaelic texts were also beginning to appear in print there from the early 1830s, although these were not the earliest Gaelic texts to be published on North American soil, with North Carolina laying claim to this in the form of Rev. Dougal Crawford's sermons, published in Fayetteville in 1791.[16] Gaelic publishing in Canada initially took the form of religious works which had originally appeared in Scotland and the earliest volumes were published in Pictou, Nova Scotia and Charlottetown, Prince Edward Island in 1832, with others printed in Toronto and Montreal in the middle years of the decade. The first original Canadian publication was published in Pictou in 1836, Alexander McGillivray's translation of *The Youth's Companion, Companach an Oganaich*. There was also a Gaelic column in the early issues of the short-lived *Prince Edward Island Times* in 1836, much of the material being drawn from the Glasgow periodical, *An Teachdaire Gae'lach*. All of this points to demand in these emigrant communities for printed Gaelic texts and, in particular, to spiritual community building

---

[12] Meg Bateman, 'Boats in the Gaelic imagination', *Scottish Gaelic Studies*, 24 (2008), pp. 53–72 (64).
[13] Tormaid Macleod, *Co'Chruinneachadh, air a chur ri chéile air iarrtus Comuinn Ard-Sheanadh Eagluis na h-Alba arson an Sgoilean* ... (Glasgow: A. Young, 1828), pp. 79–88.
[14] *Inverness Courier*, 2 September 1840, p. 2.
[15] *Glasgow Herald*, 14 June 1847, p. 2.
[16] Donald E. Meek, 'The pulpit and the pen: Clergy, orality and print in the Scottish Gaelic world', in Adam Fox and Daniel Woolf (eds), *The Spoken Word. Oral Culture in Britain, 1500–1850* (Manchester: Manchester University Press, 2002), pp. 84–118 (97–8).

within and across Gaelic-speaking settlements in Canada, based primarily on existing Scottish publications.[17]

The overriding aim of Norman MacLeod's *Teachdaire* was a moral and educative one – to provide suitable reading material for the increasing numbers being educated in Gaelic schools. MacLeod was, nonetheless, very conscious of the potential international reach of the journal, positioning it as a conduit for communication among Gaels in the Highlands and islands, the urban Lowlands, "'s am barrachd mòr fad o thìr an eòlais, fo ghréin loisgich nan Innsean, no fo dhubhar choiltean fàsail America' (*'and the many more far from their native land, under the blazing skies of the Indies or under the darkness of the desolate American forests'*).[18]

Word of the new publication reached North America quickly through the editor's personal networks, with Rev. Alexander Matheson of St Andrew's Church, Montreal, sending the prospectus to the *Kingston Chronicle*. Matheson's father had been a close friend of MacLeod during the latter's years as minister in Campsie.[19] In Matheson's accompanying letter to the editor he makes clear that he saw the *Teachdaire* as well suited to a North American Gaelic-speaking audience as a Scottish one and 'if extensively circulated, will eventually contribute greatly to the removal of many disadvantages under which the Highland settlers in these provinces labour'.[20] The importance of church networks is further underlined when Matheson asks potential subscribers to the periodical to contact him directly. Support from North America was specifically noted by MacLeod after the first issue of the *Teachdaire* had appeared, when he referred to having 'received communications from a number of their expatriated countrymen in that quarter, stating that its progress was watched with the greatest anxiety [...] and there was a fair prospect that as many would be required for America as for Scotland'.[21] There was, therefore, a clear transatlantic dimension to these emerging periodicals and, given the financial precarity of all Gaelic publications, this had added importance.

Scarcity of evidence makes it hard to establish the true extent of the literary connections anticipated by MacLeod. No information on subscribers survives and the identity of contributors is frequently obscured by pen names or the

---

[17] Kenneth E. Nilsen, 'Some notes on pre-*Mac-Talla* Gaelic publishing in Nova Scotia (with references to early Gaelic publishing in Prince Edward Island, Quebec and Ontario)', in Colm Ó Baoill and Nancy R. McGuire (eds), *Rannsachadh na Gàidhlig 2000: Papers Read at the Conference Scottish Gaelic Studies 2000* (An Clò Gaidhealach: Obar Dheathain, 2002), pp. 127–40 (127–31); Charles W. Dunn, *Highland Settler. A Portrait of the Scottish Gael in Cape Breton and Eastern Nova Scotia* (Wreck Cove, Cape Breton Island: Breton Books, 1991, 1st edn, 1953), pp. 74–7.

[18] *An Teachdaire Gae'lach*, 1 (May 1829), p. 2.

[19] Alexander Mackenzie, *History of the Mathesons with Genealogies of the Various Families*, 2nd edn edited by Alexander MacBain (Stirling: Eneas Mackay, 1900), p. 159.

[20] *Kingston Chronicle*, 6 June 1829, p. 1.

[21] *Scotsman*, 30 May 1829, p. 7.

anonymity of contributions. The only article which can be identified as having been written by a North American Gael was 'Litir o America' ('*Letter from America*') by Eoghann Cameron (Ewan Cameron), apparently based in Cape Breton. He enumerates the various ways in which the emigrants maintain their language and culture, speaking only Gaelic, celebrating Christmas and New Year as they would at home, including with a game of shinty, and with winter night entertainment including tales and music. Even their boat had been given a Gaelic name, 'A Ghruagach Ghaelach' ('*The Highland Maiden*'), reinforcing their sense of identity in their new home, noting that it would make the reader laugh to see the French people on the pier trying – and failing – to read the boat's name. The letter culminates in his description of the emotional welcome given to the periodical, with it described as a bridge:

> Nach dubhairt mi riut, arsa mo bhean fein, sud agad brìgh a bhruadair a chunnaic mise. Bhruadair mi gu'm faca mi drochaid eadar mis agus mo dhùthaich, agus gu'm faca mi Pegie mo phiuthar, agus piuthar mo mhàthar, a' tighinn thairis orra s gu'm faotainn a gabhail a nun sa nall mar thograinn fein. Saoilidh mi nis, air leam gu bheil mi dìreach aig an tigh.[22]

> (*Didn't I say to you, said my own wife, there you have the substance of the vision I saw. I dreamt that I saw a bridge between me and my homeland, and that I saw Peigi, my sister, and my mother's sister, coming across it and that I could go back and forth across it as I wished. I think now, that I'm just at home*).

While this offers no more than the merest glimpse of the periodical's reception among North American emigrant communities, the sense of the physical form of the periodical being a tangible bridge between the old world and the new acknowledges the tentative emergence of a transatlantic literary network of writers and readers focused on this nascent periodical press, a development which drew to an untimely, albeit temporary, close with the demise of the *Teachdaire* in 1831.

It was in the 1840s with the second of MacLeod's periodicals, *Cuairtear nan Gleann*, that these networks expanded as the Gaelic periodical press was revived as a means of promoting emigration in the wake of the potato famine of the later 1830s. The founding purpose of the *Cuairtear* was to encourage emigration by ensuring that Gaelic speakers had access to reliable information about emigrant destinations, and MacLeod undertook the editorial role at the behest of Highland landlords. Some contemporary reports suggest that the periodical was financed by landlords to the tune of £50 per annum for three years, with a further £10 per annum from the Canada Company, although the editor was

---

[22] Eoghann Cameron, 'Litir a America', *Cuairtear nan Gleann*, 18 (October 1830), pp. 123–6 (126).

keen to contradict such rumours, stating in the periodical's seventh issue, 'An comunn air son Gàidheil a chur do America, do Australia, do New Zealand, no do dh-aite air bith eile, cha do cheannaich uiread agus aon Chuairtear uainn, ni mò thug iad sgillinn ruadh seachad chum a chosd a dhìol' (*'the society for sending Gaels to America, to Australia, to New Zealand, or to any other place, has not bought so much as one Cuairtear from us nor have they given us a single penny to offset the cost'*).[23] Regardless of finances, the periodical's stance was very much in support of emigration, with articles about emigrant destinations in the British colonies featuring particularly prominently in the early issues.[24] In his introductory editorial, MacLeod introduces himself as an exile and therefore one who speaks with the authority of personal experience and understanding of the situation of his fellow Highlanders, 'ged tha mo dhachaidh sa' Ghalldachd, tha mo chridhe 's mo bhàigh sna glinn' (*'although my home is in the Lowlands, my heart and my attachment is in the Highlands'*).[25] The *Cuairtear* itself is presented as a hub of communications as he addresses 'gach gàidheal air feadh an t-saoghail mhóir a dh'fhosglas an leabhar beag so' (*'every Gael throughout the wide world who opens this little book'*). Readers are told 'tha luchd-eòlais measail againn anns gach cearna do n' t-saoghal d' am bheil Gàidheil a' triall' (*'we have esteemed acquaintances in every part of the world to which Gaels are travelling'*) and that information will be sought from them and shared with readers; and that the periodical will then allow acquaintance and news to be maintained 'ann an Gàilig eadar chearnabh iomallach an domhain' (*'in Gaelic between remote parts of the world'*).[26]

This idea of an interconnected, international Gàidhealtachd runs through the early issues, whether describing the physical location of the Highlands and New Zealand as being 'bonn ri bhonn' (*'sole to sole'*) at opposite sides of the world; the spiritual connection with 'Dia na dùthcha 's na thogadh sibh 'na Dhia do'n dùthaich do 'bheil sibh ag imeachd' (*'the God of the country in which you were raised is the God of the country to which you are going'*); the physical gesture of Gaels already in Canada "sìneadh a mach an lamhan riutha 's a' smèideadh orra dol a nùll' (*'stretching out their hands to them and waving to them to go over'*); and the increased proximity of North America to Scotland, with the *Cuairtear* noting the arrival of newspapers from Upper Canada, 'a bha aon uair fad as, ach a tha

---

[23] This report appeared in the *Adelaide Chronicle*, 15 July 1840, p. 5, stating that it was taken from an 'Edinburgh Paper'. I have been unable, as yet, to find reference to this financial support in the Edinburgh press, although either this, or a similar meeting, was reported, e.g. *Caledonian Mercury*, 18 January 1840, p. 2; *Cuairtear nan Gleann*, 7 (September 1840), p. 168.

[24] For a detailed discussion of the periodical's promotion of emigration, see Sheila M. Kidd, 'Caraid nan Gaidheal and "Friend of Emigration": Gaelic emigration literature of the 1840s', *Scottish Historical Review*, 81.1 (2002), pp. 52–69.

[25] *Cuairtear nan Gleann*, 1 (March 1840), pp. 1–2.

[26] Ibid.

nis aig an dorus, tre innleachd nan soithichean-smùid' ('*which was once far away but which is now at our door, through the invention of steamships*').[27]

Just as with the earlier *Teachdaire*, MacLeod looked to his network of fellow clergymen for support, addressing them specifically in the first issue of the journal. Assistance seems to have been more forthcoming from those on the other side of the Atlantic than those closer to home, judging by his comments two years later when he expressed his debt to ministers in North America, particularly those in Nova Scotia: 'nan deanadh cléir ar dùthcha féin uiread air ar son cha bhiodh e na nì dhuilich an Cuairtear a chumail air falbh' ('*if the clergy of our country were to do as much for us, it wouldn't be difficult to keep Cuairtear going*').[28] Beneath this are listed the agents for the periodical, forty-seven in total, forty-five of whom are in Scotland with some listed as schoolmaster, bookseller or postmaster, and it is only in North America that a minister is listed as an agent, Rev. R. Williamson, Pictou, alongside John McNeil, Esq., Charlotte-Town [sic], Prince Edward Island, who is described as 'General Agent for North America' and who appears to have been a school inspector. Robert Williamson, a native of Ross-shire, had only reached his Nova Scotia charge, St Andrew's Pictou, in September 1840, in all probability carrying with him copies of the new periodical.[29] Another minister mentioned is Rev. John MacLennan, minister of St John's Church, Belfast, Prince Edward Island, whose letter brought 'deòir air ar sùilean le fìor shòlas' ('*tears of pure joy to our eyes*').[30]

The challenge of identifying contributors previously mentioned holds true for the *Cuairtear*. For all that the early issues were dominated by information about emigrant destinations, there is no evidence that these were written by emigrants, although the anonymous writers may well have been drawing on Highland emigrants' accounts and letters. Robert MacDougall, an emigrant returned from three years in the Huron Tract, and author of the first Gaelic guide for emigrants, *Ceann-Iùil an Fhir-Imrich do dh'America mu Thuath; Or the Emigrant's Guide to North America* (1841), worked in the *Cuairtear*'s office for a time and may have had a hand in some of these anonymous pro-emigration texts. The first identifiable contribution from a writer outwith Scotland appears exactly a year into the periodical's three-year run, 'Mu'n Chairt-iùil' ('*About Maps*'), further underlining this connection between periodicals and movement, and had been translated into Gaelic by 'D. M. I. Iar-amhuinn Phictou'

---

[27] Ibid. p. 15; *Cuairtear nan Gleann*, 2 (April 1840), pp. 28, 31; *Cuairtear nan Gleann*, 10 (December 1840), p. 238.
[28] *Cuairtear nan Gleann*, 24 (February 1842), p. 352.
[29] Hew Scott, *Fasti Ecclesiae Scoticane* Vol. 7 (Edinburgh: Oliver and Boyd, 1928), p. 16.
[30] *Cuairtear nan Gleann*, 11 (January 1841), p. 258. For the life of MacLennan, see Jean M. MacLennan, *From Shore to Shore. The Life and Times of the Rev. John MacLennan of Belfast, P.E.I.* (Edinburgh: Knox Press, 1977).

('*D. M. I., West River of Pictou*').[31] The location, initials and strong religious underpininngs of the text suggest the author was most likely Rev. Donald MacIntosh, minister at Salt Springs and Gairloch from 1834 to 1844.[32] A trickle of items from North American Gaels continued, in addition to two from New Zealand and one from Australia.[33] MacIntosh appears to have continued writing for the *Cuairtear*, this time under the pen names 'Gaidheal' ('*Gael*') and 'Eilthireach' ('*Emigrant*'), both of whom give their location as West River of Pictou, with no other North American correspondents so specific in their location. The *Cuairtear*, then, had a greater reach than its predecessor and harnessed a wider international network of writers, with the promotion of emigration a shared aim on both sides of the Atlantic.

This periodical traffic became two-way with a counterpart to *Cuairtear nan Gleann* established in Kingston, Ontario. Six months after the first appearance of the *Cuairtear*, a prospectus for 'a Gaelic paper called Cuairtear nan Coillte (i.e. Tourist of the Woods, or Forest)' appeared in the Upper Canada press. Consciously situating itself between the old and new worlds, this fortnightly journal aimed to convey to 'the remotest corners of this and the old country every useful information relative to the resources of the different portions of the two provinces', and, in similar vein to MacLeod's *Cuairtear*, assured readers that they could trust the descriptions of Upper Canada given in its pages.[34] It is hard to assess the periodical since only a few of the later issues, from 1842, shortly before it ceased publication, appear to survive, and the fact that there is no extant issue known in Scotland may suggest that relatively few copies crossed the Atlantic. It was, nonetheless, welcomed in Scotland. *Cuairtear nan Gleann* heralded its arrival as "na naigheachd is fiach aithris' ('*news worth mentioning*'), and alluded to it republishing material from its own pages, to which it was fully welcome.[35] The English-language press also offered the Canadian publication a warm welcome, with the anonymous writer in the *Glasgow Chronicle* suggesting that it cast an embarrassing light on Gaels in Scotland: 'The conduct of Highlanders in Canada should make those who are still inheriting the land of their forefathers blush, when they scarcely support one periodical in their native language.'[36] This cultural shaming would be, as will be seen later, a feature of later periodicals, with support for Gaelic periodicals being seen, and promoted, by those involved in producing them as a marker of cultural and linguistic pride, with their regular appearance allowing for demonstrations of

---

[31] *Cuairtear nan Gleann*, 12 (February 1841), pp. 279–81.
[32] Scott, *Fasti* Vol. 7, p. 615.
[33] For a brief discussion of these Australasian contributions, see Sheila M. Kidd, 'Kangaroos and cockatoos: Gaelic literature in the nineteenth-century Antipodes', *Scottish Literary Review*, 9.2 (2017), pp. 1–18 (3–4).
[34] *Upper Canada Herald*, 15 September 1840, p. 74.
[35] *Cuairtear nan Gleann*, 8 (October 1840), p. 188.
[36] Republished in *Caledonian Mercury*, 14 March 1842, p. 4.

longer-term commitment, compared with the transient commitment shown when buying a single book.

This pride was evident among poets too, as John Maclean's eulogy to the Glasgow *Cuairtear*, composed in Nova Scotia and sent to the periodical, shows. Not only is this one of the earliest of many songs praising Gaelic journals as cultural heroes, as discussed by Robert Dunbar, but it shows how the periodicals were perceived as a conduit for communication between emigrants and those they had left behind, Maclean asking in the penultimate verse:[37]

> A 'Chuairteir' shìobhalt, ma nì thu m' iarrtas,
> 'S gun cuir thu 'n t-òran seo 'n clò nan iarann,
> Ad choibhneas giùlain don chùrsa 'n iar e,
> Don eilean ìosal, an tìr on thriall mi.

> (*O mannerly 'Traveller', if you undertake my request, / and if you put this song in the iron print-blocks, / in your kind manner carry it to the west coast, / to the low-lying island, the land from which I travelled*).[38]

The emigrant poet's depiction of the periodical as an intermediary between Gaels on either side of the Atlantic echoes the earlier writer from the *Teachdaire*, each seeing this print format as a means of connecting them to their family. It allowed the poet to communicate with his homeland in both a public role and on a personal level.

The Gaelic periodical press experienced a hiatus of some twenty years from the early 1850s, with the notable exception of the Tasmanian *An Teachdaire Gaidhealach* (*The Highland Messenger*). Ten issues appeared in Tasmania in 1857 of this publication which saw itself, similarly, as having a role in connecting the international Gaelic community, describing itself as a 'slabhraidh' ('chain') which would create an intellectual connection between Scottish and Australian Gaels.[39] The temporary lack of journals should not, however, be taken as an indication of a dearth of literary interaction between Scottish and Canadian Gaels in the middle decades of the century. One example of the maintenance of these networks and their use in reinforcing shared cultural experiences was a publication occasioned by the death of Norman MacLeod in late 1862. The following year *Caraid a' Ghaidheil* (*Friend of the Gael*) – the name by which Norman MacLeod is commonly known – was published by Maurice Ogle and Co. in Glasgow and Dawson and Sons, Montreal.[40] This text was symbolic

---

[37] Dunbar, 'Gaelic periodicals', pp. 126–8.
[38] Meek (ed.), *The Wiles of the World*, pp. 204–5.
[39] *An Teachdaire Gaidhealach*, 1 (1857), p. 1. For a brief discussion of the periodical, see Kidd, 'Kangaroos and cockatoos', pp. 6–11.
[40] John Darroch and Alexander Matheson, *Caraid a' Ghaidheil* (Glasgow: M. Ogle and Co., 1863).

of MacLeod himself and his literary work in linking Gaels on either side of the Atlantic, not only in its bilocational publication but in its content, which consisted of two Gaelic sermons: the first, on the life of MacLeod, had been preached by Rev. John Darroch in St Columba Church, Locheil, Glengarry in Canada in April 1863 and the second had been delivered in Glasgow, very shortly after MacLeod's death, by Rev. Alexander Matheson of St Andrew's Church in Montreal, whose support for MacLeod's journals in Canada was discussed above. Publications such as this provided an opportunity to reaffirm a shared culture, language and religion by celebrating the life of an internationally recognised Gael, and reinforced the place of the church at the centre of both this network and Gaelic culture.

Publishers and printers, particularly those in Glasgow, became a nexus for transatlantic literary networks, publishing material sent back to Scotland by emigrants and fostering this sense of transatlantic Gaelic literary community. With Gaelic publishing in Canada in its very earliest days in the 1830s, John Maclean sent his *Laoidhean Spioradail* (*Spiritual Hymns*) back to Glasgow, where they were published in 1835 by Maurice Ogle, with most of the copies then shipped back to Canada.[41] *Caraid a' Ghaidheil* was printed by the Glasgow-based printer and publisher, Archibald Sinclair, a native of Islay who contributed significantly to the growth of Gaelic publishing in Glasgow from the early 1850s and who was part of a wider Islay literary network. Donald Meek has described Islay as being 'the intellectual power-house of Gaelic literary development in the nineteenth century' and Sinclair was a key figure within it.[42]

In 1860 Sinclair printed *Litir bho Nial Clèireach an Canada Uachdarach gu bhràthair Coinneach Clèireach 'san Eilean Ileach* (*A Letter from Neil Clark in Upper Canada to his brother Kenneth Clark in Islay*) for another Islay publisher in Glasgow, Neil Campbell. This letter, in the form of a sixty-seven-verse poem, had been written ten years earlier but had only just come into the printer's hands and he felt it merited publication 'gu beachd cothromach a thoirt do'r luchd-dùthcha mu chuid de na doilgheasan a thachaireas riu ann am fàsaichean Chanada' ('*to give a balanced view to our compatriots about some of the difficulties they will encounter in the Canadian wilderness*').[43] Clark may well have known both Sinclair and Campbell from his Islay days, though it may equally well have been that the poet's brother served as intermediary.

---

[41] Robert Douglas Dunbar, 'The secular poetry of John MacLean, "Bàrd Thighearna Chola", Am Bàrd MacGilleain' (unpublished doctoral thesis, University of Edinburgh, 2006), p. 395.

[42] Donald E. Meek, 'The world of William Livingston', in Derrick J. McClure, John M. Kirk and Margaret C. Storrie (eds), *A Land that Lies Westward: Language and Culture in Islay and Argyll* (Edinburgh: John Donald, 2009), pp. 149–72.

[43] Nial Cleireach, *Litir bho Nial Clèireach an Canada Uachdarach gu bhràthair Coinneach Clèireach 'san Eilean Ileach* (Glasgow: N. Campbell, 1860).

We cannot know for certain if Clark, who was living in Cheltenham, Ontario when he composed the piece, had anticipated publication of his letter-poem, particularly given the lapse of time between its composition and its publication; on the other hand, it begins with a somewhat self-conscious contextualisation of the transatlantic dialogue between the brothers. It explains that Niall's brother had sought information from him about Canada and outlines how Coinneach had told him about Islay tenants being evicted. This, and the public, communal nature of much Gaelic verse, would suggest that the poet was conscious of the potential wider reach of his *Litir*. For his part, and speaking to the flow of information between the Highlands and Canada, Niall refers to having heard about the owner of Islay, Walter Frederick Campbell of Shawfield, having departed for France. Given that this departure, as a result of Campbell's insolvency, occurred in 1847, this helps date the composition to that year or fairly shortly after.[44] The letter-poem, in which the poet's overall advice is that his brother is better to remain in Islay, merits more detailed consideration than can be given here, where its interest lies primarily in its illustration of transatlantic publishing networks.

Clark was not the only emigrant Islay poet published in Glasgow at this time. John McCorkindale's dialogue poem, *Comhradh eadar Dun-Bhrusgraig agus Fear-turais* (*Conversation between Dun Nosebridge and a Visitor*), was published by Neil Campbell in 1861.[45] The conversation between this anthropomorphised Islay hill near McCorkindale's home at Cluanach in Islay, and the poet's literary persona, a returning native who had been living 'measg nan Gallaibh' ('*among the Lowlanders*'), laments the changes brought about in Islay since the sequestration of the estate.[46] The poet had spent around six years working for an Edinburgh draper before departing in 1855 for Ontario, where two of his brothers and his sister had already settled.[47] We do not know if this poem was left with the publisher or a family member before McCorkindale emigrated or sent back after he settled in Canada. Nonetheless, the publication in Glasgow of a composition by a poet on the other side of the Atlantic underlines the mobility of Gaelic literary production in the nineteenth century, in this case linking Islay, Edinburgh and Ontario, and it shows how networks – Islay ones in this case – nurtured a transatlantic Gaelic literary community. McCorkindale, along with his brother Hugh, who was also a poet, retained a literary connection with their native land and language through contributing

---

[44] For this departure date, see David Caldwell, *Islay. The Land of the Lordship* (Edinburgh: Birlinn, 2017), p. 116.

[45] It is of passing interest to note another connection the poet had to Gaelic literature with his father acting as an agent for *Cuairtear nan Gleann*, e.g. *Cuairtear nan Gleann*, 2 (April 1840), p. 48.

[46] On these changes, see David Caldwell, *Islay*, pp. 115–17.

[47] I am very grateful to the poet's great-granddaughter, Mary Kearns Trace, for kindly sharing with me details about the poet's emigration, along with much other information about him.

to later periodicals, as will be seen in this next section, which considers the literary networks that emerged in the 1870s.

The Gaelic, and Gaelic-oriented, periodicals which emerged in the 1870s were just as conscious of their dispersed readership as their predecessors had been. The radical weekly *Highlander* (1873–81), with its prominent Gaelic column, was specifically aimed at 'Highlanders at home and abroad', and the primarily English-language *Celtic Magazine* (1875–88) twice referenced 'Celts at home and abroad' in the opening paragraph of its first editorial.[48] Of particular interest, however, is the monthly *An Gaidheal*, a Gaelic journal with an English supplement, which launched in similar vein, welcoming an international Gaelic audience: 'gach co-bhràthair Gaidhealach, air feadh an t-shaoghail fharsaing, a thuigeas an canain a tha e labhairt' (*'every fellow Highlander, throughout the wide world, who understands the language he [the periodical] speaks'*).[49] It was in the vanguard of those building a more culturally confident Highlands in the 1870s, and it played a key role in maintaining and expanding a mutually supportive transatlantic literary network.

The second part of its title, *'Paipear-naidheachd agus Leabhar-Sgeoil'* (*'a Newspaper and Book of Tales'*), marks it out from previous journals. Its primary interest was neither in promoting emigration nor in providing morally and religiously uplifting reading material, although both would feature in its pages. Rather, it reflected the growing cultural confidence of its time, and its mission was one of cultural rehabilitation and advancement, citing the dearth of Gaelic journals as undermining the language's status to non-Gaels,

> mar dhearbhadh nach 'eil a chainnt no na sgriobhuidhean againn airidh air an cur a mach no 'n cumail air chuimhne ann an leabhraichean no paipeirean naigheachd agus nach robh anns na Gaidheil ach sluagh fiadhaich, borb, aig nach robh suim da leithid.[50]

> (*as proof that our language and writings are not worthy of publication or preservation in books or newspapers and that the Gaels were but a wild, barbarous people who had no interest in the like*)

An Gaidheal epitomises the transatlantic nature of Gaelic periodical publishing. It was established in Toronto in 1871 by Alexander Nicholson, a native of Ness in Lewis, and then itself became an emigrant when its founder and editor was appointed as an emigration agent by the Canadian government. As Nicholson told John Francis Campbell, the appointment was a necessary one,

---

[48] Prospectus for the *Highlander*, <https://archive.org/details/gaidhealpaipeirn06glas/page/320/mode/2up>; Introduction, *Celtic Magazine*, 1.1 (November 1875), p. 1.
[49] Roimhradh, *An Gaidheal*, 1.1 (1871), p. 1.
[50] Ibid.

'not finding my connection with Gaelic literature sufficiently remunerative to support me without some such outside aid'.[51] From its fourth issue, *An Gaidheal* was published in Glasgow, Nicholson's Scottish base.[52] Even before the move to Scotland, Nicholson positioned his literary activities as transatlantic, with his company described as, 'Nicholson & Co., Publishers, Booksellers, and Printers, Toronto, Canada and Glasgow, Scotland', and he quickly established an international network of agents for *An Gaidheal*, sixteen in Canada (including the poet Hugh McCorkindale, and John McNeil who had been agent for *Cuairtear nan Gleann* three decades earlier); three in the United States; four in Scotland (one of whom was John Campbell, Bàrd na Ledaig (*The Ledaig Poet*)); and one each in Australia and New Zealand, the agent for the former, Donald Beaton, being a regular contributor to the journal.[53]

Although *An Gaidheal* was not established to promote emigration in the way that *Cuairtear nan Gleann* had been three decades earlier, there was nonetheless a strand of pro-emigration material in its pages, unsurprisingly given its editor's new duties. This took various forms, including the republication of articles from the *Cuairtear*, letters and songs from emigrants about their new homeland, news and advertisements, for example, from the Dominion's Department of Immigration offering free land to emigrants.[54] In keeping with its cultural ambitions, the content of *An Gaidheal* was strongly weighted towards the secular, including Highland history, tales and verse, in contrast with earlier periodicals where religious texts featured prominently as a result of editors and many writers being drawn from the ranks of the clergy.

The content of the early issues, as might be expected, had a stronger Canadian flavour than later ones, and in the first three issues a new cohort of writers and poets emerges with contributors on both sides of the Atlantic, some of whom would continue to be stalwart contributors to *An Gaidheal* in later years, as well as to other Gaelic publications. The three Toronto-published issues included contributions from Rev. Duncan Black Blair, Laggan, Nova Scotia, the first in a series of essays entitled 'Mu na Seann Ghaidheil' ('*About the Old Gaels*'); songs

---

[51] Letter contained within a copy of *An Gaidheal* Vol. 1 held by the National Library of Scotland, <https://archive.org/details/gaidhealpaipeirn06glas/page/n5/mode/2up>.

[52] 'Angus Nicholson, Esq. of "The Gael"', *Highland Echo*, 8 December 1877, pp. 1–2. This biographical sketch, probably written by Nigel MacNeill, editor of the *Highland Echo*, who also helped with the editing of *An Gaidheal*, states that Nicholson was born 'at Asmigarry, parish of Ness, Lewis in 1843' and emigrated along with an older brother in 1855. Old Parish Records, however, show that he was born in 1842, OPR 086/20 109. His Canadian government appointment continued until 1881 or 1882, when he is recorded as receiving a refund of expenses, Sessional Papers of the Dominion of Canada Vol. 4 Sessional Papers (No. 6), p. 150.

[53] *An Gaidheal*, 1.2 (1871), cover; *An Gaidheal*, 1.3 (1871), p. 74.

[54] For discussion of the ways in which emigration is represented in *An Gaidheal* and the *Celtic Magazine*, see Olivia Linda Klee, '"B' fhearr dhoibh a bhi 'n America": Beachdan air às-imrich às a' Ghàidhealtachd ann an irisean ag amas air Gàidheil, 1871–1883', *Proceedings of the Association of Celtic Students of Ireland and Britain*, 8 (forthcoming).

by the Argyll poet, Evan MacColl, by then living in Kingston, Ontario; the late Bàrd Maclean's poem 'An Gaidheal am measg nan Gall' (*'The Gael among the Lowlanders'*), composed before his departure for Canada in 1819 but which, given its subject matter, still clearly resonated with Gaelic speakers; a song by Donald Grant in praise of the Glengarry (Canada) Highland Society; John McCorkindale's dialogue-poem, which has already been discussed, followed by a second part which had been composed after his emigration as well as two poems by his brother Hugh. One of these was a eulogy to *An Gaidheal*, celebrating the fact it would bring news from the old world and describing how it had sparked Hugh's literary creativity:

'N uair a chuala mise an sgeul',
Lheum (*sic*) gach cuisle feadh mo chleibh,
'S chaidh mo chlarsach air ghleus;
   'S na h-uile teud gu h-ealanta.[55]

(*When I heard the news,*
Every vein in my chest leapt,
And my harp was tuned,
And every string skilful.)

Scottish contributors included the poets John Campbell, Ledaig and Dr John MacLachlan, Rahoy; the folklorist Alexander Carmichael, who would appear to have been the author of an article entitled 'Beath'-Eachdraidh Choluim Chille' (*'The Life-Story of Columba'*), contributed under the name 'A. C., Lochmaddy';[56] and Farquhar D. MacDonell, under his pen name 'Loch-aillse' (*'Lochalsh'*), whose verse also appeared in the *Oban Times* and the *Highlander* in the early 1870s; and further afield, Donald Beaton in New South Wales, underlining the wide, international spread of contributors. The balance, however – in so far as contributors can be identified – is towards Canada, a balance which changed with the journal's move to Glasgow.

There are glimpses in the journal's pages of transatlantic dialogue between readers and editors. 'Oran do Shir Seumas MacMhathain, Bart., Leoghas' (*'A Song to Sir James Matheson, Bart., Lewis'*) by 'D. G. S.' appeared in the first issue of *An Gaidheal*, praising the owner of the island of Lewis as a kindly landlord who would 'Bhi togail suas nan diobarach, / Le innleachdan fiughantail' ('Be elevating the needy / With his charitable ways').[57] The poet was clearly in Canada,

---

[55] *An Gaidheal*, 1.1 (1871), p. 17.
[56] Domhnall Uilleam Stiùbhart, 'Alexander Carmichael and Carmina Gadelica', in Domhnall Uilleam Stiùbhart (ed.), *The Life and Legacy of Alexander Carmichael* (Port of Ness: The Islands Book Trust, 2008), pp. 1–39 (36, fn. 71).
[57] *An Gaidheal*, 1.1 (1871), pp. 16–17.

as he refers to there being many around him whose fares had been paid by Matheson. The Lewis landlord was not entirely the kindly benefactor depicted here and the conduct of his factor, Donald Munro, was what would cause the Bernera Riot in 1874.[58] This eulogy was not well received by a reader in Lewis, with the third issue of the periodical mentioning receipt of a letter directing them 'gun a bhi ri miodal nan tighearnan Gaidhealach, daoine 's miosa a tha ri fhaighinn' ('not to be flattering Highland landlords, the worst people to be found'). The letter is not published, but a robust defence of the poem and of Matheson is given, presumably by Nicholson given this related to his native island, while also agreeing that some landlords did merit censure.[59]

Highland and territorial associations on both sides of the Atlantic were regularly mentioned in the pages of *An Gaidheal*, adding to the sense of an interconnected, international Gàidhealtachd. Iain Sinclair, Bàrd Ghlinn-da-Ruadhail (*The Poet of Glendaruel*), who had left Cowal in 1840 and settled in Prince Edward Island, composed a song to Glasgow's Cowal Society in 1874 which he sent to D. C. Maclean, President of the Society, a poem which allowed him to share publicly his enduring connection to his native district over thirty years after his departure.[60] The song, praising Cowal and encouraging emigration to North America, was then sent to *An Gaidheal* by 'Glinneach' ('a Glendaruel man'), who was presumably Maclean, with an accompanying account of the Society's meeting at which it was performed before an audience of over nine hundred.[61] The periodical was part of an ever-widening process of transmission of the song, first shared through personal correspondence, then through public performance among Cowal natives in Glasgow and, finally, with an extended Gaelic community, *An Gaidheal*'s international readership, which offered public acknowledgement and recognition to the Prince Edward Island poet who may well himself have read the account.

Evan MacColl, from Kenmore, Loch Fyne, is another interesting figure, a lauded poet on both sides of the Atlantic whose songs and poems had first appeared in print before his emigration, in *An Teachdaire Ùr Gaidhealach* (*The New Gaelic Messenger*) in 1835–6 and in his collection *Clàrsach nam Beann* (*The Harp of the Mountains*),[62] published first in 1836 with English and Gaelic poems, then in revised form in 1839 with Gaelic poems only. His growing reputation earned him a place in John Mackenzie's 1841 landmark anthology of Gaelic poetry, *Sar-Obair nam Bard Gaelach; or the Beauties of Gaelic Poetry*. After his departure for Kingston in the 1850s he continued to compose Gaelic

---

[58] Joni Buchanan, *The Lewis Land Struggle. Na Gaisgich* (Stornoway: Acair, 1996), pp. 7–14.
[59] *An Gaidheal*, 1.3 (1871), p. 59.
[60] Alexander Maclean Sinclair (ed.), *The Gaelic Bards from 1825 to 1875* (Sydney, CB: Mac-Talla Publishing Co., 1904), p. 138.
[61] *An Gaidheal*, 3.25 (1874), pp. 19–20.
[62] The title of the first edition had an English title, *The Mountain Minstrel*.

poetry and fulfilled roles such as poet to the Gaelic Society of Toronto. Eight of his songs, spanning both his pre- and post-emigration compositions, were published in *An Gàidheal*, as were a portrait and biographical sketch. Even after the periodical's demise at the end of 1877 he remained in contact with Highland periodicals and their editors. When Alexander Mackenzie, editor of the *Celtic Magazine*, undertook a tour of Canada in 1879, an account of which was serialised in the journal, a visit to MacColl was a cultural pilgrimage for Mackenzie, who explained that 'to see the sweet bard of Lochfyne in the flesh, and in his own house, was the central object in my Canadian tour'.[63] The following year Mackenzie proceeded to publish his 'memoir' of the poet in the *Celtic Magazine*, followed by extracts from MacColl's diary from a tour in the north of Scotland in 1838–9 when he was collecting subscriptions to support the publication of the second edition of his poems, all of this cementing MacColl's reputation as one of the foremost Gaelic literary figures of the day, in the eyes of both Scottish and Canadian Gaels.[64]

When the President of the Toronto Gaelic Society and fellow contributor to *An Gaidheal* and the *Celtic Magazine*, Patrick MacGregor, died in 1882, Evan MacColl's elegy to him was published in the *Oban Times*.[65] MacColl's lament to his Canadian compatriot, whom he describes as "n Gaidheal thar gach Gaidheal' ('*the Gael over every Gael*'), places this death in the wider context of Gaelic literature by reaching out a hand of sympathy to Gaels in Scotland by mentioning the death the previous year of Inverness contributor to *An Gaidheal* and co-founder with Mackenzie of the *Celtic Magazine*, Rev. Alexander MacGregor, who is referred to by one of his pen names, 'Sgiathanach' ('Skyeman'):

'S beag an t-ioghna a càirdean [càirdean na Gàidhlig]
    Anns gach àite bhi gruamach.
'N déigh an dochunn do-chàradh
    O cheann ràidhe a fhuair i.
'S gann a dh-fhuaraich fo'n talamh
    An deagh "Sgiathanach" suairce,
'Nuair a thilgte 'n gath guineach
    'Rinn 'fhear-cinnidh a bhualadh.[66]

---

[63] A[lexander] M[ackenzie], 'The Editor in Canada V', *Celtic Magazine*, 5.53 (March 1880), pp. 183–93 (191).
[64] It is interesting to note that Mackenzie's travels enabled him to extend the reach of his periodical with a list of sixteen Canadian agents and one in New York published, 'Our agents in Canada', *Celtic Magazine*, 5.52 (February 1880), p. 168.
[65] MacGregor, a native of Perthshire, contributed no fewer than eight items to *An Gaidheal*. The two MacGregors were not related.
[66] *Oban Times*, 22 March 1882. A further elegy to Patrick MacGregor, by a poet using the initials 'I. M.', was published in the *Oban Times*, 29 April 1882.

(*It is little wonder its [Gaelic's] friends / in every place are sorrowful. / After the grievous injury / It received last quarter. / The good, civil 'Sgiathanach' / was scarcely cold in the grave, / When the piercing dart would be thrown / That struck his kinsman.*)

Gaelic elegies traditionally served as a means of expressing communal grief and loss, and in this instance the transatlantic Gaelic literary community is the one addressed by the poet, and through the platform which nurtured it, the press.

While on tour, Mackenzie also visited Rev. Alexander Maclean Sinclair, grandson of the John Maclean, in Springville, Nova Scotia. Maclean Sinclair would be one of the most prodigious contributors to Gaelic literature in the following decades and was at the centre of a very extensive network of Gaelic poets, writers, editors and publishers which included some of the most prominent Gaelic literary figures in Scotland.[67] Although the majority of Maclean Sinclair's periodical contributions, well over five hundred between those in English and Gaelic, would appear in later Canadian publications, some of his earliest writing appeared in Alexander Nicholson's short-lived *Canada Scotsman* and then occasionally in *An Gaidheal*, the *Highlander*, the *Celtic Magazine* and the *Oban Times*.[68] The supportive and nurturing environment which *An Gaidheal* provided for Gaelic literature and scholarship is evident in exchanges involving Maclean Sinclair. In 1875, 'Abrach' (the pen name of Edinburgh librarian, Donald C. MacPherson) sent the sixteenth-century song 'Caismeachd Ailein-nan-Sop' ('*A War Song for Ailean nan Sop*') by Hector Maclean to *An Gaidheal*. MacPherson outlined the travels of the text across the Atlantic and then back as he authenticated it for readers. He had received it from Rev. Dr Thomas MacLauchlan, Edinburgh, who had in turn received it from Alexander Maclean Sinclair, to whom it came through his grandfather, John Maclean, who had acquired it before leaving Scotland in a manuscript collection of poems belonging to a Maclean doctor in Mull.[69] Two years later, Maclean Sinclair sent *An Gaidheal* a detailed breakdown of the contents of this eighteenth-century manuscript, which had belonged to Dr Hector Maclean of Grulin, Mull, concluding with his wish to publish it. In response, a letter from a Niall Campbell encourages him to do so, suggesting:

iarraidh e 'mach gach Gàidheal, agus gach comunn Gàidhealach, agus ma tha boinne de dh-fhuil an fhìor Ghàidhil na 'n cuislean, cuiridh iad an ainm sìos, oir 's e 'n gnìomh a bheir dearbhadh air a' chùis.[70]

---

[67] See Linkletter, '*Bu dual dha sin*', pp. 247–58, for discussion of his network of correspondents in both Scotland and Canada.
[68] See Appendix B in Linkletter, '*Bu dual dha sin*' for a catalogue of most of his periodical contributions.
[69] Abrach, 'Ailein-nan-Sop', *An Gaidheal*, 4.39 (1875), pp. 76–8.
[70] Nial Caimbeal, 'An Cochruinneachadh Muileach', *An Gaidheal*, 6.62 (1877), pp. 263–4.

(*let him seek out every Gael and every Highland society and if there is a drop of true Highland blood in their veins, they will put their names down [for a copy] for the deed will prove the matter.*)

Supporting Gaelic literature and publishing was promoted as a shared patriotic duty and as a way of demonstrating one was a true Gael, with the implicit message that engagement with, and support for, the periodicals was too. Maclean Sinclair would include material from this manuscript in later publications. Mackenzie's account of his visit to Maclean Sinclair in 1879 touches on this manuscript among others in the minister's possession as well as marvelling at the minister's personal library and suggesting that 'his collection of Celtic works is the best private one on the American Continent, and very few indeed can surpass it even at home'.[71] Mackenzie's writings about MacColl and Maclean Sinclair ensured recognition for Canadian Gaels who were active in Gaelic literary circles, and Maclean Sinclair's transatlantic exchanges would continue through the following decades, and included the publication of his first poetry anthology, *Clàrsach na Coille*, in 1881 by Archibald Sinclair in Glasgow.

An Gaidheal's sense of a collective cultural mission spanning the Atlantic was shared by regular contributors such as 'Cona' in Canada, who saw the journal as a vindication of the Gaels, their language and culture: 'Co a nis, a their nach 'eil sgoilearan Gaidhlig ann; nach 'eil ar canain dheas-chainnteach airidh air saothair air bith' (*'who now will say that there are no Gaelic scholars; that our eloquent language is not worthy of any labour'*).[72] It was also an opportunity for North American Gaels to proudly demonstrate the vitality of the language among emigrant communities. 'Gaidheal anns na Coilltibh' (*'A Gael in the Woods'*) told readers that in Pictou, 'saoilidh neach gu 'r h-ann an siorrachd Rois, no Ionar Nis no Chataobh a tha e leis na choinnicheas ris de na Gàidhil, agus de 'n Ghàilig' (*'a person will think that he is in Ross-shire, Inverness-shire or Sutherland with all the Gaels and Gaelic he encounters'*).[73] On occasions there was even a hint of competitiveness between old world and new world Gaels when the anonymous writer of 'Na Gaidheil an Canada' (*'The Gaels in Canada'*) claimed 'tha e air aithris gu minig le daoine a tha eolach gun d'theid Gaidhealtachd America a Tuath faisg air dubhlan a thoirt do 'n t-seann Gaidhealtachd fhein an diugh' (*'it is often said by those who know that the Gaidhealtachd of North America will come close to challenging the old Gaidhealtachd itself today'*).[74]

In the course of the nineteenth century, Gaelic periodicals evolved from vehicles for emigration propaganda which fostered tentative links between literary Gaels in Scotland and Canada to become a medium for the maintenance of

---

[71] A. M., 'The Editor in Canada. II', *Celtic Magazine*, 5.50 (December 1879), pp. 69–77 (72).
[72] Cona, 'Litir a Canada', *An Gaidheal*, 2.22 (1873), pp. 304–6 (304).
[73] Gaidheal anns na Coilltibh, ''Litir a America', *An Gaidheal*, 4.40 (1875), pp. 114–15 (115).
[74] 'Na Gaidheil an Canada', *An Gaidheal*, 1.1 (1871), pp. 7–8 (7).

Gaelic literature, based on mutually supportive networks which embraced and nurtured an international Gàidhealtachd, with Canadian Gaels' contribution second only to those in Scotland. Although *An Gaidheal* ceased publication in 1877, transatlantic literary exchanges continued to feature in the growing numbers of Gaelic columns in Highland newspapers, including the *Oban Times*, the *Highland News* and Canadian publications such as the *Toronto Daily Mail* and Antigonish, NS's *Casket*, and created solid foundations for the first Gaelic newspaper to appear on either side of the Atlantic, *Mac-Talla*, in 1892, a publication which would also be dependent on an international network of Gaelic readers and writers.

After *Mac-Talla*'s demise well over a century ago, and with the influx of Highland emigrants to Canada all but drying up, transatlantic literary networks ebbed and flowed, but never vanished through the twentieth century and into the twenty-first. The enduring richness of Nova Scotia's Gaelic oral tradition was captured by, among others, John Lorne Campbell and Margaret Fay Shaw on a visit there in the late 1930s and a selection of these recordings was subsequently published in Scotland.[75] And scholars of Gaelic literature, culture and folklore have crossed the Atlantic in both directions, both temporarily and permanently. New connections and mutually supportive networks – literary, musical, educational and scholarly – evolved as opportunities arose. Where some nineteenth-century Canada-based poets made use of publishers in Scotland, more recent developments include Bradan Press, established in Halifax, Nova Scotia in 2016, collaborating with a Scottish-based Gaelic translator, Mòrag Anna NicNèill, to produce *Anna Ruadh*, a translation of L. M. Montgomery's *Anne of Green Gables*. This was crowdfunded internationally by an appeal to Gaelic speakers through social media, and the volume was subsequently shortlisted for the Gaelic literary awards run by Scottish organisation Comhairle nan Leabhraichean (The Gaelic Books Council). Gaelic networks have endured and reinvented themselves over the course of two centuries to maintain a transatlantic literary community.

---

[75] John L. Campbell (ed.), *Songs Remembered in Exile* (Aberdeen: Aberdeen University Press, 1990); Rob Dunbar, 'John Lorne Campbell, Jonathan G. MacKinnon, and the transatlantic ties that bind Scotland and Canada', Saltire Society's Fletcher of Saltoun Lecture (Edinburgh, 2020).

FIVE

The Scottish Highlands and Warfare in the British Atlantic World, c. 1740–1815

Matthew Dziennik

In October 1773, the factor of the estate of Sir Alexander Macdonald of Sleat invited Samuel Johnson and James Boswell to stay with him at a house in Armadale formerly occupied by his chief. That evening 'the company danced as usual. We performed, with great activity, a dance which, I suppose, the emigration from Sky[e] has occasioned. They call it *America*.' It was not the only time that Boswell and Johnson experienced Highland elation at the possibilities of reaching America. Boswell's recollections of the visit are replete with references of Highlanders gone or planning to go to America.[1] But this 'dance called America' has become a staple of understanding connections between the Gàidhealtachd and North America, used as titles for everything from popular histories of Highland emigration to a song on Runrig's 1985 album *Heartland*.[2] The potential of America as a land of opportunity for Gaels in the eighteenth and nineteenth centuries is well established and has shaped academic and popular understandings of the relationship between the Scottish Highlands and the Atlantic world.[3] Emigration agents and emigrants themselves were keen to portray North America

---

[1] J. Boswell, *The Journal of a Tour to the Hebrides with Samuel Johnson, LL.D.* (London, 1785), pp. 150, 245, 341.

[2] J. Hunter, *A Dance Called America: The Scottish Highlands, the United States, and Canada* (Edinburgh: Mainstream, 1994); Runrig, 'Dance Called America', track #5 on *Heartland* (Soundcastle Studios, 1985).

[3] A. Epperson, '"It would be my earnest desire that you all would come": Networks, the migration process and Highland emigration', *Scottish Historical Review*, 88:2 (2009), pp. 313–31; M. Bennett, *Oatmeal and the Catechism: Scottish Gaelic Settlers in Quebec* (Edinburgh: John Donald, 1998); A. Murdoch, 'Emigration from the Scottish Highlands to America in the eighteenth century', *British Journal for Eighteenth Century Studies*, 21:2 (1998), pp. 161–74; A. W. Parker, *Scottish Highlanders in Colonial Georgia: The Recruitment, Emigration, and Settlement at Darien, 1735–1748* (Athens, GA: University of Georgia Press, 1997); D. Dobson, *Scottish Emigration to Colonial America, 1607–1785* (Athens, GA: University of Georgia Press, 1994); T. M. Devine (ed.), *Scottish Emigration and Scottish Society* (Edinburgh: John Donald, 1992); J. M. Bumsted, *The People's Clearance: Highland Emigration to British North America, 1770–1815* (Edinburgh: Edinburgh University Press, 1992); M. McLean, *The People of Glengarry: Highlanders in Transition, 1745–1820* (Montreal: McGill-Queen's University Press, 1991).

as a land ideally suited to Gaels where, in the words of one promoter, 'Is iad na tuaidh luchd-uailse na duthcha. Tha iad gun mhàl 's gun bhacadh seilge / The tenantry are the gentlemen of the country. They pay no rent and there is no restriction on hunting.' Or, as one early emigrant told a correspondent on Islay, America 'is one of the best poor mans [sic] Country you ever heard of'.[4]

This assumption that Gaels interpreted America as a panacea to dispossession, marginalisation and the aggressive imposition of rural capitalism, however, requires careful consideration. The purpose of this chapter is to highlight the uneasiness and ambiguity that stood at the centre of Gaelic contacts with the Atlantic world. As powerful as America was as a possibility for many Highland emigrants, it was also a place where the tragedy of displacement and transitory movement became harsh reality. Just as North America was constructed in the minds of potential emigrants and emigration agents – or by dancers in Armadale – it was equally made in the lived experiences of emigrants who struggled to carve out new lives in an exacting and unforgiving environment. Indeed, it was precisely America's role as an abstracted location – a tabula rasa upon which to project ideas, hopes and bitterness – that made it so appealing and so central to the Gaelic experience in the eighteenth and early nineteenth centuries.[5]

One means of understanding the full range and complexity of Gaelic attitudes to movement is through one of the most consequential groups of Highlanders and Islanders to live and work in the Atlantic world: soldiers. From the mid-eighteenth century through to the end of the Napoleonic Wars, Gaels were recruited and dispatched in large numbers across the Atlantic in the furtherance of British imperial ambitions. Their songs and writings – which both lauded the contributions of Gaels towards British imperialism and acknowledged the brutality of war and civil strife in the empire – constitute a distinct and crucial corpus of sources for Scottish contacts with the Atlantic world that are only now starting to be fully appreciated.[6] Often written by serving officers and soldiers and published through the assistance of fellow military men, these

---

[4] S. M. Kidd, 'Caraid nan Gaidheal and "Friend of Emigration": Gaelic emigration literature of the 1840s', *Scottish Historical Review*, 81:1 (2002), pp. 52–69; Alexander McAllister to Angus McCuaig, 29 November 1770, PC.1738, McAllister Family Papers, North Carolina State Archives.

[5] Emerging studies have identified the problems of settlement and the desire of many emigrants to return to the land of their birth; see A. Murdoch, 'Hector McAllister in North Carolina, Argyll and Arran: Family and memory in return migration to Scotland in the eighteenth century', *Journal of Scottish Historical Studies*, 33:1 (2013), pp. 1–19; M. Harper (ed.), *Emigrant Homecomings: The Return Movement of Emigrants, 1600–2000* (Manchester: Manchester University Press, 2005).

[6] S. Innes and G. Parsons (eds), *Seumas MacLathagain agus a Làmh-Sgrìobhainnean / James McLagan and his Manuscripts* (Glasgow: Scottish Gaelic Texts Society, 2019); M. Dziennik and M. Newton, 'Egypt, empire and the Gaelic literary imagination', *International Review of Scottish Studies*, 43 (2019), pp. 1–40; R. I. Maciver, 'The Gaelic Poet and the British Military Experience, 1756–1856' (PhD thesis, University of Glasgow, 2018); W. McLeod, 'Gaelic poetry and the British military enterprise, 1756–1945', in C. Sassi and T. van Heijnsbergen (eds), *Within and Without Empire: Scotland Across the (Post)colonial Borderline* (Newcastle: Cambridge Scholars, 2013), pp. 61–76.

songs reveal the importance of military service in shaping Gaelic attitudes to the Atlantic world and the intellectual and material networks that facilitated connections between Scotland and the Americas.

The songs are infinitely complex. Some songs expressed high-spirited support for the British imperial project and contained vicious denunciations of the empire's enemies. Others considered politics secondary or even irrelevant to the celebration of Gaelic martial achievements consistent with the older codes of Gaelic panegyric verse. What they shared, however, was an acceptance of violence as an integral part of the relationship between the Scottish Highlands and the Atlantic world. And they devoted considerable attention to negative views of North America and its peoples as a foil for Gaelic triumphs. The result was a more troubled and ambiguous attitude to the Americas than those typically found in emigration literature. A critical reading of military songs can be used to enliven debates about Highland engagement with empire and the costs of such entanglements on both sides of the Atlantic Ocean.

Furthermore, these songs were not intended simply for military audiences; they were critical to Gaelic views of North America in a wider sense. Warfare in the Atlantic world was profoundly destructive to the lives and hopes of many Gaels. But it was also creative and decisive for Gaelic and for the Scottish Highlands and Islands as the region attempted to make sense of its place within an imperial world. In a telling irony, the commitment of Gaels to the military and their brutal suffering in the expansion of the British Empire may also have created the conditions for the renewed celebration of Gaelic martial exploits seen in the literary output of Gaels in the late eighteenth and early nineteenth centuries. It is in these ambiguities – a reluctance to serve, songs of war and loss, and celebrations of Gaelic militarism – that the Gàidhealtachd's uneasy relationship to the Atlantic world comes into sharper focus.

Highland military service in the Atlantic world

Before analysing the songs, it is crucial to place them in context. The ambiguities of Gaelic entanglements in North America are first revealed through the lived experiences of Highland recruits and the brutalities of imperial conflict. Highland military participation with the Atlantic world largely reflected the political needs of the British state. For much of the first half of the eighteenth century, Gaels were a marginal presence in the British Army and the government showed little interest in recruitment other than to sustain a regional police force and as a mechanism for local patronage.[7] Some Gaels did serve in the British

---

[7] P. Simpson, *The Independent Highland Companies, 1603–1760* (Edinburgh: John Donald, 1996). More Gaels were typically found in the armies of the French monarchy and the Dutch republic

Army and were recognised as crucial interlocuters between the British state and the Gàidhealtachd but their numbers were probably small.[8] Military contacts between the Scottish Highlands and North America were necessarily limited as a result. The recruitment of Highlanders for overseas expeditions tended to be localised and ad hoc, such as the 1735 effort to recruit members of the Clan Chattan Confederacy for a buffer-zone colony in Georgia between the Spanish in Florida and the British settlements in the Carolinas. In a world where styles of warfare were seen as elemental to the division between 'civilised' and 'savage' societies, English commanders such as General James Oglethorpe (the architect of the Georgia settlement) saw in the social system of the Highlands a means of matching the supposed savagery and ruthlessness of the Spanish and their Indigenous allies. The grim reality was that the members of the Confederacy who settled in Georgia were just as vulnerable to slaughter and disease as any other group of transplanted Europeans and many were killed or captured by the Spanish at the siege of Fort Mose in June 1740.[9]

Yet the state's interest in the Scottish Highlands expanded dramatically in the 1740s as the wars with France and Spain exposed the evident vulnerabilities of British colonies abroad. The need for soldiers during the period of the War of Austrian Succession (1740–8) witnessed the formation of the 43rd Foot (Black Watch) in 1739 out of the independent companies assigned to keep the peace in the region since the 1720s. It was an important step. For the first time, a regiment of Gaels was formally incorporated into the regular British Army for potential foreign service. Other regiments followed. At the same time that the Black Watch was demonstrating its use to the British state on the battlefields of Flanders in May 1745, beating orders for the 64th (Loudoun's) Foot were being distributed in the Gàidhealtachd. The story of the 64th Foot evidences a clear connection between the Highlands and British concerns for the security of North America. Raised during the Jacobite Rebellion, the regiment was actively involved in the search for Jacobite fugitives in 1746 before being deployed to Flanders, where it fought at the siege of Bergen Op Zoom in 1747. In 1748 it was proposed that the regiment be demobilised in Nova Scotia in order to counteract the presence of French-speaking Acadians. Other proposals for

---

despite efforts by the government in London to periodically restrict foreign recruiting parties in the Highlands; see S. Conway, 'The Scots Brigade in the eighteenth century', *Northern Scotland*, 1:1 (2010), pp. 30–41. Scots were also actively involved in recruiting for other European services. Admiral Thomas Gordon was involved in a scheme to recruit officers for the Russian Navy; see William Cooper to Thomas Gordon, 14 March 1720, GD24/1/856, f. 33, Papers of the Family of Stirling Home Drummond Moray of Abercairny, National Records of Scotland [hereafter NRS].

[8] Bland to Beauclerck, 24 July 1755, MS 305, f. 56, Letter Book of Humphrey Bland, National Library of Scotland [hereafter NLS].

[9] G. Plank, 'Deploying tribes and clans: Mohawks in Nova Scotia and Scottish Highlanders in Georgia', in W. E. Lee (ed.), *Empires and Indigenes: Intercultural Alliance, Colonial Expansion, and Warfare in the Early Modern World* (New York: New York University Press, 2011), pp. 221–49.

recruiting Highlanders to secure the newly conquered region were also entertained and, while no settlement plans were physically enacted, it is clear that the link between Highland recruitment and imperial security was becoming increasingly evident.[10]

Such concerns only increased with the opening of the Seven Years War in 1756. The war's global scope and the desire of the Pitt government to contest the war on all fronts gave rise to a threefold expansion of the regular army to over 90,000 men. Seeking to protect the burgeoning industrial centres of England from the loss of labour, significant efforts were directed towards northern Scotland, where ten battalions were raised for service in North America, the West Indies, Germany and India. The slow trickle of military migrants arriving in North America in the first half of the eighteenth century became a flood. In the three decades between the beginning of the Seven Years War and the end of the War for American Independence in 1783, over 12,000 Gaels served in British uniform against both France and the American revolutionaries, of whom at least 5,000 remained in North America as settlers with the peace.[11]

What is striking about these numbers is that, before the 1760s at least, there is very little evidence that Gaels had any desire to enlist for service outside of Scotland, to say nothing of being sent to the Americas. Recruiting in Inverness-shire for the Georgia Plan in the 1730s, for example, had proved difficult and those who did come forward only did so with great trepidation.[12] For many early military migrants, service in North America and the Caribbean was a form of punishment rather than a choice. Jacobite prisoners from the 1715 and 1745 rebellions – perhaps as many as 1,400 in total– were forced into indentured servitude in Maryland, Virginia, South Carolina, Barbados and Antigua, where they materially added to the numbers of white settlers.[13] Recruiters after the 1745 rebellion also combed the prison hulks for recruits or used the courts to enforce enlistments. Those found guilty of contravening the 1746 Disarming Act were impressed into regiments bound for America, while deserters from British regiments who had joined the rebel army were

---

[10] A. Mackillop, *More Fruitful Than the Soil: Army, Empire and the Scottish Highlands, 1715–1815* (East Linton: Tuckwell, 2000), p. 57; Proposals for Raising a Highland Company, n.d., 296/7, f. 8, Townshend Papers, W. L. Clements Library. For planter settlement of Nova Scotia, see J. Reid, '*Pax Britannica* or *Pax Indigena*? Planter Nova Scotia (1760–1782) and competing strategies of pacification', *Canadian Historical Review*, 85:4 (2004), pp. 669–92.
[11] For a full discussion, see M. P. Dziennik, *The Fatal Land; War, Empire, and the Highland Soldier in British America* (New Haven: Yale University Press, 2015), p. 140.
[12] Parker, *Scottish Highlanders in Colonial Georgia*, p. 3.
[13] Sam Smith to Andrew Stone, 22 October 1747, SP36/102/38, f. 40, State Papers Domestic, National Archives [hereafter NA]; B. G. Seton and J. G. Arnot, *Prisoners of the '45*, 3 vols (Edinburgh: Scottish History Society, 1928-9); G. Plank, *Rebellion and Savagery: The Jacobite Rising of 1745 and the British Empire* (Philadelphia: University of Pennsylvania Press, 2005), p. 51.

offered clemency provided they re-enlisted for overseas service.[14] Still more were enlisted into Independent Companies bound for America after a request by Sir William Pepperell, the governor of Massachusetts Bay, for Jacobite prisoners in order to make up shortfalls in recruiting in North America.[15] No less a figure than the Duke of Cumberland declared that he 'wished that these people [Jacobite prisoners] may be disposed of in such a manner as to be of service to the government, instead of a detriment to it'.[16] One senior officer considered sending the relatives of Jacobite fugitives to the West Indies in order to force their kin out of hiding.[17]

Even among would-be volunteers for the army there was also an evident disdain for service in the Americas. Rumours of a regiment being sent to America were usually enough to set off bitter resistance on the part of enlisted Gaels. The famous mutiny of the Black Watch in 1743 had been set off by rumours that the men were to be shipped to the West Indies. In a deeply bitter yet revealing irony, it is likely that the first Highland soldiers sent to the Americas were thirty-eight prisoners from the 1743 mutiny who were drafted into Dalzell's regiment based in the Leeward Islands.[18] Nor was 1743 an isolated incident. During the 1745 rebellion, Captain Alexander Mackenzie witnessed more than two-thirds of his independent company desert when a rumour spread that the men were to be shipped to America to assist in the occupation of Cape Breton Island by New England forces.[19] Such resistance encouraged officers to ensure their men understood that they might be required to serve overseas. Lord John Murray, the colonel of the Black Watch in the 1750s, required that officers explain the conditions of service to recruits before their attestation.[20]

Of course, other officers were far less scrupulous and there are innumerable examples of nefarious means used to recruit men for the regiments. There were a number of major mutinies in the Highland regiments across the Age of Revolutions, which usually occurred upon a regiment being dispatched overseas. John Clark, an author and translator, complained to the Secretary at War that 'Many an innocent [Highland] man has been dragged from a feeble and

[14] List of rebels and deserters, January 1747, LOmss10231 (Box 38), Loudoun Papers, Huntington Library [hereafter HL]; I. A. Davison, 'Some notes on the participation of the three additional companies of Lord John Murray's Highland regiment during the 1745 Rebellion and its aftermath', *Journal of the Society for Army Historical Research*, 82:3 (2004), p. 257.
[15] J. D. Oats, *The Jacobite Campaigns* (Abingdon: Routledge, 2011), p. 11.
[16] Lord J. Russell (ed.), *The Correspondence of John, Fourth Duke of Bedford*, Vol. 1 (London, 1842), p. 564.
[17] Bland to Lord George Beauclerck, 24 July 1755, MS305, f. 56, Letter Book of Humphrey Bland, NLS.
[18] J. Prebble, *Mutiny: The Highland Regiments in Revolt* (London: Secker & Warburg, 1975), p. 86.
[19] Memorial of Captain Alexander Mackenzie, n.d. [1746], LOmss9145 (Box 35), Loudoun Papers, HL.
[20] Orders for the 42nd Foot Additional Companies, 15 July 1757, BAG/5/1, f. 11, Bagshawe Family Muniments, John Rylands Library.

helpless family, to serve in the army.'[21] Other recruiters attempted to remove recruits from their home districts so they could be attested in front of less sympathetic magistrates as required by the law. The result of such practices was sometimes scuffles between recruiters and the inhabitants of villages and market towns.[22]

The reluctance of young men to serve overseas did not change with the advent of the wars against revolutionary and Napoleonic France. Once again, the British state turned to its Gaelic margins for troops, recruiting some nine new Highland regiments in the 1790s. Some of these new troops were Catholics and, while the numbers of Catholics recruited in Ireland or from Irish regiments formerly in the service of the French king were much larger than those from northern Scotland, a sizeable number of officers came from Catholic families who had been previously excluded from purchasing commissions. Predominantly Catholic regiments also appeared, such as the Glengarry Fencibles under Alexander Macdonell of Glengarry, which fought in Ireland in the 1798 rebellion. The subsequent emigration of many of the regiment to Upper Canada after 1802 provided the British state with experienced soldiers during the War of 1812 and provides an Atlantic dimension to the service of Catholics in Britain's armed forces.[23]

By and large, however, the importance of the West Indies and India as major fronts in Britain's wars made enlistment an unappealing prospect for Catholics and Protestants alike. Depending on the care taken by senior officers for newly arrived regiments and the season in which they arrived in the West Indies, casualty rates could be appalling. The superintendent of Jamaican hospitals in the 1780s determined that disease could kill as many as half of newly arrived soldiers within six months and could destroy entire regiments within three years.[24] It is estimated that over 50 per cent of the 88,000 troops sent

---

[21] J. Clark, *A Letter to the Right Honourable Charles Jenkinson, esq, Secretary At War; Animadverting on the Late Mutinies in the Highland Regiments. By the Translator of the Caledonian Bards* (Edinburgh, 1780), p. 25.

[22] Colonel Robert Skene to Sir James Grant, 6 November 1775, GD248/52/1, ff. 96–99, Seafield Papers, NRS. For the emphasis on coercion, see A. Mackillop, 'Continuity, coercion and myth: The recruitment of Highland regiments in the latter eighteenth century', *Scottish Tradition*, 26 (2001), pp. 43–4; S. Brumwell, *Redcoats: The British Soldier and War in the Americas, 1755–1763* (Cambridge: Cambridge University Press, 2001), pp. 273–4; R. A. A. McGeachy, *Argyll, 1730–1850* (Edinburgh: Birlinn, 2005), p. 230.

[23] A. Roberts, 'Faith restored: Highland Catholics and the King's Commission,' *Journal of the Society for Army Historical Research*, 85:2 (2007), pp. 146–61; McLean, *People of Glengarry*, pp. 128–50. For British efforts to exploit Catholic military resources, see S. K. Kehoe, *Empire and Emancipation: Scottish and Irish Catholics at the Atlantic Fringe, 1780–1850* (Toronto: University of Toronto Press, 2022), pp. 99–122.

[24] J. Hunter, *Observations on the Diseases of the Army in Jamaica; and on the Best Means of Preserving the Health of Europeans in that Climate* (London, 1788), pp. 45–54.

by Britain to the Caribbean died there between 1793 and 1801.[25] The newly raised regiments of the 1790s were largely saved the horrors of the West Indies (though parts of the Black Watch and the 79th Foot spent several years in Martinique, Barbados and St Lucia). However, newly raised regiments such as the 71st, 72nd, 73rd, 75th and 78th were sent to India, where mortality rates were around half of what they were in the West Indies, but were still more than four times the rates seen in Britain.[26]

These concerns drew a long shadow over recruitment. Men were unlikely to enlist in the army when their most likely destinations would be garrisons in the West Indies and India. This was especially true if the same benefits of enlistment could be met by service in forces raised only for service in Scotland or the wider British Isles and Ireland. By 1797 there were over thirty Fencible regiments raised for home serve, where pay and bounties were not dissimilar to those offered by the rest of the army. There was also the risk of men being forcibly drafted into other regiments. Numerous 'Highland' regiments such as the 97th Foot were recruited only to be disbanded and the men forcibly drafted into other regiments in violation of their terms of service. Promises that recruits would 'LIVE and DIE together' and would not 'be DRAUGHTED into different regiments' were not always honoured and memories of recruits being forcibly transferred to India at the end of the War for American Independence were not easily forgotten. It is little wonder that Highland enlistments for foreign service declined significantly during the French Revolutionary Wars.[27]

Analysis of recruiting patterns supports the contention that Highland military commitments to the Atlantic world were mixed and inconsistent across this period. Recruitment into the regular army during the Seven Years War and the War for American Independence was about as consistent in the Scottish Highlands as it was elsewhere in the British Isles. But owing to the far greater numbers of volunteer forces and militias in England, it is likely that Gaels were disproportionately represented in the regular army between the 1750s and the 1780s. During the Seven Years War, for example, Scots comprised almost a third of the British Army deployed in North America, despite making up less than one in five of the British and Irish populations.[28] But the proportion of Highlanders in the army declined from the high seen in the mid-eighteenth century. The state still placed great emphasis on Highland regiments and the

---

[25] M. Duffy, *Soldiers, Sugar, and Seapower: The British Expeditions to the West Indies and the War Against Revolutionary France* (Oxford: Oxford University Press, 1987), pp. 328–30.

[26] P. Burroughs, 'An unreformed army? 1815–1868', in D. G. Chandler and I. Beckett (eds), *The Oxford History of the British Army* (Oxford: Oxford University Press, 2003), p. 165.

[27] R. M. Sunter, 'The problems of recruitment for Scottish line regiments during the Napoleonic Wars', *Scottish Tradition*, 26 (2001), pp. 59, 62, 65–6; A. Mackenzie, 'The Highland regiments', *Transactions of the Gaelic Society of Inverness*, 10 (1881–3), p. 177.

[28] S. Conway, 'British mobilization in the War of American Independence', *Historical Research*, 72:177 (1999), pp. 65–6; Brumwell, *Redcoats*, p. 318.

number of new Highland regiments raised during the French Revolutionary Wars was entirely disproportionate to the regiments raised elsewhere in Britain in 1793 and 1794. In large measure, this resulted from Catholic relief legislation passed in the years after 1778 that allowed recruiters to target Catholics for enlistment for the first time in a century.[29] The problem was that the ability of Highland recruits to sustain such regiments was minimal. By 1809, such was the limited success of recruiting in northern Scotland that around half of the new regiments had lost their titles as 'Highland' regiments and had exchanged their kilts for the standard grey woollen trousers of the rest of the British Army in order to encourage English and Irish recruitment.

The early colonels of the Highland regiments were keen to present their regiments as entirely 'Highland' in geographic origin. Returns from the era of the Seven Years War seem to suggest that recruiting was confined to Gaelic-speaking communities – or, at least, that officers were keen to present their regiments as such. By the War for American Independence, however, the ability of such communities to sustain recruitment was in decline. Gaelic speakers remained an important minority within many regiments but the majority of recruits were being drawn from places as diverse as Lincoln, Newcastle, London, Dublin and Belfast. Only around half of the recruits enlisted into the 77th Foot in 1778 came from Highland counties while, by the French Revolutionary Wars, proprietary colonels such as Sir James Grant were happy to advertise their regiments as 'Highland' while deliberately recruiting almost exclusively in Lowland Scotland, England and Ireland. It is also estimated that as many as one-third of 'Highland' regiments consisted of Irish recruits.[30] Kevin Linch's careful assessment of recruiting patterns during the Napoleonic Wars reveals that while the War Office put a great deal of focus on Scotland, Scotland as a whole provided only around 13 per cent of recruits for the army – a significant percentage decline from the era of the Seven Years War. Highland counties were still profitable areas for army recruiters – lagging only behind industrialising cities such as Manchester in terms of recruiting parties versus returns – but it was becoming harder and harder to find Highland men willing to enlist.[31]

Yet, in spite of the difficulties of recruitment, Highland regiments continued to be a highly visible part of the British military establishment in the Atlantic world. Regiments such as the 42nd (Black Watch), the 71st (Glasgow Highland), 79th Foot (Cameron Highlanders), 91st Foot (Argyllshire Highlanders) and the

---

[29] M. L. Sanderson, '"Our Own Catholic Countrymen": Religion, Loyalism, and Subjecthood in Britain and its Empire, 1755–1829' (PhD thesis, Vanderbilt University, 2010), pp. 142–209.

[30] Dziennik, *The Fatal Land*, p. 100; Sunter, 'Recruiting problems', p. 62; T. Denman, 'Hibernia, Officina militum: Irish recruitment to the British regular army, 1660–1815', *Irish Sword*, 20 (1996), pp. 148–66.

[31] K. Linch, *Britain and Wellington's Army: Recruitment, Society, and Tradition, 1807–15* (Basingstoke: Palgrave MacMillan, 2011), pp. 60–1, 66.

92nd Foot (Gordon Highlanders) fought with distinction during the Peninsular War in Portugal and Spain from 1809 to 1814. Of the five regiments mentioned by the Duke of Wellington in his dispatches the day after the Battle of Waterloo, three were Highland regiments.[32] The presence and visibility of Highland regiments within the British Atlantic world remained high. The 71st Foot, for example, took a lead in both the capture of the Cape of Good Hope in 1795 and in the disastrous defeat at Buenos Aires in 1806 and 1807. Hoping to take advantage of the Royal Navy's unassailable command of the oceans, in 1805 the British government authorised an attack on Dutch and Spanish possessions in the Cape of Good Hope and the Río de la Plata. Cape Town was taken after hard fighting in which the 'Highland Brigade' of the 71st, 72nd (Seaforth) and 93rd (Sutherland) regiments were heavily engaged. The commander of the land forces, Major General David Baird, put great stock in the Highland regiments, having served with the 73rd (Macleod's) Foot in India in the 1780s and witnessed their performance in South Africa.[33] With Cape Town secured, Baird crossed the Atlantic to the Río de la Plata (in present-day Argentina) to take what was assumed to be an easy target and a good opportunity for City of London merchants to secure advantageous access to South American trade. It did not go as planned. The city was easily taken in June 1806 but, by early August, the British occupiers were themselves besieged as Spanish reinforcements under Santiago de Liniers arrived in numbers. Heavy street fighting took place over several days before the British surrendered on 14 August. The 71st Foot was taken prisoner and lost its regimental colours, which were dragged through the gutters by the triumphant inhabitants.[34]

A similar sacrifice of Highland soldiers occurred several thousand miles to the north-west in 1815 during another doomed British invasion of the Americas. The Battle of New Orleans was the last battle fought during the War of 1812. One of the regiments involved was the 93rd Foot. Joining General Sir Edward Pakenham's army of Peninsular veterans, the 93rd was at the forefront of the assault on New Orleans during an operation designed to secure access to the Mississippi River. The British army outnumbered the Americans dug in along the Rodriguez Canal near Chalmette Plantation but vastly underestimated their opponents. A dawn assault on 8 January 1815 – after peace had already been signed between the combatants – was a catastrophe. The advancing British

---

[32] The 42nd Foot, the 79th Foot, and the 92nd Foot. The other regiments mentioned were the 28th (North Gloucestershire) Foot and the Hanoverian Brigade.

[33] B. Hughes, *The British Invasion of the River Plate* (Barnsley: Pen & Sword, 2014), p. 22. See also J. Sinclair, *A Soldier of the Seventy-First: From De La Plata to Waterloo, 1806–1815*, ed. S. Reid (Barnsley: Pen & Sword, 2010).

[34] It seems as though approximately two hundred soldiers of the 71st either deserted or chose to accept an offer of land in Argentina provided they enlisted in Spanish service; see S. Schwamenfeld, 'The Foundation of British Strength: National Identity and the British Common Soldier' (PhD thesis, Florida State University, 2007), p. 179.

regiments were mown down in the early morning light. The 93rd was exposed to gruelling enfilade fire and took 60 per cent casualties without ever reaching the American lines.[35] According to one account, 'most of the men [were] crying from rage and vexation at seeing their comrades fall so fast, with no chance of a fight'.[36] Perhaps revealing the broad transatlantic significance of Highland soldiers, the kilt-clad 93rd Foot became a significant part of memorialising the American victory in painting, re-enactment and in film, despite the fact that they did not wear kilts during the campaign.[37] At both Buenos Aires and New Orleans – and on dozens of other battlefields in the Age of Revolutions – the British state's desire for Atlantic hegemony exposed young Highlanders to brutality and slaughter on a monumental scale.

Songs of war

The horrors of combat across the Atlantic world encouraged soldiers to reflect on their experiences in both prose and poetry. Gaels were not simply contributors to British military forces in the Atlantic world. They were also active participants in the cultural construction of the Atlantic world as an arena of violence. Just as in English-speaking Britain, the late eighteenth and early nineteenth centuries witnessed an increase in texts, memoirs and reflections by soldiers and poets that sought to make sense of the enhanced level of violence that marked the Age of Revolutions.[38] Gaels either serving in British regiments or closely connected with military service produced a significant corpus of songs that provide an intimate insight into attitudes to warfare in the Gàidhealtachd. Ruairidh Maciver has identified some 178 Gaelic songs written between 1756 and 1856 that explored military topics.[39] Unlike English-language memoirs, such as James Thompson's account of the Seven Years War, Donald McLeod's ghost-written narrative of the American Revolution or Joseph Sinclair's account of the Napoleonic Wars, these songs speak explicitly to communal attitudes and reveal the deep engagement of the Gàidhealtachd with imperial expansion in the Atlantic world.[40]

---

[35] For a recent survey, see D. R. Hickey, *Glorious Victory: Andrew Jackson and the Battle of New Orleans* (Baltimore: Johns Hopkins University Press, 2015), esp. p. 109.

[36] Quoted in B. R. Patterson, *The Generals: Andrew Jackson, Sir Edward Packenham, and the Road to the Battle of New Orleans* (New York: New York University Press, 2005), p. 245.

[37] J. F. Stoltz III, *A Bloodless Victory: The Battle of New Orleans in History and Memory* (Baltimore: Johns Hopkins University Press, 2017), pp. 83, 102.

[38] For analysis of these works, see M. Brown, A. M. Barry and J. Begiato (eds), *Martial Masculinities: Experiencing and Imagining the Military in the Long Nineteenth Century* (Manchester: Manchester University Press, 2019); N. Ramsey, *The Military Memoir and Romantic Literary Culture, 1780–1835* (Farnham: Ashgate, 2011).

[39] Maciver, 'The Gaelic poet and the British military experience'.

[40] E. J. Chapman and I. M. McCulloch (eds), *A Bard of Wolfe's Army: James Thompson, Gentleman Volunteer, 1733–1830* (Montreal: Robin Bass Studio, 2010); [William Thompson], *Memoirs of the*

The songs are far from uniform and borrowed heavily from both the panegyric tradition and Romantic-era literary styles. But it was their engagement with the Atlantic world that formed an important subset of themes that made them distinct from other Gaelic songs of this period. If emigration songs could and frequently did emphasise America's potential as a safe haven for Gaels where security could be found "S cha bhi mail ga chur suas / and the rents won't be raised', military songs displayed a far grimmer view of life across the ocean.[41] First, the songs celebrated violence consistent with the themes of an older Gaelic tradition. Many took the form of praise poems and described how the protagonist triumphed in gruesome and bloody battle. Coinneach MacCoinnich's [Kenneth Mackenzie's] praise poem for Colonel Duncan Macpherson, who commanded a Highland regiment during the War for American Independence, reported that 'Fuil ga dòrta se chleachd è / He was accustomed to spilling blood'.[42] Entire regiments also became the subject of praise poetry, with songs by Seumas MacLathagain [James MacLagan] and Iain MacGriogair [John Mcgregor] utilising regiments such as the Black Watch and Fraser's Highlanders in place of traditional clan chiefs as the subject of praise.[43] Within the songs there was an acceptance of violence as integral to the participation of Gaels in British imperial expansion.

Second, one of the more striking aspects of these songs was the vehement derision and hatred directed at a range of enemies throughout the Atlantic world. Some of these denunciations meshed easily with the panegyric tradition and carried little in the way of political connotations. Maighread Chamshron's [Margaret Cameron's] praise poem for the sons of John Campbell of Achalader raised no political objection to the American revolutionaries whom they were sent to fight but only hoped that the brothers would 'Thoirt teine air 'ur naimhdibh ... Mar sin agus buaidh làrach / Wreck fire on your enemy ... and gain victory as a result'.[44] Other songs, however, were much more direct and politicised. A song attributed to Iain mac Mhurchaidh [John McRae], a North Carolina settler who fought against the revolutionaries, chided opponents of the British Empire and warned them that 'Chan fhaighear lagh no reusan, Do Reubalaich ann / No law or reason will be available, To any rebels'. McRae's song is also interesting as it appears to have been composed while he was a prisoner and is full of longing for Scotland, the hardship of life in America and the conditions to which he was subjected. As McRae told it:

Life and Gallant Exploits of the Old Highlander Sergeant Donald MacLeod (London, 1791); Sinclair, *Soldier of the Seventy-First*.

[41] 'Oran air fonn ... le fear a bha dol a dh' America', in D. MacCallum, *Co-chruinneacha Dhàn, Òrain* (Inbhirnis, 1821), p. 120.

[42] 'Oran do Choirneal Donnacha' Mac Phearson', in Coinneach MacCoinnich, *Orain Ghaidhealach, agus Bearla air an Eadar-Theangacha* (Duneadainn, 1792), p. 40.

[43] 'Oran do'n Chath-Bhuithinn Rioghail Ghai'leach', in ibid. pp. 10–18; Iain MacGhrigair, *Orain Ghaelach* (Edin-bruaich, 1801), pp. 35–41.

[44] Maciver, 'The Gaelic poet and the British military experience', p. 241.

Tha mi sgìth dhen fhògairt seo,	I am tired of this exile,
Tha mi sgìth dhen t-srì,	I am tired of this fight,
Seo an tìom dhòrainneach,	This is a trying time,
Tha mi sgìth dhen fhògairt seo.⁴⁵	I am tired of this exile.

Another song by an Argyll schoolmaster, Donnchadh Ceanaideach [Duncan Kennedy], similarly castigated the American rebels and their French allies for their follies and lamented that Gaels had been sent to America to suppress 'Chan ìocadh na h-ìochdrain ud cìsean no càin / Those ignoble folk who would not render their taxes or tribute'. Kennedy's song is particularly revealing since he described in detail how the war in America had affected the Highlands, writing that not only had men been taken away but that 'Chaidh ceairdean is malairt, is ceannachd gun fheum / Trade-skills, commerce and sales have become useless'.⁴⁶ Kennedy's song suggests that Gaels were aware of the symbiotic nature of the Highlands relationship with North America and the way in which warfare affected both.

A song by Ailein Dùghallach [Allan MacDougall] – who is otherwise famous for his bitter denunciations of social change – spoke equally to the cost borne by Gaelic communities as they served the state; something that MacDougall interpreted as akin to a tax. In his lament for John Cameron of Fassifern, killed at Quatres Bras in 1815, MacDougall explains that:

'S iomadh laoch bu mhor pris,	Many a valuable hero,
A thuit leis an stri 's an Fhraing,	Fell in the fight in France,
Phaigh Cloinn Camshroin a chìs,	Clan Cameron paid the price,
'S cha d' thig iad air tir gun chall;	And they will not come ashore without loss;
'S ged a thàinig an t-shith,	And although peace has come,
'S daor a h-èiric 's an diol a bh'ann.⁴⁷	Expensive is the retribution that followed.

This equating of troops with a tax perfectly captures what Andrew Mackillop has described as an exchange of human capital for political and economic capital as Highland elites exchanged what they lacked – capital and status – for what they believed they could pay: labour.⁴⁸

---

⁴⁵ M. MacDonell, *The Emigrant Experience: Songs of Highland Emigrants in North America* (Toronto: University of Toronto Press, 1982), pp. 28–9; M. Newton, *We're Indians Sure Enough: The Legacy of the Scottish Highlanders in the United States* (Auburn, NH: Saorsa, 2001), pp. 142–3.
⁴⁶ Ibid. pp. 150–1, 154.
⁴⁷ 'Cumha do Choirneal Iain Camshron', in Ailein Dùghallach, *Orain, Marbhrannan agus Duanagan, Ghaidhelach* (Inbheirnis, 1829), p. 185.
⁴⁸ A. Mackillop, 'Subsidy state or drawback province? Eighteenth-century Scotland and the British fiscal–military complex', in A. Graham and P. Walsh (eds), *The British Fiscal–Military States, 1660–c.1783* (Abingdon: Routledge, 2016), pp. 179–200.

Third, the cost of Gaelic contributions allowed the writers of Gaelic song to debate the merits of North America and its potential for Highland emigrants. In many of these military songs, North America was not a land of opportunity but a place of suffering where blood and treasure were spilt and where the merits of Gaelic sacrifices were debated. In a letter written from Long Island in 1778, James MacLagan questioned whether the government in London had sold their souls to the devil over the handling of the War for Independence before suggesting that 'Ata a' chre anois breoite, lobhta, is dual d'eagal agus do bhas leantuin. B'e so diol gach tir thruailte o thosach / The soil is now sick, rotten; disease and death are sure to follow. This was ever the requital of every polluted land.'[49] This stood in contrast to MacLagan's earlier exhortations in the 1750s in which he suggested that America could be a bucolic or idyllic rest for Highland warriors.[50] And it seems as if MacLagan's frustration with war and the causes which had brought Highland men to America were not unique. Upon the arrival of over two hundred Highlanders from the 71st Foot who arrived as prisoners of war in Williamsburg in June 1776, Edmund Randolph reported to Thomas Jefferson that 'among them, we are told, are many valuable Artificers. Measures are in Agitation to reconcile them to prosecute their different Occupations in this Country. Some of them are violent vs. America, others tolerably moderate, and many from contending Passions curse the Parliament and Congress in the same Breath.'[51] Even allowing for the utility of portraying British soldiers as resentful of their government, it is evidence that there may have been some ambiguity among enlisted Gaels regarding the war.

Similar reservations about sending young men to fight across the Atlantic Ocean are captured in one of the earlier extant emigration songs, which takes as its subject men of Clan Fraser who joined the 78th Foot in 1757. The unknown poet begins with a lament for Colonel Simon Fraser's departure in a way consistent with praise poetry of old. In the second stanza, however, it takes aim at how Gaels have been drawn to war across the ocean:

'S bochd an naidheachd 's gur truagh	Terrible the news
Na fir-thaighe b' fhearr snuadh	As the finest men of our country
'S iad gun aighear, gun uaill, gun sùgradh	Are cheerless and humiliated
Toirbheir thugad an clan	Surrendering their children to you
...	...

---

[49] James MacLagan to Hugh MacDiarmid, 20 September 1778, GD/We/5, f. 12, Wedderburn Papers, Dundee City Archives [hereafter DCA].

[50] 'Oran a rinneadh d'an chath-bhuidhinn Rioghai' Ghaoidheallach', in J. Gillies, *Sean Dain agus Orain Ghaidhealach* (Peairt, 1786), p. 116.

[51] Randolph to Jefferson, 23 June 1776, in *The Papers of Thomas Jefferson*, Vol. 1, *1760–1776*, ed. Julian P. Boyd (Princeton: Princeton University Press, 1950), pp. 407–8.

'S ann an Griannaig 's an àm
Thionail gaisgich nam beann
Chum an iomain thar sàil fo d' chùram.⁵²

First to Greenock
Do the warriors of the mountains gather
So they may be driven overseas under your care.

Such frustration needs to be read as consistent with earlier resistance on the part of Gaels to soldiering in North America and suggests that while individuals may have seen merits in military service, poets often interpreted the communal effects – either in young men or taxation – as ruinous to the Gàidhealtachd.

An interesting insight into this frustration can be found in a song written by Major Dugald MacNicol on St Lucia in 1816. MacNicol was an officer of the Royal Scots and his songs comprise of the only extant songs known to have been written in the West Indies.⁵³ Heavily laced with lament for his homeland, MacNicol equated the Gael to "'S a' ghaoth gan sgaoileadh air crìonadh / Withered leaves driven by the wind' and decried the state of Scotland and the heavy taxes levied upon 'saothair na Tuath / the farmer's labours' during the Napoleonic Wars.⁵⁴ While not specifically focused on soldiers, MacNicol's status as an officer and his station in the West Indies was a clear indication of the heavy weight that war was enforcing on the Gaelic community and the unhinging of that community from its socioeconomic moorings.

And finally, some of the military songs connected with the Atlantic world contain an important undercurrent of intense regret at having served. One Glenmorison song of the Napoleonic era stated that: 'Gur a mise tha fo mhulad, Giùlan cular Righ Deòrsa / I am unhappy, Carrying the colours of King George'.⁵⁵ Many songs were cognisant of the hardship that military service brought to both individuals and their communities. Probably the most remarkable song of this nature was written by Alasdair mac Iain Bhàin [Alexander Grant] of his service during the Napoleonic Wars. Entitled Òran an t-Saighdear, the song spoke about his enlisting while 'iomrall sa cheò / lost in a mist' and coming to regret the decision. In his song, Grant lamented the promises he had believed from the recruiters:

---

⁵² Newton, We're Indians Sure Enough, p. 85.
⁵³ S. Kidd, 'Gaelic books as cultural icons: The maintenance of cultural links between the Highlands and the West Indies,' in C. Sassi and T. van Heijnsbergen (eds), Within and Without Empire: Scotland Across the (Post)colonial Borderline (Newcastle: Cambridge Scholars, 2013), p. 48.
⁵⁴ G. Henderson, 'Làmh-sgrìobhainnean Mhic-Neacail', Transactions of the Gaelic Society of Inverness, 27 (1908–11), p. 369.
⁵⁵ 'An Gille Donn', in D. Macpherson, An Duanaire (Dun-Eidin, 1868), pp. 68–70. This song was later republished in An t-Òranaiche (1879) but with many of the complaints and horrors of military service softened or edited; see Maciver, 'The Gaelic poet and the British military experience', p. 149.

Fhuair mi gealltanas mòr	I received a great promise
Le boinn agus còir	With coins and the right
Air nighean Rìgh Deòrsa	Of the daughter of King George
Mar chèile;	As a wife;
Nan creidinn an glòir	If I were to believe their speech
Cha b' eagal ri m' bheò	I wouldn't worry all my life
Dhomh an airgead no 'n òr	About silver or gold
No 'n èideadh.[56]	Or clothing.

But it went much further. The horrors of military service, the lack of security, the absence of good comradeship and even his dislike of bagpipes were all factors that Grant explored in ways that challenge the stereotype of loyal and willing service. He warned young men that 'Ma is math leat bhith buan, Gun èist thu / If you want to live, Make sure you listen'. Somewhat unusually, Grant extended his comments beyond his own suffering to describe the suffering he had inflicted upon others while wearing a British uniform. He noted that:

Cha robh seud san robh luach	There was no precious stone of any value
Eadar luingeas is shluagh	Whether of fleet or people
Nach do ghlac sinn an cluain	Which we didn't take
A chèile;	By ambush;
Loisg sinn aitreabh na ghual	We burnt his palace to cinders
Chuir sinn gaiseadh na sguaib	We blighted his crops
Thug sinn creach às le ruaig	We plundered him
Beum-sgèithe.	With a challenging attack.

Regret at what these young men had left behind was also a theme of many songs. The suffering of wives and children, similar to that which increasingly appeared in English songs of this era, was a popular refrain, driven in large measure by the broader rise in sentiment and the sentimentalisation of the victims of war.[57] A popular Napoleonic-era marching song lamented:

'S iomadh màthair tha gun mhac	Many a mother is without son,
Is piuthar tha gun bhràthair,	Many a sister without brother,

---

[56] 'Òran an t-Saighdear', in Macpherson, *An Duanaire*, pp. 63–7. My sincere thanks go to Domhnall Uilleam Stiùbhart for supplying me with this source.

[57] C. Kennedy, *Narratives of the Revolutionary and Napoleonic Wars: Military and Civilian Experience in Britain and Ireland* (Basingstoke: Palgrave MacMillan, 2013), pp. 33–68; J. Rendall, 'Women writing war and empire: Gender, poetry, and politics in Britain during the Napoleonic Wars', in K. Hagemann, G. Mettele and J. Rendall (eds), *Gender, War, and Politics: Transatlantic Perspectives, 1775–1830* (Basingstoke: Palgrave MacMillan, 2010), pp. 265–83.

| Is nighneag òg a tha gun leannan, | Many a young girl without lover, |
| O'n sheòl sinn thar sàile. | Since we sailed over the sea.[58] |

Such sentiments were echoed in numerous songs across the era. A waulking song dating to around 1799 takes as its theme a letter sent by a Gaelic soldier to his lover in which he details the suffering that will be experienced by many women when they learn of who had died in battle.[59] Another song by a Mull poet of the same year described the bodies of the dead and the many mothers, sisters and sweethearts who would mourn them.[60] Even songs ostensibly praising the activities of military Gaels could not escape the realities of soldiering, as evidenced in the following song by Kenneth Mackenzie:

Slionnar bean a bha fo' bhròn,	Plenty are the wives who are sad,
Air a lèon airson macain,	Who are wounded for a son,
Cianail muladach gu leoir,	Misery and sorrow enough,
Agus sròin do 'n Tomhac orr.'	And noses of Tobacco on them.[61]

Songs by women about military service were particularly focused on the negative effects of war. Mairearad Ghriogarach [Margaret MacGregor], whose work from the 1780s and 1790s appeared in an 1831 collection, wrote several military-related poems to members of her household and the Perthshire gentry. In them, she regrets the losses in battle and the suffering caused by war. And indeed, in an atypical and unique commentary on war in the Gaelic language, she attacks war in general terms:

Cha nann gu fabhar a dhuine	It is not for the good of man
Chaidh na blàrabh a chumail,	That wars are waged,
Ach bhi gu namhadach fuileach	But to be hostile and bloody
Chum sgu n cailta na h urrad.[62]	So that many would be lost.

It would be quite wrong to assert that most military songs shared MacGregor's general sentiments on war. It is, nevertheless, essential to consider these songs as an important representation of Gaelic views on military service and its cost to

---

[58] 'Tha sinn a' falbh 's gum bi sinn a' falbh', available at <www.smo.uhi.ac.uk/gaidhlig/alltandubh/orain/Tha_Sinn_Falbh.html> (last accessed 14 December 2020).

[59] Ò'Horò 'Ille Dhuinn', in J. L. Campbell and F. Collinson, *Hebridean Folksongs: Waulking Songs from Vatersay, Barra, Eriskay, South Uist and Benbecula*, Vol. 3 (Oxford: Clarendon Press, 1969), p. 172.

[60] 'Mo Mhallachd aig Gillean', available at <http://tobarandualchais.co.uk/en/fullrecord/44> (last accessed 10 December 2020).

[61] 'Oran don Fhreiceadan Dubh', in MacCoinnich, *Orain Ghaidhealach*, p. 36. See also a similar sentiment in 'An Gille Donn', in Macpherson, *An Duanaire*, pp. 68–70.

[62] Maciver, 'The Gaelic poet and the British military experience', p. 251.

the Highlands and Islands. Generally neglected among studies of Gaelic verse, these songs offer a very different perspective on the connections between the Gàidhealtachd and the British Empire. Compared at least to historic emigration literature, these songs offered a much more negative or at least ambivalent view of the advantages of emigration and service.[63]

Military service and the wider Gaelic community

There is no doubt that military service in the Atlantic world was violent and immensely destructive. But it would be wrong to see it as wholly detrimental. Warfare can be generative in terms of societal norms, technologies, political identifications and attitudes. And this was no different with Gaelic poetry. To fully appreciate the complexity of Gaelic views of warfare in the British Atlantic world not only requires us to recognise the violence and suffering of military service but also the way in which such suffering was mobilised to Gaelic ends. It also requires us to recognise the depth, sophistication and variances within the corpus of military songs and even among songs by the same poet. Many of the songs previously cited were not uniformly negative about military service and contained elements of praise as well as of sorrow for the activities of the Highland regiments. The reasons for this sophistication were the varied needs of the audience, who were both trying to celebrate Gaelic successes as well as attempting to understand the sacrifices that such successes required.

One of the first problems the songs were forced to confront was the very fact of Gaelic military service for the Hanoverian state, given the historical adherence of many clans to Jacobitism. Explanations for this tended to focus on service to a king as being consistent with the Gaelic tradition, particularly in the face of anti-monarchical revolutionary enemies. But efforts were also made to explain the reciprocal relationship between service and reward, with Gaels being duly recognised and rewarded for their loyalty by George III.[64] The idea that donning a British uniform potentially betrayed Gaelic tradition may not have been as prominent as we might expect, given just how many of the officers came from reliable Whig families, but it did cause some writers to attempt to justify why young men should serve the British state.[65] This probably explains efforts to define imperial wars in America as an opportunity for Gaels. Kenneth Mackenzie, who had served in the Royal Navy, spoke of the flowering of new branches, making use of the widely popular allusion to trees in Gaelic song

---

[63] See, for example, [Scotus Americanus], *Informations Concerning the Province of North Carolina Addressed to Emigrants from the Highlands and Western Isles of Scotland, Written by an Impartial Hand* (Glasgow, 1773).

[64] A. Macleod (ed.), *Orain Dhonnchaidh Bhàin* (Edinburgh: Scottish Gaelic Texts Society, 1978), p. 23.

[65] List of Officers, [1757], LO6324, Loudoun Papers, HL.

to suggest a new beginning. He went on to argue that 'O 'n stoc a tha uasal lan buaghana gràidh ... An onair sa'n èididh, cha treig iad gu bràth / A new stock is coming with the virtues of love ... Their honour and clothing will not betray them'. Here Mackenzie was attempting to show that the uniforms of the British Army would not betray their wearers and that a new age for Gaels was coming.[66]

There was equally an effort to suggest that military service somehow elevated Gaelic and gave it broad recognition in Britain and the wider world. The Gaelic language was often portrayed as a weapon or as a piece of military equipment.[67] Prima facie, there should have been little reason for Gaelic to be enhanced by military service. Gaelic was not the language of command and a number of commentators made the point that the mutinies in the Highland regiments were a direct result of officers who could not speak the language. According to one officer, even those who were willing to learn it were discouraged from doing so by senior officers in order to enforce the primacy of English within the regiments.[68] At the same time, the ability to speak Gaelic was deemed important if not essential to officers serving in Highland regiments. It was particularly crucial for both surgeons and chaplains, who were so intimately acquainted with the men who made up the rank and file. The prominent lawyer and Comptroller of Taxes in Scotland, Henry Mackenzie, informed Lady Grant of Grant (his sister-in-law) that there were vacancies for surgeons in the Black Watch and the Gordon Highlanders but that they had to be able to speak Gaelic in order to fulfil the role.[69] As a result, writers were able to imagine that Gaelic was being heard across the battlefields of the Atlantic world.

It is equally critical not to neglect the role of military officers in the study, recording, publication, and safeguarding of Gaelic and Gaelic texts in this period. The late eighteenth century saw a flourishing of Gaelic secular texts and the publication of numerous collections of songs. Service in the army was not usually conducive to the processes of publication, and deployment overseas often removed scholars of Gaelic from their materials. Donald McNicol, an important collector and transcriber, explained that James MacLagan's deployment to North America during the War for American Independence was the greatest impediment to getting a scheme going to publish a Gaelic dictionary.[70]

---

[66] 'Oran do na Chath-Bhuithinn cheudna', in MacCoinnich, *Orain Ghaidhealach*, p. 17. My sincere thanks go to Donald Meek for his suggestion of this interpretation.

[67] 'Oran do'n Chath-Bhuithinn Rioghail Ghaileach', in MacCoinnich, *Orain Ghaidhealach*, pp. 11, 14; Maciver, 'The Gaelic poet and the British military experience', p. 225.

[68] J. Clark, *A Letter to the Right Honourable Charles Jenkinson, esq, Secretary At War*, pp. 10, 18; S. Graham, *Memoirs of General Graham with Notices of the Campaigns in Which He was Engaged from 1779–1801*, ed. J. Graham (Edinburgh, 1862), pp. 10–11.

[69] Henry Mackenzie to Jean Grant, 1 October 1803, GD248/65/2, f. 51, Seafield Papers, NRS.

[70] McNicol to MacLagan, 3 March 1779, GD/We/5/13, Wedderburn Papers, DCA. For the formulation of the Gaelic dictionary, see Kidd, 'Gaelic books as cultural icons', pp. 46–60.

At the same time, the networks forged by Gaelic-speaking military officers were crucial to the collection of materials and their publication. MacLagan, the long-time chaplain of the 42nd Foot, stood at the centre of a network of collectors who secured an invaluable collection of materials from across the Gàidhealtachd. Mobilising his church and military contacts, MacLagan was able to accrue an extensive collection of some 250 manuscripts and was actively involved in the publication of important texts such as the 1786 Gillies Collection.[71] But he was not alone in mobilising military networks in the furtherance of Gaelic texts. Some forty-six serving military officers were among the subscribers to Kenneth Mackenzie's 1792 collection and military networks were probably vital to his publication project.[72] Another important figure was Major John Small who, in his role as a member of Sir Henry Clinton's staff during the War for American Independence, was a crucial conduit between the army's high command and the activities of collectors. It was Small who advocated for MacLagan to be returned to Britain so as to help with the publication of a Gaelic dictionary.[73]

The array of army officers and officials involved in the promotion of Gaelic probably extended beyond the networks of MacNicol, MacLagan and Mackenzie. Fragmentary evidence suggests that many members of the military took an interest in Gaelic song and culture. The substitute chaplain in the Duke of Gordon's Fencible corps, for example, argued to the Duke that providing him with a permanent chaplaincy in the regiment would enable him to continue his research into Gaelic antiquities, suggesting that the study of Gaelic was something that was important enough to be leveraged in seeking a post in the army.[74] Army officers were also helpful bridgeheads in efforts to establish arenas for the use of Gaelic in the Americas. General Hugh Carmichael, for example, was petitioned during the late Napoleonic Wars to assist in the development of a Gaelic chapel in the Leeward Islands and responded that it would

---

[71] D. S. Thomson, 'McLagan, James (1728–1805)', *Oxford Dictionary of National Biography*, Oxford University Press, <https://doi.org/10.1093/ref:odnb/54067> (last accessed 20 December 2020). For these networks, see C. Savonius-Wroth, 'Bardic ministers: Scotland's Gaelic-speaking clergy in the Ossian controversy', *Eighteenth-Century Studies*, 52:2 (2019), pp. 225–43; V. Henshaw, 'James Macpherson and his contemporaries: The methods and networks of collectors of Gaelic poetry in late eighteenth-century Scotland', *Journal of Eighteenth-Century Studies*, 39:2 (2016), pp. 197–209.

[72] J. Mackenzie, *Sàr-Obair nam Bard Gaelach, or the Beauties of Gaelic Poetry and Lives of the Highland Bards* (Glasgow, 1841), pp. 270–1; MacCoinnich, *Orain Ghaidhealach*, pp. 242–73. Matilda Greig notes that in the English-speaking world, soldiers were critical to the creation of an influential and commercially successful genre of war memoirs and were deeply knowledgeable and keen for recognition within a literary world; see M. Greig, 'Accidental authors?: Soldiers' tales of the Peninsular War and the secrets of the publishing process', *History Workshop Journal*, 86:1 (2018), pp. 224–44.

[73] McNicol to MacLagan, 3 March 1779, GD/We/5/13, Wedderburn Papers, DCA.

[74] John Buchanan to Duke of Gordon, 28 November 1796, GD44/47/15/2, f. 38, Gordon Castle Muniments, NRS.

'afford me a very great satisfaction in any way in my power to promote that most important object in which I am happy to see your exertions have been so successful'.[75] More work is certainly needed on the role of military networks in the study and promotion of Gaelic in the eighteenth and nineteenth centuries but it seems clear that military figures were not incidental to the promotion of Gaelic in this period.

The military connections between the Scottish Highlands and the Atlantic world were complex and multi-dimensional. While North America may have been seen through the lens of emigration as a land of unlimited potential, in the context of the military a more ambiguous picture emerges. While efforts were certainly made to encourage recruits through appeals to land grants in America, British regiments struggled to recruit men throughout this period. The active resistance of soldiers to deployment overseas cautions against any simple explanation of military service as a form of emigration.

The complexity of views of the Atlantic world within the Gàidhealtachd are made clear in the large number of military songs that offer an unparalleled insight into the attitudes of soldiers. These songs recognised that violence was an elemental part of the relationship between the Highlands and the Americas and used the celebration of martial triumphs to emphasise the role of violence in the contemporary imperial world. In expressing doubt and regret over the choice to serve or by denouncing the horrors that combat required against the peoples living in North America, Gaelic poets countered the more positive representations of America seen elsewhere in Gaelic song. What is particularly revealing is the range of motifs, emotions and attitudes displayed within a hugely varied corpus of songs. Few of these songs were wholly supportive of military service but nor were they wholly negative. Gaelic poets of the Age of Revolutions often captured the ambiguities of the British imperial world better than we have been able to do. The military was not the only means of Gaelic engagement with the Atlantic world. Indeed, to an extent, our focus on the military reifies a traditional narrative of Highland martial prowess and ignores the productive – rather than destructive – role of Gaels in the Americas as explorers, traders, officials, educators and settlers. But the military was an important zone of contact which produced a distinctive and illuminating set of perspectives on the British Atlantic world.

It is appropriate then that military contacts with the British Atlantic world should have produced two seemingly contradictory responses in the Gàidhealtachd. The first was the acknowledgement that Gaelic involvement in imperial activities was based on the application of violence. The suffering of Indigenous peoples in North America was rarely considered; it was the

---

[75] Carmichael to Unknown, 28 August 1810, Hugh Carmichael Letterbook, National Army Museum.

hardships and losses to the Gaelic community that were centred in this regard. But the second response was an effort to mobilise military service as a means of protecting and enhancing the station of Gaels within an imperial world. Ironically, the violence of the Atlantic world was generative as well as destructive in the sense that it created space for the celebration of the Gael and of Gaelic even as the forces of Anglo-British colonialism were also taking their toll on the region.[76] Views of America could not be uniformly positive – they could not be simple or one-sided – because they had to account for the contradictory effects of Gaelic participation in the wars fought across the Atlantic Ocean in this period. Ultimately, the joy of the 'dance called America' was simply one iteration of the Gàidhealtachd's complex interactions with the Atlantic world.

---

[76] For Gaelic and colonialism, see I. Mackinnon, 'Colonialism and the Highland Clearances', *Northern Scotland*, 8:1 (2017), pp. 22–48; S. Stroh, *Uneasy Subjects: Postcolonialism and Scottish Gaelic Poetry* (Amsterdam: Rodopi, 2011).

Part Three

Networks of Empowerment and Oppression

SIX

Christian Robertson (1780–1842) and a Highland Network in the Caribbean: A Study of Complicity

David Alston

This is an account of a Highland family in the Caribbean, Liverpool and Scotland, explored through a focus on Christy (Christian) Robertson, whose life, although she never travelled beyond the shores of Britain and Ireland, was shaped by involvements in the West Indies. These involvements were a source of material wealth – and from relatively modest beginnings she came to move in elite circles in Liverpool, Edinburgh and elsewhere – but also of personal loss. Two brothers and two of the five children of her first marriage died in, or returning from, the Caribbean; and two other brothers and two other sons spent many years there. In these human terms she was as much an investor in the Caribbean as any man of money.

Christy was married twice and her second husband, Thomas Stewart Traill, wrote a 'Memoir of Mrs Traill' immediately after her death in 1842, a private record of her life composed for himself and for her family. Traill, who was a friend before he was her husband, also preserved much of Christy's correspondence, including letters from her brothers and sons in Guyana. These sources make it possible to understand Christy's life in unusual detail.[1] This might be described as an example of what Emma Rothschild in *The Inner Life of Empires* has called 'a micro-history of the uneminent'.[2] But Rothschild's study is of more prominent individuals active across the British Empire – the four sisters and seven brothers of the Johnstone family of Westerhall. Christy was truly a minor player on the stage of Britain's empire; a woman whose life illuminates both the long reach of the Highlands into networks of commerce and influence within and beyond Scotland – and the continuing importance of a Highland identity and connections within these networks.

---

[1] National Library of Scotland [hereafter NLS] Traill Papers, MS 19391 'Memoir of Mrs Traill' and correspondence in MSS 19329–19334. Orkney Archives hold a typescript copy of the 'Memoir' presented by descendants of Mrs Traill. Page numbers refer to Traill's numbering in the MS.

[2] E. Rothschild, *The Inner Life of Empires* (Princeton and Oxford: Princeton University Press, 2011), p. 277.

Kiltearn and *Kiltearn*

Christy Robertson, the sixth of ten children of Anne Forbes (1753-1826) and the Reverend Harry Robertson (1748-1815), was born and brought up at the manse of Kiltearn, on the north shore of the Cromarty Firth in the Highlands of Scotland. Her mother, who came from Golspie in Sutherland, was a daughter of William Forbes, gardener to the Earl of Sutherland at Dunrobin Castle and later the tenant of a farm on the estate. She married Christy's father, Harry Robertson, when he was the minister of Clyne, the neighbouring parish in Sutherland, and in 1776 the couple moved to his native Kiltearn, where he served for almost forty years as a diligent and well-regarded pastor.

Christy was brought up in an emotionally and intellectually nurturing family. Her parents employed a governess and Alexander McGregor, the rector of Inverness Academy and a man of 'taste, learning and integrity', spent all his holidays with them until his sudden death in 1805. There were numerous other guests at the manse and they socialised with the families of Sir Hector Munro of Novar and other local landowners.[3] It was also a physically attractive environment and almost a century later a prominent local clergyman recalled the family and their home:

> I always heard my mother say that Dr. Robertson was an uncommonly handsome man and Mrs. Robertson particularly good-looking, and both had a fine taste. The manse was close to the Cromarty Firth, the soil was beautifully laid out with shrubs and splendid flowers, and the garden stocked with apple and pear trees.[4]

The Robertsons were broad-minded in matters of religion. There is a striking example in one of Mrs Robertson's letters to Christy, written in November 1800 from Aberdeen, where Harry had gone to receive a Doctorate in Divinity from his old college. She remarked that, on their first Sunday in Aberdeen, while 'your Father and the boys went to our own church' – that is, the Church of Scotland – Annie (Christy's older sister) went 'with the Miss Boyles to the English [i.e. Episcopalian] Chapel [and] in the evening to the Roman Catholic and Methodist Chapel which shows she wants to see everything she can'. And the following day, when they dined with a Professor Stewart, Mrs Robertson and Annie 'slipt away' to the theatre to see Sheridan's latest play *Pizarro*.[5] This is markedly different to the strictness of much Scottish Presbyterianism and a similar openness to new experiences would characterise Christy's later life.

[3] 'Memoir', pp. 1-5.
[4] Rev. Dr Aird to Raymond Tinné Berthon, 3 January 1894, in George Sherwood, *The Pedigree Register* (London: George Sherwood, 1910-13), pp. ii, 81-2.
[5] Mrs Anne Robertson, from Aberdeen, to her daughter Christian (Mrs Watson), Crantit, Orkney, 7 November 1800, MS 19331, f. 59, Traill Papers, NLS.

Yet there was a disturbing side to Christy's family in their involvement with the slave trade and the enslaved-worked plantations of the Caribbean. Mrs Robertson's brothers George Forbes (1740–86) and William Forbes (d. 1789) had been among the first purchasers of land in Tobago after it was ceded to Britain by France in 1763, at the end of the Seven Years War.[6] George died there in 1786; William became Attorney General of Barbados, where he died in 1789; and two other brothers, Duncan (1746–92) and James, also died in Barbados.[7]

On her father's side, Harry Robertson's cousin Gilbert Robertson (1759–1836) worked in Trinidad before moving to Philadelphia, where he served as British consul from 1817 until his death.[8] Harry's two brothers, John and George, also pursued opportunities in the Caribbean. John Robertson (1751–98) was a lawyer who died in Tobago, while George Robertson (1756–99), the most successful of these relations, had gone to Grenada and by the late 1780s was one of the merchants taking advantage of the town of St George's recently acquired status as a free port to extend trade into the Spanish colonies of Caracas and New Grenada.[9]

George Robertson's business partnerships would have a significant impact on the lives of his niece Christy, and her brothers and sisters. To assist him in Grenada, he had engaged a young clerk, Charles Stewart Parker (1771–1828), the American-born son of James Parker, a British loyalist who had lost his property in Virginia and returned to Scotland. Charles became Robertson's partner in 1789, bringing to the business both his own skills – he had learned Spanish – and additional capital. In 1790 they joined with Samuel Sandbach (1769–1851) from Cheshire and James McInroy (1759–1825) from Highland Perthshire, in what was to be a successful venture into plantation ownership and trade in the Dutch colony of Demerara (Guyana).[10] Two subsequent marriages converted this business partnership into an extended kinship network, which continued long after George Robertson's death in Demerara in 1799. First, in 1797, Charles Parker married Christy's cousin Margaret Rainy (1774–1844), the daughter of Ann Robertson and the Reverend George Rainy of Creich;

---

[6] J. Fowler, *A Summary Account of the Present Flourishing State of the Respectable Colony of Tobago, in the British West Indies* (London, 1774).

[7] *Pedigree Register*, p. 185; 'Memoir', p. 9; MS 19399, f. 18, Traill Papers, NLS.

[8] E. R. Purple, *Contributions to the History of Ancient Families of New Amsterdam and New York* (New York, 1881).

[9] E. H. Gould and P. S. Onuf (eds), *Empire and Nation: The American Revolution in the Atlantic World* (Baltimore: Johns Hopkins University Press, 2015).

[10] The principal sources for the partnerships which became Sandbach Parker & Co. are the Parker Papers, PAR 920, Liverpool Central Library Archives [hereafter LCLA]; and business papers of Sandbach Tinné & Co., D/SAN, Liverpool Maritime Museum. I am grateful to Alison Clark for sharing her current doctoral research on the partnerships and to Malik al Nasir for discussions on his research.

and then, in 1802, Christy's sister Betsy (Elizabeth) Robertson (1782–1859) married Samuel Sandbach.

The Parkers established themselves at Blochairn, near Glasgow, and later in the coastal village of Fairlie, in Ayrshire; while the Sandbachs lived at Aigburth, in Liverpool, and later owned property at Hafodunos, in Denbighshire. These networks provided opportunities for Christy's brothers and then for her sons and made possible the creation of a second *Kiltearn*, a cotton plantation on the Corentyne Coast of Berbice (Guyana), owned by Christy's brother Gilbert Robertson and their cousin Gilbert Rainy. Berbice was one of the unhealthiest places in the Caribbean and, for enslaved Africans, one of the most brutal, where survival was itself an achievement.[11] Yet, in February 1806, there was a palpable sense of family pride when news reached the Kiltearn manse that a cargo of *Kiltearn* cotton had arrived in the Clyde.[12] It had been shipped by Sandbach & McBean, the Demerara-based branch of the Parker/Sandbach business network – William McBean (1776–1822) was from Tomatin in Inverness-shire – on their new, fast-sailing, copper-bottomed vessel, appropriately named *The Highlander*.[13]

Was Christy's family unusual among those of 'the middling sorts' in the Highlands in having these connections to the Caribbean? One perspective on this is to consider the families of other Church of Scotland ministers in the area. Kiltearn was one of eight parishes which formed the Presbytery of Dingwall and when Harry Robertson was appointed to Kiltearn in 1776, another minister, Angus Bethune in Alness, had similarly extensive connections to the Caribbean, in his case through his wife's family, the Munros of Lemlair. Another, John Fraser in Kilmorack, would later have a son who became a planter in Berbice. Further north, in the nine parishes of the Presbytery of Tain, Joseph Munro in Edderton had a son, Matthew (1761/2–97), who went to Grenada and, at his death, owned plantations there and in Demerara and St Lucia. And George Douglas the minister of Tain, who had married a sister of Matthew Munro, had a brother and son-in-law who owned Demerara plantations. In the nine parishes of the Presbytery of Dornoch, both George Rainy in Creich and George McCulloch in Loth had Caribbean involvements. However, to the south, in the eleven parishes of the Presbytery of Inverness, no ministers appear to have had such interests. An analysis for 1815, the year of Harry Robertson's death, shows a similar pattern and we can conclude that the involvement of the families of Church of Scotland ministers with Caribbean plantations was not exceptional

[11] R. M. Browne, *Surviving Slavery in the British Caribbean* (Philadelphia: University of Pennsylvania Press, 2017), pp. 1–10.

[12] Mrs Anne Robertson, Kiltearn, to her daughter Christian (Mrs Watson), Crantit, Orkney, 31 March 1806, MS 19331, f. 115, Traill Papers, NLS; arrival of *The Highlander* in the Clyde from Demerara, *Hibernian Journal*, 21 February 1806.

[13] *The Essequebo and Demerary Gazette*, 15 June 1805.

but neither was it the norm. Of more significance is the fact that the Robertsons in Kiltearn, the Rainy family in Creich and the McCullochs in Loth were closely related to each other, and there was a more distant relationship, but close friendship, between the Robertson and Douglas families.[14]

Growing up at Kiltearn and married life in Orkney

In 1790 George Robertson, writing from Grenada, opined that his brother Harry's children were all 'too delicate for this climate' and so he would not 'ever recommend [them] to come across the Atlantick'.[15] Nevertheless, Christy's early years were punctuated by the departure of her three older brothers for the Caribbean. Gilbert (1774–1839) probably left home about 1790, when Christy was ten years old, and later established himself in Demerara. The eldest, William (1773–1837), trained as a lawyer and worked for some time as a public notary in British-occupied Dutch Suriname before joining Gilbert in Demerara. Then, in early 1793, Christy said goodbye to Harry (1776–95), who left by sea from Foulis Point, two miles west of the manse. By late February he was in Glasgow, about to sail for Demerara, and sent an affectionate letter to Christy:

> My last promise to you at the Storehouse of Fowlis was to write you. I therefore sit down to do it very hurriedly. I send you as a token that I do not forget you, a pair of gloves & cissors [sic].

Christy kept this letter, along with the last he wrote to her in November 1795. By the time she received it, Harry was dead – having survived two bouts of yellow fever, he had drowned.[16] Christy was now fifteen and Harry had flattered her by called her a 'big woman', that is a grown-up, and had given her brotherly advice and encouragement:

> I hope you are as attentive as possible to improve yourself in everything within your reach, tho' your Father cannot afford you Inverness Court Education, yet with some attention you'll all cut as good a figure as your neighbours.

There is an indication here of the family's relatively modest means. Although Harry's reference to an 'Inverness Court Education' is opaque, he was probably

---

[14] H. Scott, *Fasti Ecclesiae Scoticanae: The Succession of Ministers in the Church of Scotland from the Reformation* (Edinburgh: Oliver and Boyd, 1915); for details of these families, see D. Alston, 'Slaves & Highlanders', available at <http://www.spanglefish.com/slavesandhighlanders/> (last accessed 17 April 2022).

[15] George Robertson to George Rainy, 15 December 1790, microfiche 3300, 14.1, Parker Family Papers, University of Edinburgh Special Collections. The original of this microfiche collection is held in PAR 920, Liverpool Central Library Archives (LCLA).

[16] MS 19332, ff. 23, 24, Traill Papers, NLS.

referring to the social circles in Inverness in which his sisters would aspire to move. Three years later Christy duly made her mark when, aged eighteen, she appeared at the Northern Meeting Ball and caught the eye of James Watson, ten years her senior and serving as a lieutenant in the newly formed Regiment of the Isles. Watson, the son of a house carpenter in Dumfries, had been in partnership in a drapery and haberdashery business there but in 1799 he was appointed chamberlain to Lord Dundas on the estates of the Earldom of Orkney.

With a secure future, he proposed to Christy. They were engaged in April 1800 and married at Kiltearn in June.[17] Christy moved with her husband to Crantit, near Kirkwall, where four sons were born, a period of personal happiness brought to an end by the sudden death of James Watson in December 1808, when Christy was pregnant with their fifth child, also a boy. Although they had formed a circle of supportive friends in Orkney, Watson had not been universally popular.[18] As chamberlain he deputised for Lord Dundas as Vice-Admiral of Orkney, responsible for the court which had jurisdiction over the lucrative matter of wrecked ships. This brought him into conflict with both the town councillors of Kirkwall, who had authority over the town's port, and with those islanders who, in Watson's view, regarded pillaging wrecks as a right. In a report to the Admiralty Office he was damning in his account of some of the inhabitants of the island of Sanday for their conduct after the wreck of the *Utrecht* in 1807. Some of the crew were refused shelter and died during the night.[19]

Lord Dundas was also the principal heritor in Orkney and, since the heritors (the main landowners) were responsible for the payments of ministers' stipends and the upkeep of manses and churches, Watson was also brought into conflict with a number of clergymen. One of them circulated a pamphlet attacking Watson, describing him as 'a broken down pedlar of Dumfries'.[20]

Yet it was a happy time for the couple and from these years Christy kept thirty-eight letters from her mother and two from her father, along with eighteen letters her husband had received from her father. These fifty-eight letters provide a remarkably detailed account of family and social affairs at Kiltearn – especially given Mrs Robertson's garrulous style – and illustrate the extent to

---

[17] 'Memoir', pp. 5–8.
[18] S. J. Rosie, *Saints and Sinners: The Memorials of Saint Magnus Cathedral* (Kirkwall: The Orcadian Ltd, 2015), entry 83.
[19] Draft letter to William Marsden, Admiralty Office, from James Watson, Vice Admiral Depute of Orkney and Shetland, summarising the proceedings regarding the wreck and salvage of the *Utrecht* [1807], D1/46/48, Orkney Archives [hereafter OA]. Quoted in Rosie, *Saints and Sinners*, p. 172.
[20] The circular was written in 1805 by Rev. Francis Liddell against James Watson and entitled, 'To the Humane and Generous Inhabitants of Britain; the Groans of the Poor Oppressed Clergy of the Orkney Islands'. D13/6/12, OA.

which the Caribbean was part of day-to-day life. There was, of course, news of their own family. Christy's brother William had left Demerara in May 1802 and returned to London in poor health, while Gilbert remained at plantation *Kiltearn* in Berbice. Her cousins Tom and William McCulloch, from Loth, were in Demerara and about 1806 her cousin George Rainy from Creich went out to the colony to join his older brother Gilbert. Close to the Kiltearn manse was the farm of Balcony, which had been tenanted by a Robert Douglas. While Robert's older son George, a contemporary of Harry Robertson, had become minister of Tain, the younger son, Gilbert, became a planter in Demerara, where he was joined in 1802 by his own son, Robert. Mrs Robertson conveyed frequent news of the Douglas family, who were closely enough related for her to describe Robert as Christy's cousin. They had used their wealth to acquire a substantial house outside Glasgow, named Douglas Park, and Christy's sister, Betsy, spent three or four weeks there in the spring of 1802. Later, in 1807, Gilbert Douglas's wife, Cecilia – 'a most amiable lady' – stayed at the Kiltearn manse. Her collection of paintings would later be the basis of Glasgow's Kelvingrove Art Gallery.

Christy's parents took a particular interest in the children of other ministers. At one point John Bethune, the son of the Alness parish minister, was home from Demerara, the 'same fine agreeable lad we knew of old', as was Hector Downie, son of the minister at Urray, a 'fine young man & very intimate with our friends'. There was also news of Innes Arthur, son of the minister of Resolis, who was in Berbice where he had 'grown a tall genteel looking lad'.[21] And a Berbice planter, Mr Labalmondiere, had married Betsy Douglas, daughter of the Tain minister.

In 1806 one of the Robertsons' own domestic servants, a boy named Hugh Munro, went to Demerara under a three-year indenture which paid for his passage, along with two other young men known to Christy; and three other men from the parish went out in the same year at their own expense.[22] Meanwhile, guests at the manse included visitors from Guyana such as Dr William Munro – from Easter Ross but by then established in Berbice – and, from the same colony, Simon Fraser of Belladrum with his Dutch wife. Since there were frequent reports of deaths, perhaps the most welcome news to be passed on from any letter was that 'our friends at Demerara are all well'.[23]

But there were connections to other parts of the West Indies. In 1801 Dr Robertson wrote of expecting 'a friend from Jamaica who has hardly an acquaintance in this country but myself and depends a good deal on our society

---

[21] Mrs Anne Robertson, Kiltearn, to her daughter Christian (Mrs Watson), Crantit, Orkney, 20 April 1802, MS 19331, f. 67, Traill Papers, NLS.

[22] Mrs Anne Robertson, Kiltearn, to her daughter Christian (Mrs Watson), Crantit, Orkney, 21 October 1808, MS 19331, f. 129, Traill Papers, NLS.

[23] Rev. Harry Robertson to James Watson, from Kiltearn, 18 March 1801, MS 19331, f. 7, Traill Papers, NLS.

for enjoyment while here' and Mrs Robertson wrote of a visit from 'Collector Tulloch & his son Harry from Jamaica', noting that Harry Tulloch reminded her of their own son Gilbert.[24] In later letters there was news of others in the colony, such as their distant relative William Munro, who had become 'solicitor to the Customs at Kingston'.[25] William's brother, Gilbert Munro, was in Trinidad and later in St Vincent.[26] Some visitors were unexpected, such as an old school friend of their son Harry, whom they had known as 'Jock McLean' and was now 'Mr John McLean of Carriacou'. His brother George McLean was to become the largest enslaver on this very Scottish Caribbean island.[27]

There were also many references to the Robertsons' close friend, Elizabeth Baillie, wife of Colonel James Sutherland of Uppat (near Dunrobin). The Sutherlands' son Robert was a plantation owner in St Vincent and this island was also the base for Elizabeth's brother George Baillie, who, until his financial collapse in 1805, was one of the major slave-factors in the West Indies.[28]

Hugh Munro Robertson

During these years the Robertson family had to consider a career for Christy's only younger brother, Hugh Munro Robertson (1787–1819). In August 1802 their brother Gilbert wrote from Demerara to Charles Parker saying that Hugh had expressed an interest in coming to the colony. Gilbert, however, felt 'he would be better in a counting house for some time' and asked for Parker's help in arranging this.[29] Hugh was able to visit James and Christy in Orkney in the summer of 1803 and it was not until late 1804 that he moved to Liverpool, to work under the direction of his brother-in-law, Samuel Sandbach. Writing to her cousin Mrs Parker, Christy was pleased that he had also made a good impression when he visited them.[30]

---

[24] Rev. Harry Robertson to James Watson, from Kiltearn, 22 July 1801, MS 19331, f. 11, Traill Papers, NLS; and Mrs Anne Robertson, Kiltearn, to her daughter Christian (Mrs Watson), Crantit, Orkney, 19 July 1800, MS 19331, f. 55, Traill Papers, NLS.

[25] Rev. Harry Robertson to James Watson, from Kiltearn, 2 October 1802, MS 19331, f. 21, Traill Papers, NLS.

[26] William Robertson, London, to his sister, Christy, 1 February 1812, MS 19332, f. 11, Traill Papers, NLS.

[27] Mrs Anne Robertson, Kiltearn, to her daughter Christian (Mrs Watson), Crantit, Orkney, 20 November 1805, MS 19331, f. 111, Traill Papers, NLS.

[28] Mrs Anne Robertson, Kiltearn, to her daughter Christian (Mrs Watson), Crantit, Orkney, 25 November 1809, MS 19331, f. 145, Traill Papers, NLS.

[29] Gilbert Robertson (Demerary) to Charles Stewart Parker (Glasgow), 28 August 1802, PAR 920/II/6/2, Parker Papers, LCLA.

[30] Rev. Harry Robertson to James Watson, from Kiltearn, 24 May 1803, MS 19331, f. 25, Traill Papers, NLS; Anne Robertson (Kiltearn) to Mrs Parker (Blackhearn [sic]), 28 February 1805, PAR 920/II/17, Parker Papers, LCLA.

A year later, when Hugh was eighteen, the time for decisions had come. But there were differences of opinion. Christy's mother wrote to her in November 1805:

> As to my dear Hugh going to Demerary I am entirely of Mr Watson's mind and yours on this subject it depresses me much the thought of his going. But strange as it may seem his Father is quite keen about it and presses him on.[31]

Her father's view prevailed and by March the matter was concluded: 'My dear Hugh goes for Dem^{ry}. Indeed it touches me to the heart that no other plan has cast up for him.'[32] Hugh attempted to explain his situation in a letter to James Watson in April:

> I have now fully made up my mind about going to Dem^{ry} yet it is not a measure of choice with me if I could help it: but what is to be done in this Country without money & strong interest?

And so, despite their connections to the Sandbach and Parker families, the Robertsons thought they had insufficient influence or means to ensure Hugh a career at home.[33] In July 1806 Sandbach wrote to confirm that Hugh was on his way. He hoped that 'in the course of time ... Hugh will relieve his brother Gilbert who will retire and transfer his present commission in his favour – Gilbert must now be well on towards independence, altho' the crops for two seasons back have been very short'.[34] The hope of financial 'independence' was a recurring theme of family discussions. On her marriage the Robertsons' wish for Christy's husband had been that 'by a prudent attention to your affairs [you] may in a few years attain a genteel independency' and they later observed that a legacy from an uncle to Samuel Sandbach had been 'the foundation of his being arrived so early in life at independence'.[35]

In Kirkwall, Christy had come to know her husband's Orkney friend, Thomas Stewart Traill (1781–1862). Traill had graduated in medicine from Edinburgh University in 1802 and, on his return to Kirkwall, gave a series of public lectures

---

[31] Mrs Anne Robertson, Kiltearn, to her daughter Christian (Mrs Watson), Crantit, Orkney, 20 November 1805, MS 19331, f. 111, Traill Papers, NLS.

[32] Mrs Anne Robertson, Kiltearn, to her daughter Christian (Mrs Watson), Crantit, Orkney, 26 February 1806, MS 19331, f. 115, Traill Papers, NLS.

[33] Mrs Anne Robertson, Kiltearn, to her daughter Christian (Mrs Watson), Crantit, Orkney, 23 November 1801, MS 19332, f. 65, Traill Papers, NLS.

[34] Rev. Harry Robertson to Mrs Traill (Christy Robertson), from Kiltearn, 29 March and 22 April 1814, MS 19332, f. 51, Traill Papers, NLS.

[35] Rev. Harry Robertson to James Watson, from Kiltearn, 19 July 1800, MS 19331, f. 3, Traill Papers, NLS; Mrs Anne Robertson, Kiltearn, to her daughter Christian (Mrs Watson), Crantit, Orkney, 14 February 1805, MS 19331, f. 96, Traill Papers, NLS.

on chemistry to raise funds for the poor following a failure of the harvest. The Watsons were among those who attended and Traill repeated the practical part of his course at the Watsons' house, remarking that Christy was 'a neat and successful experimentalist'.[36] When Traill found it difficult to progress his career in medicine, Christy's connection to the Sandbach family in Liverpool allowed Traill to set up his practice in the city in 1804.

Hugh Munro Robertson's departure for Demerara in 1806 was even more difficult because in Liverpool he had formed an intense friendship with Dr Traill, six years his senior. From his arrival in the colony he wrote a series of affectionate letters, ending the first:

> Write me soon ... when you want to write anything on snug subjects regarding either of ourselves, you might (to avoid any being the wiser) call yourself Marcus & me Julius.

And he signed himself, 'Yours to the end of time'. Was he in love with Traill? Perhaps.

Hugh observed and collected on Traill's behalf, describing for him the climate, people, flora and fauna of Guyana and sending him soil samples, snake skins, a jaguar skin, weapons from the region's Indigenous peoples, and a number of preserved birds, including a wild duck which was his own first attempt at taxidermy.[37] But along with this there are disturbing elements in his letters, including a callous acceptance of the sexual abuse of enslaved women, revealed in one of his comments to Dr Traill:

> [You would be] astonished to know how common the venereal disease is among the Negroes – not an estate almost but has some of its people labouring under one of its stages; in fact a person runs a greater risque in this Country than among the fair nymphs [i.e. prostitutes] at home, unless they are very wary.

And one can only feel distaste at his enthusiastic and sentimental response to his brother Gilbert's present of 'a little boy newly imported from the Gold Coast'.[38]

Hugh's arrival in Demerara had also brought him into an entirely different network through his brother Gilbert's relationship with the free woman of colour, Eliza Thomas. She was a daughter of the remarkable Dorothy 'Doll' Thomas, sometimes known in the colony as the 'Queen of Demerara'.

---

[36] Thomas Traill, Kirkwall, to Mr and Mrs Watson, 10 June 1804, MS19329, f. 2, Traill Papers, NLS.
[37] M. Jasanoff, *Edge of Empire: Conquest and Collecting in the East 1750–1850* (London and New York: Harper, 2006).
[38] Mrs Anne Robertson, Kiltearn, to her daughter Christian (Mrs Watson), Crantit, Orkney, 20 April 1802, MS 19332, f. 67, Traill Papers, NLS; Mrs Anne Robertson, Kiltearn, to her daughter Christian (Mrs Watson), Crantit, Orkney, 2 May 1802, MS 19332, f. 69, Traill Papers, NLS.

'Doll' Thomas and the Robertsons

No one forgot their first meeting with Dorothy 'Doll' Thomas. John Castlefranc Cheveley, who worked as a clerk in Georgetown, encountered her in 1821 and recorded his impressions in his diary. She had, he thought, 'the deportment of an empress' and was especially noted for the 'balls and entertainments' over which she presided.[39] She had borne at least ten children to five white men and had, to use Cheveley's terms, 'disposed' of her daughters to suitable 'white young gentlemen'. These included Christy's brother Gilbert who, by 1804, was living with Dorothy's daughter Eliza; and Ayrshire-born John Fullarton, like Gilbert a 'son of the manse', who was in a relationship with Eliza's half-sister, Charlotte Thomas.[40] When Gilbert was joined by his brother Hugh in 1806, he was living on Doll Thomas's *Kensington* plantation.[41]

Gilbert became the joint owner with Gilbert Rainy of the *Kiltearn* plantation in Berbice, managed *Woodlands* in Demerara for Charles Parker, and with Parker acquired *L'Amitie en Libertie* next to *Kensington*. However, by 1810 Parker, writing to his wife, expressed concerns about Gilbert's management of their interests:

> I am sorry to say that accounts of Gilbert Robertson (from him we have heard nothing) are far from flattering, he is over his head in debt. I see nothing for it but compulsive measures to get what can be got out of his hands.[42]

In contrast, Gilbert's cousin George Rainy was on his way to becoming a partner in McInroy Sandbach & Co. and rose to be its main representative in Demerara, where he lived for more than thirty years.[43] While George provided some protection for his cousin, it may have been Dorothy Thomas's family which kept Gilbert from financial disaster.

Second marriage and life in Liverpool

After James Watson's death in 1808, Christy spent more than a year in Orkney settling her husband's affairs and then returned to her parents' home at Kiltearn,

---

[39] C. C. Thornburn, *No Messing, The Story of an Essex Man: The Autobiography of John Castlefranc Cheveley I, 1795–1870*, 2 vols (Chichester: The Memoir Club, 2012), pp. ii, 76.
[40] K. Candlin and C. Pybus, *Enterprising Women: Gender, Race and Power in the Revolutionary Atlantic* (London: University of Georgia Press, 2015), p. 116, quoting Slave Returns, Demerara, 1820, T71/407, The National Archives [hereafter TNA].
[41] Hugh M. Robertson, Kensington, Demerary, to Thomas Traill, physician, 21 Islington, Liverpool, 17 August 1806, MS 19332, f. 67, Traill Papers, NLS.
[42] C. S. Parker to E. Parker, 28 June 1810, PAR 920 1/53, Parker Papers, LCLA.
[43] *Oxford Dictionary of National Biography*, entry for George Rainy. Available at <https://doi-org.nls.idm.oclc.org/10.1093/ref:odnb/107415> (last accessed 17 April 2022).

where her children could be cared for and where they had already spent long holidays. Dr Traill, who had been in Liverpool since 1804, had remained close to the Watsons and had visited them in Orkney in 1807. Christy wrote afterwards to say that his 'departure made a blank in our little society'.[44] On 5 July 1810, as he left for Liverpool after spending some time with the family at Kiltearn, Traill left a letter for Christy asking 'leave to offer my hand, and what I trust shall ever accompany it, my heart'. She demurred, reminding him of her lack of possessions and her five children, and asking him not to feel committed to his proposal. Traill repeated his offer, telling her that he would regard her children as his own, and with this assurance Christy accepted. However, they agreed to keep their engagement secret, telling only Christy's sister, Mrs Sandbach, and her husband. Over the next year they wrote seventy-two letters, growing closer, exchanging verses, discussing poetry and other literature, and often teasing each other.[45] Traill sent her a ring and told her he was looking for a suitable house in Liverpool. But it was not until the end of April 1811 that Christy told her parents. Her father wrote to Traill giving his enthusiastic consent but asked that Christy's five boys continue to live with them at Kiltearn. The couple were married at Kiltearn at the end of July and travelled south to Liverpool through the west Highlands.[46]

One old school friend of Traill's, Samuel Laing, disapproved of the match, describing Christy as 'a vulgar woman; [who] will always keep him down in society'. Although he had in 1808 described her as 'gay, agreeable and lively, and of a very hospitable turn', Laing strongly disapproved of what he regarded as Christy's match-making among the Watsons' circle of friends and described her as a 'dangerous busy woman'. In particular, he believed she had encouraged his sister May to enter into an unhappy marriage with an army captain, Alexander Mackenzie Shaw of Muirton, in Inverness.[47] He also thought Traill had been inveigled into his marriage with Christy 'in the prime of youth', describing her as 'a woman with five children older considerably than himself'. This was untrue. Traill was a year older than Christy – an unusually small age difference when on average men of this class were twelve years older than their

[44] Christian Watson, Crantit, to Dr Traill, 31 January 1807, MS 19329, f. 11, Traill Papers, NLS.
[45] MS 19329, ff. 13–159, Traill Papers, NLS.
[46] Dr Traill to Christian Watson, 5 July 1810, MS 19329, f. 13, Traill Papers, NLS; for continued correspondence until Christy informed her parents, see MS 19329, ff. 15–113, Traill Papers, NLS; Rev. Harry Robertson to Dr Traill, from Kiltearn, 15 May 1811, MS 19331, f. 43, Traill Papers, NLS; for further correspondence of Traill and Christy until the eve of their marriage, see MS 19329 ff. 117–159, Traill Papers, NLS; 'Memoir', pp. 37–48/3.
[47] R. P. Fereday, *The Autobiography of Samuel Laing of Papdale* (Kirkwall: Bellavista Publications, 2000), pp. 43, 180.

wives – and he delighted in her lively mind and agreeable manner in society.[48] Their marriage was happy.

Although the Robertsons had offered to keep the five boys with them at Kiltearn, Christy wanted the youngest, James – whom she called 'the child of her affliction' – to be with her in Liverpool. Christy would go on to have five children with Traill, three girls and two boys. They set up home in fashionable St Anne Street and in 1812 moved to a larger house there, closer to that of her sister. Although not as wealthy as Eliza and Samuel Sandbach, the two families spent much time together. Christy and Eliza had always written to each other. Now they met often and, when they wanted to talk privately, they would sometimes revert to their native Gaelic. Traill joked that whatever the subject, they would make sure their husbands at least felt they were included by interspersing their talk with the occasional *'agus* [and] Dr Traill' or *'agus* Mr Sandbach'.[49]

How should we best understand the life of this comfortable, Scottish family in Liverpool? Christy Robertson lived during a period in which new middle-class identities were emerging. Leonore Davidoff and Catherine Hall described this process in 1987 in their *Family Fortunes: Men and Women of the English Middle Class 1780–1850*, a book which was pioneering in the rich detail it gave of the lives of individuals, couples and their families. They argued that gender – as well as class – was a critical tool in understanding what was to become modern British society and that class and gender could only be understood in interaction with each other. To understand people's lives – in this case those of the middle classes – was to explore what it meant to be a man or woman at this time and in this society. There was, they showed, an increasing 'separation of the sexes in all institutions and an ideology to support that division' in the form of 'a new masculinity and a new femininity and new ideals of home and family'. The 'new masculinity' valued active, autonomous roles in industry, commerce, public affairs and worthy occupations; the 'new femininity' fostered dependence, obedience, gentility, the creation of a harmonious domestic sphere and, beyond that, charitable work.[50]

Catherine Hall's introduction to the 2018 edition of *Family Fortunes* provides a useful and concise review of relevant scholarship in the thirty years since the book was first published. She notes that these forms of family life had a much longer history than they had thought, with origins in the earlier eighteenth century; that there was a much greater diversity than they had suggested – a variety of 'middling sorts' rather than a single middle class; and that ideals

---

[48] For age differences, see K. Barclay, *Love, Intimacy and Power: Marriage and Patriarchy in Scotland, 1650–1850* (Manchester: Manchester University Press, 2011), pp. 20–1.
[49] 'Memoir', p. 77.
[50] L. Davidoff and C. Hall, *Family Fortunes: Men and Women of the English Middle Class 1780–1850* [1987], 3rd edn (London: Routledge, 2018), pp. 75, 143.

of manliness and femininity were but one part of the multiple ways in which identities and roles were created and sustained. Hall also notes the importance of understanding white middle-class families in the wider context of nation, empire and colonial rule, with its increasingly rigid conceptions of racial difference and hierarchy. And Hall welcomes the 'decentering' of England in studies such as Katie Barclay's *Love, Intimacy and Power: Marriage and Patriarchy in Scotland, 1650–1850* published in 2011, in which Barclay shows some differences in the relationship between gender and power in Scottish society.[51]

Barclay began her study by drawing attention to an important difference between class structures in England and Scotland. While there was a clear distinction in England between the nobility on the one hand and the substantial class of gentry who were the backbone of rural society on the other, in Scotland before industrialisation there was 'a relatively small, closely connected group, ranging from wealthy, middling sorts to nobility' without such clear lines of demarcation. What held them together was a link, however tenuous, to landownership and the status which was derived from this. But the small size of many Scottish estates and the relatively small incomes derived from even the largest meant that 'even the most prestigious families had to look beyond land ownership to supplement their incomes'. Consequently landowners combined estate incomes with other occupations and their children went into 'law, medicine, the army or navy, government service or university posts' – as did members of the wider 'middling sorts', including the families of Church of Scotland ministers. One outcome of this was wider connections among this group to agricultural improvement, banking, manufacturing and the growth of Scottish industries, including coal mining. Indeed, this connectedness might be part of the explantation for Scotland's unprecedented rate of industrialisation and subsequent urban growth.[52] And a similar desire to secure other sources of income would, in part, account for the greater involvement of Scots of all the 'middling sorts' with enslavement and the plantation economies.

Distinctions of wealth and status, which were real but subtle, were subject to continual change and redefinition, and Barclay argues that Scottish elites were characterised by a greater sense of vulnerability than their English neighbours. Frugality was therefore 'prized at all social levels ... and seen as a necessary quality in a wife'.[53] This is borne out in Traill and Christy's exchange of letters between his proposal in July 1810 and their marriage in July 1811.[54] Since, in her own words, she brought 'in place of a fortune ... only a family', Christy pledged 'to endeavour, by the strictest economy, to make the best appearance on a limited income'. On his part, Traill admitted that he had not 'paid that

---

[51] Barclay, *Love, Intimacy and Power*.
[52] Barclay, *Love, Intimacy and Power*, pp. 10–13.
[53] Barclay, *Love, Intimacy and Power*, p. 17.
[54] MS 19329, ff. 13–159, Traill Papers, NLS.

attention to economy which would have been prudent' and resolved to bring to an end the amusement of 'expensive pursuits', such as the purchase of paintings. He declared himself content to exchange the 'tiresome variety' of company for 'your more agreeable society at our own fireside'.[55] Traill was expressing that ideal of a harmonious domestic sphere which was at the core of the separation of masculine and feminine roles. Yet Christy's skill as a hostess in their home would be an important part of the development of Traill's academic and scientific network. In the words of the architect Thomas Rickman, one of their earliest guests in Liverpool, she was 'a very clever & at the same time very domestic woman'.[56]

Although it took some time for him to build up his medical practice, Dr Traill was soon at the heart of the flowering of intellectual and cultural life in Liverpool. In 1812 he was a founding member of the Literary and Philosophical Society and in early 1814, at a dinner held in the house of the cotton broker, William Corrie, Traill proposed the establishment of a Liverpool Scientific Institution. Traill drew up a prospectus, Corrie took on the role of chairman of the Society and over £20,000 was raised from donations for what became the Liverpool Royal Institution for the Promotion of Literature, Science and the Arts. When it opened in Colquitt Street in November 1817, Traill gave the first course of lectures and lent his extensive collection of minerals to the Institution's museum.[57] Traill also served on the committees of the Botanic Garden, the Ophthalmic Infirmary and the School for the Blind, and he was the founding president of the Liverpool Mechanics' Institute in 1825.[58] Christie's role in these ventures was as a 'patroness' of balls and bazaars which raised funds to support the running of the Royal Institution, a role commonly judged suitable for ladies of her class.[59]

Traill's interaction with many leading thinkers included inviting them to his home and in his 'Memoir' he consistently refers to guests being entertained at 'Mrs Traill's table'. He valued her social skills, referring to her cordiality, easy dignity, taste, tact, playful humour and elasticity of mind. In this way they met, and sometimes formed or continued friendships, with many influential individuals, including the American naturalist John James Audubon; the Scottish philosopher Dugald Stewart (who had taught Traill at Edinburgh University); the American physician and naturalist Thomas Horsefield, who had travelled extensively in Indonesia and had become curator of the East India Company's

---

[55] Christy to Traill, 22 August 1810, MS 19329, f. 19, Traill Papers, NLS; and his reply, 29 August 1810, MS 19329, f. 21, Traill Papers, NLS.
[56] MS 19399, f. 50, Traill Papers, NLS. Notes extracted from the unpublished *Journal of Thomas Rickman*.
[57] 'Memoir', p. 96.
[58] *Liverpool Mercury*, 8 May 1818, 3 August 1821, 18 January 1822 and 12 September 1828.
[59] *Liverpool Mercury*, 15 December 1820; F. Prochaska, *Women and Philanthropy in 19th Century England* (Oxford: Oxford University Press, 1980).

museum in London; the Swiss mineralogist, Necker de Saussure; the Irish dramatist and actor James Sheridan Knowles; the poet Thomas Campbell, whose lectures at the Liverpool Royal Institution were enjoyed by Christy; and a number of Italian and French politicians. Later, in Edinburgh, the Traills entertained the scientists John Dalton, originator of modern atomic theory, and John Jacob Bezelius, regarded as one of the founders of modern chemistry.[60]

Two of their dinner guests, John Franklin (1786-1847) and William Scoresby (1789-1857), played important roles in the exploration and study of the arctic regions of the North Atlantic. When Franklin set off from Liverpool for British North America in 1825, on what was known as the Mackenzie River Expedition, Christy 'seemed no less interested than her husband' and Traill noted that 'on the return of the intrepid voyagers, two years afterwards, their first call was on Mrs Traill'.[61] While Franklin's arctic expeditions were organised by the Royal Navy and were focused on finding and mapping the supposed 'North West Passage' as a new trade route to the Pacific, it was the whaler William Scoresby who brought that fusion of practical experience and university study of the sciences which enabled him to conduct experiments which would 'not be rivalled by any of the Victorian gentlemen-explorers who followed him north'.[62] The Traills met Scoresby in 1818 and he was soon among their 'most intimate and esteemed friends'.[63] Traill helped Scoresby publicise his work through the *Edinburgh Philosophical Journal*, joined Scoresby on a trip to Ireland, and when Scoresby made a voyage to Greenland in 1822, on the Liverpool-built *Baffin*, Traill was present at the launch. On his return, it was Thomas and Christy who had to break the news of Scoresby's wife's death during his absence.[64] Scoresby named Traill Island, in north-east Greenland, after his friend. Later, Scoresby's son William studied at Edinburgh, where the Traills found him a 'fine warm-hearted youth'. Sadly he fell ill and died of a haemorrhage in 1838. Christy sat with him during his illness and laid out the body after his death.[65]

Many women of Christy's class – including her own sister – were married to merchants and assisted them through entertaining those with whom they did business. If we think of Traill as being in the business of science and learning, then Christy was providing similar support. But beyond this she played a particularly significant role in two of Traill's endeavours. In 1816 Traill met with Alexander Scott, a sailor from Liverpool who had been shipwrecked on the

---

[60] 'Memoir', p. 235.
[61] 'Memoir', p. 181.
[62] C. L. Devlin, 'The influence of whaler William Scoresby, Jr. on the Arctic observations of Sir James Lamont', *Arctic*, 68:3 (2015), pp. 317–30.
[63] 'Memoir', p. 175.
[64] William Scoresby, *The Arctic Whaling Journals of William Scoresby the Younger* (ed. C. I. Jackson), 3 vols (Hakluyt Society: Routledge, 2009), pp. iii, xxxvii, 135.
[65] 'Memoir', p. 283.

coast of Africa and had recently returned after being held for almost six years as a slave 'among the Wandering Arabs of the Great African Desert'. Traill was the author of the 'Account of the Captivity of Alexander Scott' published in 1820 and 1821.[66] Traill edited Scott's narrative, writing in such a way that he limited Scott's presence in the text in order to prevent the Liverpudlian's unrefined 'voice' from distracting readers from the scientific veracity of the account. Major Rennell, whom Traill described as a 'veteran geographer', provided corroboration by showing the general consonance of Scott's evidence with the emerging map of Africa.[67] Yet Traill had, of course, no other primary source than the interviews which he and his collaborator, William Lawson, had conducted with Scott. Christy, as a woman, received no public acknowledgement but in his 'Memoir of Mrs Traill' her husband credited her contribution, recording that she 'often saw and conversed with Scott … [and] obtained information which it would probably have escaped her husband to elicit'.[68]

In 1825 she played a similar role after Te Pehi Kupe, a Māori paramount chief of the Ngāti Toa tribe, arrived in Liverpool on the *Urania*. The ship's master, Captain Reynolds, with whom the Māori had formed a close bond, asked Traill to attend Te Pehi Kupe during an attack of measles. He was soon 'a frequent guest at Mrs Traill's table' and she 'assisted in collecting the information which was afterwards published in the Library of Entertaining Knowledge'.[69] This 'Account of Tupai Cupa' – as his name was rendered – was a chapter in George Craik's *The Newzealanders*, published in 1830.[70] It included reproductions of Te Pehi Kupe's drawing of his own facial tattoo – his *moko* – and a portrait drawing of him in formal European dress. It was partly on this work that Hermann Melville later based the character of Queequeg in *Moby-Dick*.[71]

Love, obedience and friendship

Barclay makes the point that love did not mean equality and that for women of the time the phrase 'loving and obedient' could be used 'without any sense of incongruity'.[72] There is no doubt that the Traills' marriage was loving.

---

[66] T. S. Traill and W. Lawson, 'Account of the Captivity of Alexander Scott, among the Wandering Arabs of the Great African Desert, for a period of nearly Six Years. With Geographical Observations on his Routes, and Remarks on the Currents of the Ocean on the North-Western Coast of Africa, by Major Rennell FRS & &', *The Edinburgh Philosophical Journal*, 4 (1821), pp. 38–54, 235–46.

[67] S. Outram-Leman, 'Alexander Scott: Constructing a legitimate geography of the Sahara from a captivity narrative, 1821,' *History in Africa*, 43 (2016), pp. 63–94.

[68] 'Memoir', pp. 168–9.

[69] 'Memoir', p. 182.

[70] G. L. Craik, *The Newzealanders* (London, 1830), pp. 317–36.

[71] J. Ellis, *Tattooing the World: Pacific Designs in Print & Skin* (New York: Columbia University Press, 2008), especially '"The Original Queequeg"? Te Pehi Kupe, Toi Moko, and Moby-Dick', pp. 52–73.

[72] Barclay, *Love, Intimacy and Power*, p. 1.

The couple wrote to each other frequently during any period of absence and until the end of Christy's life their letters were both affectionate and an expression of their common intellectual interests. But to what extent was there an equality between them which might be described as friendship?

They shared many interests. His first gift to her, as a family friend in 1802, had been a 'portable chemical apparatus as a small but sincere mark of friendship & esteem' and immediately before his proposal of marriage in 1810 he had given her a copy of *Reliques of Robert Burns*, which they discussed in their letters.[73] In the early years of their marriage Traill set aside time in the evenings to read with Christy and commented that 'although she had not read extensively, her judgement in such matters was seldom erroneous'.[74] Traill was at pains to include in his 'Memoir' a number of 'extracts from our correspondence ... [which] will show how I loved and esteemed this most affectionate wife, and the high opinion I ever entertained of her judgement and understanding'.[75] However, it was always clear, to Traill, that his was the superior intellect. Yet he conceded that, in some matters, Christy exercised a 'cooler' and more prudent judgement. Thus she successfully persuaded him to appear often in public when the position of 'senior physician' in Liverpool was about to become available and she dissuaded him from a rash response when one of his scientific papers was suppressed by a rival.[76]

Christy was obedient – as required by her marriage vows – but there was scope for negotiation of their relationship. In 1814 Traill had the opportunity, which Christy encouraged him to take, to spend a number of months in Spain. He left Liverpool only two weeks after the birth of their second child and his tour was extended to six months rather than the expected three or four. It was a difficult and anxious time for Christy and her letters to her husband carefully balanced expressions of her unhappiness at his absence with the desire that he use the opportunity of travel to expand his knowledge. The following is one example which illustrates the way in which love was both expressed and used to negotiate the terms of their relationship:

> This letter savours more of longing for your return, than any I have yet written; but do not, my dearest love, suppose that I write to hurry you, or to deprive you of any enjoyment that you can overtake at present; so far from that, I really wish you to see all you have in your power; and I am content to wait, because I believe you are happy.

---

[73] Thomas Traill, Kirkwall, to Mr and Mrs Watson, 10 June 1804, MS19329, f. 2, Traill Papers, NLS; Mrs Watson, Kiltearn, to Thomas Traill, Liverpool, 5 August 1810, MS19329, f. 17, Traill Papers, NLS.
[74] 'Memoir', p. 79.
[75] 'Memoir', p. 120.
[76] 'Memoir', pp. 145, 175.

Christy extracted from him the promise that he would respect her wishes: 'In short, I never will part with you again. If you will travel, I shall do so also.' And Traill felt himself bound by this commitment.[77]

Christy's views of marriage – and of friendship within it – would have been informed by her upbringing and an important insight comes from her father's writing. In 1802 he published *The Scotch Minister's Assistant; Or, a Collection of Forms for Celebrating the Ordinances of Marriage, Baptism, and the Lord's Supper etc.* In the introduction he explained that there were 'no Forms prescribed by the Church of Scotland ... [and] every Clergyman is left to exercise his own talents on such occasions'. The only requirement was to follow the Directory of Public Worship which required the exchange of vows, with the man promising to be 'loving and faithful' and the woman to be 'loving, faithful and obedient'. Harry Robertson provided three suggested Forms for Marriage, all of which stressed the importance of love and mutual esteem. While recognising 'a certain superiority' in the husband, this was to be 'so tempered with an equality in other respects' that 'a happy marriage affords all the pleasures of friendship, all the enjoyments of sense and reason, and indeed all the sweets of domestic life'.[78]

Limits to empathy

Christy had shown her ability to engage with strangers from different societies or with widely different experiences, overcoming barriers of class, language, religion and culture. And yet there is nothing to suggest that Alexander Scott's experience of being enslaved, with which she seems to have empathised, had any impact on her view of her family's involvement with slavery. Nor did reaching across what would have been thought of as a racial boundary to Te Pehi Kupe lead her to reach out to the situation of her family's enslaved labourers and their children.

Indeed, some of Traill's activities in Liverpool directly assisted planters in the Caribbean. In 1830, for example, at the request of the West India merchants John Gladstone and John Moss, both slave-owners on a large scale, he advised on the application of Edward Charles Howard's patented process of refining sugar in a container, known as a Howard vacuum pan. Moss and Gladstone introduced this in the West Indies, producing white sugar from one boiling which, when it arrived in Britain, required no further refining. Christy 'had pride and pleasure in exhibiting at tea or breakfast this new sugar'.[79]

---

[77] 'Memoir', pp. 98–146.
[78] H. Robertson, *The Scotch Minister's Assistant: Or, a Collection of Forms for Celebrating the Ordinances of Marriage, Baptism, and the Lord's Supper, According to the Usage of the Church of Scotland. With Suitable Devotions for Church and Family Worship* (Inverness, 1802).
[79] 'Memoir', p. 191.

This was at a time when women were increasingly active in campaigning for the immediate abolition of slavery. In 1824 Elizabeth Heyrick published her pamphlet *Immediate not Gradual Abolition* and called for a boycott of sugar produced by enslaved labour; and, in Birmingham in 1825, Lucy Townsend founded the first of a network of Ladies Societies – later often called Female Societies – which promoted the sugar boycott, canvassed for support door to door, and were independent of the national Anti-Slavery Society, which favoured a gradual approach.[80] The Liverpool Ladies' Anti-Slavery Association was founded in the town in 1827 and placed advertisements in the local newspapers promoting the sale of 'free labour produce' from India.[81]

Anthony Tibbles argues that in Liverpool 'social, business and family connections were always stronger than views on the slave trade' and that the differences between abolitionists and defenders of slavery did not cause a major social divide.[82] This seems to be borne out by the Traills' close friendships both with the abolitionist William Roscoe (1753–31) and with the merchant and slave-holder John Gladstone (1764–1851), and by his service on the committee of the Botanic Garden along with Roscoe and the slave-owner William Earle (1787–1864).[83] Radical action such as the sugar boycott was more closely associated with Quakers and Methodists, who were not part of this social circle.

Roscoe was an historian, poet, botanist, art collector, lawyer, banker and, briefly, a Member of Parliament. Traill became an acquaintance in 1806 and his doctor in 1810. He attended Roscoe during his last illness in 1831 and after Roscoe's death Traill wrote and published a *Memoir*, the first published account of Roscoe's life.[84] In this he referred to Roscoe's 'generous sympathy with the suffering sons of Africa' expressed in his poem *Mount Pleasant* (1777).[85] Traill noted 'how early Roscoe denounced the traffic in human flesh' and how 'this required no inconsiderable share of moral courage … in the chief seat of the odious traffic'.[86] Yet, when Traill wrote the *Memoir*, four of Traill's five stepsons were working in Demerara, one of them an overseer on a plantation.

---

[80] C. Midgley, *Women Against Slavery: The British Campaigns, 1780–1870* (London: Routledge, 1992).
[81] B. Howman, 'Abolitionism in Liverpool', in D. Richardson, S. Schwarz and A. Tibbles (eds), *Liverpool and Transatlantic Slavery* (Liverpool: Liverpool University Press, 2007), pp. 277–96; *Liverpool Mercury*, 8 February 1828.
[82] A. Tibbles, *Liverpool and the Slave Trade* (Liverpool: Liverpool University Press, 2018), p. 83.
[83] *Liverpool Mercury*, 8 May 1818.
[84] T. S. Traill, 'Memoir of William Roscoe', *Edinburgh New Philosophical Journal*, Vol. 13 (1832), pp. 193–221; reprinted as *Memoir of William Roscoe* (Liverpool, 1853).
[85] W. Roscoe, *Mount Pleasant: A Descriptive Poem. To which is added, an Ode* (London; Liverpool, 1777).
[86] Traill, *Memoir of William Roscoe*, pp. 14–15.

The Watson boys: 'your young folks in Demerary & Berbice'

Her family's Caribbean involvements had exacted a further toll on Christy. On Christmas Day 1819, while she was with her husband, their children and her mother at the Sandbach house, the firm's ship *Demerary*, bound for the Clyde, struck the Wicklow banks off the coast of Waterford and sank with the loss of all on board – except, according to local lore, a Black sailor and a Newfoundland dog.[87] The passengers included Christy's 'favourite brother' Hugh Munro Robertson, who had first sailed to Demerara in 1806 on the same vessel. They had last seen Hugh five years before on his only visit home in these thirteen years. His body was found in his dressing gown, identified by the name on his underclothes. 'This was', wrote Traill, 'an overwhelming blow to his aged mother, who after it scarcely ever rallied; and it was most terrible to his affectionate sisters.'

Christy was also in the slow process of parting with the sons of her first marriage. All her children, except James, had remained in the Highlands after her remarriage in 1811, and Christy's father wrote in 1812 that the boys were 'fine promising young creatures closely attended to by their aunt [Christy's sister Anne] who is looked up to with reverence'. Christy's mother ensured that all the children learned at least some Gaelic.[88] In the autumn of 1815, after the death of Dr Robertson, all Christy's children were reunited with their mother in Liverpool, while Christy's mother and her sister Anne went to live with the Sandbach family.[89]

Her eldest boy, Harry Watson (1801–36), had continued his schooling at Inverness Royal Academy, which he had attended since 1808, lodging with family friends in the town. This was one of a number of academies in the north of Scotland whose creation or expansion had been supported by donations from Highland planters in the Caribbean. These institutions benefited directly from Highland participation in the exploitation of enslaved Africans, became symbols of Highland participation in the growth of British educational culture, demonstrated continued commitment to the survival of the home communities – and, in this and other cases, trained individuals for further exploitation of the colonies.[90] Harry Watson sailed for Demerara in March 1817 to work 'under the auspices of Mr Gladstone after serving in the counting houses of John Gladstone and of Messrs Ewart & Rutson'.[91]

---

[87] T. M. Tate, *Tales and Legends of Lecale, County Down* (Downpatrick: unknown, 1930).
[88] Rev. Harry Robertson to Dr Traill, from Kiltearn, 3 March 1812, MS 19331, f. 49, Traill Papers, NLS.
[89] 'Memoir', p. 150.
[90] S. K. Kehoe, 'From the Caribbean to the Scottish Highlands: Charitable enterprise in the Age of Improvement, c. 1750 to c. 1820', *Rural History*, 27:1 (2016), pp. 37–59.
[91] 'Memoir', p. 156.

By 1818 it had been decided that the 'lively and volatile' Andrew Watson (1803-37) should be sent to a school near Macclesfield run by a John Williams. He remained there for a year and returned 'improved in every thing, and became a clever, well instructed youth, of very engaging disposition', before going on to Bahia in Brazil to work as a clerk in the house of Messrs Gilfillan.[92] Peter Miller Watson (1805-69), after two years in the Sandbach counting house in Liverpool, left for Demerara in November 1822 to work under his cousin George Rainy in the house of McInroy, Parker & Sandbach.[93] And William Robertson Watson (1807-76) arrived there in 1827 to work as an overseer on a plantation 'some distance from Georgetown', despite having had the ambition to enter a 'learned profession'.[94] This was in part because at the age of eighteen he had lost his right thumb in an accident in Liverpool, and could not write well enough even to take up a position as a clerk.[95] Only the youngest, James Watson (1809-?), who had been brought up in the Traill family, pursued a career in Britain, becoming a 'Chancery barrister' in London, and this was in part as a result of support provided from Demerara by Harry.[96]

The progress of Harry and Peter in Demerara 'reconciled Mrs Traill to some extent to parting with her dear children, and diminished the pain of so early a separation'.[97] The still 'volatile' Andrew, however, had a disagreement with his employers in Brazil, moved to Berbice and then to to a position in Demerara, where he lasted little more than six months, and finally worked as a clerk in Fullarton & Macdonald's business in Georgetown.[98] Relations between the brothers were sometimes strained, with Andrew commenting in 1824 that he was 'better anywhere else than with his brother' and a few years later writing that 'Peter is just the same crabbed body he was at home, must have his own way in everything'.[99] In 1832 Christy's brother Gilbert wrote from Demerara to Dr Traill with the news that the Watson boys were 'in excellent health and

---

[92] 'Memoir', pp. 161, 163.
[93] Peter Watson to Dr Traill, from City of George Town, Demerary, 16 April 1843, MS 19334, f. 75, Traill Papers, NLS; 'Memoir', p. 174.
[94] Peter Miller Watson to his mother (Mrs Traill, Liverpool), 11 August 1827, MS 19334, f. 67, Traill Papers, NLS; Gilbert Robertson, 19 Queen Street, Soho Square, London, to his sister Christy, Liverpool, 18 May 1824, MS 19332, f. 19, Traill Papers, NLS.
[95] Peter Watson, Demerara, to his mother (Mrs Traill), 11 August 1827, MS 19334, f. 67, Traill Papers, NLS.
[96] 'Memoir', p. 314; William Robertson Watson to his mother (Mrs Traill, Liverpool) from Demerara, 27 September 1828, MS 19334, f. 103, Traill Papers, NLS.
[97] 'Memoir', p. 174.
[98] Andrew Watson to his mother (Mrs Traill), from Bahia, 7 December 1821, MS 19334, f. 45, Traill Papers, NLS; Andrew Watson to his mother (Mrs Traill), from Berbice, 1 August 1824, MS 19334, f. 53, Traill Papers, NLS; Andrew Watson to his mother (Mrs Traill), from George Town, 15 October 1828, MS 19334, f. 57, Traill Papers, NLS.
[99] Gilbert Robertson, London, to his sister Christy, 18 May 1824, MS 19332, f. 19, Traill Papers, NLS; Andrew Watson to his mother (Mrs Traill), from George Town, 15 October 1828, MS 19334, f. 57, Traill Papers, NLS.

all very industrious' but he added 'it will be a good many years before they can arrive at independence if times don't mend here'.[100]

After the death of Hugh Munro Robertson, Traill's nephew Harry had taken on the role of seeking out exotic specimens for him. He sent minerals, poison-tipped arrows, plants, a snake skin, a live Trumpeter bird, and humming birds preserved in rum.[101] Traill also collected through other contacts and in 1819 he published articles on what he claimed as two new species from Demerara, which he called the Jacketed Monkey and the Spotless Cat, both based on his examination of specimens brought back in 1817 by Charles Edmonstone, of Cardross in Dunbartonshire. In 1823 he expanded the former into a longer article on jaguars, having by then seen a live specimen brought from Paraguay to Liverpool by a ship's captain. He also published notes on the Trumpeter bird.[102] All this is indicative of the way in which participation in the expanding networks of the Atlantic world created the opportunities for collecting and enabled the advancement of scientific knowledge. And this, as Maya Jasanoff argues in *Edge of Empire*, in which she explores imperial expansion in the East Indies, could give collectors a new identity.[103] Collecting was 'a means of self-fashioning' and Hugh and Harry in Demerara were self-fashioning themselves as men of education and enlightenment, expanding the boundaries of knowledge in the mould of Traill himself. Their participation in this project gave them the solace of an identity other than that of enslaver and exploiter.

The inter-related Robertsons, Watsons and Traills were like those large 'baggy' families which Margot Flinn has described in relation to the East India Company, families who lived across metropole and colony 'with their numbers of children, their bachelors and spinsters, aunts, nephews and cousins'.[104] Much could be hidden or ignored within that bagginess. And it was a large receptacle in which there was room for many contradictions. Christy, in letters to relatives,

---

[100] Gilbert Robertson to Doctor Traill, St Ann Street, Liverpool, from Plantation Brothers, Demerary, 23 October 1832, MS 19332, f. 21, Traill Papers, NLS.

[101] Harry Robertson Watson to his stepfather (Dr Traill, Liverpool) from Demerary, 20 May 1820, MS 19334, f. 6, Traill Papers, NLS; Harry Robertson Watson to his mother (Liverpool) from Demerary, 2 July 1820, MS 19334, f. 8, Traill Papers, NLS; Harry Robertson Watson to his stepfather (Dr Traill, Liverpool) from Demerary, 30 March 1821, MS 19334, f. 14, Traill Papers, NLS; Harry Robertson Watson to his stepfather (Dr Traill, Liverpool) from George Town, Demerary, 21 July 1821, MS 19334, f. 16, Traill Papers, NLS.

[102] 'Report of Proceeding of the Wernerian Natural History Society, 27 November 1819', *The Edinburgh New Philosophical Journal*, Vol. 2 (1820), p. 181; T. S. Traill, 'Remarks on some of the American Animals of the Genus Felis, particularly on the Jaguar', *Memoirs of the Wernerian Natural History Society*, Vol. 4 (1823), pp. 468–74; T. S. Traill, 'The Trumpeter-bird, a true Ventriloquist', *Edinburgh Philosophical Journal*, Vol. 6 (1824), p. 417; T. S. Traill, 'Observations on the Habits, Appearance, and Anatomical Structure of the Bird named The Trumpeter', *Memoirs of the Wernerian Natural History Society*, Vol. 5:2 (1826), pp. 523–32.

[103] Jasanoff, *Edge of Empire*.

[104] Quoted by Davidoff and Hall in *Family Fortunes*, introduction to the 3rd edition (2018), pp. xiii–xxvi.

often referred to 'my dear Lads in Demerary' but there is nothing to hint at any qualms over their involvement in the enslaved-worked plantations. Peter wrote to her in September 1823, just after the Demerara enslaved uprising, and was uncompromising in his condemnation of missionaries who he believed had fomented the rebellion.[105] Ten years later, after emancipation, Christy made one of her rare comments about those who had been formerly enslaved. In a letter to her aunt in Orkney she remarked that 'the poor deluded blacks have got idle and independence & freedom has not as yet had a good effect upon them'.[106] Despite her intelligence and the warmth of her personality, none of the horrors of chattel slavery impinged on her view of the colonies – or on her view of her children's roles there.

Edinburgh

In 1832 Traill was appointed Professor of Medical Jurisprudence at the University of Edinburgh and the family left Liverpool the following April. This followed an extended period of ill health in 1829 and a desire for a 'less laborious life' than that required by his growing medical practice. Traill was attracted by academic life, although there would be a substantial reduction in his income, and Christy agreed despite her attachment to her friends and family in Liverpool. Traill described this as a joint decision but recognised that she had made 'a great sacrifice of her own feelings and predilections'.[107]

It also gave them more opportunity to visit friends and relations. That autumn they made a ten-week trip to Orkney, accompanied by their three daughters, and Traill returned to Orkney the following year.[108] In 1835 there was a visit to Dublin for the annual meeting of the British Association, the learned society founded in 1831, where they were guests at the mansion house of Robert Hutton MP, along with the eminent geologists Louis Agassiz and George Bellas Greenough.[109] This was followed by a trip around Wicklow – which since they went alone, Christy referred to as their second 'marriage jaunt' – and a few weeks in Liverpool, before returning to Edinburgh.[110] The British Association would also take them on visits to Liverpool in 1837 and Newcastle in 1838.

In September 1834 the Traills' daughter Anne became engaged to her second cousin, George Parker, the son of Margaret Rainy and Charles Parker. Anne had known George since childhood and had become better acquainted through

---

[105] Peter Watson to his mother (Mrs Traill), Demerara, 4 September 1823, MS 19334, f. 63, Traill Papers, NLS.
[106] Christy (Mrs Traill) to Mrs Yule, Kirkwall, 8 December 1834, MS 19330, f. 6, Traill Papers, NLS.
[107] 'Memoir', pp. 205–6.
[108] 'Memoir', pp. 216–30.
[109] 'Memoir', p. 243.
[110] 'Memoir', p. 244.

visits to their house at Fairlie, on the Ayrshire coast. Traill found George's 'manners gentlemanly – the delicacy and generosity of his conduct, on all occasions, everything that fond parents could desire for a favourite daughter'.[111] Their wedding took place in May 1836 but the occasion was bittersweet – at the end of March news had come that Harry Watson had died of fever in Demerara. 'It is impossible', wrote Traill, 'to describe the anguish which this afflicting intelligence caused to the most affectionate of mothers.'[112] And in September 1837 came the second blow, news of the death of Andrew Watson, which reached the Traills in Liverpool on the last day of the meeting of the British Association. It was a turning point in Christy's life:

> Those who knew Mrs Traill the best have confessed that after the death of her two eldest born, her excellent and affectionate sons, she never was the same being she had been before. Calm placidity of manner, and affection for her family & friends, remained but that elasticity of mind, that playful amenity of disposition, which rendered her so agreeable a companion, and made her a general favourite in every society, were obscured by mental distress.[113]

In an attempt to relieve her distress the Sandbach family invited her to Hafodunos, their newly acquired estate in North Wales, where Christy's nephew, Henry Robertson Sandbach, and his wife, Margaret Roscoe (a granddaughter of William Roscoe), had set up home. Henry and Margaret were patrons of the arts, especially of the sculptor John Gibson. Margaret was herself an accomplished poet and would later commemorate Christy in her poem 'She never can be there'.[114]

In the following year, 1838, Christy went to London for the first time, visiting her newly married daughter Lucia and, as it turned out, seeing her son James for the last time. Her brother William had died the previous year but he seems to have become increasingly distant from his family. As long ago as 1812 he had told Christy that, other than to see his mother, he had 'not the most distant inclination to visit Ross-shire again', referring in the same letter to his father only as 'the Dr.'.[115] William's death in 1837 did not merit mention in Traill's 'Memoir'.

---

[111] 'Memoir', p. 237.
[112] 'Memoir', p. 262.
[113] 'Memoir', p. 279.
[114] Bound in with Traill's 'Memoir', pp. 428–9.
[115] William Robertson, London, to his sister, Christy (Mrs Traill), Liverpool, 1 February 1812, MS 19332, f. 11, Traill Papers, NLS.

Fairlie: the 'Clyde Clapham'

From the time of Traill and Christy's move to Edinburgh, the Parkers' home in Fairlie became an even more important part of Christy's life and a further chilling example of that 'coexistence of enlightenment and oppression' which Emma Rothschild describes in *The Inner Lives of Empire*.[116] She found companionship and solace with the Parkers, an explicitly pious family. Although her father had had a low opinion of Charles Parker, whom he regarded as 'truly a strange fish ... the parting with money is like losing his vital blood', Christy remained on good terms with Parker's wife, her cousin Margaret Rainy.[117] Margaret had a deep religious faith and later formed a close friendship with Dr Thomas Chalmers, perhaps the most influential Scottish churchman of the nineteenth century. Chalmers became the leader of the Evangelical party within the Church of Scotland, served as Moderator of the General Assembly, and was the first moderator of the Free Church, formed under his leadership at the Disruption of 1843. Chalmers held Margaret in the highest regard and after her death wrote, 'such a friendship, so steadfast, so exuberant of all that was kind and beautiful and generous to me and mine, I never expect to see replaced in this world'.[118]

In *'Send Back the Money!': The Free Church of Scotland and American Slavery*, Iain Whyte has argued that the Free Church, under Chalmers, was compromised immediately after the Disruption by accepting financial support from Presbyterian churches in southern slave states of the United States.[119] Chalmers' earlier career shows that this compromise was long-standing, with his own supporters combining evangelical principles with the 'ownership' of enslaved people. The Parkers' support for Chalmers was evident as early as 1814 when the minister of Glasgow's Tron Kirk resigned to take up the post of Professor of Divinity at the University. Moves were soon made to promote the candidacy of Chalmers, then a young evangelical preacher, as his successor. This campaign originated with the brothers John and Robert Tennent (Margaret Rainy's sister Christian was married to Robert's son, Hugh Tennent) and gained the support of Margaret's husband, Charles Parker, then a member of the Town Council, which had the right of appointment. When the Council finally voted in November 1814, Chalmers was elected but only after an intense campaign during which one of Chalmers' supporters had been offered a bribe by a Glasgow West India

---

[116] Rothschild, *The Inner Life of Empires*, pp. 258–66.
[117] MS 19331, ff. 23–25, 37, Traill Papers, NLS.
[118] P. C. Simpson, *The Life of Principal Rainy* (London: Hodder and Stoughton, 1909), p. 13.
[119] I. Whyte, *'Send Back the Money!': The Free Church of Scotland and American Slavery* (Cambridge: James Clarke & Co., 2012).

merchant house to cast his vote against Chalmers.[120] Parker was thereafter a key figure in securing funds to build a new church for Chalmers, followed by a chapel of ease to accommodate the growing population, and in the appointment of an assistant minister, through all of which Chalmers implemented his theories of parish-based poor relief and education.[121] One of the elders from 1819 to 1832 was the merchant Robert Brown, who was married to Margaret's other sister, Ann Rainy.

Chalmers found that his health suffered from living in the polluted atmosphere of the city and he used the country homes of his middle-class supporters for recuperation. He stayed for a week with the Parkers at Blochairn in the summer of 1820, becoming 'strongly and tenderly attached' to the couple, and occupied Blochairn House in the summer of 1823 before he moved to become a professor at St Andrews.[122] The Parker, Tennent and Brown families, inter-related through the Rainy sisters, all had villas at Fairlie, which is said to have been referred to as the 'Clyde Clapham' – after the group of aristocratic evangelical Anglicans associated with Clapham (London) from about 1790 to 1830.[123] If so, it was a deeply ironic epithet. Although both were 'evangelicals', the Clapham Sect was led by William Wilberforce and was committed to the abolition of slavery, while the coterie at Fairlie was founded on fortunes made in the West Indies.

Charles Parker continued to oppose abolition. In a debate in the House of Commons in 1826, James Blair MP, who like Parker had substantial plantations in Guyana, spoke on the anti-slavery petition which had been presented:

> [It] was another instance of the tricks which the Methodists and Dissenters had recourse to for the purpose of inflaming the public mind by misrepresentation. In order to swell the number of signatures to that petition, the subscribers were in ninety-nine cases out of an hundred, schoolboys, carters, and colliers, persons who had no property ... Mr. Blair was perfectly certain he spoke from good authority, indeed he had been fully authorised to use the name of his informant, Charles S. Parker, a man of great respectability.[124]

As in Liverpool, there is nothing to suggest that this continuing connection to slavery caused any moral problems for the Traills.

---

[120] M. T. Furgol, 'Thomas Chalmers' Poor Relief Theories and their Implementation in the Early Nineteenth Century' (PhD thesis, University of Edinburgh, 1987), pp. 60–6.
[121] Furgol, 'Thomas Chalmers' Poor Relief Theories', pp. 107–9, 180–4.
[122] W. Hanna, *Memoirs of the Life and Writings of Thomas Chalmers*, 2 vols (Edinburgh, 1881), pp. ii, 274, 472.
[123] Furgol, 'Thomas Chalmers' Poor Relief Theories', p. 413. Furgol wrongly identifies Robert Tennent as the father-in-law of Charles S. Parker.
[124] *Dublin Evening Mail*, 24 May 1826.

The circle of friends and relations at Fairlie were not only pious but rich, leisured and refined – and the lives of its younger members were very different from those of the Watson boys. For a few months in 1829/30 young George Parker had worked in Demerara for his uncle, George Rainy of McInroy, Sandbach & Co. But Rainy was not impressed by his nephew, whom he thought exhibited a 'lack of spirit or ... want of self will' and young George soon left the colony, travelling through the Caribbean islands to Philadelphia, and visiting Niagara Falls before returning to England.[125] George's older brother, Charles Stewart Parker junior (1800–68), had also been in the West Indies but his main activity had been collecting botanical specimens. He had studied botany in Geneva and Traill described him as 'a zealous and accomplished naturalist'.[126] In 1824 he chartered his own ship in order to bring back his extensive collection from Demerara. The vessel was lost in a storm but his collections from Barbados, Trinidad and St Vincent were safely brought to Britain.[127]

When Ann Traill and George Parker married in 1836, their 'marriage jaunt' was a year of travel in Germany, Switzerland, Italy and France. Their first child was born in Genoa, christened George but known in the family by the Italian name Doria.[128] Initially, they set up home in Liverpool but moved to Fairlie in 1838.[129] George Parker was an accomplished yachtsman and in 1839 the Parkers and Dr Traill made a trip through the West Highlands on Parker's yacht *The Phantom*, sailing as far north as Lochalsh. Christy's son, Peter Miller Watson, made an extended visit home in 1840 and that summer saw three generations of the Traill family gather at the Parkers' house. It was among 'the happiest moments of their lives'.[130]

In the autumn Parker oversaw the launch of a fifty-eight-foot yacht built to his own design and named the *Doria*, which was to be 'one of the swiftest yachts on the Clyde' and in which, in the same year, they again cruised in the West Highlands, this time with Christy on board. On Iona she went alone to attend a church service in Gaelic.[131]

---

[125] George Parker to his mother, Mrs Parker, Fairlie, from Barbados (14 March 1830), Demerary River (24 April 1830) and Philadelphia (22 July 1830), PAR 920/II/12/6, 7 and 8, Parker Papers, LCLA.
[126] T. S. Traill, 'Observations on the Habits, Appearance, and Anatomical Structure of the Bird named The Trumpeter', *Memoirs of the Wernerian Natural History Society*, Vol. 5:2 (1826), pp. 523–32.
[127] *The Edinburgh Journal of Science*, Vol. 2 (Edinburgh, 1825), p. 183.
[128] Letters from Anne Traill (Mrs Parker) to her mother-in-law, Mrs Parker, Fairlie, PAR 920/II/13/1–26, Parker Papers, LCLA.
[129] 'Memoir', p. 322.
[130] 'Memoir', p. 336.
[131] 'Memoir', p. 338; M. F. McCallum, *'Fast and Bonnie': A History of William Fife and Son Yachtbuilders* (Edinburgh: John Donald, 1998), p. 15.

'Baggy' families and relations in the shadows

The Robertson, Watson and Traill family network included some individuals who were seldom, or never, mentioned. Neither Christy's uncle – the George Robertson who died in Demerara in 1799 – nor his brother John who had died in Tobago in 1798, left legitimate children. But George had two acknowledged children, Gilbert (1794–1851) and Antoinette, with a 'free coloured' woman, Fanchine Dubrulon. Gilbert was born in Trinidad, educated in Sutherland, became a farmer in Gladsmuir (Haddingtonshire), married and then emigrated to Tasmania. Antoinette, probably born in Demerara, was in Inverness in 1813 and may have attended school there.[132] George also had a son, known as 'Black George', who was educated in London, and John had two 'mulatto boys', Charles and Daniel, who had been sent to an unnamed school in Glasgow. And so, at the time of Christy's marriage to James Watson in 1800 she had at least five Black Robertson cousins. Christy's mother, although favourably disposed towards Antoinette, made her views about such children clear in a letter written in 1804 following a visit to friends in Dingwall:

> They had just got home two little Foreigners children of their Brother the late Doctor George Bethune. Their mother was a Brigand. They are yellow, ugly things. I think it would be best to leave them in their own country but their aunt seems very tender of them and much interested.[133]

Dr Bethune had died in Demerara the previous year – and 'brigand' was a term sometimes applied to 'free coloured' women.

From Christy's brother Gilbert's relationship with Eliza Thomas in Demerara there were at least two children. This was at a time when Gilbert's mother, writing to her cousin Mrs Parker, observed that 'it is most extraordinary that we seldom hear from Gilbert now who used to be so punctual a correspondent'.[134] However, Hugh Munro Robertson's intimate letters to Dr Traill did contain information about Gilbert:

---

[132] Copy of the will of George Robertson, 20 February 1798, MS 19399, ff. 6–7, Traill Papers, NLS. For reference to Antoinette by Christy's mother, see Mrs Anne Robertson, Kiltearn, to her daughter Christian (Mrs Traill), Liverpool, 1 January 1813, MS 19331, f. 151, Traill Papers, NLS. For Gilbert Robertson, see 'Robertson, Gilbert (1794–1851)', *Australian Dictionary of Biography*, Vol. 2 (Melbourne: Melbourne University Press, 1967), which mistakenly gives his father as Gilbert Robertson.

[133] Mrs Anne Robertson, Kiltearn, to her daughter Christian (Mrs Watson), Crantit, Orkney, 20 April 1804, MS 19331, f. 83, Traill Papers, NLS.

[134] Anne Robertson (Kiltearn) to Mrs Parker (Blackhearn [sic]), 28 February 1805, PAR 920/II/17, Parker Family Papers, LCLA.

> He is distressed at present by the loss of a sweet little girl of his called Ann; she was indeed one of the finest engaging children I ever saw. She was quite fair haired, & at first sight struck me as being very like little Ann Sandbach. She died after 14 days illness of a teething fever.[135]

The other child was Henry Robertson (1807–81).[136] In 1810, in a letter to his wife, Charles Parker observed caustically, 'Who do you think is in Glasgow but Gilbert Robertson's Mother-in-Law Doll Thomas, with about 19 of her children & grandchildren come home for education.'[137] These may have included three-year-old Henry, since it was Doll – not Gilbert – who became Henry's guardian after the death of his mother Eliza.[138] Eliza had certainly died before 1817 when her sister Charlotte, acting on behalf of Doll, entered ten-year-old Henry's 'ownership' of three females in the Register of Slaves.[139]

Surprisingly, given his comments, Charles Parker had himself fathered two 'mulatto' boys, Charles and James, who were sent to Scotland for education in 1791, again to unnamed schools. It may have been Doll Thomas's blatant breach of decorum which irked him.[140] In contrast, when Parker had arrived in Greenock from Demerara in September 1805 accompanied by 'Jim' – perhaps his son James who must have joined him on the voyage – his wife had thoughtfully and discreetly made suitable arrangements:

> I have formed a plan some time ago of you sending him to Kate Warden who now lives in the same house at Port Glasgow as your aunt did some time ago – if you approve of this plan you can adopt it. I mention it in case you would be at a loss what to do with him on your landing & she will be happy to take charge of him.[141]

---

[135] Hugh M. Robertson to Thomas Traill, physician, 21 Islington, Liverpool from Demerary, Kensington, 17 August 1806, MS 19332, f. 67, Traill Papers, NLS.

[136] In her study of another Gilbert Robertson (1794–1851) – a Tasmanian farmer, newspaper editor and fiery opponent of the colony's Lieutenant-Governor – Cassandra Pybus argues that he was also a son of Christy's brother, Gilbert, born in Trinidad and sent home for education at Kiltearn around 1799. Mrs Robertson's comments above make the latter claim very unlikely but the assertion about his parentage is supported by the entry in the *Australian Dictionary of Biography* (see note 134 above). Whatever the truth, this Gilbert is not mentioned in the surviving family correspondence.

[137] C. S. Parker to E. Parker, 11 August 1810, PAR 920 I/53, Parker Papers, LCLA.

[138] D. Alston, 'A forgotten diaspora: The children of enslaved and 'free coloured' women and Highland Scots in Guyana before Emancipation', *Northern Scotland*, 6:1 (Edinburgh: Edinburgh University Press, 2015), pp. 49–69.

[139] 'A list of slaves belonging to Henry Robertson a minor, in the lawful possession of Charlotte Fullarton representative of D Thomas Guardn', T. 71/393, f. 1324, no. 1285, Slave Registers, Demerara, 1817, TNA.

[140] C. Pybus, 'The colourful life of Gilbert Robertson', available at <www.launcestonhistory.org.au/wp-content/uploads/2012/03/CassandraPybus20112.pdf> (last accessed 19 April 2022).

[141] Margaret Rainy [Mrs Parker] (Blochairn) to Mr Parker (on board the *Brilliant* arrived in Greenock), 24 September 1805, PAR 920/II/3/2, Parker Papers, LCLA.

When Gilbert came to London in 1824 to seek medical treatment, he wrote to Dr Traill saying that he was 'very much rejoiced to find my poor boy Henry settled with so respectable a man as Mr Bowman of Harley Street', a surgeon and apothecary whose clients included the Duke of Dorset and the Marquis of Waterford. It was Henry's grandmother, Doll Thomas, who had found him the position and paid the £400 fee for the seven-year apprenticeship. Although Eliza may have died, Gilbert clearly wished his relationship, and his son Henry, to be accepted by his family.[142] Charles Parker's earlier reference to Mrs Thomas as Gilbert's mother-in-law makes it clear that the relationship between Gilbert and Eliza was for him a marriage, albeit an irregular one. One could, after all, marry in Scotland simply by declaration in front of two witnesses.

Henry, at the second attempt, passed the examinations of the Society of Apothecaries in 1828 and soon joined his father in Demerara. In October 1832 Gilbert concluded a letter to Traill with the words, 'Henry begs to be affectionately remembered to you & yours'. If the family did acknowledge Henry – or his mother and grandmother – there is no record in their letters. Despite a bankruptcy in 1832, Henry became a general medical practitioner in England, married, had three children and died in 1881. Doll Thomas was ultimately disappointed in him, pointedly leaving him nothing in her will.[143]

Andrew Watson's last letter from Demerara in May 1837 had included news for Christy that her brother Gilbert had recovered his health and was 'as merry as I ever saw him'.[144] But the following September Gilbert, now aged sixty-four, arrived in Liverpool having been so feeble that it had been doubtful if he would survive the voyage.[145] He was cared for in the Sandbach household until he was well enough to join the Traills in Edinburgh. However, Christy was, in her husband's words, 'once again destined to mourn'. Gilbert died in September 1839, having undergone an unsuccessful operation by the eminent surgeon Charles Bell, who had performed the same operation on him in 1824.[146] Gilbert – 'this the last son of her father' to whom she was 'much attached' – had spent well over forty of his sixty-five years in the Caribbean, without achieving the 'independence' to which he, his brothers and his nephews had aspired.

Christy's own physical and mental health began to deteriorate. During the family cruise in the West Highlands in 1840 she 'exhibited traits of timidity which were not natural to her' and during the next year there was a 'diminution of her calm composure and mental intrepidity'. She did not join the long family

[142] Gilbert Robertson, London, to Thomas Stewart Traill, Liverpool, 30 January 1824, MS 19332, f. 17, Traill Papers, NLS.
[143] Will of Dorothy Thomas born Kirwan, PROB 11/2077, Prerogative Court of Canterbury Wills, TNA.
[144] Andrew Watson to his mother (Mrs Traill), 16 May 1837, MS 19334, f. 59, Traill Papers, NLS.
[145] Christy Traill to her daughter Mary Eliza Omond, Edinburgh, from Dingle Lane, Liverpool, 22 September 1838, MS 19330, f. 78, Traill Papers, NLS.
[146] 'Memoir', p. 321.

cruise in 1841 but Traill, as affectionate as ever, shared the experience in ten letters to her sent from different harbours on their route.[147] Over the following months her general health declined and she sometimes appeared confused. Then in April 1842, following a minor operation to remove a small corn from between her toes, the wound became infected and gangrene developed. Amputation was considered but she died in the early hours of the morning of 7 May 1842 with her family around her. Her husband held her hand and, as she gazed into his eyes and unable to speak, she pressed his fingers twice 'as if she would have said farewell'.[148]

Conclusions

This focus on a woman in Scotland as part of a Caribbean network allows us to see more clearly the extent to which middle-class families like the Robertsons were involved with the enslavement of Black Africans – and the extent to which, as shown in the Robertson/Watson letters, this involvement was accepted as part of everyday life in the north of Scotland. It also goes part of the way to explaining the disproportionately large involvement of such Scots in the exploitation of enslaved people in the Caribbean. Christy's family background – and both of her marriages – provide evidence of the insecurity of the 'middling sorts' and of their perceived need to secure sources of income other than from land and inherited wealth. The families of Church of Scotland ministers, like the Robertsons, are but one example of this.

Christy's second marriage to Thomas Traill, and her life in Liverpool, illustrate the growing importance of the separation of new masculine and feminine roles in middle-class society, with Christy at the heart of – and largely confined to – the domestic sphere. The importance of cultural and intellectual endeavours to them both, however, allowed them a closer friendship within their marriage than was common, although this remained an unequal partnership. This brought Christy and her husband into contact with a number of the leading thinkers of the time, something which makes even more startling their moral blindness to their family's continued involvement with and dependence on slavery. Yet, this was not unusual. The coexistence of enlightenment and oppression was common in middle-class society in Liverpool and, as is shown here, in the Evangelical circles which became the leadership of the nascent Free Church of Scotland.

Christy's was an extended and complex family, which took pride in its Highland origins and left vestiges of the Highlands in the names of Guyanese plantations, in the names of the ships which transported the produce of

---

[147] 'Memoir', pp. 352, 377; MS 19329, Traill Papers, NLS.
[148] 'Memoir', p. 423.

plantations, and in the personal names imposed on numerous enslaved Africans and their descendants. It was also what has been called a 'baggy' family, which contained not only the comfortable middle-class lives of the Traills in Liverpool and Edinburgh, but also 'free coloured' women, mixed-race children, a range of aunts, sisters, cousins and nieces in polite society at home and – living at least part of their lives at the brutal and brutalising edge of British colonial expansion – their uncles, sons, cousins and nephews. There was much which it was more convenient to silence or ignore.

This chapter has also been a study of complicity. The operation of all plantations worked by the enslaved relied on what can be accurately described as an 'apparatus of terror'.[149] That apparatus was not always and everywhere physically in action, except in the important sense that it was there as a constant and effective threat. Nevertheless, no one who worked on a plantation, or lived in a Caribbean colony whose economy was based on enslaved labour, could be unaware of its existence. In particular, any enslaved person who rebelled against their status as a slave knew they would feel its full force. Christy and her family were complicit in the operation of that 'apparatus of terror' but sought to construct a view of themselves which did not diminish their sense of self-worth and bridged the gap – perhaps a chasm – between what they had done, or failed to do, and the values which they believed defined them. Christy's life highlights the coexistence of enlightenment and oppression, the dependence of artistic and scientific endeavours on wealth gained from enslavement, and the surprising entanglement of evangelical faith with pro-slavery attitudes.

Coda

I find it impossible to end without mention of a legacy of the Robertsons' involvement in Guyana which Christy never knew. After her death, her son, Peter Miller Watson, had a son and a daughter with Hannah Rose, a woman of colour in Demerara. Andrew Watson (1856–1921), who attended Glasgow University and later worked as a marine engineer, is now recognised as the first Black person to play association football at international level, representing Scotland three times between 1881 and 1882.[150]

---

[149] M. Fulbrook, *Reckonings: Legacies of Nazi Persecution and the Quest for Justice* (Oxford: Oxford University Press, 2018).

[150] L. Walker, *A Straggling Life: Andrew Watson, the Story of the World's First Black International Footballer* (Worthing: Pitch Publishing, 2021).

SEVEN

The Gaelic Club of Glasgow: Gateway from the Scottish Highlands to the British Atlantic World, 1780–1838

Stephen Mullen

During a grand tour of Scotland in the summer of 1799, Virginian born merchant Littleton Dennis Teackle attended an exclusive meeting of the Gaelic Club of Glasgow,[1] held in the Black Bull Inn in the commercial centre near the Trongate:

> By appointment, I [was] accompanied ... to a Meeting of the Gaelic Society. My friend C_ was excluded from partaking of the feast, by the charter of the Society, which forbids all inhabitants of the City who are not members from attending their meetings. The father is of the fraternity. I was ushered into a large Room amidst 40 or 50 gentlemen. Those that were members were distinguishable by their Tartan Dresses. The Strangers were equally numerous with the Members. I was introduced to the President & the officers of the Fraternity ... This Society is chiefly composed of the first Merchants in this place & every member of it is a person of property & respectability. The president is our consul here, he showed me much civility.[2]

Established in March 1780, the Gaelic Club's surviving minutes – held in Glasgow City Archives – confirm Teackle's attendance as a 'stranger' alongside a 'numerous and highly respectable company' on 18 July 1799.[3] The group of

---

[1] An earlier version of this paper was presented to 'Comann-rannsachaidh air Eachdraidh nan Gàidheal ann an Alba/Discussion Group on the History of Gaelic Scotland' at the University of Glasgow in May 2019. The author is grateful to attendees for feedback and suggestions, especially Martin Macgregor, Aonghas MacCoinnich, Iain Mackinnon and Kate Mathis.

[2] Diary, 1799–1800, Vol. 1, pp. 112–15, 17 July 1799, MMC-1956, Littleton Dennis Teackle papers, Library of Congress [hereafter LoC]. The author is grateful to Marenka Thompson-Odlum for providing a copy of this source.

[3] 'Minutes of the Gaelic Club, vol. 1', 1780–1817, TD746/1, Glasgow City Archives [hereafter GCA]; 'Minutes of Gaelic Club, vol. 2', 1780–1842, TD746/2, GCA. There is no pagination with either source and, where possible, the dates of meetings are cited for reference purposes in lieu of page numbers. For Teackle's attendance, see 'Minutes, vol. 1', 17 July 1799, TD746/1, GCA. The author is grateful to Allan Macinnes for drawing my attention to these sources.

prominent merchants and manufacturers enjoyed an evening of 'great harmony and conviviality' in the company of Teackle, a transatlantic merchant who would go on to become an enslaver in Virginia and ultimately a member of the Maryland House of Delegates.[4] These events brought together not only those of Highland descent in Glasgow but established relationships between commercial luminaries in Scotland and across the Atlantic world.

Recounting how guests from Virginia dined on calipee and calipash with tartan-clad Highlanders at a club in eighteenth-century Glasgow reveals a colonial *mentalité* better than any ledger book.[5] On the evening of 18 July 1799, one of Glasgow's most prominent West India merchants, Alexander Campbell of Hallyards, 'presented the club with a Turtle', one that was likely brought back alive from the Caribbean as a fresh, luxury item for the elite dinner table.[6] Teackle was invited 'to partake of their mirth and hilarity' and enjoy the feast:

> The steward announced that the dinner was ready. The visitors were first requested to go & take their seats & then follow'd the members, as well as their servants – all habited in Tartan Dresses. The Dinner was large & excellent. One dish whereof was the back shell of Green Turtle nearly 3 feet long. There appeared by no means that scarcity which the English people say universally prevails in Scotland.[7]

The membership included some of the most important figures in commercial Glasgow (as discussed in detail below). Of the members that evening of July 1799, eight had connections with the West Indies. The merchant fraternity was well represented: Campbell of Hallyards was a co-partner in prominent Glasgow-West India firm John Campbell senior & Co., while James McInroy was a partner in McInroy, Parker & Co.[8] Absentee planter Gilbert Douglas, who owned *Mount Pleasant* estate in St Vincent, was also in attendance.[9] Of the seventeen named 'strangers' in attendance (that is, residents outside Glasgow

---

[4] For a biography of Teackle, see Somerset County Historical Society website, 'Littleton Dennis Teackle', available at <http://somersetcountyhistoricalsociety.org/teackle_mansion/littleton_dennis_teackle> (last accessed 24 December 2017). Teackle was an enslaver in 1820, see *Laws of Maryland Made and Passed at a Session of Assembly, 1820* (Annapolis: Jonas Green, 1824), p. 186.

[5] Calipee and calipash were cartilaginous substances underneath a turtle's shell that gave turtle soup consistency. For turtle soup, see: *The Household Encyclopædia; or, Family Dictionary of Everything Connected with Housekeeping and Domestic Medicine, by an Association of Heads of Families and Men of Science*, Vol. 2 (London: W. Kent & Co., 1859), p. 513.

[6] 'Minutes, vol. 1', 18 July 1799, TD746/1, GCA.

[7] 'Teackle Diary, 1799–1800, vol. 1', pp. 113–14, MMC-1956, Littleton Dennis Teackle papers, LoC.

[8] For an account of the firm John Campbell senior & Co., see S. Mullen, 'The Great Glasgow West India house of John Campbell senior & Co.', in T. M. Devine (ed.), *Recovering Scotland's Slavery Past: The Caribbean Connection* (Edinburgh: Edinburgh University Press, 2015), pp. 124–45.

[9] 'Gilbert Douglas', in *Legacies of British Slave-ownership Database*, available at <http://wwwdepts-live.ucl.ac.uk/lbs/person/view/2146654761> (last accessed 15 October 2018).

personally admitted to the club on a one-off basis at the discretion of the Preses), around six had West India connections. For example, Walter Ewing MacLae was a West India broker in Glasgow (and whose son, James Ewing, was also a West India merchant), while Robert Glasgow owned the *Mountgreenan* and *Sans Souci* estates in St Vincent.[10] Other strangers simply named Haggart and Parker were likely Charles Hagart of Bantaskine and Charles Stewart Parker, both at the commanding heights of the Glasgow-West India trades at the end of the eighteenth century.[11] In all, around 40 per cent of the attendees that night had connections with the West India trades, which would surely have promoted valuable discussion with those in attendance such as Archibald Graham of the Thistle Bank in Glasgow and, of course, Virginia merchant Littleton Dennis Teackle.[12]

Gentleman's social clubs – often formed for the 'improvement' of members – exemplified the associational culture of eighteenth-century Great Britain. The clubs operated as organised social networks, integrating men of similar rank and occupational status.[13] There was a long tradition of networks and associations in Glasgow. Perhaps the most famous was the Hodge Podge club, frequented by the city's famous 'tobacco lords' in the lead-up to the American War of Independence (1775–83).[14] There was also a long-established Highland/Gaelic network in Glasgow. The Highland Society was founded in 1724 (continuing to 1876) and operated with distinctly charitable aims to promote education and apprenticeships. The society erected the Black Bull as a place for Highlanders and Lowlanders to socialise and it subsequently served as a shop. This also became the home to the Gaelic Club, a 'socially elite offshoot' of the original society.[15] The Gaelic Club served many important functions. On the one hand, the elite membership and structure was similar to many clubs of eighteenth-century Great Britain. On the other, it had a distinctive social role that connected prominent citizens of Highland stock in Glasgow in order to

---

[10] See S. D. Smith, 'Slavery's heritage footprint: Links between British country houses and St Vincent plantations, 1814–34', in M. Dresser and A. Hann (eds), *Slavery and the British Country House* (Swindon: English Heritage, 2013), p. 62.

[11] A. Cooke, 'An elite revisited: Glasgow West India Merchants, 1783–1877', *Journal of Scottish Historical Studies*, 32:2 (2012), pp. 127–65.

[12] 'Minutes, vol. 1', 18 July 1799, TD746/1, GCA.

[13] P. Clark, *British Clubs and Societies, 1580–1800: The Origins of an Associational World* (Oxford: Oxford University Press, 2000).

[14] J. Strang, *Glasgow and its Clubs* (Glasgow: Richard Griffin & Company, 1857), p. 40; T. M. Devine, *The Tobacco Lords* (Edinburgh: John Donald, 1975), p. 9; A. Hook and R. Sher, 'Introduction: Glasgow and the Enlightenment', in A. Hook and R. Sher (eds), *The Glasgow Enlightenment* (Edinburgh: Tuckwell Press, 1995), p. 5; T. F. Donald (ed.), *The Hodge Podge Club 1752–1900: Compiled from the Records of the Club* (Glasgow: James MacLehose and Sons, 1900), pp. 59–65.

[15] A. I. Macinnes, 'Contacts and tensions: Highlands and Lowlands in the nineteenth century', in C. MacLachlan and R. W. Renton (eds), *Gael and Lowlander in Scottish Literature: Cross-currents in Scottish Writing in the Nineteenth Century* (Glasgow: Scottish Literature International, 2015), pp. 16–17.

promote the interests of their community and wider culture, although, as will be shown, this came second to self-interest.

In a classic account of Glasgow's clubs, John Strang noted how successful Highlanders involved with the Gaelic Club had 'by their industry, won a prominent position amongst their Lowland competitors for fortune or power in Glasgow – a knot of rather remarkable men'.[16] Similarly, for Charles Withers the role of the club was to draw 'together a middle-class elite to exert hegemony over the urban working classes', while Douglas Hamilton claimed that most of the leading West India merchants in Glasgow joined a club 'less concerned with the promotion of Gaelic than in securing the interests of its influential members'.[17] Exactly what the main industry of these Highlanders was based upon, or how the club served the interests of its members, remained largely unexplored. Given the increasing historiographical interest in the connections between the Scottish Highlands and chattel slavery in the Caribbean and South America,[18]

---

[16] Strang, *Glasgow and its Clubs*, p. 40.

[17] C. Withers, 'Class culture and migrant identity: Gaelic Highlanders in Urban Scotland', in G. Kearns and C. W. J. Withers (eds), *Urbanising Britain* (Cambridge: Cambridge University Press, 1991), p. 76; D. Hamilton, *Scotland, the Caribbean and the Atlantic World, 1750–1820* (Manchester: Manchester University Press, 2005), p. 187.

[18] See, for example: A. I. Macinnes, 'Landownership, land use and elite enterprise in Scottish Gaeldom: From clanship to clearance in Argyllshire, 1688-1858', in T. M. Devine (ed.), *Scottish Elites* (Edinburgh, 1994), pp. 1–42; D. Alston, 'Very rapid and splendid fortunes? Highland Scots in Berbice (Guyana) in the early nineteenth century', *Transactions of the Gaelic Society of Inverness*, 63 (2002), pp. 208–36; D. Hamilton, *Scotland, the Caribbean and the Atlantic World, 1750–1820* (Manchester: Manchester University Press, 2005); D. Hamilton, 'Transatlantic ties: Scottish migration networks in the Caribbean, 1750–1800', in A. McCarthy (ed.), *A Global Clan, Scottish Migrant Networks and Identities since the Eighteenth Century* (London: Taurus, 2006); A. I. Macinnes, 'Landownership, land use and elite enterprise in Scottish Gaeldom: From clanship to clearance in Argyllshire, 1688-c.1858', in J. Pan-Montojo and F. Pedersen (eds), *Communities in European History: Representations, Jurisdictions, Conflicts* (Pisa, 2007), pp. 47–64; F. McKichan, 'Lord Seaforth: Highland proprietor, Caribbean governor and slave owner', *The Scottish Historical Review*, 90:2 (2011), pp. 204–35; S. Kidd, 'Gaelic books as cultural icons: The maintenance of cultural links between the Highlands and the West Indies', in C. Sassi and T. van Heijnsbergen (eds), *Within and Without Empire: Scotland Across the (Post)colonial Borderline* (Newcastle: Cambridge Scholars Publishing, 2013), pp. 46–60; Mullen, 'The Great Glasgow West India house of John Campbell senior & Co.'; D. Alston, '"The habits of these creatures in clinging one to the other": Enslaved Africans, Scots and the plantations of Guyana', in T. M. Devine (ed.), *Recovering Scotland's Slavery Past: The Caribbean Connection* (Edinburgh: Edinburgh University Press, 2015), pp. 99–124; S. K. Kehoe, 'From the Caribbean to the Scottish Highlands: Charitable enterprise in the Age of Improvement, c.1750 to c.1820', *Rural History*, 27:1 (2016), pp. 37–59; D. Alston, 'Scottish slave-owners in Suriname: 1651–1863', *Northern Scotland*, 9:1 (2018), pp. 17–43; S. Mullen, 'John Lamont of Benmore: A Highland planter who died "in harness" in Trinidad', *Northern Scotland*, 9:1 (2018), pp. 44–66; C. Rosenthal, *Accounting for Slavery* (Cambridge, MA: Harvard University Press, 2018), pp. 75–9; F. McKichan, *Lord Seaforth: Highland Landowner, Caribbean Governor* (Edinburgh, 2018); D. Worthington, 'Sugar, slave-owning, Suriname and the Dutch imperial entanglement of the Scottish Highlands before 1707', *Dutch Crossing*, 44:1 (2020), pp. 3–20; Iain MacKinnon and Andrew Mackillop, 'Plantation slavery and landownership in the west Highlands and Islands: Legacies and lessons – A discussion paper', *Community Land Scotland*, available at <https://www.communitylandscotland.org.uk/

it seems both appropriate and timely to unravel these interests – firstly, by tracing the Gaelic Club's membership from its establishment in 1780 until the end of Caribbean slavery in 1838, and secondly, by examining connections between membership, visitors and transatlantic commerce. This chapter reveals – by a detailed analysis of surviving club minutes and other sources – an elite Highland–Caribbean nexus in Glasgow with high-level connections stretching across the British Atlantic world.[19]

Club business

The Gaelic Club (at first named the 'Gaelic Society') was established on 7 March 1780. 'A number of the Highland Gentlemen', the surviving minutes record, 'met to form themselves into a society', including the first Preses Mr George McIntosh and secretary Hugh McDiarmid, a Gaelic clergyman. A native of Ross-shire, Dr Hugh MacLeod, Professor of Church History at the University of Glasgow, was also among the early figures in the club. A charter from the Highland Society of London on 20 April 1780 confirmed the establishment of the Gaelic Club, which was intended to encourage 'native company occasionally and promoting whatever shall do honour to the name of Highlander in general or benefit any individual Gael'. In response, the Highland gentleman of Glasgow thanked the parent society 'as natives of the same Land, and as connected together by Dùthchas they wish'd to enlist themselves under the banner of such honourable and respectable Leaders'.[20] While the initial group were mainly Highland manufacturers and professionals in Glasgow, the transformation in membership of the Gaelic Club reflects the increasing involvement of Highlanders in the colonial trades in Glasgow and across the British Atlantic world more generally.

---

wp-content/uploads/2020/11/Plantation-slavery-and-landownership-in-the-west-Highlands-and-Islands-legacies-and-lessons.pdf> (last accessed 1 June 2021). David Alston, *Slaves and Highlanders* (Edinburgh: Edinburgh University Press, 2021).

[19] For Glasgow's elite society, see S. Nenadic, 'Middle rank consumers and domestic culture in Edinburgh and Glasgow, 1720–1840', *Past and Present*, 145 (1994), pp. 122–56; S. Nenadic, 'The rise of the urban middle class,' in T. M. Devine and R. Mitchison (eds), *People and Society in Scotland, vol. 1, 1760–1830* (Edinburgh: John Donald, 1994), pp. 109–26; I. Maver, *Glasgow* (Edinburgh: Edinburgh University Press, 2000). For Highland elites, see S. Nenadic, *Lairds and Luxury: The Highland Gentry in Eighteenth Century Scotland* (Edinburgh: John Donald, 2007).

[20] 'Minutes, vol. 1', 7 March 1780, 20 April 1780, 8 July 1780, TD746/1, GCA. For a recent account of the Highland Society in London, see K. L. McCullough, 'Building the Highland Empire: The Highland Society of London and the Formation of Charitable Networks in Great Britain and Canada, 1778–1857' (PhD thesis, University of Guelph, 2014). Traditionally, Dùthchas (up to c. 1800) was tied up with land and the hereditary right to land. By the twentieth century, the concept was also understood to mean 'birth tie'. *The Scottish National Dictionary* defines Dùthchas as: 1: 'The paternal seat, the dwelling of a person's ancestors', and 2: 'The possession of land by whatever right, whether by inheritance, by wadset, or by lease; if one's ancestors have lived in the same place.' Available at <https://www.dsl.ac.uk/entry/snd/duchas> (last accessed 3 April 2021).

With the parliamentary union of 1707, Scots gained access to the already established English Empire in the Americas. The English (then British) West Indies were created in successive eras of colonial expansion.[21] In the first phase from the 1600s, the islands of Barbados and Jamaica were settled – including by Scots holding proprietary grants and indentured servants – as well as St Kitts, Nevis and Antigua. Jamaica became renowned for well-established Scottish networks, including Highlanders.[22] Opportunities undoubtedly increased after the Seven Years War (1756–63), as Great Britain gained control of Grenada, Dominica, St Vincent and Tobago, while Trinidad, St Lucia and Demerara were added after victories in the Napoleonic and Revolutionary Wars (1793–1815). On the South American coast, the third-phase colonies of Berbice and Essequibo merged with Demerara to become British Guiana (now Guyana) in 1831. Recent work has underlined that Scottish Highlanders were pervasive across the latter colony.[23]

In North America, colonies such as Virginia and Maryland became British in 1707, and with the addition of the Carolinas and Georgia, Scots were presented with a vista of exploitative opportunities in what became the Thirteen Colonies. Between 1700 and 1815, around 90,000 Scots emigrated to North America, often as family units, with one-third departing from the Scottish Highlands.[24] The American War of Independence (1775–83) radically reshaped the British Atlantic world and in the process ended British control over America and the Glasgow merchants' monopoly in Chesapeake tobacco. What has been described as the city's tobacco era was over.[25] Though monopoly trade with the Thirteen Colonies was lost, Glasgow's West India merchants imported sugar and cotton, thus ensuring that slave economies powered Scotland's economic development up to 1838.

During Glasgow's successive colonial eras, many of the city's Highlanders resident focused on trade with British imperial zones. The establishment of the Gaelic Club on 7 March 1780 therefore coincided with the congregation of an increasingly powerful group of Highlanders in the commercial hub. At the first meeting, eight rules were established. The first stipulated the club was to meet on the first Tuesday of every month in Mrs Scheid's home at seven o'clock in the evening. For the first two hours of the meeting, the members were to 'converse in Gaelic, according to their abilities'. A Preses and secretary

---

[21] B. W. Higman, *Slave Populations of the British Caribbean, 1807–1834* (Kingston, Jamaica: University of West Indies Press, 1995), pp. 43–4.

[22] A. Karras, *Sojourners in the Sun* (Ithaca: Cornell Press, 1992).

[23] See Alston, '"The habits of these creatures in clinging one to the other"'.

[24] T. C. Smout, N. C. Landsman and T. M. Devine, 'Scottish emigration in the Early Modern Period', in N. Canny (ed.), *Europeans on the Move: Studies on European Migration, 1500–1800* (Oxford: Oxford University Press, 1996), pp. 76–112.

[25] T. M. Devine, 'The golden age of tobacco', in T. M. Devine and Gordon Jackson (eds), *Glasgow. Volume I: Beginnings to 1830* (Manchester: Manchester University Press, 1995), pp. 139–84.

were to be chosen biannually while new members – nominated by existing members – only gained successful entry if approved by a unanimous ballot. Strangers – also to be introduced by members – paid the same nightly fees as members. Members present at meetings paid bills (for food and drink) at eleven o'clock and if absent, a fine of one shilling was imposed, with fines collected biannually. Further regulations were added in the years to come. In November 1781, for example, the admission of strangers was regulated and from then on none entered without the permission of the Preses.[26] In June 1787, the developing Highland-Caribbean ethos of the club was confirmed as, from then on, all members had to attend the meetings in a 'tartan short coat … under the penalty of a bottle of rum'. If members chose additional Highland dress, they would be considered a 'more meritorious member of the society of the descendants of the clans of Caledonia'.[27]

Across the eighteenth century, tartan was an elite commodity used – by the Highland people themselves – as a marker of social status, to reinforce masculine identities and as a visual cultural emblem, including in portraiture.[28] The Gaelic Club adopted tartan dress not only to underline Highland identity but to associate its exclusively male membership with the region's burgeoning reputation for martial excellence. In spring 1802, the Gaelic Club members approved a uniform based upon the tartan plaid of the 42nd Regiment (Royal Highlanders), as their 'good conduct … [was] very flattering to the national character of the Scots Highlanders'.[29] Regulations relative to the club uniform were later broadened. In 1815 the Highland Society of London compiled a list of clan tartans and it seems the Gaelic Club's members were free to make the choice.[30] By 1831 members chose their own tartan trousers (although a kilt was acceptable), while each adopted the plaid of the clan they were 'entitled to use'. The uniform was complemented with dark-green short coats with an upright collar and silver buttons, and finished with black stockings and dirk, a handkerchief, tartan hose, shoes and a bonnet.[31] Highland dress remained part of the club's traditions at the same time as attitudes towards the geographical origins of the members were increasingly relaxed.

On 7 March 1798, the Gaelic Club was dissolved and re-established with new regulations that opened up the membership. From then, the club met on

---

[26] 'Minutes, vol. 2', 7 March 1780, 6 November 1781, TD746/2, GCA.
[27] 'Minutes, vol. 1', 7 June 1787, TD746/1, GCA.
[28] S. Tuckett, 'National dress, gender and Scotland: 1745–1822', *Textile History*, 40:2 (2009), pp. 140–51; M. P. Dziennik, 'Whig tartan: Material culture and its use in the Scottish Highlands, 1746–1815', *Past & Present*, 217:1 (2012), pp. 117–47; V. Coltman, 'Party-coloured plaid? Portraits of eighteenth-century Scots in tartan', *Textile History*, 41:2 (2010), pp. 182–216.
[29] 'Minutes, vol. 1', 15 January 1802, 10 February 1802, TD746/1, GCA.
[30] S. Tuckett, 'Reassessing the romance: Tartan as a popular commodity, c. 1770–1830', *The Scottish Historical Review*, 95:2 (2016), p. 198.
[31] 'Minutes, vol. 2', 10 January 1831, TD746/2, GCA.

the second Wednesday of every month between October and April.³² Existing members automatically gained entry, while new members had to be proposed and put to ballot (although two black balls were sufficient for refusal of entry). All members of the Gaelic Club were encouraged to join the Highland Society of Glasgow and meetings were afterwards held in the Black Bull at 640 Argyle Street in the city, property of the said society.³³ Thus, by making membership of the Highland Society compulsory, the Gaelic Club committee seemingly harnessed the wealth of its membership to support the education and clothing of Highland boys and girls. Also, and perhaps relatedly, the strict terms for membership were relaxed, opening the club up to new members. As noted, the ability to speak Gaelic was the initial criterion for membership, although by 1798, regulation five stated:

> That persons eligible to become members of the Club must be such as are Highlanders & speaking the Gaelic Language, or descended of Highland parents, or having landed property in the Highlands or who have served his Majesty in Highland or at least in Scots Regiments or who are *otherwise connected with or interested in the Highlands* [my italics].³⁴

This opened the club's doors to a new clientele and attendance was strictly enforced: if any member did not attend for a season they were automatically removed from membership. The new regulations stipulated only three strangers were allowed entry at any meeting although, as will be shown, this rule was not always adhered to. Nevertheless, visiting strangers were aware of the rules as soon as they arrived. As Littleton Dennis Teackle strolled into the club in July 1799, one of the members thrust into his hands a 'copy of the Regulations of the Society'.³⁵

After the rule change in 1798, the club met at four o'clock in the afternoon for dining.³⁶ Recording his visit in great detail, Littleton Dennis Teackle's journal provides a rare insight not only of the food on offer, but also the bespoke plates on which the turtle was served and the wider customs in the club:

> Altho, the Entertainment was in a Hotel the plate & everything the Fare was served up on appertain'd to the Society & each piece had this motto inscribed on it 'Commun nan Gael' in the Galic language it signifies 'the meeting of Highlanders' many emblems

---

³² 'Minutes, vol. 2', 7 March 1798, TD746/2, GCA.
³³ Strang, *Glasgow and its Clubs*, p. 112; see also C. Withers, 'Kirk, club and culture change: Gaelic chapels, Highland societies and the urban Gaelic subculture in eighteenth-century Scotland,' *Social History*, 10:2 (1985), pp. 171–92.
³⁴ 'Minutes, vol. 2', 7 March 1798, TD746/2, GCA.
³⁵ 'Teackle Diary, 1799–1800, vol. 1', pp. 112–15, MMC-1956, Littleton Dennis Teackle papers, LoC.
³⁶ 'Minutes, vol. 2', 7 March 1798, TD746/2, GCA.

were displayed. A curious horn containing snuff, with a spoon suspended, to feed the nostrils, and a brush to remove the superfluous particles. This vehicle was passed round the Table & used by every person present to keep up an established custom as likewise many other such like outre' ceremonies were performed to the infinite merriment of the company.[37]

This merriment lasted for hours, with the bill for food and drink collected from members exactly four hours later.[38] A more active form of socialising ensued; Highland dancing to the skirl of the bagpipes, as Teackle noted:

At 8 in the evening the glasses were removed which had been copiously used & a Troop of Bag-pipers were introduced who instantly began to tune their instruments the table was removed & the whole company, promiscuously, began to dance Highland reels & truly many of the Sawnies were excellent proficients in the active art. I was a willing witness of this capering for a little time.[39]

Less than a year after Teackle's visit, however, as 'frequent altercations take place amongst members in presence of strangers', a committee decided that club affairs (elections, nominations, ballots) should be held before dinner in order to retain some discretion. From then, strangers – carefully vetted in advance and invited only with 'approbation and consent of the Preses' – would attend only the club's social events.[40]

Club membership

Verifying individual attendees of the Gaelic Club has proven a more complex task than identifying the rules they had to abide by. Given the ubiquity of surnames such as McKenzie, Stewart, Robertson and especially Campbell among club members – with individuals sometimes identified only by surname – it is impossible to identify the full membership between 1780 and 1817. Membership seemed to peak at forty-one in 1800, although it was restricted to thirty in 1805.[41] Total membership from establishment up to 1817 is likely to have been close to one hundred. While Douglas Hamilton's claim that most of the leading West India merchants in Glasgow were members of the Gaelic Club is an exaggeration, it is evident this commercial grouping attended in increasing

---

[37] 'Teackle Diary, 1799–1800, vol. 1', p. 114, MMC-1956, Littleton Dennis Teackle papers, LoC.
[38] 'Minutes, vol. 2', 7 March 1798, TD746/2, GCA.
[39] 'Teackle Diary, 1799–1800, vol. 1', pp. 114–15, MMC-1956, Littleton Dennis Teackle papers, LoC.
[40] 'Minutes, vol. 1', 3 March 1800, TD746/1, GCA.
[41] 'Minutes, vol. 1', 3 March 1800; Strang, *Glasgow and its Clubs*, p. 114, TD746/1, GCA.

numbers after it was established.[42] Of the sixteen initial members in March 1780, just two – Robert Mackay of Robert McKay & Co. and John Robertson of Plantation – were prominent West India merchants in Glasgow. Another, Dugald Thomson, was in Jamaica by the time the minutes were recorded.[43] In 1784 Andrew Houston of Jordanhill, Robert Dunmore and John Campbell senior were all members, hinting at the post-war prominence of the West India interest in the club and the city in general.[44] When Littleton Dennis Teackle visited the club in July 1799 (after reconstitution of the rules around one year previously), eight of eighteen members in attendance (44 per cent) were probably involved with the West India trades in Glasgow.[45]

In November 1817, new regulations were again drawn up and a recorded census allows the historian to glimpse into the social background of the membership.[46] Between 1817 and 1838, fifty-four individuals were recorded as members of the Gaelic Club. Twenty were of the landed ranks, including major figures like Kirkman Finlay of Castle Toward. Duncan Macfarlan (1771–1857), the Principal of the University of Glasgow, became a member in 1827. Of the total membership of fifty-four registered between 1817 and 1838, seventeen (31 per cent) were connected to the West India trades in Glasgow, although there was a slight decline over the period. Of the twenty-seven members in the year 1817, ten (37 per cent) were West India merchants, while of the twenty-seven new members registered up to 1838, seven (25 per cent) were West India merchants. Especially after 1784, West India merchants and planters in Glasgow regularly attended, and often constituted over one-third of the membership the Gaelic Club up to 1838.

One Glasgow-West India dynasty stands out from the rest in the minutes of the club: those associated with the firm John Campbell senior & Co. The founder of the firm, John Campbell senior (c. 1735–1807), was the son of a Black Watch captain, Alexander Campbell of Kinloch. Initially John Campbell senior held shares in one of Glasgow's tobacco firms, although he established a West India firm that became a major force in the city.[47] In March 1784, John Campbell senior became a member of the Gaelic Club and his brother, Colin

---

[42] Hamilton, *Scotland, the Caribbean and the Atlantic World*, p. 187. The extent of merchants in the Glasgow West India trades hailing from the Highlands should not be overstated. Of the known residences of the fathers of 150 West India merchants in Glasgow between 1775 and 1838, only eleven (7 per cent) hailed from the Scottish Highlands or Hebrides. Of course, this does not factor in those of Highland descent like the second-generation Campbells whose fathers had relocated to Glasgow and surrounding areas. See S. Mullen, *The Glasgow Sugar Aristocracy: Scotland and Caribbean Slavery, 1775–1838* (London: University of London, 2022).
[43] 'Minutes, vol. 2', 7 March 1780, TD746/2, GCA.
[44] 'Minutes, vol. 1', 6 March 1784, TD746/1, GCA.
[45] 'Minutes, vol. 1', 18 July 1799, TD746/1, GCA.
[46] 'Minutes, vol. 2: Members, 1817–1870', TD746/2, GCA.
[47] Devine, *The Tobacco Lords*, p. 178.

Campbell of Park, followed in February 1790.[48] John Campbell senior's nephew and co-partner in the firm – 'Alexander Campbell junior of Grenada' – was also admitted a full member in 1792, although he was essentially a temporary attendee, living a transient Atlantic lifestyle between Scotland and Grenada, where he owned the estate *Marran* from which he took his nickname (in time he would be known as Alexander Campbell of Haylodge).[49]

Given this group were admitted to the Gaelic Club when conversation in Gaelic was a prerequisite for entry, some Glasgow merchants were evidently native speakers, while others took their language to the British West Indies with them. In return, Glasgow merchants introduced a taste of the Caribbean to the proceedings of the Gaelic Club. On 11 July 1798, John Campbell senior's cousin and senior co-partner Alexander Campbell of Hallyards 'very politely provided the Club with a Turtle ... upon which the above Gent[leme]n feasted like Aldermen!'.[50] After the death of Campbell of Hallyards in 1817, the club mourned a 'loss they so deeply regret'.[51] Others joined as initial members passed on. Overall, around ten of John Campbell senior's immediate relations were members of the Gaelic Club between 1790 and 1838. Several were involved with the family firm. Mungo Nutter Campbell (1785–1862) was the son of Alexander Campbell of Dallingburn, Collector of Customs at Port Glasgow (also a member of the club). Aged twenty-one in 1806, Mungo Nutter assumed co-partnership status in John Campbell senior & Co. and took up membership of the Gaelic Club on 8 December that year.[52] Across the duration of his membership of the Gaelic Club, he was prominent in commercial organisations: as a founding member of the pro-slavery lobbying group, the Glasgow West India Association in 1807, as Dean of Guild of the Merchants House in 1822 and as Lord Provost of Glasgow in 1824. Like some other West India merchants in Glasgow, Campbell retained a Highland connection with the purchase of Ballimore landed estate in Argyll.

A second generation of Campbells joined the Gaelic Club too. At least three of John Campbell senior's sons became members: Colin Campbell was admitted on 13 November 1809, his brother Alex Campbell of Possil sometime before 1813, and Thomas Campbell became a member on 13 November 1815.[53] Cousins also joined the club and West India firms almost concurrently. 'Black Mungo' Campbell (1793–1860) was a member of the Gaelic Club from October 1816.[54] He was the son of Alexander Campbell of Haylodge

---

[48] 'Minutes, vol. 1', 6 March 1784, 17 February 1790, TD746/1, GCA.
[49] 'Minutes, vol. 1', 11 January 1792, TD746/1, GCA.
[50] 'Minutes, vol. 1', 11 July 1798, TD746/1, GCA.
[51] 'Minutes, vol. 2', 13 October 1817, TD746/2, GCA.
[52] 'Minutes, vol. 1', 8 December 1806, TD746/1, GCA.
[53] 'Minutes, vol. 1', 13 November 1809, 8 March 1813, 13 November 1815, TD746/1, GCA.
[54] 'Minutes, vol. 1', 26 October 1816, TD746/1, GCA.

('Marran'), who returned from Grenada to Scotland and lived in luxury on a landed estate in Peeblesshire. In 1817 – the year after 'Black' Mungo joined the club – he matriculated as a burgess and guild brethren in Glasgow and was a co-partner in Glasgow-West India firm Robert Dennistoun & Company (some of this family were also members of the Gaelic Club).[55] In 1828 he became a co-partner in John Campbell senior & Co. when his father gifted him stock and shares.[56] He retained significant capital stock in the firm for over twenty years. Another co-partner of the firm, 'White' Mungo Campbell junior (1805–66) – so-called to distinguish him from his cousin 'Black' Mungo – was the son of Alexander Campbell of Hallyards and Barbara Campbell, daughter of Archibald Campbell of Jura.[57] He took up his deceased father's share in 1828 and became a member of the Gaelic Club the same year.[58] In addition to paternal relations among the membership, his maternal uncle, Colin Campbell of Jura, another prominent West India merchant in Glasgow, was also a full member.[59] 'Black' Mungo retained a senior role in John Campbell senior & Co. in the years leading up to the closing of the firm on 30 May 1858. By comparing when the Campbells took up co-partnerships in the firm and membership of the club, it is clear the young merchants marked their status as West India traders by also joining the club in an important rite of passage.

Other prominent West India merchants in Glasgow with Highland connections took up membership. James McInroy of Lude (1759–1825) was born near Pitlochry, Perthshire. By 1782 McInroy was in Demerara and came into the possession of large sugar estates and enslaved people. In 1790, with Charles Stewart Parker and others, he established McInroy Sandbach & Co. – known as McInroy Parker & Co. in Glasgow where the firm was based. A Liverpool office was established in 1804 – the company ultimately relocated and was renamed Sandbach, Tinné & Co. (discussed below in more detail). However, James McInroy remained in Glasgow and was a member of the Gaelic Club from 11 July 1798 until at least 1817. His son, James Patrick McInroy – also a co-partner in Sandbach, Tinné & Co. – also became a member of the club around 1820.[60]

---

[55] J. Anderson (ed.), *The Burgesses and Guild Brethren of Glasgow, 1751–1846* (Edinburgh: J. Skinner and Co., 1935), p. 307.
[56] 'Contract of Copartnery of Messrs John Campbell senior & Company, 1828', TD96, GCA.
[57] J. Burke and B. Burke, *A Genealogical and Heraldic Dictionary of the Landed Gentry of Great Britain & Ireland* (London: Holborn, 1847), p. 179.
[58] 'Minutes, vol. 2, Members 1817–1870', TD746/2, GCA; 'Contract of Copartnery of Messrs John Campbell senior & Company, 1828', TD96, GCA.
[59] 'Minutes, vol. 2, Members 1817–1870', TD746/2, GCA.
[60] 'Minutes, vol. 1', 11 July 1798, TD746/1, GCA; 'Minutes, vol. 2, Members 1817–1870', TD746/2, GCA; D. Alston, 'James McInroy', *Slaves & Highlanders*, available at <http://www.spanglefish.com/slavesandhighlanders/index.asp?pageid=552969> (last accessed 13 October 2018).

After the Jacobite Rising of 1745, Highland culture was increasingly assimilated into wider Scottish society, as Lowland elites absorbed the imagery of a romanticised Highlands to construct a new, late-eighteenth-century Scots-British identity (a process described as 'Highlandism'). The Lowland takeover of the Gaelic Club is a prime example: prominent merchants came to dominate a Gaelic Club which subsequently served as the cornerstone for an elite Highland-Caribbean identity in Glasgow.[61] Indeed, some Glasgow-West India merchants who frequented the Gaelic Club seem to have had geographically tenuous connections to the Scottish Highlands. Charles Stewart Parker – a member of the club at least from 1811 and likely before – was the son of James Parker of Glasgow, formerly of Virginia.[62] Charles Stewart Parker was senior partner in the firm McInroy, Parker & Co. – with James McInroy of Lude – that carried on business at Liverpool, Demerara and Glasgow.[63] He was chairman of the pro-slavery lobbying group, the Glasgow West India Association in 1825. His landed estate was located in Fairlie in Ayrshire. Another prominent West India merchant, Charles Stirling junior of Gargunnock (1796–1839), was a member of the Gaelic Club from 1820.[64] The son of John Stirling of Kippendavie in Stirlingshire, he was a partner in Stirling, Gordon & Co. and co-owner of *Content* estate in St James, Jamaica (and a claimant of slave compensation in 1834).[65] Another, William Leckie Ewing, was born in Broich, near Stirling, and became a partner in Stirling, Gordon & Co. His father was close personal friends with Kirkman Finlay who, of course, was a prominent merchant and member of the Gaelic Club. Leckie Ewing became a member around 1832.[66] The membership of Parker, Stirling and Leckie Ewing supports the view of John Strang, who argued the Gaelic Club became a 'most aristocratic brotherhood' of mercantile luminaries, especially after 1798 when an individual's status and connections rather than Highland origins decided membership.[67]

---

[61] T. M. Devine, *Clanship to Crofter's War: The Social Transformation of the Scottish Highlands* (Manchester: Manchester University Press, 1994), pp. 84–100; for an account of Highland imagery, see A. McLeod, *From an Antique Land: Visual Representations of the Highlands and Islands 1700–1880* (Edinburgh: John Donald, 2012).

[62] 'Minutes, vol. 1', 14 January 1811, TD746/1, GCA; *A List of Matriculated Members of the Merchant's House, From 3d October 1768, to 5th October 1857* (Glasgow: James McNab, 1858), p. 10.

[63] *Cases Decided in the Court of Session 1826–1827*, Vol. 5 (Edinburgh: William Blackwood, 1827), p. 389.

[64] 'Minutes, vol. 2, Members 1817–1870', TD746/2, GCA.

[65] W. Fraser, *The Stirlings of Keir, and their Family Papers* (Edinburgh, 1858), p. 109; 'Charles Stirling of Gargunnock,' in *Legacies of British Slave-ownership Database*, available at <http://wwwdepts-live.ucl.ac.uk/lbs/person/view/13388> (last accessed 13 October 2018).

[66] 'Minutes, vol. 2, Members 1817–1870', TD746/2, GCA; J. MacLehose, *Memoirs and Portraits of 100 Glasgow Men* (Glasgow: James MacLehose and Sons, 1886); 'William Leckie Ewing', in *Legacies of British Slave-ownership Database*, available at <http://wwwdepts-live.ucl.ac.uk/lbs/person/view/46466> (last accessed 13 October 2018).

[67] Strang, *Glasgow and its Clubs*, p. 108.

The Gaelic Club-West India cohort hailed mainly from middling backgrounds. The exception seems to be Colin Campbell of Jura and Craignish, one of the leading cadet families of the house of Argyll. Others had more modest backgrounds, while the majority were sons of established colonial merchants.[68] Robert Dunmore and Charles Stewart Parker were sons of 'tobacco lords' in Glasgow. The rise of John Campbell senior & Co.'s co-partners provides an instructive model: the first generation (John Campbell senior and brother Colin Campbell) were sons of the military from Argyll. Becoming successful West India merchants in Glasgow, relations – cousins and nephews – joined them in the firm and the club and subsequently introduced their sons, who became a second-generation West India cohort in their own right. In this way, membership of the Gaelic Club can be viewed as part of an improving process as Highlanders of middling stock entered Glasgow's elite mercantile ranks.

Connecting the Highlands and the Caribbean

Although the results of interactions at the Gaelic Club are impossible to gauge, frequenting the elite club likely enhanced reputations, engendered trust, consolidated personal relationships and, on occasion, underpinned transatlantic business dealings. Archibald Grahame, Cashier of the Thistle Bank, was admitted as a full member of the Gaelic Club of Glasgow on 1 October 1783.[69] As discussed below, the first visitor from the West Indies – William McAllan of Grenada – joined the club soon after in December that year. While their connection is unknown, Archibald Grahame afterwards entered into the West India business – likely with no experience of the colonies – via fellow club members. And his profiteering occurred – perhaps not coincidentally – at a time of internal warfare on the south-eastern island of Grenada. Grahame sent goods for sale to the colony during the uprising known as Fedon's Rebellion (1795–6), in which the island's economy was decimated with losses estimated at £2.5 million sterling.[70]

On 23 December 1795, Archibald Grahame sent a box of muslins to Grenada under the charge of the firm John Campbell senior & Co. Grahame requested the firm to 'give directions to your Correspondent in the West Indies to make the most of them'.[71] Grahame therefore requested his fellow club

---

[68] Of the twenty-three known West India merchants who were members in the Gaelic Club 1780–1838, occupations of fathers were known in eighteen cases: West India merchants or planters (10), military (2), 'tobacco lords' (2), Scottish laird (1), general merchant (1), farmer (1) and customs officer (1).

[69] 'Minutes, vol. 1', 1 October 1783, TD746/1, GCA.

[70] E. Cox, 'Fedon's Rebellion, 1795–96: Causes and consequences', *Journal of Negro History*, 67:1 (1982), p. 15.

[71] 'Copy Invoice of Goods Consigned to Mer[chants] J. Campbell sen. & Co. & letter from Arch. Grahame', 23 December 1795, GB1830 THI/14/10, Lloyds Banking Group Archives (Edinburgh).

members and prominent merchants to compel associates in the colonies to sell his goods for the highest prices. This was not a one-off. On 30 October 1797, Archibald Grahame wrote to Alexander Stewart in St George's, Grenada, revealing their 'mutual friend' Mr Alexander Campbell (likely Hallyards) had passed him the account. For his own records, Grahame annotated the side of the letter: 'forwarded through the hands of Mr. Alex. Campbell, whom I requested to use his influence with Mr. Stewart to make the most of goods and remit'.[72] Once again, Grahame compelled fellow club members to influence connections in Grenada – Scots he had likely never met resident on an island he never set foot on – to achieve the highest price possible and send the profits to Scotland. The goods were eventually sold in 1801 – including to several Campbells on the island, the wives or daughters of the firm's representatives – and the proceeds of £365 Grenada currency (c. £237 sterling) sent to Glasgow. A contemporary estimate suggests this could be worth around £272,000 in 2019 values.[73]

This example is significant for two reasons. Firstly, it shows how the firm of John Campbell senior & Co. profited from business generated by those unconnected to the West India trades. Secondly, Archibald Grahame was able to take advantage of the resources in the Gaelic Club's commercial network for personal gain. This bank cashier, with limited or no experience of the West Indies and certainly no mercantile reputation in Glasgow, accessed colonial markets by accessing the networks of fellow members of the club. He was provided access to transatlantic shipping and markets in Grenada. In the process, he requested the firm influence colonial representatives for his advantage, while on another occasion, Grahame cited a prominent West India merchant as a mutual friend to promote his own interests. Although it was common for business to be undertaken in the colonies by direct kin connections, on this occasion friendships underpinned by membership of the Gaelic Club generated trust and ultimately capital in the colonies. Facilitated by commercial networks of the Gaelic Club, this huckster-type arrangement remains largely invisible in the historiography of the economics of Scotland and the Caribbean.

(hereafter LBGAE). I am grateful to Siân Yates, Archivist, Group Archives & Museum at Lloyds Banking Group for permission to quote.

[72] 'Copy Letter from Archibald Grahame Thistle Bank, Glasgow to Alex. Stewart, St George's, Grenada', 30 October 1793, GB1830 THI/14/10, LBGAE.

[73] 'A/C Sales Muslins, Thornton, Orr & Co.', GB1830 THI/14/10, LBGAE. According to one contemporary source, 'the currency of Grenada, or rate of exchange, is commonly sixty-five per cent worse than sterling'. See W. Winterbottom, *Historical, Geographical, Commercial and Philosophical View of the American United States*, 2nd edn, Vol. 4 (London: J. Ridgeway, 1795), p. 264. Modern values of £267 sterling in 1801 (estimated here using a Relative Wage Income: Average Earnings, 2019 values) are derived from L. H. Officer and S. H. Williamson, 'Five Ways to Compute the Relative Value of a UK Pound Amount, 1270 to Present', *Measuring Worth 2021*, available at <www.measuringworth.com/ukcompare/> (last accessed 4 April 2021).

There is some evidence that the Gaelic Club-West India cohort were relatively more successful than others. Large-scale merchants like Charles Stewart Parker (£117,329), James McInroy (£172,912) and Colin Campbell (£169,350) were supremely successful and left nationally significant fortunes, while others such as 'Black' Mungo Campbell and William Leckie Ewing left much less and James Robert Dennistoun was almost bankrupt on death. However, the average fortunes (£48,353) left by this group were almost 20 per cent more than those left on death (£40,352) by the subscribers of the pro-slavery Glasgow West India Association (an organisation some of this cohort also subscribed to).[74] Thus, West India merchants of Highland stock in Glasgow tended to be more financially successful than the average. Wealth did not always convert to social status, however, although the Gaelic Club allowed the merchants and their guests to mix with high society at elite events.

Members of the Gaelic Club enjoyed the privilege of inviting guests to events – as 'strangers' – although these individuals were carefully vetted in advance, presumably to verify rank and status.[75] Examination of such invitees in the period 1780 to 1838 reveals a cross-section of high society, merchants, manufacturers as well as imperial statesmen and commercial adventurers returned from the British colonies. Members of the Scottish aristocracy sometimes attended. On 10 January 1804, an 'extra meeting' was hastily organised as the Duke of Montrose had accepted an invitation to attend. Of the Gaelic Club-West India cohort, Alexander Campbell of Haylodge was in attendance, as well as Archibald Campbell of Jamaica and Colin Campbell of Jura. Ten strangers attended, including the Duke of Montrose and the Lord Provost of Glasgow. The club thus acted as an important platform that facilitated connections with the Scottish gentry, influential politicians and Highlanders, sometimes of lesser rank.[76] Imperial statesmen of the highest importance also attended the club.

At a meeting of the Gaelic Club held in the Black Bull Inn on 13 February 1799, thirteen members of the club were in attendance alongside six strangers. Among the members was Archibald Campbell of Jamaica, while the strangers included John Alston (possibly West India merchant John Alston of Westerton) and the Right Honourable Dundas.[77] This was almost certainly Henry Dundas, MP for Edinburgh, Home Secretary (1791–4), Secretary of State for War (1794–1801) and the leading Scottish imperial statesman. The Gaelic Club's members were

---

[74] Of the twenty-three known West India merchants who were members of the Gaelic Club 1780–1838, confirmation inventories generated on death were found for fifteen. The total wealth was £725,308, with an average wealth of £48,353. This compares favourably to the average wealth left by sixty-eight subscribers of the Glasgow-West India Association. See S. S. Mullen, 'The Glasgow West India Interest: Integration, Collaboration and Exploitation in the British Atlantic World, 1776–1846' (PhD thesis, University of Glasgow, 2015), p. 217.
[75] 'Minutes, vol. 1', 3 March 1800, TD746/1, GCA.
[76] 'Minutes, vol. 1', 10 January 1804, TD746/1, GCA.
[77] 'Minutes, vol. 1', 13 February 1799, TD746/1, GCA.

Table 7.1 Residence of Atlantic world-based 'Strangers' at the Gaelic Club, 1780–1838

Colony	1780–99	1800–10	1811–20	1821–30	1831–8	Total
Berbice	0	3	0	0	1	4 (10%)
Demerara	0	3	10	6	0	19 (49%)
Essequibo	0	0	3	0	0	3 (8%)
Grenada	1	1	0	0	0	2 (5%)
Jamaica	3	1	1	1	2	8 (20%)
Trinidad	0	0	0	0	1	1 (3%)
'West Indies'	0	1	1	0	0	2 (5%)
	4	9	15	7	4	39

Source: Glasgow City Archives (hereafter GCA) TD746/1, 'Minutes of the Gaelic Club, Vol. 1'; TD746/2, 'Minutes of Gaelic Club, Vol. 2'.

'highly satisfied with Lord Dundasses [sic] good humour & happiness & much gratified with the Honour of his company'.[78] While it is difficult to ascertain the outcome of the Dundas visit, his widespread dispensation of patronage to Scots across the British Empire was well known and perhaps some favours were granted. That he visited at all confirms the club's status as an elite venue in Glasgow for imperial statesmen and those involved with the colonial trades.

Individuals who had returned from the Caribbean and South America seem to be the most frequent group of strangers to attend the Gaelic Club between 1780 and 1838, with almost forty named in the surviving minutes.[79] In the minutes, the secretary noted the guests' various home residences or at least where they had recently arrived from. As Table 7.1 shows, these men mainly hailed from Demerara followed by Jamaica and Berbice, although Grenada, Trinidad and Essequibo were numbered among the locations too. These

---

[78] 'Minutes, vol. 1', 13 February 1799, TD746/1, GCA.

[79] The following individuals and colonies were identified in 'Minutes, vol. 1', TD746/1, GCA: Wm Lammie, Jamaica, 1 December 1783; Wm McAllan, Grenada, 1 December 1783; Mr Garden, Jamaica, 12 December 1798; Archibald Campbell, Jamaica, 13 February 1799; Thomson, West Indies, 8 January 1800; Houston, Grenada, 13 January 1806; Alex Campbell, 7 March 1808; Evan Fraser, Demerara, 11 October 1808; McPherson, Demerara, 11 December 1809; Pat Rose, Berbice, 13 February 1810; Simon Fraser, Berbice, 16 April 1810; Simon Fraser, Berbice, 8 October 1810; Thomas Cumin, Demerara, 12 November 1810; Hugh Mackenzie, Demerara, 14 October 1811; Crawford, West Indies, 13 January 1812; Tinné, Demerara, 11 January 1813; John McIntosh, Demerara, 11 October 1813; Hugh Mackenzie, Demerara, 11 October 1813; Francis Abeyars, Demerara, 15 November 1813; H. McKenzie, Demerara, 15 November 1813; Chas. McIntosh, Demerara, 13 December 1813; Wm McPherson, Demerara, 13 December 1813; Jas McPherson, Essequibo, 10 October 1814; Jas McPherson, Essequibo, 14 November 1814; Wm Robertson, Demerara, 9 January 1815; McLean, Jamaica, 9 January 1815; Jas McPherson, Essequibo, 13 February 1815; Simson, Demerara, 10 February 1817. The following individuals and colonies were identified in 'Minutes, vol. 2', TD746/2, GCA: McPherson, Demerara, 10 December 1821; McLaggan, Demerara, 11 November 1822; Evan Fraser, Demerara, 13 October 1823; Alex Munro, Demerara, 12 October 1823; E. B. Manson, Demerara, 10 January 1825; Colin MacRae, Demerara, 7 March 1827; Ferguson, Jamaica, 13 December 1830; McLennan, Berbice, 10 January 1831; M. Campbell, Trinidad, 20 April 1835; W. C. Campbell, Jamaica, 11 January 1836; M. Campbell, Jamaica, 10 December 1838.

individuals were invited by club members, which adds a transatlantic dimension to the argument that Highlanders clung together in Demerara.[80] The Scottish Highland's Guiana merchants, planters and returned sojourners clung together in Glasgow too.

The first known visitors from the West Indies – William McAllan from Grenada and Wm Lammie from Jamaica – attended the club on 1 December 1783 and were voted in as full members.[81] The first stranger (that is, who attended on an ad hoc basis) was 'Mr Thomson from the West Indies', which could have been former club member Dugald Thomson.[82] Another in 1806, simply titled 'Houston of Grenada', was likely Alexander Houston of Clerkington, MP for Glasgow Burghs (1802–3) and Lieutenant-Governor of Grenada (1796–1802).[83] The names of other strangers were recorded in full, which makes it easier for the historian to identify both individuals and business connections. On 11 October 1808, Mr Evan Fraser of Demerara visited the club as a stranger alongside eight members, including two co-partners of John Campbell senior & Co.: Alexander Campbell of Hallyards (who was Preses that evening) and Mungo Nutter Campbell.[84] By 1822, Evan Fraser was the owner of two estates in Demerara and was heavily indebted to the firm, which perhaps formed the basis of discussions during his second visit to the Gaelic Club on 13 October 1823.[85] The long-term commercial dealings between the powerful Glasgow-West India merchants and the Demerara planter might have been sealed during a night of merriment in the Black Bull Inn.

On average, strangers from the Caribbean and South America visited the Gaelic Club every eighteen months. Most of these strangers were Scotsmen likely visiting the Gaelic Club for social purposes but in doing so supplied an important flow of information. On 12 November 1810, 'Thomas Cuming Esq of Demerara' was unanimously admitted as an honorary club member following recommendation by Campbell of Hallyards.[86] Formerly of Morayshire, Cuming spent fifty years in Demerara – as 'the patriarch and benefactor' of the colony – acquiring several large plantations before leaving for good in 1810.[87] Perhaps Cuming and others like him arrived at Clyde ports on their way home

---

[80] Alston, '"The habits of these creatures in clinging one to the other"', pp. 99–124.
[81] 'Minutes, vol. 1', 1 December 1783, TD746/1, GCA.
[82] 'Minutes, vol. 1', 8 January 1800, TD746/1, GCA.
[83] 'Minutes, vol. 1', 13 January 1806, TD746/1, GCA; W. I. Addison, *The Matriculation Albums of the University of Glasgow, From 1728 to 1858* (Glasgow: James Maclehose and Sons, 1913), p. 139.
[84] 'Minutes, vol. 1', 10 October 1808, TD746/1, GCA.
[85] E. Moore, *Reports of Cases Heard and Determined by the Judicial Committee and the Lords of Her Majesty's Most Honourable Privy Council, vol. 2, 1837–1838* (London: V&R Stevens, 1840), pp. 276, 293; 'Minutes, vol. 2', 13 October 1823, TD746/2, GCA.
[86] 'Minutes, vol. 1', 12 November 1810, TD746/1, GCA.
[87] *The Essequibo and Demerary Royal Gazette*, 15 June 1813; see Alston, 'Very rapid and splendid fortunes?'.

and made a point of visiting fellow Highlanders at the Gaelic Club to discuss commercial business and the prosperity of kith and kin in the colonies.

Not all of these strangers were Scots. At a monthly meeting of the Gaelic Club on 11 January 1813, James McInroy was acting as Preses while his co-partner in McInroy, Parker & Co., Charles Stewart Parker, was present alongside twelve ordinary members. Among the three strangers in attendance was a man simply recorded as 'Tinné Esq. of Demerary'.[88] This was almost certainly Philip Frederick Tinné (1772–1844), born in the Netherlands and a large-scale merchant and planter in Demerara.[89] There was a long transatlantic history behind this meeting. As noted above, James McInroy had been resident in Demerara in 1782 and eventually established McInroy, Parker & Co. in Glasgow with a Liverpool office. In 1813 Philip Frederick Tinné became a partner and afterwards the firm became known as Sandbach, Tinné & Co., the second-largest mercantile beneficiary of compensation from the British government when slavery was abolished in the British West Indies in 1834.[90]

In the firm's surviving records – now held in the University of London – the first mention of Sandbach, Tinné & Co. was on 22 July 1813, almost six months to the day after the meeting in the Gaelic Club. This letter revealed plans for the new business, including the sale of offices in late January. It is probable, therefore, that the visit of Mr 'Tinné Esq. of Demerary' to the Gaelic Club in January 1813 confirmed the establishment of what became one of the major West India merchant firms in the nineteenth-century British Atlantic world. The Gaelic Club of Glasgow seems an appropriate venue for a Dutch planter to discuss the formation of a firm in Demerara, one whose expansion would have grim consequences for the lives of many hundreds of enslaved people in what became British Guiana.[91]

Another 'stranger', Colin Macrae, visited the Gaelic Club on 7 March 1827, alongside full member Mungo Campbell.[92] Macrae had strong commercial links with Campbell's firm, John Campbell senior & Co., over several years. Macrae was based in Demerara as an attorney for the firm, but resided in London from June 1826 and attended meetings of the London West India Committee – the most powerful pro-slavery group in the British Atlantic world – and was heavily involved with the Berbice and Demerara sub-committee established in

---

[88] 'Minutes, vol. 1', 11 January 1813, TD746/1, GCA.
[89] 'Philip Frederick Tinné', *Legacies of British Slave-ownership Database*, available at <http://wwwdepts-live.ucl.ac.uk/lbs/person/view/8963> (last accessed 13 October 2018).
[90] D. Alston, 'James McInroy', in *Slaves & Highlanders*. For Sandbach, Tinné & Co., see N. Draper, *The Price of Emancipation: Slave-Ownership, Compensation and British Society at the End of Slavery* (Cambridge: Cambridge University Press, 2010), p. 236.
[91] 'Letter to Sandbach Tinné & Co. from McInroy Parker & Co. re insurance and shipping', 22 July 1813, ICS70/14, University of London; 'Minutes, vol. 1', 11 January 1813, TD746/1, GCA.
[92] 'Minutes, vol. 2', 7 March 1827, TD746/2, GCA.

November that year.[93] Thus, what appears in the club minutes as a social visit by a Demerara-based attorney, also presented Glasgow West India merchants with the opportunity to shape opinion at the highest level.

While there was an obvious colonial dimension to the Gaelic Club networks, events hosted in Glasgow reinforced the ranks and elite status of the members in the west of Scotland. At a monthly meeting on 1 February 1792, the hierarchy of the Gaelic Club 'resolved to give as Entertainment to the Ladies' an elite ball on the club's anniversary, 7 March. A committee laid out rules which included invitations to ensure only ladies of the correct sort would be in attendance:

> The company shall consist of the members & honorary members of the club, with their wives, and such of their families, and ladies being with their families as are of a proper age to attend and should any of the married Ladies find it inconvenient to be present, their husbands, as well as the unmarried members shall be entitled each to name a Lady who shall be invited.

The event on 7 March 1792 passed off with festivity.[94] Grand balls became a recurrent event in club business: another was held on 21 April 1821 – organised by Mungo Nutter Campbell – which was said to have been held in 'style and splendour hitherto unequalled in this Country'. Held in the Assembly Rooms on the north side of Ingram Street, members appeared in club uniform, whilethe club piper played the traditional tune 'The Gathering of the Clans' in a ballroom surrounded by a border of Scottish thistles. There was a crowd of around 160 ladies and gentlemen in attendance.[95]

Another ball held on 23 March 1831 attracted 230 guests. The minutes recorded: 'never did a Ball in the City of Glasgow cause much an anxiety it may be said ferment amongst the Ladies, all wishful that it might be their happy lot to be present'.[96] The outcomes of pairing eligible young people in elite venues is difficult to ascertain. Nevertheless, it seems likely the Gaelic Club-West India cohort tended to marry among themselves. Of the twenty-three known West India merchants attending the club, five (21 per cent) married daughters of other Highland families associated with the Gaelic Club between 1780 and 1838. Colin Campbell of Jura married Isabella Hamilton Dundas Dennistoun, daughter of Richard Dennistoun (although it is unclear if he was a member, several of his family line were). In 1800 Alexander Campbell of Hallyards married Barbara, the daughter of Colin Campbell of Jura. Alexander Campbell

---

[93] 'West India Committee Records: Minutes of the Demerara & Berbice Committee', 13 November 1826, SC89 6/4, Alma Jordan Library, The University of the West Indies, St Augustine (Trinidad and Tobago).
[94] 'Minutes, vol. 1', 1 February 1792, 7 March 1792, TD746/1, GCA.
[95] 'Minutes, vol. 2', 24 April 1821, TD746/2, GCA.
[96] 'Minutes, vol. 2', 23 March 1831, TD746/2, GCA.

of Haylodge married the daughter of John Robertson. In 1809 Mungo Nutter Campbell married his first cousin, Helen, daughter of John Campbell senior. Thomas Campbell, son of John Campbell senior, married Agnes, daughter of Kirkman Finlay.[97] These balls, therefore, were not only public expressions of Highland identity in Glasgow, but perhaps encouraged intermarriage among sons and daughters of the mercantile ranks, creating an elite Highland community in the city.

Conclusion

This article has approached the study of the Gaelic Club as a social network in its broadest sense.[98] In this context, a number of conclusions can be made. In theory, there were three distinct levels of social networks at play in the Gaelic Club of Glasgow. The inclusion of individuals in each grouping was based on social rank, gender and occupation.

Firstly, the regulations of 1780 created a permanent (by endorsement) male-only membership of Gaelic speakers – initially manufacturers and merchants – although rule changes in 1798 allowed incorporation of the wider mercantile elite. In practical terms, the club created an elite Highland community in late eighteenth- and early nineteenth-century Glasgow. Many of the first generation of West India merchants – such as John Campbell senior – were of modest backgrounds and had no connections to Glasgow. Membership of the Gaelic Club had considerable reputational consequences for its members, many of whom included the wealthiest West India merchants in the city. This article underlines Highlanders and those of Highland descent were at the commanding heights of the West India trades during Glasgow's 'golden age' of sugar (1790–1838). The many influential Highland West India merchants tended to congregate around the Gaelic Club. The interaction within the club network was important too. The banker Archibald Grahame's profiteering in Grenada during Fedon's Rebellion could not have been undertaken without fellow club members associated with John Campbell senior & Co. There was also considerable interaction with local and national political networks. In Glasgow, some of the Gaelic Club members took up influential political office, such as Dean of Guild and the Lord Provost, while others were involved with the Glasgow West India Association.

Secondly, there was a temporary (by appointment) male-only network of 'strangers' invited to the club. The strangers brought information from the

---

[97] Mullen, 'The Great Glasgow West India house of John Campbell senior & Co.', pp. 127–8.
[98] For a discussion of eighteenth-century networks and the study of them, see I. Baird, 'Introduction: Social Networks in the Long Eighteenth Century: The public sphere revisited', in I. Baird, *Social Networks in the Long Eighteenth Century* (Newcastle: Cambridge Scholars Publishing, 2014), pp. 1–31.

Caribbean and, in conjunction with the intelligence of the club's West India membership, this meant the Scottish Highlands were only ever one or two steps from the Caribbean towards the end of slavery in the British colonies. The transfer of information and more importantly influence can only be surmised.

Thirdly, the club was annually opened up to a temporary (by invitation) group of female attendees who appeared at grand balls each anniversary on 7 March. The invitation of ladies of the proper rank introduced them to eligible club members, including many affluent West India merchants. In turn, there was a high incidence of the Gaelic-West India cohort marrying daughters of other Highlanders in Glasgow, thus retaining slavery-derived fortunes within the community.

The Gaelic Club therefore promoted the interests of the West India cohort in two important ways; by generating business opportunities for the merchants and also attendees not involved with West India commerce, while the social events created a community and likely encouraged pairings which meant fortunes derived from slavery remained in the hands of the second- and third-generation Highland families. In this way, the Gaelic Club of Glasgow helped maximise the accumulation of wealth derived from Caribbean slavery among its members, as well as promoting the long-term retention of such fortunes among the elite Highland community in the west of Scotland.

EIGHT

Family, Society and Highland Identity in an Industrial World

Don Nerbas

Hugh MacLennan set his 1951 novel *Each Man's Son* in the town of his birth, early twentieth-century Glace Bay, Nova Scotia. At the time he was born, in 1907, Glace Bay was a booming coal town in the fast-growing industrial area at the eastern tip of Cape Breton Island, and his father, Samuel, was a colliery doctor for the Dominion Coal Company. The century before, in 1832, MacLennan's great-grandfather, Neil, had arrived in Cape Breton with the great wave of Highland migration to the island in the 1820s and 1830s and settled in Malagawatch. *Each Man's Son* is situated within a common experience of outmigration from the countryside, which had shaped MacLennan's own family history. It is, in MacLennan's telling, a tragic story of Highlanders leaving behind bucolic home communities for the 'country of coal', where they experienced a sudden and disorienting departure from a past 'unblighted by the mines'.[1] Fighting and drinking appear in the novel as symptoms of cultural despair and displacement among Gaelic-speaking miners lost in the modern world. Archie MacNeil, a brawny prize fighter and would-be miner living away in the United States, embodies this incapacity. Dan Ainslie, a local doctor tortured by his Calvinism, is closer to MacLennan's own experience. These two characters, Ainslie and MacNeil, drive the narrative arc of *Each Man's Son* to its tragic conclusion and stand for the profound class divisions of the mining town: 'It was hard to believe, in the grounds of the doctor's house, that the beginning of the miners' row was less than a quarter mile away.'[2] Though born in Glace Bay, MacLennan resided in Montreal and had limited direct experience with the coal town. His romantic, tragic representation of Glace Bay and its Highland residents was itself a metropolitan projection upon a hinterland community, reconstructed through ethnic essentialism and class stereotypes. Nonetheless, the

---

[1] H. MacLennan, *Each Man's Son*, with introduction by R. Marchand (Montreal and Kingston: McGill-Queen's University Press, 2018 [1951]), p. 39; for MacLennan's family history, see Marchand's introduction, pp. xviii–xxi.
[2] MacLennan, *Each Man's Son*, p. 26.

novel and MacLennan's own social origins suggest an important, yet often understated, historical fact: those who migrated from Highland settlements in rural Cape Breton were not all destined to work underground; a significant number joined a middle class that expanded with the making of industrial Cape Breton and constituted an important element of the social order.[3]

Historians have noted the impact of the Highland majority that emerged at the mines during the nineteenth century in the shaping of a distinctive working-class culture in Cape Breton's coal towns.[4] But what of individuals such as Samuel MacLennan and their families? What of their participation in the emerging middle class? Answers to this question are not only underdeveloped in this specific instance. In the broader Canadian literature, 'Highland enclave settlements' have often been treated as outside and conceptually distinct from urban-industrial society.[5] Through a close reading of the papers of William McDonald, a businessman and Conservative politician in the Glace Bay area during the later nineteenth and early twentieth centuries, this chapter reconstructs the making of a prominent family from the composite Highland community that developed in Cape Breton's coal district.[6] In so doing, it provides a case study of how industrialism, class formation and colonial nationalism recast Highland identities in the Atlantic world during the long nineteenth century.

---

[3] For a corrective to MacLennan's depiction of Glace Bay, see D. MacGillivray, 'Glace Bay: Images and impressions', in B. H. D. Buchloh and R. Wilkie (eds), *Mining Photographs and Other Pictures, 1948–1968* (Halifax and Sydney: Nova Scotia College of Art & Design Press and University College of Cape Breton Press, 1983), pp. 170–91.

[4] See D. MacGillivray, 'The Scottish Factor in Cape Breton Labour' (unpublished paper, 1979); D. Muise, 'The making of an industrial community: Cape Breton coal towns, 1867–1900', in D. Macgillivray and B. Tennyson (eds), *Cape Breton Historical Essays* (Sydney: University College of Cape Breton Press, 1980), pp. 76–94; D. Frank, 'Tradition and culture in the Cape Breton mining community in the early twentieth century', in K. Donovan (ed.), *Cape Breton at 200: Historical Essays in Honour of the Island's Bicentennial* (Sydney: UCCB Press, 1985), pp. 203–18. For a historiographical discussion and consideration of some new evidence on the Highland factor in Cape Breton's country of coal, see D. Nerbas, 'Scots, capitalism, and the colonial countryside: Impressions from nineteenth-century Cape Breton', *History Compass*, 18:11 (2020), pp. 1–12.

[5] See, for instance, C. W. Dunn, *Highland Settler: A Portrait of the Scottish Gael in Cape Breton and Eastern Nova Scotia* (Toronto: University of Toronto Press, 1953); D. Campell and R. A. MacLean, *Beyond the Atlantic Roar: A Study of the Nova Scotia Scots* (Toronto: McClelland and Stewart, 1974); J. M. Bumsted, *The Peoples' Clearance: Highland Emigration to British North America, 1770–1815* (Edinburgh: Edinburgh University Press, 1982); M. McLean, *The People of Glengarry: Highlanders in Transition, 1745–1820* (Montreal and Kingston: McGill-Queen's University Press, 1991); J. I. Little, *Crofters and Habitants: Settler Society, Economy, and Culture in a Quebec Township, 1848–1881* (Montreal and Kingston: McGill-Queen's University Press, 1991); L. H. Campey, 'The Regional Characteristics of Scottish Emigration to British North America, 1784–1854' (PhD thesis, University of Aberdeen, 1997); M. Bennett, *Oatmeal and the Catechism: Scottish Gaelic Settlers in Quebec*, revised edn (Edinburgh: John Donald Publishers, 2003 [1998]).

[6] William McDonald fonds, MG 9.23, Cape Breton University, Beaton Institute Archives [hereafter BI].

I

William McDonald was born in the backlands at River Denys Mountain in 1837. His father, grandparents and relatives had left South Uist a decade before, in 1826, departing from Greenock aboard a vessel that unceremoniously deposited them at St Andrew's, New Brunswick, to take on a load of timber. They eventually made it to their Cape Breton destination and acquired land grants, participating in a dramatic acceleration of settler colonialism in which recently displaced Highlanders became dispossessors of Mi'kmaw people.[7] These McDonalds were of a Clan Ranald sept – *Sliochd Iain Dubh nan Cathan* (The Tribe of Black John of the Battles) – likely descended from the third tackman of Howbeg. In South Uist, William's grandfather, Donald McDonald, had been responsible for the keeping of the partially restored Ormacleit Castle, a position inherited from his father, Aodh.[8] William's grandmother, Catherine MacLellan, also came from a family that 'had a high rating in the native land'.[9] A significant number of Donald and Catherine's grandchildren, like William, left backland farms in Cape Breton to assume positions of importance, which suggests the transfer of social advantages to the colonial environment. William's mother, Mary, arrived in Nova Scotia around 1829 with her father William McDonald of Barra. Young William grew up on a homestead surrounded by kin and acquired sufficient education to begin teaching by sixteen years of age before moving on to St Francis Xavier College in Antigonish, the educational centre for the training of the priests and lay leaders of the Scottish-Catholic communities of north-eastern Nova Scotia. He briefly attended the College, until June 1859, and then relocated to the Grand Narrows area, at Iona, to teach school.[10]

---

[7] A. Parnaby, 'The cultural economy of survival: The Mi'kmaq of Cape Breton in the mid-19th century', *Labour / Le Travail*, 61 (Spring 2008), pp. 69–98; W. C. Wicken, *The Colonization of Mi'kmaw Memory and History, 1794–1928: The King v. Gabriel Sylliboy* (Toronto: University of Toronto Press, 2012); J. G. Reid, 'Scots, settler colonization, and Indigenous displacement: Mi'kma'ki, 1770–1820, in comparative context', *Journal of Scottish Historical Studies*, 38:1 (2018), pp. 178–96; S. K. Kehoe, 'Catholic Highland Scots and the colonisation of Prince Edward Island and Cape Breton Island, 1772–1830', in S. K. Kehoe and M. E. Vance (eds), *Reappraisals of British Colonisation in Atlantic Canada, 1700–1930* (Edinburgh: Edinburgh University Press, 2020), pp. 77–92.

[8] J. L. MacDougall, *History of Inverness County, Nova Scotia* (Truro: Truro News Print, 1922), pp. 503–7; D. E. Rea and A. J. Gillis, 'Origins of some pioneer families of River Denys Mtn. and Area, Inverness Co., Cape Breton Island', p. 19, Allan J. Gillis fonds, MG 6, 9 J (1), BI; 'The Hon. W. MacDonald, Senator', *The Fiery Cross: A Monthly Illustrated Magazine for Scottish Canadians*, May 1896, p. 1. See also the description of River Denys Mountain within the context of piping in J. G. Gibson, *Old and New World Highland Bagpiping* (Montreal and Kingston: McGill-Queen's University Press, 2002), pp. 244–6.

[9] MacDougall, *History of Inverness County*, p. 508.

[10] 'William McDonald', typescript, n.d., p. 2, and clipping 'Hon. William McDonald, Glace Bay, N.S.', *The Newspaper Reference Book*, p. 177, William McDonald B & G file, MS 9, 23, BI; A. A.

Around 1861 William McDonald arrived in Lingan. He initially found work as a teacher, but he was most likely drawn there by the mining boom.[11] The London-based General Mining Association (GMA) had commenced mining in Lingan in 1854. By the time of McDonald's arrival, production at the mines was fast expanding. In 1861 coal shipped from Lingan Mines more than doubled the previous year's output, exceeding 35,000 tons.[12] An end to the GMA's monopoly over Nova Scotia's coal had been negotiated only a few years earlier, and new mines nearby at Little Glace Bay and Cow Bay were evidence of a wider boom on the Sydney coalfield.[13] As early as 1863 he was named by Donald McDonald and James McNeil to act for them in their efforts, ultimately unsuccessful, to procure a mining lease at Little Glace Bay.[14]

Before his arrival in Lingan, McDonald's life had been spent in a countryside dominated by Highland settlement. Lingan was a somewhat more diverse environment by comparison. Families such as the Laffins and Youngs had settled in the area before the development of the coal mine.[15] Writing from Grand Narrows in 1862, Malcolm MacNeil teased McDonald: 'I see that you forgot your old Comrade since you Convert[ed] to be an Irishman.'[16] Yet, McDonald was one among many other Gaelic-speaking Highlanders who left rural Cape Breton for the mining district during the 1860s. In Lingan, he would have undoubtedly become acquainted with Ronald McDonald, who oversaw the company store.[17] Ronald came from the East Bay area, where McDonald families of *clann Lachlainn* had settled. His mother, Teresa Gillis, was supposed to be 'the first white child born in East Bay'.[18] In 1865 William McDonald married Ronald's

---

Johnston, *A History of the Catholic Church in Eastern Nova Scotia*, Vol. 2 (Antigonish: St Francis Xavier University Press, 1971), p. 337. For the early history of St Francis Xavier University, see J. D. Cameron, *For the People: A History of St Francis Xavier University* (Montreal and Kingston: McGill-Queen's University Press, 1996), pp. 11–43.

[11] The following correspondence reveals that McDonald was working as a schoolteacher in Lingan by 1861: Angus I. Cameron, Bridgeport, to Mr McDonald, 4 July 1861, item 1, series 14, McDonald fonds, BI.

[12] *Journal and Proceedings of the House of Assembly of the Province of Nova Scotia*, Session 1862 (Halifax, 1862) [hereafter *JHA*], Appendix No. 35, p. 6.

[13] See D. Nerbas, 'Empire, colonial enterprise, and speculation: Cape Breton's coal boom of the 1860s', *Journal of Imperial and Commonwealth History*, 46:6 (2018), pp. 1067–95.

[14] Donald McDonald and James McNeil, 25 January 1863, item 1a, series 25, McDonald fonds, BI; The Petition of Donald MacDonald and James McNeil of Glace Bay in County of Cape Breton, 12 April 1863, and also Memo, March 1864, RG 21, file 'Coal Mines, 1859–1867', Vol. 13, Nova Scotia Archives [hereafter NSA].

[15] See B. White, 'The Irish of Lingan' (unpublished paper, 1976), BI.

[16] Malcolm MacNeil (Neil's son), North Side Grand Narrows, to William McDonald, Lingan Mines, 18 April 1862, item 1, series 21, McDonald fonds, BI.

[17] Nova Scotia, Vol. 12, p. 624 (Ronald McDonald, Lingan, 28 November 1860 and October 1867), R. G. Dun & Co. Credit Report Volumes, Baker Library, Harvard Business School [hereafter Dun & Co., BL].

[18] A. J. MacMillan, *A West Wind to East Bay* (Sydney: Music Hill Publications, 2001), pp. 249–56; quotation from p. 256.

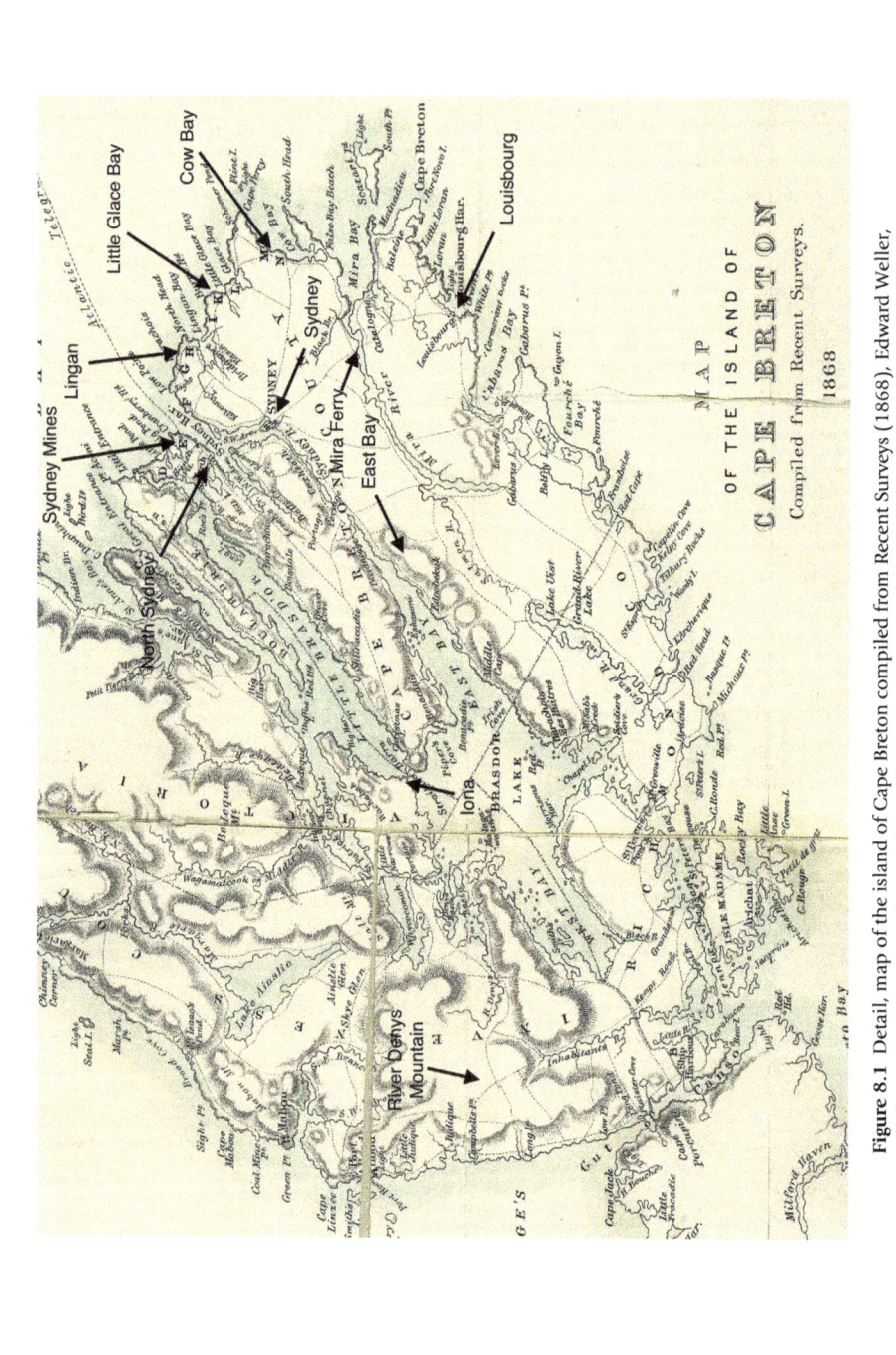

Figure 8.1 Detail, map of the island of Cape Breton compiled from Recent Surveys (1868), Edward Weller, Lithographer, Beaton Institute Archives, Cape Breton University (with relevant place names indicated)

sister, Kate. By this time, McDonald had relocated to neighbouring Little Glace Bay, where he engaged in trade. Because McDonald arrived in Little Glace Bay as part of a broader wave of Highland migration to the mines, he operated in commercial and political networks that were transferred from the countryside.[19] This pattern of migration also helped produce a Catholic majority in the area.[20] When Little Glace Bay received a resident pastor in 1866, it was McDonald who was given responsibility of securing a house for the arriving priest, Father John Shaw, who had roots in McDonald's home county of Inverness and had been, in 1861, one of the earliest students at St Francis Xavier College to be ordained.[21] By 1870 a local Caledonian Club had been organised and was holding 'Athletic Games'.[22] Highland settlements in Cape Breton not only supplied the mines with goods and labour; they decisively shaped the character of Little Glace Bay.

Nova Scotia's entry into Confederation in 1867 created a new, distant government in Ottawa that made important decisions touching various local issues, from mail service and the maintenance of harbours, to the operation of customs houses and tariff policy. It also represented an important new source of patronage and commercial opportunity. By the early 1870s, in addition to being a dealer in dry goods and groceries, McDonald was postmaster, telegraph operator and registrar at Little Glace Bay, whose estimated population of 400 (in 1871) fluctuated with the shipping season as itinerant labourers arrived from the countryside to find work at the mines.[23] The McDonald household had also grown. Kate gave birth to the couple's first child, Teresa, in 1866, followed by Allan Joseph (Allan J.) in 1868, and Dan Lewis (Dan L.) in 1870.[24] As the 1872 Dominion election approached, McDonald reported: 'The leaders of the people, round here, of every class, urge me to try for the position of representative, and as I have already, [sic] some claim, I intend to consult my friends, [sic] in other parts of the County.'[25]

---

[19] For example, McDonald was selling goods for Christmas Island merchant, Malcolm McDougall, in 1864. See Malcolm McDougall, Christmas Island, to William McDonald, 20 July 1864, series 25, item 4, McDonald fonds, BI.

[20] See Muise, 'Making of an industrial community', Appendix IV.

[21] James Quinan, P. P., Sydney, to William McDonald, 3 April 1866, item 6, series 26, McDonald fonds, BI; Johnston, *A History of the Catholic Church in Eastern Nova Scotia*, Vol. 2, p. 269. McDonald knew Shaw well. See John Shaw, P. P., Ingonish to Wm. McDonald, 9 June 1862, item 2, series 26, McDonald fonds, BI.

[22] *Cape Breton News*, 17 September 1870. McDonald was a member of the club. See J. C. Morrison, Washington, to William McDonald, item 51, series 26, McDonald fonds, BI.

[23] *Dominion and Provincial Directories for 1871* (John Lovell, c. 1871), p. 1676.

[24] Province of Nova Scotia, Registration of Death, Rev. Sr Mary Aquinas MacDonald, 5 July 1955, and Allan Joseph McDonald, 7 June 1943; Birth Registry Book, Cape Breton County, 'Danl. Louis McDonald', p. 110, NSA. Documents identified through <https://archives.novascotia.ca/vital-statistics/> (last accessed 10 June 2021).

[25] William McDonald to ?, 8 April 1872, item 3, series 29, McDonald fonds, BI.

McDonald ran and was elected as a Conservative member for Cape Breton County in 1872, and was re-elected three more times before his appointment to the Senate in 1884. In an era when the organisational structure of political parties and party discipline remained limited, McDonald relied upon a dense web of personal networks to mobilise support. In Cape Breton County, a two-seat constituency since the 1872 election, McDonald ran as the Catholic on a Catholic-Protestant ticket that sought to unite the Highland vote. His running mate, Hugh McLeod, was elected with him in the 1878 election. Hugh's untimely death triggered a by-election the following year, and his brother, Dr William McKenzie McLeod, ran successfully in his place.[26] Hugh and William were the sons of Reverend Hugh McLeod, a senior Presbyterian minister who in the middle years of the nineteenth century was sent to Cape Breton by the Edinburgh Ladies' Association and summoned to the congregation at Mira Ferry.[27] By 1871 he had relocated to Sydney and was 'an extensive landowner and entrepreneur', having commenced development of coal properties at Mira Bay during the boom of the 1860s.[28] The McDonald-McLeod ticket thus commanded support in the county's outlying rural areas and was connected to notions of ethnic loyalism. Declared one observer to McDonald, 'The Scotch Catholics of this Noble County and the Scotch Presbyterians must be united, "United we Stand, divided we fall!["] ... Together – that is, the Scotch Catholics and the Presbyterians, can carry this county at all times.'[29] The colonial environment of Cape Breton County thus produced a remarkably different political and cultural space for Catholicism than was the case in Scotland.[30] In the mining district itself, McDonald's appeal was powerful.

---

[26] See series 29, 30, 31 and 32, McDonald fonds, BI. See also J. A. MacDougall, *Cape Breton County Election Returns: Dominion Elections Complete from 1867 to 1904; Local Elections from 1879 to 1906* (Glace Bay, c. 1906), pp. 4–8, PAM 100, BI.

[27] L. Stanley, *The Well-Watered Garden: The Presbyterian Church in Cape Breton, 1798–1860* (Sydney: University College of Cape Breton Press, 1983), pp. 123–4.

[28] Mines Report by P. S. Hamilton, Chief Commissioner, 12 December 1865, Appendix No. 6, JHA (Halifax, 1865), p. 7; *Dominion and Provincial Directories for 1871*, p. 1762; quotation from Stanley, *The Well-Watered Garden*, p. 126.

[29] Rod McKinnon, North Sydney, to William McDonald, 30 August 1879, item 3, series 31, McDonald fonds, BI.

[30] For the Scottish situation, see C. Johnson, *Developments in the Roman Catholic Church in Scotland, 1789–1829* (Edinburgh: John Donald, 1983); L. O. Macdonald, *A Unique and Glorious Mission: Women and Presbyterianism in Scotland 1830–1930* (Edinburgh: John Donald, 2000); S. K. Kehoe, *Creating a Scottish Church: Catholicism, Gender and Ethnicity in Nineteenth-Century Scotland* (Manchester: Manchester University Press, 2010), especially Chapter 5; G. Vaughan, 'The distinctiveness of Catholic schooling in the West of Scotland before the Education (Scotland) Act, 1918', in S. J. McKinney and R. McCluskey (eds), *A History of Catholic Education and Schooling in Scotland: New Perspectives* (London: Palgrave, 2019), pp. 43–60; S. J. McKinney, 'The Presbyterian Campaign (1923–1930) against the Education (Scotland) Act, 1918', in *A History of Catholic Education and Schooling in Scotland*, pp. 149–73; M. McHugh, 'The Education (Scotland) Act, 1918, revisited: The Act and its legal implications', in *A History of Catholic Education and Schooling in Scotland*, pp. 175–99.

Figure 8.2 William McDonald, MP, April 1873 (Library and Archives Canada)

Following the collapse of the coal trade in the mid-1870s, he emerged as a strong advocate for tariff protection on coal, presenting himself as a loyal defender of the demoralised and crisis-stricken mining communities.[31] His political power was tied to his ability to represent the Highland majority and to act independently of the coal operators.[32] And after the return to power of the John A. Macdonald Conservatives on the National Policy platform in the decisive 1878 election, McDonald exercised considerable power in the dispensation of patronage.

Kate gave birth to four more children during this period: Minnie (1872), Cassie (1874), Willie (1877) and Agnes (1880). All lived to adulthood with the exception of Agnes, who died in 1884.[33] McDonald's political standing in the county was bolstered by his wife's connections to East Bay, and sinecures flowed in the other direction as well. Kate's brother, Ronald, was appointed Collector of Customs at the county seat of Sydney in 1882, acquiring the nickname 'Ronald Customs'.[34] Before this, in Lingan, Ronald had purchased the store debts held by the GMA's Halifax agents, the Cunards, to become an independent merchant in Lingan; 'he has been successful in collecting', reported a local observer in 1871.[35] A few years earlier, Hector McDonald, a Glace Bay coal cutter originally from River Denys, wed Ronald and Kate's sister, Mary, in East Bay.[36] The marriages of William McDonald and Hector McDonald to the McDonald sisters of East Bay was characteristic of the importance of rural home communities in the selection of marriage partners in the coal district.[37] It is likely that Hector

---

[31] *Debates of the House of Commons of the Dominion of Canada, Third Session–Third Parliament* [hereafter *Debates*] (Ottawa, MacLean, Roger & Co., 1876), p. 648; *Debates* (1877), pp. 381, 544; *Debates* (1878), Vol. 1, p. 1064, and Vol. 2, pp. 2165, 2168; D. Muise, 'Elections and Constituencies: Federal Politics in Nova Scotia, 1867–1878' (PhD thesis, University of Western Ontario, 1971), p. 301.

[32] This was made especially clear by the endorsement he received from the Provincial Workmen's Association in the 1882 Dominion election. See *Trades Journal* (Stellarton, NS), 7 June 1882.

[33] Province of Nova Scotia, Registration of Death, William MacDonald, 11 October 1959, NSA; 'William McDonald', typescript, p. 4.

[34] MacMillan, *A West Wind to East Bay*, p. 257.

[35] Nova Scotia, Vol. 12, p. 624 (Ronald McDonald, Lingan, 1 August 1871), Dun & Co., BL.

[36] Marriage Register, Cape Breton County 1867–8, p. 26: Hector McDonald and Mary McDonald, 10 February 1868, East Bay, NSA.

[37] See Muise, 'Making of an industrial community'.

McDonald's marriage played a role in him later becoming a Harbour Master and merchant in Cow Bay.[38] William, Ronald and Hector were, for a time, spread across the principal coal-mining villages on the south side of Sydney Harbour. They were exemplars of the independent mercantile interests that served the new mining communities of Cape Breton County, which emerged from the composite Highland communities that formed at the coal mines.

The rise of these men was embedded in kin relations and sustained by households that buttressed the commercial achievement of individual patriarchs. The McDonald household in Little Glace Bay was not limited to the nuclear family. We find in the 1871 census a seventeen-year-old telegraph operator named Stephen McDonald, and Jane and Mary McDonald, twenty-six and twenty-one years of age respectively. Stephen lived with the family and assumed responsibility for the operation of McDonald's store throughout the 1870s while parliament was in session. He does not appear to have been a close relation, but he may have come from the Grand Narrows area, and his family was known to the McDonald household, if not distantly related. Mary is difficult to identify definitively, but may have been Kate's sister; the McDonald papers indeed reveal the coming and going of family as a common occurrence. The Jane in the 1871 census may have been William's adopted sister.[39] A Jane also appears at the River Denys homestead in 1871 and 1881, and William's daughter Teresa reported upon receipt of a letter from 'Auntie Jane' in 1881: 'They are all well at Grandpa's.'[40] In the 1891 census Jane appears in the McDonald household at Little Glace Bay and is explicitly identified as 'Sister'.[41] Jane's situation was not unique. Fosterage appears to have been a common practice that persisted throughout different generational cohorts. Kate's youngest sister Agnes was married to Patrick Young, a harbour pilot at Lingan.[42] In the spring of 1892, he suddenly fell ill and died, leaving behind Agnes and five children; William and Kate McDonald afterwards adopted one of Agnes's daughters, Clara Agnes, who would later become Sister Mary Agnes.[43] The practice is also suggested in a laconic comment from Teresa to her father in 1877: 'They have a stranger at Uncle Hector's[,] a little girl[,] they got her last night but she is

---

[38] Census of Canada, 1881, Nova Scotia, Cape Breton, Cow Bay, p. 8.
[39] Census of Canada, 1871, Nova Scotia, Cape Breton, Lingan Mines (div. no. 2), p. 47.
[40] Teresa to Papa, 28 January 1881, item 207, series 207, McDonald fonds, BI; Census of Canada, 1871, Inverness, River Dennis (div. no. 2), p. 4; Census of Canada, 1881, Inverness, River Dennis, p. 10.
[41] Census of Canada, 1891, Nova Scotia, Cape Breton County, Little Glace Bay, p. 11.
[42] Census of Canada, 1891, Nova Scotia, Cape Breton County, Lingan (div. no. 1), p. 26; MacMillan, *A West Wind to East Bay*, p. 259.
[43] Dan L., Little Glace Bay, to Papa, 23 May 1892, item 447, series 26, McDonald fonds, BI; Census of Canada, 1901, Nova Scotia, Cape Breton, Glace Bay, p. 32; 'Obsequies of Late Senator McDonald', *Glace Bay Gazette*, 7 July 1916, McDonald B & G file, BI; Teresa, St Patrick's Convent, to Papa, 7 June 1892, item 450, series 26, McDonald fonds, BI.

not christened yet.'⁴⁴ Moving into the early twentieth century, the sisters Cassie and Minnie took responsibility for Allan J.'s son, Willie Jr, who suffered from a chronic illness, possibly disseminated tuberculosis. Fosterage evinced the operation of meaningful kin ties.

The McDonald children thus grew up surrounded by aunts, uncles and grandparents. On Kate's side of the family, 'uncle Ronald' and 'aunt Alice', and later 'aunt Aggie' and 'uncle Pad' from Lingan, as well as 'uncle Hector' and 'aunt Mary' from Cow Bay, appear in accounts of daily life in letters from the children. Because the letters were generally written when McDonald was away in Ottawa, they offer an incomplete account of events. The death of aunt Alice around 1880, for instance, is never directly mentioned in the surviving letters. But Ronald is listed as widowed in the 1881 census in a household with nine children.⁴⁵ Ronald's sister Aggie moved in for a time.⁴⁶ And they soon after moved to Sydney, coincident with Ronald's appointment as Collector of Customs. 'I received letters today from Aggie and Essie,' reported Teresa in January 1883. 'They do not seem to like Sydney as much as Lingan but of course they will not for a while until they get used to it ... Grandma and Grandpa are staying with them now.'⁴⁷ In addition to 'aunt Jane', William's three brothers also appear in correspondence. Michael McDonald – 'uncle Mick', and typically referred to as 'the Doctor' from the early 1880s onwards – was a Sydney physician who in 1880 wed Eunice McInnis, daughter of the Sydney merchant Alex McInnis, a cousin of Bishop Colin F. MacKinnon.⁴⁸ By 1891 William McDonald's parents, Allan and Mary, had themselves relocated from River Denys to Sydney and had moved in with Michael and Eunice.⁴⁹ Daniel, 'uncle Dan', a coal merchant and bachelor in Halifax, was an occasional visitor to the McDonald household and kept in regular contact with the children. John A., 'uncle John', provided news from the farm at River Denys Mountain in the late 1870s. He remained in Inverness County, married and was appointed Light House Keeper at Port Hood.⁵⁰

In the 1870s and 1880s, there were few strangers at Little Glace Bay. Migration to the coal district was not a solitary experience, and individuals were regularly

---

⁴⁴ Teresa to Papa, 10 April 1878, item 83, series 26, McDonald fonds, BI.
⁴⁵ Census of Canada, 1881, Cape Breton, Lingan, p. 80.
⁴⁶ Teresa, Mt St Vincent, to Mama, 24 December 1882, item 292, series 26, McDonald fonds, BI.
⁴⁷ Teresa, Mt St Vincent, to Papa, 2 January 1883, item 294, series 26, McDonald fonds, BI.
⁴⁸ Marriage Register, County of Cape Breton 1880, p. 149, no. 20: Michael McDonald and Eunice McInnis, NSA. Alex McInnis's connection to the Bishop was mentioned within the context of credit reports: Nova Scotia, Vol. 12, p. 623 (Alex McInnis, Trader Sydney, 4 September 1858 and 24 January 1860), Dun & Co., BL.
⁴⁹ 'William McDonald', typescript, p. 2; Census of Canada, 1891, Nova Scotia, Cape Breton County, Town of Sydney, p. 10.
⁵⁰ MacDougall, *History of Inverness County*, pp. 506–7; A. D. MacDonald, *Mabou Pioneers*, Vol. 1 (Halifax: Formac Publishing Company Limited, 2014 [1977]), p. 634.

identified by their kin relations and home communities from which they had come.[51] The McDonald house was at a road junction, inland from the Glace Bay Mining Company's cliffside operations and the concentration of miners' dwellings that developed around the pithead, which was known locally as the Roost. Though the McDonalds were familiar with the people from the Roost, the McDonald household was generally more socially integrated with older settlers to the area such as their neighbours the Farrells, and Laurence Laffin of Lingan. 'I wase [sic] in your House on wednesday 24 Feb. and had dinner with Mrs McDonald,' Laffin wrote to McDonald in 1875. 'Mrs McDonald and Famley [sic] were in good health.'[52] William McDonald's land at Little Glace Bay consisted, in 1871, of a couple of acres and included reclaimed marshland. The household kept a milch cow and raised potatoes, hay and other crops as part of McDonald's mercantile enterprise. The family thus participated in local farming that served the mines, and their agricultural activities would expand in the decades to come.[53] The miners and their families at the Roost were McDonald's customers and were collectively dependent upon his political brokerage, but social visits there appear to have been rare.[54]

The Catholic chapel was near the McDonald home, and the church played a vital role in the locality and in the life of the McDonald family. The local chapter of the League of the Cross, a Catholic total abstinence society, was especially active. McDonald's eldest son, Allan J., joined the League of the Cross in 1878 at around the age of ten.[55] It was a major subject not only in Allan J.'s correspondence to his father, but in correspondence McDonald received from his daughter Teresa and others in the community. The society acquired regalia and conducted marches through the mining district, held balls and hosted regular lectures, and constructed a local hall. The group was a fixture of local life, which offered leisure and sociability meant as an alternative to the rum sellers and tavernkeepers.[56] School was also a point of broader

---

[51] See also W. Davey and R. MacKinnon, 'Nicknaming patterns and traditions among Cape Breton coal miners', *Acadiensis*, 30:2 (2001), pp. 71–83.

[52] Laurence Laffin, Lingan, to William McDonald, 9 March 1875, item 21, series 26, McDonald fonds, BI.

[53] Census of Canada, 1871, Nova Scotia, Cape Breton, Lingan Mines (div. no. 2), Schedule 4, p. 8; and Schedule 5, p. 8.

[54] See for mentions of the Roost from the McDonald children, McDonald fonds, BI: Dan Lewis, Little Glace Bay, to Papa, 25 February 1883, item 305, series 26; Allan J., Little Glace Bay, to Papa, 17 March 1883, item 312, series 26; Allan J., Little Glace Bay, to Papa, April 14, 1883, item 274, series 25; Willie, Little Glace Bay, to Papa, 24 February 1889, item 333, series 26; Willie, Little Glace Bay, to Papa, 12 February 1890, item 357, series 26; Minnie, Glace Bay, to Papa, 15 February 1890, item 359, series 26; D.L., Glace Bay, to Father, 23 March 1899, item 548, series 25; Minnie, Glace Bay, to Papa, 28 February 1890, item 363, series 26; Minnie, Glace Bay, to Papa, 24 September 1896, item 605, series 26.

[55] Teresa, Little Glace Bay, to Papa, 10 April 1878, item 83, series 26, McDonald fonds, BI.

[56] See McDonald fonds, BI: Teresa, Little Glace Bay, 19 February 1878, item 55, series 25; Allan J., Little Glace Bay, to Papa, 24 March 1879, item 106, series 26; Teresa, Little Glace Bay, to Papa,

social interaction for the McDonald children. In the mid- to late 1870s Teresa provided to her father regular updates on her own progress in school, as well as the progress of her siblings. The other children would do the same.[57] Education was clearly a family priority, and McDonald regularly sent books to his young children when he was away in Ottawa. Teresa excelled from an early age. Her teacher, 'Mrs Benson', also visited the McDonald home to give music lessons on the family's organ.[58] Teresa received music books from her father and wrote back to tell about what she had learned to play from them; this included, she wrote to her father, 'your favourite tune[,] Auld lang syne'.[59] The organ appears to have been situated in a parlour where musical performance was an aspect of social gathering.[60] This was a domestic environment insulated from the rough realities of the mining community, and even the popular Gaelic culture of William McDonald's younger years.[61] By the early 1880s, Teresa left home to attend Sydney Academy and then moved along to Mount St Vincent Academy, near Halifax. 'She is most attentive to her studies,' reported Mother

---

9 April 1879, item 109, series 26; Allan J., Little Glace Bay, to Papa, 11 April 1879, item 110, series 26; Allan J., Little Glace Bay, to Papa, 20 April 1879, item 112, series 26; Allan J., Little Glace Bay, to Papa, 17 January 1880, item 125, series 26; Allan J., Little Glace Bay, to Papa, 20 Jan 1880, item 127, series 26; Allan J., Little Glace Bay, to Papa, 18 Feb 1880 (second letter), item 133, series 26; Allan J., Little Glace Bay, to Papa, 18 March 1880, item 137, series 26; M. McKinnon, Little Glace Bay, to Wm. McDonald, 29 March 1880, item 140, series 26; Allan J., Little Glace Bay, to Papa, 5 December 1880, item 164, series 26; Allan J., Little Glace Bay, to Papa, 24 December 1880, item 178, series 26; Allan J., Little Glace Bay, to Papa, 27 January 1881, item 205, series 26; Allan J., Little Glace Bay, to Papa, 3 March 1882, item 247, series 26; Minnie, Glace Bay, to Papa, 15 February 1890, item 359, series 26; Minnie, Glace Bay, to Papa, 20 March 1890, item 375, series 26; Willie, L.G. Bay, to Papa, 19 March 1892, item 425, series 26; Minnie, Glace Bay, to Papa, 19 March 1896, item 572, series 26; Cassie, Glace Bay, to Papa, 16 June 1897, item 641, series 26.

[57] See, for instance, series 26, McDonald fonds, BI: Theresa, Little Glace Bay, to Papa, 5 March 1875, item 20; Theresa, Little Glace Bay, to Papa, 4 February 1877, item 33; Teresa McDonald to Papa, 11 March 1877, item 41; Teresa, Little Glace Bay, to Papa, 27 February 1878, item 64; Allan J., Little Glace Bay, to Papa, 28 February 1879, item 101; Teresa, Little Glace Bay, to Papa, 17 March 1879, item 105a; Teresa, Little Glace Bay, to Papa, 17 February 1880, item 131; Allan J., Little Glace Bay, to Papa, 18 February 1880, item 133; Allan J., Little Glace Bay, to Papa, 19 December 1880, item 174; Allan J., Little Glace Bay, to Papa, 22 March 1882, item 258; Daniel L., Little Glace Bay, to Papa, 13 April 1882, item 269; Willie, Little Glace Bay, to Papa, 24 February 1889, item 333. See also Dan L., Little Glace Bay, to Papa, 14 March 1885, item 292, series 25, McDonald fonds, BI.

[58] Teresa, Little Glace Bay, to Papa, 2 April 1877, item 48, series 26, McDonald fonds, BI.

[59] Teresa, Little Glace Bay, to Papa, 28 February 1879, item 102, series 26, McDonald fonds, BI.

[60] Teresa, Little Glace Bay, to Papa, 22 February 1877, item 36, series 26, McDonald fonds, BI; Teresa, Little Glace Bay, to Papa, 26 February 1877, item 37, series 26, McDonald fonds, BI.

[61] See, for instance, the scene described by Alex McKinnon, Grand Narrows, to William McDonald, 30 January 1862, item 1, series 26, McDonald fonds, BI.

Benedicta in December 1882.⁶² By the end of the decade, Teresa had become Sister Aquinas.⁶³

The education of the children coincided with anglicisation. William and Kate were native Gaelic speakers. A satirical song narrating local events around the turn of the century indeed declared the following about a man who was likely William McDonald: 'Curious English he spouted rarely.'⁶⁴ But the children were raised in English, though Gaelic would have been everywhere around them. This was characteristic of a more widespread programme of anglicisation that was embraced by aspiring, middle-class families such as the McDonalds, and was also evident in the curriculum at St Francis Xavier College. According to the university's historian, James D. Cameron, 'Highland culture and traditions were not a priority; social advancement and integration were.'⁶⁵ Gaelic was indeed not offered until 1894, and afterwards remained consigned to a marginal role.⁶⁶ The family's connections to the College were considerable, and William's cousin Angus G. – son of his father's brother, Eugene (Aodh) – had been a professor of natural philosophy and mathematics at the College between 1877 and 1885 and afterwards moved to the Normal School of Truro and served as a school inspector.⁶⁷ William McDonald was a member of the College's board of directors and became an active member of the alumni association and benefactor. He also sent his three boys there.⁶⁸

Higher education would take the boys out of the community for periods and was a fundamental basis for their prospective entries into professional and business life. Allan J. studied law at Dalhousie University in Halifax, and in the early 1890s his father had secured for him a place in the Sydney law firm of J. A. Gillies and A. J. G. MacEchen.⁶⁹ Dan L. went for medical training at Bellevue Medical College in Brooklyn, where his uncle Michael had gone. However, Dan L. squandered the money his father had given him on alcohol and unreliable friends and returned home embarrassed by the experience.⁷⁰ By 1896 he was

---

⁶² Mother Benedicta, Mount St Vincent, to William McDonald, 21 December 1882, item 291, series 26, McDonald fonds, BI.

⁶³ Allan J., Halifax, to Father, 18 December 1889, item 334, series 26, McDonald fonds, BI.

⁶⁴ Broadside, 'Doing a Sheriff' (c. 1901), item 584, series 25, McDonald fonds, BI.

⁶⁵ Cameron, *For the People*, p. 32.

⁶⁶ Cameron, *For the People*, p. 416 (fn. 38).

⁶⁷ Cameron, *For the People*, pp. 65, 79; MacDougall, *History of Inverness County*, p. 505.

⁶⁸ *St Francis Xavier's College: Prospectus and Course of Studies* (Pictou: Colonial Standard Book and Job Print, 1878), p. 3; see the historical sketch in *Calendar of the University of St Francis Xavier* (1921–2), p. 13.

⁶⁹ Allan J.'s time at law school can be glimpsed at in series 26, McDonald fonds, BI: Allan J., Hollis St. [Halifax], to Father, 26 January 1890, item 343; Allan J., Hollis St. [Halifax], to Father, 28 January 1890, item 345 (a); Allan J., Hollis St. [Halifax], to Father, 31 January 1890, item 347; Allan J., Hollis St., Halifax, to Father, 6 February 1890, item 352; Allan J., Hollis St., Halifax, to Father, 18 February 1890, item 360.

⁷⁰ See series 26, McDonald fonds, BI: Dan L., 90 Fourth Avenue, Brooklyn, to Uncle Dan, 29 October 1893, item 482; Dan McDonald, Halifax, to William McDonald, 7 November 1893,

helping to run his father's local business interests, including a drugstore in Glace Bay by the following year.[71] And Willie, after obtaining a BA degree from St Francis Xavier College in 1896, completed a year in applied science at McGill University.[72] He too returned home before the end of the century; still only in his twenties, he was a clerk for the Glace Bay branch of the Union Bank of Halifax and dabbled in stock speculation.[73] Minnie and Cassie did not have such opportunities, reflective of the Senator's conservative adherence to the normative gender roles of 'separate spheres' ideology. Minnie and Cassie both taught school for periods in Little Glace Bay, but otherwise were unable to pursue professional careers outside the home. Cassie aspired to study music at the Boston Conservatory. But she did not receive support from her father.[74]

II

With his appointment to the Senate in 1884, William McDonald was no longer dependent upon elections, and by 1896 the Conservatives had been displaced by the Liberals in both provincial and Dominion government. McDonald's stature as a popular political figure consequently dissipated. By the time of his death in 1916, he was remembered as a figure 'better known to people a generation ago'.[75] Yet, the Senator's business activities grew in scope. The formation of the Dominion Coal Company in 1893 consolidated the operations of seven different mining companies on the south side of Sydney Harbour and ushered in an era of dramatic expansion on the coalfield. Initially led by Boston capitalist Henry Melville Whitney, the company had been taken over by Montreal interests by the end of the nineteenth century. It was from its inception a modern corporation with financial resources that far exceeded the capacities of the old operators, and which could extract favourable treatment from a Nova Scotia government desirous of raising government revenue from

---

item 486; Teresa, St Patrick's Convent, to Papa, 12 November 1893, item 488; Teresa, St Patrick's Convent, to Papa and Mama, 26 November 1893, item 491; Dan L., 90 Fourth Avenue, Brooklyn, to Papa, 29 December 1893, item 496, series 26; Dan L., Halifax, 17 April 1895, item 502.

[71] Dan L., Glace Bay, to McDonald, 21 August 1896, item 481, series 25, McDonald fonds, BI.

[72] Willie, Glace Bay, to Father, 4 September 1896, item 596, series 26, McDonald fonds; Willie, 60 University St., Montreal, to Father, 20 September 1896, item 603, series 26, McDonald fonds, BI.

[73] For one of many examples, see Willie, Union Bank of Halifax, Glace Bay, to McDonald, 24 March 1899, item 550, series 25, McDonald fonds, BI. Reference to Willie's stock speculation is made in J. W. Ryan, Glace Bay, to Wm. McDonald, 5 March 1905, item 821, series 26, McDonald fonds, BI.

[74] See series 26, McDonald fonds, BI: Minnie, Glace Bay, to Papa, 18 February 1895, item 499; Teresa, St Patrick's Convent, to Papa, 5 August 1895, item 535; Cassie, Glace Bay, to Papa, 18 August 1896, item 591; Cassie, Glace Bay, to Papa, 28 August 1896, item 592.

[75] 'Death of Senator William M'Donald', *Sydney Post*, 5 July 1916, clipping, McDonald B & G file, BI.

Figure 8.3 Senator's Corner, Glace Bay, 1906 (Beaton Institute Archives, Cape Breton University)

coal production.[76] In 1896 the company shipped over 500,000 tons of coal to the St Lawrence ports, the large majority destined for Montreal; less than two decades later, in 1913, Dominion Coal shipped nearly 1.5 million tons to Montreal alone.[77] The formation of the Dominion Iron and Steel Company and its construction of a steel plant in Sydney at the turn of the century also increased the demand for coal and dramatically expanded industrial employment. With these developments, Little Glace Bay became absorbed into the town of Glace Bay, incorporated in 1901. The local population of the area almost tripled between 1891 and 1901 to reach just under 7,000, and more than doubled during the decade that followed.[78] By the early twentieth century, land connected to the McDonald household occupied the central commercial junction of a sprawling town, known locally as Senator's Corner.

At the beginning of the twentieth century, the Senator's adult children as well as Clara Agnes remained at home.[79] Teresa (Sister Aquinas) and Allan J. were the only exceptions. Allan J. established his own legal practice in Sydney by late 1893, and married Florence A. (Fawnie) Hearn, daughter of Sydney barrister James H. Hearn, and set up home in Sydney.[80] In 1895 a child was born of the couple; '"Baby Willie" is growing so nicely and has two teeth of which he is extremely proud,' Fawnie reported the following spring.[81] Senator McDonald invested in real estate, loaned out money and became a landlord of some significance in Glace Bay. Allan J. aided and represented his father in these various dealings. He also kept a branch of his practice in Glace Bay and became involved in moneylending himself. 'The people will always be borrowing,' he declared.[82] In addition to his responsibilities at the drugstore, Dan L. tracked and collected rents, and supervised the employment of a farm labourer, William Willis, who maintained the family's farm and did odd jobs.[83] The family often employed a female servant in the house, and also employed additional labour as necessitated by the seasonal demands of the farm. Dan L., for instance, reported to his father in June 1904:

---

[76] D. MacGillivray, 'Henry Melville Whitney comes to Cape Breton: The saga of a Gilded Age entrepreneur', *Acadiensis*, 9:1 (1977), pp. 44–70.

[77] 'Nova Scotia coal', *Monetary Times* (Montreal), 7 August 1896; 'Dominion Shipments to St. Lawrence', *Coal and Coal Trade Journal*, 27 January 1915.

[78] *The Canada Year Book, 1914* (Ottawa: J. de L. Tache, 1915), p. 50.

[79] Census of Canada, 1901, Nova Scotia, Cape Breton, Glace Bay, p. 32.

[80] Certificate of Registration of Death, Nova Scotia, Florence A. MacDonald, 7 December 1933, NSA; *A Cyclopedia of Canadian Biography: Being Chiefly Men of the Time* (Toronto: Rose Publishing Company, 1888), p. 225.

[81] Fawnie A. Macdonald, Sydney, to William Macdonald, 19 April 1896, item 584, series 26, McDonald fonds, BI.

[82] Allan J., Sydney, to Father, 17 May 1897, item 530, series 25, McDonald fonds, BI.

[83] Census of Canada, 1891, Nova Scotia, Cape Breton County, Little Glace Bay, p. 14; Census of Canada, 1901, Nova Scotia, Cape Breton, Glace Bay, p. 35.

> McInnis and Willis and Campbell are working at the Marsh. Willis has been weeding the garden at the house. Campbell has been picking the potatoes and McInnis clearing and cleaning up on the marsh. There will be nothing for Campbell after today. The frenchman is getting on well with his work and it is looking very well. I had the horse in the waggon a couple of times and McInnis was doing some harrowing with him.[84]

Again, May 1905:

> Willis has the ground ready at the house to put plants and seeds in. ... Roy is getting the ground ready at the Marsh. He put in 100 Asparagus plants on Saturday. The marsh is very wet yet and not fit to harrow. Willis has spread some of the manure. McNeil is getting on first rate with the cellar and should have all the earth out this week.[85]

And, again, June 1906:

> Willis has the turnips planted and is now fencing around the barn. Campbell worked 8½ days since you left. Mick McNeil did not work any. I think he is up the country.[86]

The farm was one aspect of a number of commercial activities run by the McDonald children, and its operation was not only facilitated by labour drawn from 'up the country' but also through commercial exchange with the farms of nearby Highland settlers. 'The two cows calved – will write Angus McDonald Benacadie and tell him to take one of them,' wrote Dan L. in a commonplace piece of correspondence.[87] The activities of the farm also provided occasion for the sisters, especially Minnie, to play an active role in the economic life of the coal town, not well visible in a male-dominated public sphere. Minnie shared in Dan L.'s tasks. She wrote to her father, 'I did not sell any potatoes yet. We will sell them later when they get scarce.'[88] This was not merely the execution of instruction, but entrepreneurial calculation. The Senator was a patriarchal figurehead of an expansive household economy.

This was not entirely new. In the 1870s, Stephen McDonald had aided in the operation of McDonald's store before the children were old enough to do so. He lived in the McDonald household for at least a decade. Teresa's comment in 1877 suggests that he may have been a relation: 'Stephen had a letter from uncle John to day too from River Dennis and they are all well.'[89] Certainly, he was written about by the children as a member of the family. Stephen's sudden

---

[84] Dan L., Glace Bay, to Father, 15 June 1904, item 808, series 26, McDonald fonds, BI.
[85] Dan L., Glace Bay, to Father, 15 May 1905, item 833, series 26, McDonald fonds, BI.
[86] Dan L., Glace Bay, to Father, 27 June 1906, item 866, series 26, McDonald fonds, BI.
[87] Dan L., Glace Bay, to Father, 15 April 1902, item 756, series 26, McDonald fonds, BI.
[88] Minnie, Glace Bay, to Papa, 8 June 1904, item 797, series 26, McDonald fonds, BI.
[89] Teresa, Little Glace Bay, to Papa, 16 March 1877, item 45, series 26, McDonald fonds, BI.

disappearance in 1880 must, then, have come as a shock. On 4 June, McDonald received a telegram from Murdo McRae in St Peters: 'Stephen McDonald arrived here Tuesday[,] departed westward yesterday[,] assumes name James McNeil.'[90] Rumours circulated that he had drowned, but clearly he was running from some type of fraud or financial embarrassment. 'I am pleased to learn for his own and especially your own sake,' wrote Rod McKinnon from North Sydney, 'that the savings bank is all o.k.'[91] In late January 1881, Teresa relayed a story she had received in a letter from Dan L.: 'He was telling me that Archie McDonald put two men in jail and they broke the windows and he put a board up to the window with Stephen McDonald on it and everyone came to the house and wanted to know if it was Stephen was [sic] in jail.'[92] What followed is not entirely clear. But a week later, Teresa reported that Stephen's goods were to be sold at auction and that his father's land had been seized for debts owed to Montreal firms.[93] Allan J.'s letters reveal that he was beginning to assume more responsibility in his father's business following Stephen's abrupt departure. 'I marked every thing that I sell out of the shop in the book and I give the money to mama,' Allan J. wrote.[94] The price of butter, sale of hay, purchase of coal, collection of debts and feed for the mare: these were among the subjects addressed in his letters from this period.[95] McDonald's business enterprise had long been rooted in a household economy that operated on the collective labour of family.

Senator McDonald's embeddedness in the Highland community and connections to the countryside remained an important aspect of business into the late nineteenth and early twentieth centuries. In the summer of 1893, only months after the incorporation of the Dominion Coal Company, McDonald began building houses in Glace Bay in anticipation of growing demand for dwellings.[96] His tenants were principally Highlanders moving to the fast-growing mining town. And they were often known by the family through kin

---

[90] Murdo McRae, St Peters, to Wm. McDonald, MP, L.G. Bay, 4 June 1880, item 150, series 26, McDonald fonds, BI.

[91] Rod McKinnon, North Sydney, to Wm. McDonald, 5 June 1880, item 151, series 26, McDonald fonds, BI.

[92] Teresa, Sydney, to Papa, 28 January 1881, item 207, series 26, McDonald fonds, BI.

[93] Teresa, Sydney, to Papa, 5 February 1881, item 215, series 26, McDonald fonds, BI.

[94] Allan J., Little Glace Bay, to Papa, 12 April 1882, item 268, series 26, McDonald fonds, BI.

[95] See series 26, McDonald fonds, BI: Allan J., Little Glace Bay, to Papa, 10 May 1882, item 277; Allan J., Little Glace Bay, to Papa, 12 February 1883, item 299; Allan J., Little Glace Bay, to Papa, 24 February 1883, item 304; Allan J., Little Glace Bay, to Papa, 25 February 1883, item 306; Allan J., Little Glace Bay, to Papa, 11 March 1883, item 310; Allan J., Little Glace Bay to Papa, 17 March 1883, item 312.

[96] See series 25, McDonald fonds, BI: John Millard (Manufacturer of Lumber), Liverpool, NS, to McDonald, 15 August 1893, item 381; Millard, Liverpool, to McDonald, 31 August 1893, item 386; Millard, Liverpool, to McDonald, 16 September 1893, item 388; Millard, Liverpool, to McDonald, 17 October 1893, item 394; Millard, Liverpool, to McDonald, 30 November 1893, item 405.

and social networks. 'Dan McIsaac + a McNeil wanted to know yesterday if you had any houses to rent or land to sell,' Cassie wrote in 1895.[97] Nearly a decade later, similar dynamics persisted. Minnie reported in 1903 that 'a Mrs Michael McNeil (widow) of Iona' was looking for a house to rent: 'She said you would know her Malcolm McNeil who lived in Glace Bay [and] was her brother in law, and another one is Red Stephen. Her son is working in the mine for two years, and he wants her to come and settle here.'[98] These were also potential customers for the purchase of farm produce or loans. Allan J., as an agent of the Toronto-based Canadian Mutual Loan & Investment Company, attempted to work out an arrangement with the Dominion Coal Company whereby debts could be collected directly from the pay of miners.[99] Such efforts suggest that local economic life was hardly paternalistic. The old politics of paternalism and ethnic loyalism, which had served McDonald as an MP, were indeed less relevant by the end of the century.

This was an aspect of a broader reconfiguration of social relations on the coalfield in the late nineteenth and early twentieth centuries. Local notables such as the McDonalds – merchants, barristers, medical doctors and others – made up a business and professional class in the county that had been broadened as a consequence of Highland migration to the mining district. With the arrival of the Dominion Coal Company, members of this local bourgeoisie found business and professional opportunities with the coal corporation. Most notable was David MacKeen. The proprietor and manager of the Caledonia Coal Company and its mine near Little Glace Bay, and elected Conservative MP for Cape Breton in 1887 and 1891, MacKeen became Dominion Coal's first resident manager.[100] From Minnie's correspondence, we can also get a glimpse of the growing practice of a colliery doctor in 1896: 'Dr. Sam McLennan is at [the] Dominion No. 1 [mine] now, and has part of the Bridgeport practise too.'[101] This was the father of Hugh MacLennan, later to be born in Glace Bay. Dominion Coal and the interconnected steel company, Dominion Iron and Steel, were gigantic corporations that employed not only mine and steel workers, but also large bureaucracies of administrators, managers, supervisors and professionals. For some, these corporations offered the possibility for upward mobility. Dan Hugh McDougall's story is familiar, though also exceptional. Born in St Peter's in 1879 to Catholic, Gaelic-speaking parents, he

[97] Cassie, Glace Bay, to Papa, 24 April 1895, item 504, series 26, McDonald fonds, BI.
[98] Minnie, Glace Bay, to Papa, 29 September 1903, item 652, series 25, McDonald fonds, BI.
[99] Letter draft, Allan J. MacDonald to Canadian Mutual Loan & Investment Company, 51 Yonge Street, Toronto, 20 February 1897, attached to Allan J., Sydney, to Father, 25 February 1897, item 508, series 25, McDonald fonds, BI.
[100] D. MacGillivray, 'David MacKeen', *Dictionary of Canadian Biography/Dictionnaire biographique du Canada* (University of Toronto Press/Université Laval, 1998), Vol. 14, available at <http://www.biographi.ca/en/bio/mackeen_david_14E.html> (last accessed 25 April 2022).
[101] Minnie, Glace Bay, to Papa, 16 April 1896, item 583, series 26, McDonald fonds, BI.

was brought to Little Glace Bay with his family, where his father, John J., was a policeman and later a truckman.[102] Dan Hugh began as a mechanic's apprentice and assistant mine and railway surveyor, and became a civil and mining engineer who rapidly ascended in the corporate world to become Assistant General Manager of Dominion Coal by 1909.[103] With plans to combine the coal and steel operations under one general manager, he appealed to Senator McDonald – a familiar figure from Dan Hugh's youth in Little Glace Bay – to use his influence with powerful men to secure fair consideration for the post. The Senator's intervention was apparently successful.[104] Dan Hugh is better known to historians as D. H. McDougall, as opposed to his contemporary and adversary in the major coal strike of 1909–10, Dan McDougall, president of District 26 of the United Mine Workers of America.[105] Highland identities were powerfully fractured by the class divisions of the early twentieth century.

The new coal and steel corporations not only created business and professional opportunities, they also contributed towards the recasting of social and cultural life as the scattered mining settlements became integrated into a wider industrial area with the development of railway and tram services and the establishment of the steel plant in Sydney. In late May 1895, the new general manager of the Dominion Coal Company, Hiram Donkin, invited Cassie and Minnie on an evening outing by train to Louisbourg with company officials and their families and other locals of note. Mrs Donkin helped prepare the tea that was served to the party of about forty in the car.[106] Coal and steel company officials participated with the McDonalds in a local social and cultural life that was facilitated by easy travel, which made trips to destinations such as Sydney, Louisbourg and North Sydney more frequent, and allowed Minnie, Cassie and Willie to frequent balls, teas and literary society meetings across the industrial area.[107] No institution better captured the social and cultural coalescence between coal and steel company newcomers and county elites than the yacht club in Sydney, established in 1901 and incorporated as the Royal Cape Breton

---

[102] Census of Canada, 1891, Nova Scotia, Cape Breton County, Little Glace Bay, p. 16; Census of Canada, 1901, Nova Scotia, Cape Breton, Glace Bay, p. 30; Marriage Register, Nova Scotia, Cape Breton County, 1906, p. 206.

[103] B. M. Greene (ed.), *Who's Who and Why, 1921* (Toronto: International Press Limited, c. 1921), pp. 885–6.

[104] Dan H. McDougall, Sydney, to Wm. McDonald, 28 November 1909, item 888, series 26, McDonald fonds, BI.

[105] For more on the two McDougalls and the 1909–10 strike, see D. Frank, *J.B. McLachlan: A Biography* (Toronto: James Lorimer & Company, 1999), pp. 89–127.

[106] Cassie, Sydney, to Papa, 29 May 1895, item 510, series 26, McDonald fonds, BI.

[107] See series 26, McDonald fonds, BI: Minnie, Glace Bay, to Papa, 14 June 1895, item 518; Minnie, Glace Bay, to Papa, 22 June 1895, item 523; Minnie, Glace Bay, to Papa, 20 February 1901, item 705; Minnie, Glace Bay, to Papa, 18 April 1901, item 731; Minnie, Glace Bay, to Papa, 6 May 1901, item 736; Minnie, Glace Bay, to Papa, 13 April 1902, item 755; Minnie, Glace Bay, to Papa, 30 September 1903, item 782.

Yacht Club in 1903. A. J. Moxham – the steel company president who arrived from Ohio to build an iconic neogothic mansion on King's Road, a choice residential location in Sydney's new urban landscape – was among the club's first officers in 1901. Senator McDonald was classified as a 'privileged' member. He had, in fact, helped secure for the club a royal warrant to fly the blue ensign and permission to use the royal prefix.[108] And the social milieu of the McDonalds was not strictly local, of course. When Willie was attending McGill University, he received requests from Senators William Ogilvie and George Drummond to call on them at their mansions in Montreal's Square Mile.[109]

Even while members of the McDonald household remained deeply embedded in the local life of Glace Bay, their social network of family and friends had gravitated towards an increasingly distinct middle-class social and cultural sphere. J. A. Gillies, the Sydney barrister in whose firm Allan J. had worked, remained a friend of the Senator's, and his wife, Josephine, visited with Minnie and Cassie regularly. 'Mrs. Gillies came out from Sydney this morning to stay a week,' Cassie reported in 1896.[110] A week later, she wrote from Sydney: 'I came in here yesterday with Minnie + Mrs. Gillies to a party at the hotel. We are invited to go on board to the Admiral's ship tomorrow afternoon and Thursday night. Mrs. Dr. Willie McLeod is giving a party for the Admiral and we are going to that.'[111] Minnie stayed with Mrs McLeod to help her with the party, then stayed with her brother, Allan J., and his wife and infant son. She also saw 'Grandma and Aunty Jane' during her time in Sydney.[112] Dr William McKenzie McLeod and J. A. Gillies, Dr Samuel McLennan and Dr Michael McDonald, 'Aunt Jane' and 'Ronald Customs': mainly migrants from rural Cape Breton, they were part of a cohort of upwardly mobile Highlanders who formed an important element of industrial Cape Breton's middle class. This was the world of the Senator's family.

III

Highland identities were embedded in the kin relations and social networks that made up Cape Breton's country of coal. Decades ago, Rosemary Ommer documented the persistence of the local kin group, *clann*, as a unit of social reproduction among Highlanders who remigrated from Cape Breton to the

---

[108] F. C. Kimber, Sydney, to McDonald, 10 February 1902, item 744, and 24 April 1902, item 763, series 26, McDonald fonds, BI; *The Constitution and Bye-laws of the Royal Cape Breton Yacht Club* (Sydney, 1907).

[109] Willie, 43 Hutchinson St., Montreal, to Father, November 1896, item 611, series 26, McDonald fonds, BI.

[110] Cassie, Glace Bay, to Papa, 1 September 1896, item 593, series 26, McDonald fonds, BI.

[111] Cassie, Sydney, to Papa, 8 September 1896, item 598, series 26, McDonald fonds, BI.

[112] Minnie, Sydney, to Papa, 10 September 1896, item 600, series 26, McDonald fonds, BI.

Codroy Valley of Newfoundland.[113] This appears to have been an aspect of the experience of the McDonalds at Little Glace Bay. And the Senator indeed remained interested in his Highland identity later in the nineteenth century. 'We saw you were at a highland meeting in Ottawa last week,' commented Minnie to her father in 1896.[114] Earlier that year, he was profiled in a Scottish-Canadian magazine, *The Fiery Cross*, published in Montreal; his family connections to Clan Ranald and to the site of Ormacleit Castle were the emphasis in the lead article.[115] Importantly, the Senator's embrace of his Highland past occurred within an immediate historical experience of assimilation and anglicisation; it was an identity divorced from local context and distanced from the working-class culture of the coal towns and their distinct interpretations and uses of Highland culture and identity.[116]

Within the intergenerational, diasporic story of Senator McDonald's family, the rural homestead was not a destination but a beachhead to a wider colonial society and an urban-industrial political economy. The timing and location of settlement – the division between frontland and backland farms, often emphasised by scholars – were not the only factors in the production of social differentiation in the colonial countryside.[117] Often, historians have emphasised where Highlanders had come from and arrived, but not where they went afterwards. William McDonald left the family homestead to leverage inherited advantages and connections, and fully embraced a capitalist modernity predicated upon colonial nationalism and the acceleration of settler colonialism. He was not alone in this. J. A. Gillies's interest in real estate was the basis of his efforts to remove the Mi'kmaq from the King's Road Reserve in the Sydney area, which actually occurred in the 1920s. McDonald too sought profit from the appreciation in landed property that accompanied the making of industrial Cape Breton. He also, in the early 1880s, speculated in Prairie West land rendered more valuable by the prospect of an accelerated settler colonialism under the National Policy; as Chairman of the Committee on Immigration

---

[113] R. E. Ommer, 'Primitive accumulation and the Scottish *clann* in the Old World and the New', *Journal of Historical Geography*, 12:2 (1986), pp. 121–41.

[114] Minnie, Glace Bay, to Papa, 24 September 1896, item 605, series 26, McDonald fonds, BI.

[115] 'The Hon. W. MacDonald, Senator', *The Fiery Cross*, May 1896, pp. 3–4. McDonald had the editor send him one hundred copies of that issue of the magazine. See T. D. McDonald, Editor, 'Fiery Cross', 2591 St Catherine St., Montreal, to W. McDonald, 1 June 1896, item 475, series 25, McDonald fonds, BI.

[116] See Frank, 'Tradition and culture'.

[117] R. Bittermann, 'The hierarchy of the soil: Land and labour in a 19th century Cape Breton community', *Acadiensis*, 18:1 (1988), pp. 33–55; S. J. Hornsby, *Nineteenth-Century Cape Breton: A Historical Geography* (Montreal and Kingston: McGill-Queen's University Press, 1992); R. Bittermann, R. A. MacKinnon and G. Wynn, 'Of inequality and interdependence in the Nova Scotian countryside, 1850–70', *Canadian Historical Review*, 74:1 (1993), pp. 1–43; Daniel Samson, *The Spirit of Industry and Improvement: Liberal Government and Rural-Industrial Society, 1790–1862* (Montreal and Kingston: McGill-Queen's University Press, 2008).

and Colonization during that period, he was indeed directly involved in the Dominion government's colonisation programme.[118] By the turn of the century, industrial Cape Breton's increasingly diverse population – which included Jewish, African-Caribbean, Lebanese and Italian migrants – may have presented new business opportunities for the McDonalds, but they appear in family correspondence as outsiders and 'others'.[119] John Yorke, an African-Nova Scotian miner in Glace Bay, was evidence of a longer Black presence in the mining district; his father, James, had been a coal cutter at Sydney Mines. When Glace Bay magistrate A. B. McGillivray was chosen by the local priest to accompany Yorke in carrying the lead banner for a League of the Cross parade, McGillivray 'refused the honour'; Willie's description of Yorke – 'the n-----' – made clear the cause.[120] In early twentieth-century Canada, Scottish and Highland identities assumed meaning in an environment saturated by the racism of an 'age of empire'.

The bourgeois, patriarchal household also generated internal strife. In the McDonald papers, there is not one piece of correspondence from Kate McDonald, a significant gap in the documentary record. An unusually candid letter from Minnie in 1895, following Dan L.'s aborted effort to complete medical school, suggests the Senator may have acted as a domineering patriarch:

> I do not see why you should worry everyone in the house about Dannie. Why not send him off some place[?] It is not our place to do it. As I said yesterday Mama has enough trouble without adding more. People all say how old she looks, and it is no wonder. She is not made of stone.[121]

If the Senator acted in a domineering manner, his daughters appear to have been able to say so. And Teresa, as a nun, freely gave advice and guidance to her father on family issues. But tensions did not go away. When the Senator's brother Michael died, a dispute erupted in the family. His sister Jane sued him over

---

[118] Wicken, *The Colonization of Mi'kmaw Memory and History*, pp. 202–28. For evidence of McDonald's purchase of land in the Prairie West, see in series 25, McDonald fonds, BI: Ross, Ross & Killam, Winnipeg, to McDonald, 1 May 1880, item 143; A. W. Ross, Winnipeg, to McDonald, 12 March 1882, item 193; Dennis Sons & Co., Winnipeg, to McDonald, 27 February 1883, item 258.

[119] On African-Caribbean migration to industrial Cape Breton, see C. Bonner, 'Industrial Island – African-Caribbean Migration to Cape Breton, Canada, 1900–1930' (MA thesis, Dalhousie University, 2017).

[120] Willie, Glace Bay, to Father, 3 April 1899, item 659, series 26, McDonald fonds, BI. Census of Canada, 1871, Cape Breton, Sydney Mines (div. no. 2), p. 62; Census of Canada, 1881, Cape Breton, Sydney Mines (div. no. 2), p. 21; Census of Canada, 1891, Cape Breton County, Little Glace Bay, p. 84; Census of Canada, 1901, Cape Breton, Glace Bay, p. 50 (Yorke's 'racial origin' is listed as 'English' in this census); Census of Canada, 1911, Cape Breton South, Town of Glace Bay, p. 16. And the census can be linked to Yorke's death certificate. See Certificate of Registration of Death, Province of Nova Scotia, John Yorke, 7 May 1942, NSA.

[121] Minnie, Glace Bay, to Papa, 12 June 1895, item 517, series 26, McDonald fonds, BI.

money she claimed was owed to her. Dan L. was on his aunt's side.[122] Afterwards he became involved in a conflict with his father and Allan J. over his attempt to purchase a house in Essex County, Massachusetts, in a foreclosure sale connected to his uncle's estate. By March 1907 the dispute had escalated. 'It would not have been wise to have had Dan arrested while you were in Boston,' Allan J. wrote to his father, 'as this would likely necessitate your appearing against him and you would have been obliged to remain there for an indefinite time.'[123] Correspondence with the family effectively ends there in the Senator's papers, though the legal dispute dragged into 1909.[124] Familial bonds were strained by unequal commercial relations within the patriarchal household, but in the years to follow Dan L. maintained a place in the commercial life of the family.[125]

In the country of coal, the McDonalds were among a stratum within the composite Highland community positioned to pursue and exploit new commercial and professional opportunity, and they joined a local elite – of county barristers, merchants, politicians, doctors and others – which constituted an important element of the emerging social order. As such, they embraced the new industrialism. Hugh MacLennan's twentieth-century depiction of the Scottish Gael as a helpless victim of the coal town defies more complex historical realities, of which, ironically, he was himself a product. Nor were the miners helpless in the face of rapid change; Allan J.'s short reign as mayor of Glace Bay was ended in 1918 in a defeat to a working coal miner, a decisive moment in Glace Bay's transition to becoming a 'labour town'.[126]

---

[122] Allan J., Sydney, to Wm. McDonald, 10 April 1906, item 746, series 25, McDonald fonds, BI; Allan J. to Wm. McDonald, 23 November 1906, item 773, series 25, McDonald fonds, BI.
[123] Allan J., Glace Bay, to Father, 23 March 1907, item 787, series 25, McDonald fonds, BI.
[124] See, for instance, Allan J. to Thos. W. Proctor, 10 June 1909, Allan J. MacDonald letterbook, B2, p. 903, William (Billy Senator) MacDonald fonds, MG 12.88, BI.
[125] See W. H. Brasbie, Glace Bay, to D. L. & W. Jr. Macdonald, 10 October 1913, file B, Bert MacLeod fonds, MG 12.274, BI; Lease, D. L. MacDonald + W. MacDonald Jr. to Brasbies Ltd, 28 May 1909, file A.12, William (Billy Senator) MacDonald fonds, BI.
[126] David Frank, 'Company town / Labour town: Local government in the Cape Breton coal towns, 1917–1926', *Histoire sociale – Social History*, 14:27 (1981), p. 182.

Epilogue
Contested Boundaries – Documenting the Socio-Cultural Dimensions of Empire
Dara Price

The complexity of colonial identity

This book reminds us how daunting an intellectual task it is to interrogate the nature of colonial identity. The authors in this volume deftly illustrate how the social and cultural dimensions of empire were – and are – multi-faceted, dynamic and conflicted. This volume is timely, for it urges the reader to pause and reflect on the complexity of our colonial past. And, indeed, our colonial *present*: as the authors explore, the legacy of transatlantic migration in the eighteenth and nineteenth centuries continues to shape the social and cultural contours of community and identity today. These ongoing influences are dynamic, real and complicated.

At the moment – at least in Canada – 'colonialism' is frequently referenced in popular social and political discourse. Usually when used, the word connotes something wholly negative. It is a heuristic for a monolithic, oppressive force that is unidirectional and fundamentally destructive. On the one hand, this shorthand is useful and important: it gives us a vocabulary for myriad social ills that have grown out of post-Enlightenment political and economic structures. European hegemony in the modern age has resulted in persistent and intersecting forms of oppression, and this legacy is recognisable across all societies touched by the Western imperialism of the fifteenth to twentieth centuries. Words are powerful: in naming this legacy 'colonialism', we hold ourselves to account and create a framework for righting some of the wrongs of the past.

On the other hand, if we are reductionist in how we talk about colonialism – by conflating the simplified heuristic with the messier reality – we do ourselves a disservice. Half a millennium of social, political and economic interaction was not monolithic and is not adequately summed up in a single term. If we are to fight the daunting, intersectional forces of racism, sexism and classism (among others) stemming from colonial experiences, we must be clear-eyed about their complexity. We must accept that colonialism was an aggregate of disparate, layered and competing human experiences. These were both positive and negative, and were constantly shifting and being negotiated in light of local circumstances – not only political and economic, but equally environmental, linguistic, social and cultural.

This volume is a compelling case study in this complexity. By examining the connections between the Scottish Highlands and the Atlantic world from a variety of different vantage points, the authors demonstrate that the roles of coloniser and colonised were not fixed. Not only did migrants from the Scottish Highlands and Islands experience imperialism *within* the British Isles before their departure, but they had also lived that experience from vastly different viewpoints in terms of their access to power, be that class, wealth, religion, language or political influence. Tindley, for example, tells of the contest in which transplanted Highland elites engaged as they attempted to recreate – indeed, augment – the power they had enjoyed at home. The primary tool in this contest was land, both the asset itself and the policy framework around its ownership. The experience of these landowners could not have been more different than the Highland Scots in Cape Breton described by Kehoe, who entered into hyperlocal struggles for subsistence in the face of brutal living conditions. These took place in systematic defiance of colonial state authorities and involved not only opportunistic, extra-legal dispossession of local Mi'kmaq, but also a widespread and persistent practice of squatting. 'Settlement', then, belies an incremental and ambivalent web of processes. Similarly, identity formation was tentative, multi-generational and – importantly – multi-directional. The chapters in this volume demonstrate how the colonial route from the Highlands to the Atlantic world created a nexus of dynamic and inter-related identities that continues to evolve today.

Interdisciplinarity and expanding 'the archive'

Nuanced appreciation for the complexity of colonial stories – such as the sociocultural relationship between the Highlands and the Atlantic world – comes from openness to hearing multiple perspectives. Case studies, like those in this volume, are a powerful means of achieving this diversity of view. Complementary to this is interdisciplinarity. While not explicit as a unifying theme across these chapters, through their expansive studies of land, language and culture, and networks of empowerment and oppression, these authors implicitly advocate for crossing boundaries between academic disciplines. Their collection of personal and community stories relies on the work of not only economic, feminist and subaltern historians (to name but a few), but also archaeologists, environmental biologists and cultural studies scholars.

This interdisciplinary, case-study approach in turn encourages us to be open in how we think about the 'archive'. This book demonstrates how the exploration of complex concepts like identity, which are so firmly rooted in disparate and conflicting individual and collective experiences, requires diverse thinking about what constitutes historical evidence. Traditionally, archives are caches of documents – usually textual – deliberately preserved for their value as authoritative accounts of events or experiences. This tradition is anchored in Western epistemology: written accounts have long been considered the gold standard of factual, reliable and authentic records, particularly if authored by someone in a position of power. Other records, such as maps and photographs – even moving images – also make the cut, because they purport to be objective and accurate facsimiles of empirical reality. Valorisation of these modern, 'trusted' records emerged from the nineteenth-century exuberant belief that 'scientific' and technical processes (like photography and cartography) captured objective 'fact'.

To some extent, this certainty was destabilised by the great social, political and intellectual upheavals of the twentieth century. For many decades now, researchers have been grappling with the concept of universal and verifiable 'truth'. The post-war crumbling of the formal European imperial framework coincided with profound intellectual disruption: the civil rights movement, second-wave feminism, and the voicing of subaltern and Indigenous perspectives (among others) urged scholars to seek, hear and somehow incorporate the experiences of those on the margins of established power structures.

We clearly still have a long way to go in this regard. Nonetheless, as this book neatly demonstrates, historians have evolved our thinking about 'evidence' and have expanded our definition of authentic and legitimate sources. For example, many scholars now take advantage of the fundamentally different information and perspectives provided by oral testimony and tradition. This has opened up new and innovative avenues of analysis, as illustrated by both Dziennik and Dunbar. Dziennik uses an archive of spoken (or, rather, sung) heritage to reveal the otherwise obscured nuance in attitudes of many Gaels to British imperialism and North American immigration. Dunbar, for his part, uses sound recordings to shed light on how Gaelic folklore was preserved, transmuted and transmitted in Canada, as well as how ties of culture and identity were perpetuated between Scotland and North America long after European settlement of Cape Breton.

In addition to oral tradition, post-modern epistemology has also integrated a variety of other sources of documentation: stamps and coins, for instance, offer information about their contemporary societies; paintings can be seen as documents that – like photographs – reveal detail not only about an actual event, but also the perspective of the artist. Whereas in the past this lens would have been suspect because it was considered biased, now this unique interpretation has intrinsic value *by virtue of* being coloured by individual experience. It not only provides complementary information about what might have been out of another's frame (deliberately or accidentally), it is also an alternative – and valid – version of the truth.

Acceptance that there are, in fact, multiple and valid perspectives on truth, and that they are rooted in real experience, is of critical importance in colonial studies. As suggested above, the success or failure of work currently taking place across various settler societies to seek reconciliation between the colonial state and Indigenous populations will hinge on society's willingness to have brave, critical and complicated conversations about our social and cultural identity and heritage. In pursuit of this, scholars have started to appreciate the informational and archival value of 'documents' of Indigenous traditional knowledge, such as textiles and a wide variety of performance and visual arts.

Let us, then, go one step further and explore the possibilities of even greater creativity in thinking about the archive and about how we gain knowledge of the past. We could argue, for example, that Tindley and Kehoe use the land *itself* as an archival repository. Their arguments are based on the idea that, inscribed in the very geography of Atlantic Canada and of the Scottish Highlands, is a story of lives lived. Struggles over identity and culture were played out in this physical space, and the record of those struggles can be glimpsed in its topography, its flora and fauna, in its archaeology. Land is a document that can be read. Likewise, other authors explore how class structures in settler societies are texts, of sorts. Social class in the Atlantic world can be read as a coda, revealing stories about the interplay between metropole and periphery, and between colonial actors vying to create, reinvent or cement power structures. Language, too, is a text: the trajectory of Gaelic in both Scotland and Canada over the past centuries is a map that charts the definition and redefinition of networks and identities.

Other examples are evident in this volume, but I digress. The point is, if we as historians are willing to think broadly about what counts as 'evidence', and to team up with experts in other fields and use a common language, we can unlock new truths about colonial experiences. If this helps to develop more nuanced vocabulary about the profoundly complex social and cultural dimensions of colonialism it will, I hope, contribute something concrete to efforts at reconciliation.

This book invites us to consider and challenge our assumptions about boundaries. This includes the physical, social and cultural boundaries between Scotland, Canada and the Caribbean, as well as the boundaries among Highlanders themselves, and between them and other communities. The authors have shown us how the Highlands and the Atlantic world were – and are – deeply connected, entangled in dynamic networks of language, family, wealth, status and culture. I have further suggested that we contest the boundaries that separate academic disciplines, as well as those that define how we think about legitimate informational and archival sources. These borders are the product of Western knowledge systems: they are, in many ways, arbitrary. By experimenting with moving back and forth across them, we can discover new paths to addressing some of the pressing social and cultural challenges we currently face.

Index

Note: bold indicates illustrations

Aberdeen, 116
abolition movement, 134, 141
absentee landowners, 22, 25, 26, 28–9
Acadians, 31, 35, 37, 48, 54, 94
'Account of the Captivity of Alexander Scott' (Traill), 131
'Account of Tupai Cupa' (Traill), 131
Act of Union, 153
African Caribbean settlers, 31–2, 192
Agassiz, Louis, 138
Age of Revolutions, 96, 101, 111
agriculture, 18, 20, 27, 39, 128, 180, 185–6, 196
Ainsley, George Robert, 34–5
Alexander, William, Earl of Stirling, 54
Alston, John, 163
L'Amitie en Libertie plantation, 125
ancestors, 1, 37, 64
anglicisation, 5, 182, 191
Anglo-Irish Ascendancy, 23
Antigonish County, 54, 57, 90, 172
Antigua, 95, 153
Anti-Slavery Society, 134
Anna Ruadh (NicNèill), 90
archives, 3, 196–8
Arctic exploration, 130
Argyllshire Highlanders, 99
aristocracy, 9, 15–30, 128, 163, 196
Arthur, Innes, 121

Audubon, John James, 129
Australia, 26, 79, 80, 84, 85, 143

Bahia, 136
Baillie, George, 122
Baird, David, 100
Baker, Colin, 59
balls, 120, 125, 129, 167–8, 169, 180, 189
banking, 128, 150, 161
bankruptcy, 22, 145
Barbados, 95, 98, 117, 142, 153
Barclay, Katie, 128, 131
Bateman, Meg, 74
Bathurst, Henry, 34
Beaton, Donald, 84, 85
Bell, Charles, 145
Bellevue Medical College, 182
Berbice, 118, 121, 125, 136, 153, 164
Bergen Op Zoom, 94
Bernera Riot, 86
Bethune, Angus, 118
Bethune, George, 143
Bethune, John, 121
Bezelius, John Jacob, 130
Birmingham, 134
Black Bull Inn, 148, 150, 155, 163, 165
Black Watch regiment, 94, 96, 98, 99, 102, 109, 110, 154, 157

INDEX

Blair, Duncan Black, 84
Blair, James, 141
Blenheim, 74
Blochairn, 118, 141
'Birlinn Chlann Raghnaill' (Mac Mhaighstir Alasdair), 73
Bòrd na Gàidhlig, 58–9
Boswell, James, 91
Botanic Garden, Liverpool, 129, 134
Bourdieu, Pierre, 68
Bradan Press, 90
Brazil, 136
British Army, 93–112
British Association, 138, 139
British North America *see* Canada
Brown, Ann (née Rainy), 141
Brown, Robert, 141
Bucholtz, Mary, 68
Buenos Aires, 100, 101
Bun is Bàrr programme, 50, 53
Burns, Robert, 9, 132

'Caismeachd Ailein-nan-Sop' (Maclean), 88
Caledonia Coal Company, 188
Caledonian Club, 175
Cameron, Eoghann, 76
Cameron, James D., 182
Cameron, John, 103
Cameron Highlanders, 98, 99
Campbell, Agnes (née Finlay), 168
Campbell, Alex (son of John senior), 158
Campbell, Alexander (of Dallingburn), 158
Campbell, Alexander (of Hallyards), 149, 158, 162, 165, 167
Campbell, Alexander (of Haylodge), 158–59, 163, 167–8
Campbell, Alexander (of Kinloch), 157
Campbell, Archibald (of Jamaica), 163
Campbell, Archibald (of Jura), 159
Campbell, Barbara, 159, 167
Campbell, 'Black' Mungo, 158–59, 163
Campbell, Colin (of Jura), 159, 161, 163, 167

Campbell, Colin (of Park), 157–8, 161, 163
Campbell, Colin (son of John senior), 158
Campbell, Helen, 168
Campbell, Isabella Hamilton Dundas (née Dennistoun), 167
Campbell, John (of Achalader), 102
Campbell, John (poet), 84, 85
Campbell, John Lorne (recorder of oral traditions), 90
Campbell, John senior (Gaelic Club member), 157–59, 161, 168
Campbell, Mungo Nutter, 158, 165, 167, 168
Campbell, Neil, 81, 82
Campbell, Niall, 88–9
Campbell, Thomas (poet), 130
Campbell, Thomas (son of John senior), 158, 168
Campbell, Sir Walter, 22, 82
Campbell, 'White' Mungo, 159
Canada
  climate, 34
  education, 8, 23, 48, 49, 50, 56, 59, 180–3
  English language, 8, 53, 55–7, 64, 182
  exploration, 130
  forests, 21, 34
  French language, 8, 49, 53, 59, 94
  Gaelic language, 7–8, 10, 47–50, 53–8, 60–70, 72, 74, 76, 78–90, 173, 182
  governance, 23–5, 34, 176–7
  Indigenous displacement, 9–10, 33, 37–8, 41–2, 172, 191, 196
  industry, 11, 31, 170–1, 173–82, 183–6, 188–91, 192, 193
  land acquisition, 9–10, 16, 21–2, 34–8, 172
  land agitation, 19, 25–30
  land reform, 28–9
  landscape, 21, 34, 37
  migration to, 2, 4, 9, 15–30, 31–43, 54–5, 57, 74, 95, 97, 170, 172, 196
  military service in, 94–5, 97

mining, 2, 4, 11, 170-1, 173-81,
    183-5, 188-89, 192
periodicals and publishing, 72, 74,
    78-90
tourism, 10, 33
see also individual locations
Canada Company, 76
Canada Scotsman, 88
Cannadine, David, 17, 18
Cape Breton Island
  agriculture, 39, 180, 196
  climate, 34
  education, 48, 180-3
  elections, 175-7
  ethnic diversity, 31-2, 192
  forests, 34
  Gaelic language, 8, 48, 56, 72, 173, 182
  governance, 34, 176-7
  Indigenous displacement, 10, 33, 37-8,
    41-2, 172, 191, 196
  industry, 11, 31, 170-1, 173-81,
    183-5, 188-90, 192, 193
  land acquisition, 10, 34-8, 172
  landscape, 34, 37
  MacLennan's writings on, 1-2, 11,
    170-1, 193
  maps, 36, 37, **174**
  migration to, 2, 16, 19, 27, 31-43,
    54-5, 170, 172, 196
  Mi'kmaq, 10, 31-4, 37-8, 41-3, 172,
    191, 196
  mining, 2, 4, 11, 170-1, 173-81,
    183-5, 188-89, 192
  periodicals and publishing, 72
  population decline, 56
  population growth, 37
  social class, 170-1, 182, 188-90, 193
  social networks, 33-4, 35-7, 171-93
  squatting, 38-40, 41, 196
  tourism, 10, 33
  transport, 189
  yacht club, 189-90
Cape of Good Hope, 100
capitalism, 20, 21, 25, 92, 191
Caraid a' Ghaidheil, 80-1

Caribbean
  climate, 119, 124
  colonisation and settlement, 153
  Gaelic language, 71, 110-11, 158
  land acquisition, 153
  migration to, 4, 95
  military service in, 95, 96, 97-8, 105
  periodical subscriptions, 71
  plantations, 3, 117-19, 121-2, 125,
    128, 134-8, 141, 146-7, 149-50,
    158-60, 165
  slavery, 2, 10, 117-19, 122, 124, 128,
    133-47, 151-2, 158-60, 166, 169
  and social networks, 10, 115-47,
    149-69
  uprisings, 138, 161, 168
  see also individual locations
Carmichael, Alexander, 85
Carmichael, Hugh, 110-11
Carriacou, 122
Casket, 90
Catholicism, 5, 37, 40, 55, 97, 99, 116,
    172, 175, 176, 180
Ceanaideach, Donnchadh (Duncan
    Kennedy), 103
*Ceann-Iùil an Fhir-Imrich do dh'America
    mu Thuath* (MacDougall), 78
Celtic Magazine, 83, 87, 88
census data, 7, 47, 55, 58, 157, 178, 179
ceremony, 18, 37, 155-6
chain migration, 55
Chalmers, Thomas, 140-1
Chamshron, Maighread (Margaret
    Cameron), 102
Cheveley, John Castlefranc, 125
Chisholm, Archie Neil, 43
Clan Chattan Confederacy, 94
Clan Ranald, 172, 191
clann Lachlainn, 173
Clark, John, 96-7
Clark, Niall, 81-2
Clàrsach nam Beann (MacColl), 86
Clàrsach na Coille (Maclean Sinclair), 89
class *see* social class
clearances *see* Highland Clearances

climate, 34, 119, 124
Clinton, Sir Henry, 110
collective memory, 21, 24–5
colonial nationalism, 11, 171, 191
Comhairle nan Leabhraichean, 90
Comhradh eadar Dun-Bhrusgraig agus Fearturais (McCorkindale), 82, 85
commerce *see* trade
commercial farming, 20
Community Land Scotland, 3
Companach an Oganaich (McGillivray), 74
compensation
  for land improvements, 26
  for slave owners, 160, 166
Conservative Party, 171, 176–7, 183, 188
Content plantation, 160
Corrie, William, 129
cotton, 118, 129, 153
Cow Bay, 173, 178, 179
Cowal, 86
Cozzens, Frederick, 40
Craik, George, 131
Crantit, 120
Crawford, Dougal, 74
Creich, 117, 118, 119, 121
Cuairtear nan Gleann, 72, 73, 76–80, 84
Cuming, Thomas, 165

Dalhousie University, 182
Dalton, John, 130
Dalzell's regiment, 96
Darroch, John, 81
Davidoff, Leonore, 127–8
Demerara, 117–19, 121–5, 134–8, 142, 143, 145, 147, 153, 159, 164–7
Demerary, 135
democracy, 23, 24
Dennistoun, James Robert, 163
Dennistoun, Richard, 167
dictionaries, 71, 109–10
Disarming Act, 95
disease, 94, 97–8, 119
displacement
  in the Highlands, 16, 19–21, 33, 38, 42–3, 54, 55
  of Indigenous peoples, 2, 9–10, 33, 37–8, 41–2, 172, 191, 196
Disruption, 140
Dominica, 153
Dominion Coal Company, 170, 183–5, 187–8
Dominion Iron and Steel Company, 185, 188
Donkin, Hiram, 189
Doria, 142
Dorian, Nancy, 68
Dörnyei, Zoltán, 53
Douglas, Betsy, 121
Douglas, Cecilia, 121
Douglas, George, 118, 121
Douglas, Gilbert, 121, 149
Douglas, Robert (father of George and Gilbert), 121
Douglas, Robert (son of Gilbert), 121
Douglas Park, 121
Downey, Hector, 121
Drummond, George, 190
Dublin, 138
Dubrulon, Fanchine, 143
Dufferin, Frederick Hamilton-Temple-Blackwood, 1st Marquess, 23–9
Dùghallach, Ailein (Allan MacDougall), 103
Dunbar, Robert, 72, 80
Dundas, Henry, 163–4
Dundas, Thomas, Lord, 120
Dunmore, Robert, 157, 161
Dunrobin Castle, 116, 122

Each Man's Son (MacLennan), 170–1
Earle, William, 134
East Bay, 173, 177
East India Company, 129–30, 137
Edinburgh, 72, 82, 88, 115, 130, 138–9, 145
Edinburgh Journal, 28
Edinburgh Ladies Association, 176
Edinburgh Philosophical Journal, 130
Edmonstone, Charles, 137

education
  in Canada, 8, 23, 48, 50, 56, 59, 180–3
  and the Gaelic language, 7, 8, 47–50, 56, 58–9, 69, 182
  higher education, 182–3
  immersion education, 48, 49–50, 58–9, 69
  institutions supported by money linked to slavery, 135
  promotion of, 150, 155
  in Scotland, 7, 48, 49, 50, 58–9, 69, 135–6, 143–4
  and social class, 182
Edwards, John, 55–6, 59, 67
emigrant guidebooks, 78
emigrant ships, 73–4
emigration schemes, 9, 10, 15–16, 19, 21–3, 72, 76–7
emigration songs, 102, 104–5
English language
  anglicisation, 5, 182, 191
  in Canada, 8, 53, 55–7, 64, 182
  as language of empire, 7
  and military service, 109
  periodicals and publishing, 71, 79, 83, 86
equality, 131–3, 146
Essequibo, 153, 164
estates
  estate management, 18, 19–21
  historical links with slavery, 3
  income from, 128
  purchase of, 158
  see also plantations
ethnic diversity, 31–2, 192
European Union, 7
evictions, 19–21, 82; *see also* Highland Clearances
Ewing, James, 150
exploitation, 2, 10, 146
exploration, 130

Fairlie, 118, 139, 140–2, 160
Fall on Your Knees (MacDonald), 31

Family Fortunes (Davidoff and Hall), 127–8
famine, 20, 22, 28, 39, 76; *see also* Great Famine; Highland Famine
Fedon's Rebellion, 161, 168
femininity, 127–8, 146
feminism, 196, 197
Fiery Cross, 191
Finlay, Kirkman, 157, 160, 168
fishing, 16, 39
Fishman, Joshua A., 49–51, 60, 67–8
Flinn, Margot, 137
Florida, 94
folklore, 85, 197
Forbes, Duncan, 117
Forbes, George, 117
Forbes, James, 117
Forbes, William, Jr, 117
Forbes, William, Sr, 116
forests, 21, 34
Fort Mose, 94
42nd Foot regiment *see* Black Watch regiment
fosterage, 178–79
France, 94, 95, 97, 117, 142
Franklin, John, 130
Fraser, Evan, 165
Fraser, John, 118
Fraser, Simon (colonel), 104
Fraser, Simon (of Belladrum), 121
Fraser's Highlanders, 102
Free Church of Scotland, 140, 146
French language, 8, 49, 53, 59, 94
French Revolutionary Wars, 98, 99, 153
Fullarton, John, 125

Gaelic Club of Glasgow, 10–11, 148–69
Gaelic identity, 60–70, 71, 76; *see also* Highland identity; Scottish identity
Gaelic language
  attitudes towards, 7, 56–7, 60–70
  in Australia, 80, 85
  in Canada, 7–8, 10, 47–50, 53–8, 60–70, 72, 74, 76, 78–90, 173, 182

on Cape Breton Island, 8, 48, 56, 72, 173, 182
in the Caribbean, 71, 110–11, 158
dictionaries, 71, 109–10
and education, 7, 8, 47–50, 56, 58–9, 69, 182
and Gaelic Club membershipo, 153, 155, 158, 168
and identity, 48, 50–1, 53–4, 57–8, 60–70, 76
immersion education, 48, 49–50, 58–9, 69
intergenerational transmission, 49, 50, 51, 55–6, 69
language policies, 47–50, 57–9, 69–70
literary networks, 10, 71–90, 110
and military service, 99, 109–10
new speakers, 8, 10, 47–54, 58, 59–70
numbers of speakers, 7, 47, 56, 58
periodicals and publishing, 10, 71–90, 109–10
poetry, 73, 81–2, 84–9, 101, 104–5, 108, 111
promotion of, 110–11
revitalisation of, 10, 47–52, 57–9, 67
in Scotland, 7, 47–8, 50, 52, 58–67
and social networks, 5, 8, 71–90
songs, 10, 43, 92–3, 101–9, 111, 197
use in professional contexts, 59, 60, 69
Gaelic associations, 10–11, 86, 87, 148–69
Gaelic Society of Toronto, 87
Gaidheal, An, 72, 73, 83–90
'Gaidheal am measg nan Gall, An' (Maclean), 85
'Gaidheal thar gach Gaidheal' (MacColl), 87–8
Gàidhlig aig Baile programme, 50, 53
Gardner, Robert C., 53
gender, 127–9, 131–2, 146
General Mining Association, (GMA), 173, 177
gentlemen's clubs, 10–11, 148–69
George III, 108

Georgetown, 125, 136
Georgia, 94, 95, 153
Germany, 95, 142
Ghriogarach, Mairearad (Margaret MacGregor), 107
Gibson, John, 139
Gillies, J. A., 182, 190, 191
Gillies, Josephine, 190
Gillies Collection, 110
Glace Bay, 2, 170–1, 173–83, 185, 187–93
Gladstone, John, 133, 134, 135
Glasgow, 10–11, 72, 80–2, 84, 86, 89, 119, 121, 140–1, 143, 144, 148–69
Glasgow, Robert, 150
Glasgow Chronicle, 79
Glasgow Highland regiment, 99, 100, 104
Glasgow West India Association, 158, 160, 163, 168
Glenaladale, 38
Glengarry County, 54–5, 81, 85
Glengarry Fencibles regiment, 97
Gloomy Memories of the Highlands of Scotland (MacLeod), 21, 28
Golspie, 116
Gordon, Alexander, 4th Duke, 110
Gordon Fencibles, 110
Gordon Highlanders, 100, 109
governance
  aristocratic conceptions of, 23–5
  in Canada, 23–5, 34, 176–7
  colonial governance, 6, 23–5, 34
  of estates *see* estate management
  Indigenous systems, 6, 32
Grahame, Archibald, 150, 161–2, 168
Grand Narrows, 172, 173, 178
Grant, Donald, 85
Grant, Sir James, 99
Great Depression, 56–7
Great Famine, 39
Greenland, 130
Greenough, George Bellas, 138
Grenada, 117, 118, 119, 153, 158, 161–2, 164, 165, 168

Guyana, 115, 117, 118, 121, 124, 141, 147, 153, 165, 166

Hafodunos, 118, 139
Hagart, Charles, 150
Halifax, 57, 90, 177, 179, 183
Haliburton, Thomas Chandler, 40
Hall, Catherine, 127–8
Hall, Kira, 68
Hamilton, Douglas, 151, 156
Hearn, James H., 185
Hebrides, 21
Heyrick, Elizabeth, 134
Highland Clearances, 16, 19–21, 24–5, 33, 42–3, 54, 55
Highland dancing, 156
Highland Famine, 20, 22, 28, 39, 76
Highland identity, 1, 31–2, 40–1, 43, 66, 115, 154, 160, 171, 189, 190–1; *see also* Gaelic identity; Scottish identity
Highland Land War, 17
Highland News, 90
Highland Society of Glasgow, 150, 155
Highland Society of London, 152, 154
Highlander (periodical), 83, 85, 88
Highlander (ship), 118
Historical Slavery Initiative, 3
Hodge Podge club, 150
Horsefield, Thomas, 129–30
housing, 22, 185, 187–8
Houston, Alexander, 165
Houston, Andrew, 157
Howard, Edward Charles, 133
Hunter, James, 38, 40
hunting, 39, 41
Hutton, Robert, 138

identity
  Gaelic identity, 60–70, 71, 76
  and gender, 127–9, 146
  Highland identity, 1, 31–2, 40–1, 43, 66, 115, 154, 160, 171, 189, 190–1
  and language, 48, 50–1, 53–4, 57–8, 60–70, 71, 76

  Scottish identity, 48, 61
  and social class, 11, 127–9, 171, 189
  and social networks, 8–9, 11, 43, 115, 189, 190–1
Immediate not Gradual Abolition (Heyrick), 134
immersion education, 48, 49–50, 58–9, 69
improvement
  of land, 19, 22, 26, 128
  personal, 7, 150, 161
India, 23, 26, 27, 95, 97, 98, 100, 134
indentured servitude, 95, 121, 153
independent military companies, 94, 96
Indigenous peoples
  attitudes towards, 111–12
  ceremonial practices, 37
  displacement of, 2, 9–10, 33, 37–8, 41–2, 172, 191, 196
  governance systems, 6, 32
  knowledge systems, 6, 198
  land use, 6, 37–8, 41
  see also Mi'kmaq
Indonesia, 129
industrialisation, 17, 128
industry, 11, 17, 18, 31, 55, 127, 128, 170–1, 173–81, 183–5, 188–90, 192, 193
inheritance, 28, 30
interdisciplinarity, 196–9
intergenerational transmission, 49, 50, 51, 55–6, 69
Inverness, 69, 118, 119–20, 126, 143
Inverness County, 31, 35, 42, 54, 57, 175, 179
Inverness Royal Academy, 116, 135
Iona, 142
Ireland, 17, 20, 23, 26, 27, 30, 39, 42, 97, 99, 130, 138
Irish settlers, 31, 35, 37
Islay, 22, 23, 72, 81–2
Italian settlers, 192
Italy, 142
Ivey, Marlene, 58

Jacobite Rebellions, 94, 95–6, 108, 160
Jaffe, Alexandra, 51, 67, 68
Jamaica, 97, 121–2, 153, 157, 160, 164, 165
Jasanoff, Maya, 137
Jefferson, Thomas, 104
Jewish settlers, 192
John Campbell senior & Co., 149, 157–59, 161–2, 165, 166, 168
Johnson, Samuel, 91
Johnson map, 36, 37
Johnstone family, 115
Joseph, John, 68

kelp industry, 16
Kennedy, Michael, 54, 55, 56
Kensington plantation, 125
Kildalton, 22
Kiltearn, 116–21, 125–7
Kiltearn plantation, 118, 121, 125
Kingston, Jamaica, 122
Kingston, Ontario, 79, 85, 86–7
Kingston Chronicle, 74
kinship networks, 8, 117–27, 134–47, 157–59, 161, 178–80, 185–93
Kirkwall, 120, 123–4
Knowles, James Sheridan, 130

labour, 10, 15–16, 95, 103, 175, 185–6
Ladies' Societies, 134
Laffin, Laurence, 180
Laing, May, 126
Laing, Samuel, 126
Lambert, Wallace E., 53
Lammie, William, 165
land acquisition, 6, 9–10, 16, 21–2, 34–8, 153, 172
land agitation, 17, 19, 25–30
land grants, 20, 21, 34–5, 111, 153, 172
land lotteries, 6, 22, 25
land management, 18–19
Land Purchase Act, 26
land reform, 6, 19, 26–30
land rights, 6, 25–30, 34–8, 41
land speculation, 191–2

land use, 6, 33, 41
landlords, 10, 15–30, 72, 76–7, 85–6, 185, 187–8
landownership, 3, 6, 10, 17, 19, 25–9, 33, 34–5, 128, 196
landscape, 4, 21, 34, 37
language acquisition, 49–54
language discrimination, 7–8
language policies, 48–50, 57–9, 69–70
language shift, 49, 50, 56–7
Laoidhean Spioradail (Maclean), 81
Lawson, William, 131
League of the Cross, 180
Lebanese settlers, 31, 192
LeBone, Oliver Thomas, 41
Leckie Ewing, William, 160, 163
Leeward Islands, 96, 110–11
legislative reform, 17, 28–9
Lewis, 83, 85–6
libraries, 3, 74
Linch, Kevin, 99
Lingan, 173, 177, 178, 179, 180
linguistic ideologies, 10, 48, 51–2, 57, 59, 68
Liniers, Santiogo de, 100
Linkletter, Michael, 72
Literary and Philosophical Society, 129
literary networks, 10, 71–90, 110
Litir bho Nial Clèireach (Cleireach), 81–2
Liverpool, 115, 118, 122, 124, 126–34, 136, 138, 142, 145, 146, 159, 166
Liverpool Ladies' Anti-Slavery Association, 134
Liverpool Mechanics Institut, 129
Liverpool Ophthalmic Infirmary, 129
Liverpool Royal Institution, 129, 130
Liverpool School for the Blind, 129
London, 22, 25, 100, 136, 139, 143, 145, 152, 154, 166
London West India Committee, 166–7
'Long Mhòr nan Eilthireach' (MacLeod), 74
Louisbourg, 189
Lowland Cove, 38

Lowland Scots, 5, 55, 61, 99, 150, 160
Loyalists, 31, 34, 35, 117

McAllan, William, 161, 164
McBean, William, 118
Macclesfield, 136
MacCoinnich, Coinneach (Kenneth Mackenzie), 102, 107, 108–9, 110
MacColl, Evan, 85, 86–8, 89
McCorkindale, Hugh, 82–3, 84, 85
McCorkindale, John, 82–3, 85
McCulloch, George, 118
McCulloch, Tom, 121
McCulloch, William, 121
MacDiarmid, Hugh, 152
McDonald, Agnes (daughter of Kate), 177
McDonald, Agnes (sister of Kate), 178, 179
MacDonald, Sir Alexander, 91
McDonald, Alice, 179
McDonald, Allan (father of William), 179
McDonald, Allan J. (son of William), 175, 179, 180, 182, 185, 187, 188, 190, 193
McDonald, Angus G., 182
MacDonald, Angus L., 42
MacDonald, Anne Marie, 31
McDonald, Aodh, 172, 182
McDonald, Augustin, 38
McDonald, Cassie, 177, 179, 183, 188, 189, 190
McDonald, Catherine (née MacLellan), 172
McDonald, Clara Agnes, 178, 185
McDonald, Daniel (brother of William), 179
McDonald, Dan L. (son of William), 175, 182–3, 185–6, 187, 192–3
McDonald, Donald, 172, 173
McDonald, Eunice (née McInnis), 179
McDonald, Florence A. (née Hearn), 185
McDonald, Hector, 177–8, 179
McDonald, Jane, 178, 190, 192–3
MacDonald, John (settler, Prince Edward Island), 38
McDonald, John A. (brother of William), 179
McDonald, Kate, 175, 177, 178–79, 192
McDonald, Mary (mother of William), 172, 179
McDonald, Mary (sister of Kate), 177, 178, 179
McDonald, Michael, 179, 182, 190, 192
McDonald, Minnie, 177, 179, 183, 186, 188, 189, 190, 191, 192
MacDonald, Rodney, 57
McDonald, Ronald, 173, 177–8, 179, 190
McDonald, Stephen, 178, 186–7
McDonald, Teresa (daughter of William), 175, 178–79, 180–2, 185, 187, 192
McDonald, Teresa (née Gillis) (mother of Ronald), 173
McDonald, William, 171–93, **177**
McDonald, William (of Barra) (grandfather of William), 172
McDonald, Willie (son of Allan J.), 179, 185
McDonald, Willie (son of William), 177, 183, 189, 190
Macdonnell, Alexander, 97
MacDonell, Farquhar, 85
McDougall, Dan Hugh, 188–89
MacDougall, Robert, 78
Macfarlan, Duncan, 157
McGill University, 183, 190
McGillivray, A. B., 192
McGillivray, Alexander, 74
MacGregor, Alexander (periodical contributor), 73, 87
McGregor, Alexander (rector, Inverness Academy), 116
MacGregor, Patrick, 87
MacGriogair, Iain (John Mcgregor), 102
mac Iain Bhàin, Alasdair (Alexander Grant), 105–6
McInnis, Alex, 179
McInroy, James, 117, 149, 159, 160, 163, 166
McInroy, James Patrick, 159
MacIntosh, Donald, 79

INDEX

McIntosh, George, 152
MacIntyre, Peter D., 53–4
Maciver, Ruairidh, 101
Mackay, Robert, 157
MacKeen, David, 188
Mackenzie, Alexander (army captain), 96
Mackenzie, Alexander (editor of *Celtic Magazine*), 87–8, 89
Mackenzie, Henry, 109
Mackenzie, John, 86
Mackenzie River Expedition, 130
Mackillop, Andrew, 103
MacKinnon, Colin F., 179
MacKinnon, Kenneth, 54, 56
MacKinnon, Rod, 187
MacLachlan, John, 85
MacLae, Walter Ewing, 150
MacLathagain, Seumas (James MacLagan), 102, 104, 109–10
MacLauchlan, Thomas, 88
Maclean, Hector, 88
McClean, John (of Carriacou), 122
Maclean, John (poet), 73, 80, 81, 85, 88
Maclean Sinclair, Alexander, 72, 88–9
MacLennan, Hugh, 1–2, 7, 11, 170–2, 188, 193
MacLennan, John, 78
MacLennan, Neil, 170
MacLennan, Samuel, 170, 171, 188, 190
MacLeod, Donald, 21, 28, 101
McLeod, Hugh (political candidate, Cape Breton), 176
MacLeod, Hugh (professor, University of Glasgow), 152
MacLeod, Norman, Jr, 73–81
MacLeod, Norman, Sr, 74
McLeod, William McKenzie, 176, 190
McLeod, Wilson, 52
Macleod's regiment, 100
Mac Mhaighstir Alasdair, Alasdair, 73
mac Mhurchaidh, Iain (John McRae), 102–3
McNeil, James, 173
McNeil, John, 78, 84
MacNeil, Malcolm, 173

McNicol, Donald, 109
MacNicol, Dugald, 105
MacPherson, Donald C., 88
Macpherson, Duncan, 102
Macrae, Colin, 166–7
McRae, Murdo, 187
Mac-Talla, 72, 90
Manchester, 99
Margaree Forks, 31, 35, 43
Marran plantation, 158
marriage, 117–18, 126–33, 146, 167–8, 169, 177–8
Martinique, 98
Maryland, 95, 149, 153
masculinity, 127–8, 146
Massachusetts Bay, 96
Matheson, Alexander, 75, 81
Matheson, Sir James, 86
Meek, Donald, 81
Melville, Hermann, 131
'Memoir of Mrs Traill' (Traill), 115, 129, 131, 132, 139
Memoir of William Roscoe (Traill), 134
memory, 21, 24–5, 41, 42
Mertz, Elizabeth, 56
metapragmatic filters, 56–7
Methodist church, 116, 134, 141
Middle River, 37–8
migration
  to Australia, 143
  to Canada, 2, 4, 9, 15–30, 31–43, 54–5, 57, 74, 95, 97, 170, 172, 196
  to Cape Breton Island, 2, 16, 19, 27, 31–43, 54–5, 170, 172, 196
  to the Caribbean, 4, 95, 96
  chain migration, 55
  emigrant guidebooks, 78
  emigrant ships, 73–4
  emigration schemes, 9, 10, 15–16, 19, 21–3, 72, 76–7
  emigration songs, 102, 104–5
  increased levels of, 4, 37
  landlord opposition to, 15–16, 20, 28
  military migrants, 94–5, 97

migration (*cont.*)
  to New Zealand, 74, 77
  to Nova Scotia, 15, 20, 27, 54–5, 57, 172
  to Prince Edward Island, 15–16, 19, 21–2, 38, 54
  promotion of, 76–9, 84, 91–2
  to the United States, 153
Mi'kmaq, 6, 10, 31–4, 37–8, 41–3, 48, 54, 172, 191, 196
military networks, 9, 110–11
military recruitment, 10, 92, 93–100, 105–6, 111
military service, 3, 9, 10, 18, 92–112
military songs, 10, 92–3, 101–9, 111
mining, 2, 4, 11, 128, 170–1, 173–81, 183–5, 188–89, 192
Moby Dick (Melville), 131
monarchy, 23, 108
moneylending, 185
Montgomery, L. M., 90
Montreal, 74, 75, 80–1, 170, 183–5, 190, 191
Montrose, James Graham, 3rd Duke, 163
Moss, John, 133
Mount Pleasant (Roscoe), 134
Mount Pleasant plantation, 149
Mount St Vincent Academy, 181
Mountgreen plantation, 150
Moxham, A. J., 190
Mull, 88, 107
Mullen, Mary, 42
Munro, Donald, 86
Munro, Gilbert, 122
Munro, Sir Hector, 116
Munro, Hugh, 121
Munro, Joseph, 118
Munro, Matthew, 118
Munro, William, 121, 122
Murdoch, Steve, 32
Murray, Lord John, 96
museums, 3, 129–30
music, 43, 76, 181
mutinies, 96–7, 109

Napoleonic Wars, 20, 92, 97, 99, 101, 105–6, 110, 153
National Trust for Scotland, 3
nationalism, 11, 171, 191
Netherlands, 100
Nevis, 153
New Orleans, Battle of, 100–1
New Zealand, 26, 74, 77, 79, 84, 131
Newcastle, 138
Newfoundland, 55, 191
newspapers, 16, 22, 24, 72, 74, 77–8, 90
Newton, Michael, 42
Newzealanders, The (Craik), 131
Niagara Falls, 142
Nicholson, Alexander, 83–4, 86, 88
NicNèill, Mòrag Anna, 90
91st Foot regiment *see* Argyllshire Highlanders
92nd Foot regiment *see* Gordon Highlanders
93rd Foot regiment *see* Sutherland regiment
97th Foot regiment, 98
North Carolina, 74, 153
North West Passage, 130
Nova Scotia
  education, 48, 56
  English language, 55–7, 64
  enters into Confederation, 175
  French language, 94
  Gaelic language, 7, 10, 47–8, 50, 53–8, 60–70, 74, 78, 80, 88, 90
  migration to, 15, 20, 27, 54–5, 57, 172
  periodicals and publishing, 74, 78, 80, 88, 90
  socioeconomic change, 56–7
  see also Canada; *and individual locations*

Oban Times, 85, 87, 88, 90
Office of Gaelic Affairs (*Oifis Iomairtean na Gàidhlig*), 48, 57
Ogilvie, William, 190
Ogle, Maurice, 80, 81
Oglethorpe, James, 94
Ommer, Rosemary, 190–1

Ontario, 55, 57, 72, 79, 82, 85, 86–7
Orkney, 120, 122–4, 125–6, 138
Ormacleit Castle, 172, 191
Ottawa, 175, 179, 181, 191
oppression, 2, 9, 10, 195, 196
oral tradition, 41, 90, 197
ornamental roles, 17–18

Pakenham, Sir Edward, 100
panegyric, 93, 102
Parker, Anne (née Traill), 138–9, 142
Parker, Charles, 144
Parker, Charles Stewart, Jr, 142
Parker, Charles Stewart, Sr, 117–18, 122, 125, 138, 140–1, 144, 150, 159, 160, 161, 163, 166
Parker, George, 138–9, 142
Parker, George 'Doria', 142
Parker, James (father of Charles Stewart Parker), 117, 160
Parker, James (son of Charles Stewart Parker), 144
Parker, Margaret (née Rainy), 117–18, 138, 140
Passenger Vessels Act, 15, 20
paternalism, 29, 188
Paul, Daniel, 32
Peninsular War, 100
Pepperell, Sir William, 96
periodicals, 10, 71–90
Phantom, 142
Philadelphia, 117, 142
Pictou County, 20, 54, 57, 74, 78–9, 89
Piesse, Jude, 71, 72
plantations, 3, 117–19, 121–2, 125, 128, 134–8, 141, 146–7, 149–50, 158–60, 165
poetry, 73, 81–2, 84–9, 101–2, 104–5, 108, 111, 132, 139; *see also* songs
Pollet's Cove, 38–9
population decline, 56
population growth, 37
Portugal, 100
power structures, 10, 17, 33, 42, 197, 198

Presbyterianism, 5, 37, 40, 116, 140, 176
press *see* newspapers; periodicals
Prince Edward Island, 15–16, 19, 21–2, 25–9, 38, 41, 54, 74, 78, 86
Prince Edward Island Times, 74
privilege, 2, 9, 27, 28
profiteering, 161–2, 168
Protestantism, 55, 97, 116, 176; *see also* Presbyterianism
publishing, 10, 71–90, 109–10

Quakers, 134
Quebec, 55

racism, 40, 138, 143, 192, 195
Rainy, Ann (née Robertson), 117
Rainy, George, 117, 118, 121, 125, 136, 142
Rainy, Gilbert, 118, 121, 125
Ramsay, John, 22–3
Randolph, Edmund, 104
real estate, 185, 187–8, 191–2
Regiment of the Isles, 120
religion, 5, 37, 40, 55, 75, 78, 81, 116, 140–1, 175, 176, 180
rents, 19, 26, 28
responsbilities, 24, 27–8
reversing language shift (RLS) model, 50–1, 67
Rickman, Thomas, 129
Río de la Plata, 100
River Denys, 172, 177, 178, 179
Robertson, Ann (daughter of Gilbert), 144
Robertson, Anne (née Forbes) (mother of Christy), 116, 120–2, 123, 135
Robertson, Anne (sister of Christy), 135
Robertson, Antoinette, 143
Robertson, 'Black George', 143
Robertson, Charles, 143
Robertson, Christy, 115–47
Robertson, Daniel, 143
Robertson, George, 117, 119, 143

Robertson, Gilbert (brother of Christy), 117, 118, 119, 121, 122–5, 136–7, 143–5
Roberston, Gilbert (son of George), 143
Robertson, Harry, 116, 118, 121–2, 123, 133, 135
Robertson, Henry, 144–5
Robertson, Hugh Munro, 122–5, 135, 137, 143–4
Robertson, John, 117, 143, 157, 168
Robertson, William, 119, 121
romanticisation, 10, 33, 39
Roscoe, William, 134, 139
Rose, Hannah, 147
Rothschild, Emma, 115, 140
Royal Cape Breton Yacht Club, 189–90
Royal Highland regiment *see* Black Watch regiment
Royal Navy, 100, 108, 130
Royal Scots regiment, 105
'rule by the best', 17, 21

St Andrews, New Brunswick, 172
St Andrews University, 141
St Francis Xavier University, 40, 172, 175, 182, 183
St George's, Grenada, 117, 162
St James, Jamaica, 160
St Kitts, 153
St Lucia, 98, 105, 153
St Peters, Cape Breton, 187, 188
St Vincent, 122, 142, 149–50, 153
Sandbach, Betsy (née Robertson), 118, 121, 126, 127
Sandbach, Henry Robertson, 139
Sandbach, Margaret (née Roscoe), 139
Sandbach, Samuel, 117, 118, 122, 123, 126, 127
Sandbach, Tinné & Co., 159, 166
Sans Souci plantation, 150
Sar-Obair nam bard Gaelach (Mackenzie), 86
Saussure, Necker de, 130
Scoresby, William, Jr, 130
Scoresby, William, Sr, 130

Scotch Minister's Assistant (Robertson), 133
Scotchman's Return (MacLennan), 1–2
Scott, Alexander, 130–1, 133
Scott, Sir Walter, 9
Scottish Enlightenment, 7
Scottish identity, 48, 61; *see also* Gaelic identity; Highland Identity
Seaforth regiment, 100
sectarianism, 40
security of tenure, 26
Selkirk, Thomas Douglas, 5th Earl, 15–16, 21–2, 24, 29–30
Senator's Corner, Glace Bay, **184**, 185
sentimentality, 106–7
service aristocracy, 17–18, 29
Seven Years War, 95, 98, 99, 101, 117, 153
1798 rebellion, 97
71st Foot regiment *see* Glasgow Highland regiment
72nd Foot regiment *see* Seaforth regiment
73rd Foot regiment *see* Macleod's regiment
77th Foot regiment, 99
78th Foot regiment, 104
79th Foot regiment *see* Cameron Highlanders
sexual abuse, 124
Shaw, Alexander Mackenzie, 126
Shaw, Fr John, 175
Shaw, John, 55
Shaw, Margaret Fay, 90
Sherbrooke, Sir John, 20
Sheridan, Richard Brinsley, 116
shinty, 76
ship metaphors, 73–4
shipping, 118, 162
shipwrecks, 120, 130–1
Silverstein, Michael, 51
Sinclair, Archibald, 81, 89
Sinclair, Iain, 86
Sinclair, Joseph, 101
64th Foot regiment, 94

Skye, 66, 87, 91
slavery
  abolition campaigns, 134, 141
  Alexander Scott's enslavement, 131, 133
  in the Caribbean, 2, 10, 117–19, 122, 124, 128, 133–47, 151–2, 158–60, 166, 169
  compensation for slave owners, 160, 166
  emancipation, 138
  institutions' links with, 2–3, 135, 140–1
  middle-class investment in, 10, 117–19, 128, 133–42, 146–7
  pro-slavery lobby groups, 158, 160, 163, 166–7
  and sexual abuse, 124
  slave trade, 3, 117, 122, 133–4
  in the United States, 140, 149
  uprisings, 138, 161, 168
  see also indentured servitude
Small, John, 110
social class, 5, 9–11, 15–30, 118–19, 127–9, 146–7, 151, 157, 161, 167, 170–1, 182, 188–90, 193, 198
social networks
  on Cape Breton Island, 33–4, 35–7, 171–93
  and the Caribbean, 10, 115–47, 149–69
  and culture, 8–9, 43
  and establishment of colonial settlements, 4–5, 33–4, 35–7
  and the Gaelic language, 5, 8, 71–90
  and gentlemen's clubs, 10–11, 148–69
  and identity, 8–9, 11, 43, 115
  kinship networks, 8, 117–27, 134–47, 157–59, 161, 178–80, 185–93
  literary networks, 10, 71–90, 110
  and marriage, 117–18, 167–8, 169, 177–8
  and military service, 9, 110–11
  and religion, 5, 37, 75, 78, 81

and social class, 5, 118–19, 127–9, 146–7, 151, 157, 161, 167, 170–1, 182, 188–90, 193
socioeconomic change, 2, 4, 56–7
songs, 10, 43, 92–3, 101–9, 111, 182, 197
South Africa, 26, 100
South Carolina, 95, 153
South Uist, 172
Spain, 94, 100, 132
specimen collection, 124, 137, 142
squatting, 38–40, 41, 196
steel industry, 185, 189–90
Stewart, Alexander, 162
Stewart, Dugald, 129
Stirling, Charles, 160
Stirling, John, 160
storytelling, 43, 76
Strang, John, 151, 160
strikes, 26, 189
subsistence farming, 39, 196
sugar, 133–4, 153, 159, 168
Suriname, 119
Sutherland, Cromartie Granville Leveson-Gower, 4th Duke, 16
Sutherland, Elizabeth (née Baillie), 122
Sutherland, George Leveson-Gower, 1st Duke, 16
Sutherland, James, 122
Sutherland Clearances, 16, 20–1
Sutherland family, 15, 16, 20–1, 116
Sutherland regiment, 100–1
Sydney, 57, 173, 176–8, 179, 182, 185, 189–90, 192
Sydney Academy, 181

tariffs, 175, 177
tartan, 31–2, 43, 148, 149, 154
Tasmania, 80, 143
taxation, 103, 105
Te Pehi Kupe, 131, 133
Teachdaire Gae'lach, An, 73, 74–6, 80
Teachdaire Gaidhealach, An, 80
Teachdaire Ùr Gaidhealach, 86

Teackle, Littleton Demmis, 148–49, 150, 155–6, 157
Tenant League, 26
Tennent, Christian (née Rainy), 140
Tennent, Hugh, 140
Tennent, John, 140
Tennent, Robert, 140
theatre, 116
Thirteen Colonies, 153
Thomas, Charlotte, 125
Thomas, Dorothy 'Doll', 124–5, 144, 145
Thomas, Eliza, 124–5, 143, 145
Thompson, F. M. L., 18
Thompson, James, 101
Thomson, Dugald, 157, 165
Tibbles, Anthony, 134
Tinné, Philip Frederick, 166
tobacco, 150, 153, 157, 161
Tobago, 117, 143, 153
Tobermory, 74
Tomah, Francis, 41
Toronto, 74, 83–4, 87, 188
Toronto Daily Mail, 90
tourism, 10, 33
Townsend, Lucy, 134
trade, 115, 117, 127, 149–50, 152, 153, 157, 161–3, 168
Traill, Lucia, 139
Traill, Thomas Stewart, 115, 123–4, 126–39, 142, 143–4, 146
Traill, William, 139
transport, 38–9, 189
Trinidad, 117, 122, 142, 143, 153, 164
Tulloch, Harry, 122

United Mine Workers of America, 189
United States, 24, 34, 74, 84, 94, 95, 100–1, 104, 140, 149, 153
University of Edinburgh, 123, 129, 130, 138–9
University of Glasgow, 2–3, 140, 147, 152
urbanisation, 17, 57, 128

Ushioda, Ema, 53
Utrecht, 120

Victoria County, 54
violence, 6, 10, 92–3, 101, 102, 108, 111–12
Virginia, 95, 117, 149, 153

Wade, George, 4
war, 10, 92–112, 161
War of American Independence, 95, 98, 99, 102, 104, 109, 110, 150, 153
War of Austrian Succession, 94
War of 1802, 97, 100–1
Waterloo, Battle of, 100
Watson, Andrew (son of Christy), 136, 139, 145
Watson, Andrew (son of Peter Miller), 147
Watson, Harry, 135, 136–7, 139
Watson, James, Jr, 127, 135, 136
Watson, James, Sr, 120, 122–4, 125–6, 143
Watson, Peter Miller, 136, 138, 142, 147
Watson, Seumas, 58
Watson, William Robertson, 136
Wellington, Arthur Wellesley, 1st Duke, 100
West Indies *see* Caribbean
Whitney, Henry Melville, 183
Whyte, Iain, 140
Wicklow, 138
Wilberforce, William, 141
William, Duke of Cumberland, 96
Williams, John, 136
Williamsburg, 104
Williamson, Robert, 78
Willis, William, 185–6
Withers, Charles, 151
Woodlands plantation, 125

Yorke, James, 192
Yorke, John, 192
Young, Patrick, 178

EU representative:
Easy Access System Europe
Mustamäe tee 50, 10621 Tallinn, Estonia
Gpsr.requests@easproject.com

www.ingramcontent.com/pod-product-compliance
Lightning Source LLC
Chambersburg PA
CBHW051122160426
43195CB00014B/2309